"A wonderful book, nourishing fo   e
reader to participate in an extensiv   ,
offering a meeting of ethical reflect.   .n
transformation of moral action. The volume proposes a dialogical and communal dimension and a dimension of personal commitment. Each of these elements contributes
to the construction of a world that is ethically responsible."

—Sandu Fruza, Professor of Communication Ethics, Babes-Bolyai University;
Executive Editor, *Journal for the Study of Religions and Ideologies*

"*Talking About Ethics: A Conversational Approach to Moral Dilemmas* by Mike Jones,
Mark Farnham, and David Saxon is a superb twenty-first-century book introducing
contemporary issues of right and wrong—ethics. The material presented is clear, comprehensive, and not only understandable for any 'student' 18–81, but also laid out in an
engaging manner. Three students with different ethnicities, religions, and study majors
meet at a local tea shop and hash out the issues being presented in an ethics class. The
authors thoroughly present and analyze topics through the thought and voices of the
three protagonists. Their personalities develop throughout the book's discussions, which
cunningly draws the reader painlessly into the abstruse topics in fifteen burning ethical
issues of today. I am putting it on my list for my introduction to world religions class!"

—Leonard Swidler, Professor of Catholic Thought
and Interreligious Dialogue, Temple University; Founder, Dialogue Institute

"*Talking About Ethics* does its readers several great services. In terms of both its expansive
scope and aerial perspective, with innovation and crystal clarity, an irenic spirit, and
jargon-free accessibility, it models for readers what substantive engagement with ethical
issues looks like. In these strident and divisive days, exhortations are all too rare to listen respectfully to the best positions on all sides of an argument. Such encouragement,
however, is the very heart and salient strength of this book. This volume can serve as a
vital and refreshing antidote to the tendentious, partisan, conversation-sabotaging ani-
mus that is such a recurring and lamentable fixture of public discourse today. Unafraid
to acknowledge complexities and explore hard questions, these inviting and enjoyable
pages provide powerful witness to the fact that ethics is no mere academic matter. It is
rather rife with practical import and real-life repercussions, and worthy of our diligent
efforts. Kudos to the writers, and highly recommended!"

—David Baggett, Professor of Philosophy and Director of the
Center for Moral Apologetics, Houston Baptist University

"*Talking About Ethics* is an excellent introduction to help readers think through ethical
theories and issues, and it offers wisdom about ethical decision-making. This book is
an accessible and practical guide in an era of moral confusion. Highly recommended!"

—Paul Copan, Pledger Family Chair of Philosophy and Ethics,
Palm Beach Atlantic University

"*Talking About Ethics* models the kinds of conversations we should be having! In a day when respectful dialogue is being replaced by complacent groupthink, this book provides a refreshing corrective. The authors artfully weave human moral dilemmas with thoughtful ethical theory, resulting in an enjoyably informative read. I can't wait to introduce this volume to my ethics students; my only dilemma is whether to require it at the beginning of class to illustrate the purpose of ethical theory, or at the end of the course as a springboard into ethical practice."

—Bryan W. Brock, Professor of Bible and Church Ministries,
Maranatha Baptist University

"This text uses an attractive students-in-dialogue/conversationalist approach to introduce students to diverse views for a broad range of ethical issues. In so doing, it takes the dialogue approach to teaching ethics to a higher level of excellence."

—James P. Sterba,
Professor of Philosophy, University of Notre Dame

"I highly recommend *Talking About Ethics: A Conversational Approach to Moral Dilemmas* by Michael S. Jones, Mark J. Farnham, and David L. Saxon. This volume is an excellent introduction to many of the morally problematic issues we face today. The authors examine and address fifteen current and relevant topics such as immigration, legalizing narcotics, abortion, capital punishment, environmentalism, world hunger, and many others. One of the best features is that the book is written in a conversational style between three fictional college students. The conversations are enjoyable to read and provide the reader with a fair and balanced discussion of the pertinent moral problems under each topic. I can see this book as a primary textbook in an undergraduate ethics class."

—Mark W. Foreman,
Professor of Philosophy and Religion, Liberty University

"While *Talking About Ethics* addresses the spectrum of topics you would expect to find in an introductory ethics text, this volume is unique in that it does so in a conversational format. Indeed, the genius of this book is that it takes complex moral issues and unfolds them in a winsome manner that makes the material accessible to any reader. I predict that this volume will become a standard text in many ethics classrooms, will become a go-to book in many pastoral studies, and will become a resource for anyone desiring to know what Scripture has to say about the moral issues confronting twenty-first-century Western culture."

—David W. Jones,
Professor of Christian Ethics,
Southeastern Baptist Theological Seminary

TALKING

ABOUT

ETHICS

A
CONVERSATIONAL
APPROACH
TO
MORAL
DILEMMAS

MICHAEL S. JONES • MARK J. FARNHAM
DAVID L. SAXON

KREGEL
ACADEMIC

Talking About Ethics: A Conversational Approach to Moral Dilemmas

© 2021 by Michael S. Jones, Mark J. Farnham, and David L. Saxon

Published by Kregel Academic, an imprint of Kregel Publications, 2450 Oak Industrial Dr. NE, Grand Rapids, MI 49505-6020.

ISBN 978-0-8254-4691-7

Printed in the United States of America

21 22 23 24 25 / 5 4 3 2 1

*We dedicate this book to Laura, Adrienne, and Jamie, who have
provided considerable support
and invaluable input in writing this book.*

*They have walked with us through the real-life
challenges of seeking to live ethically in this world.*

CONTENTS

INTERNATIONAL ISSUES

PREFACE

THE NEED

Life is fraught with ethical dilemmas. Hardly a day goes by in which we don't face some sort of moral issue. Some issues are much more significant than others; some are easily resolved, while others are quite complex. The present volume is born from the conviction that it is best to think about the difficult ones *before* we find ourselves embroiled in them. If we wait until we are caught up in a vexing moral dilemma, then we lose our distance from it, compromising our objectivity and jeopardizing the clarity of our judgment.

Another conviction that motivates this book is the belief that ethical decision-making works best when it is guided by a coherent set of principles. Many guiding moral principles have been suggested over the centuries: Aristotle had seminal accounts of Natural Law Theory and Virtue Ethics (and Thomas Aquinas developed theistic versions); Epicurus had a carefully nuanced individual hedonism; William of Ockham argued for Divine Command Theory; John Stuart Mill advocated Utilitarianism; Immanuel Kant promoted Duty Ethics; and so on. But the average person has little knowledge of such theories and therefore is prone to approaching important moral decisions in a haphazard way. A religious person might believe that his religion contains answers to moral questions but may not know how to find them. A nonreligious person may have a strong sense of right and wrong but may be left wondering just how to figure out what actions fall into which category. Both would benefit from a structured approach to ethics.

Talking About Ethics is also motivated by a shared experience: the experience of college ethics professors. While teaching ethics at various colleges and universities, the authors of *Talking About Ethics* have enjoyed the challenge of helping their students to think about moral issues in a structured, systematic way. Ethics is important, and their students grasp that intuitively. This has led to rich, deep, challenging, and very enjoyable times in the classroom.

However, the pleasure and reward of teaching undergraduate ethics has been hindered by a lack of appropriate textbooks. It seems that undergraduate ethics texts are either dominated by abstract reasoning on ethical theories or completely devoid of it. Many seem to be written as introductions to ethics for those who are majoring in ethics, philosophy, or some related field. There is a need for a book that is written for nonphilosophers, written on a university level but for beginning students—one that is at the same time both practical and imbued with the guiding principles of ethical theories.

This is, of course, asking a lot. The book needs to be theoretically informed but written on a beginner's level. It needs to be sufficiently academic to work as a textbook and yet approachable enough to hold a student's attention. And it needs to fairly and accurately present the major options and perspectives on the issues.

A UNIQUE SOLUTION
Talking About Ethics takes a unique approach to addressing these needs. After an initial chapter introducing the major ethical theories in the Western tradition, it introduces the reader to three students at Lone Mountain University. Bianca, Lauren, and Micah are enrolled in an ethics class. It's there that they first meet and become friends. Soon their in-class discussions spill over to The Grey Earl, a coffee-and-tea shop near the campus. We follow our three friends to their other classes, into their homes, and to various other parts of their daily lives as we listen in on their many discussions of moral issues. We see that ethics impacts all parts of their lives. We also see that friends will often disagree—both on how to approach ethics and on what conclusions to draw—but that they can disagree agreeably and as a result benefit from their disagreement.

Chapters two through sixteen are composed of dialogues. Each chapter involves some combination of our three friends wrestling with a new moral dilemma. By the end of the book they have discussed immigration, capital punishment, torture, animal rights, legalizing narcotics, abortion, euthanasia, organ transplantation, reproductive technology, premarital sex, homosexuality, gender identity, environmentalism, world hunger, and war. In each dialogue, multiple perspectives are presented and arguments for and against each perspective are examined. The dialogues are consistently informed and guided by the ethical theories that the students are studying in their ethics class at Lone Mountain University, but this is done in a way that flows naturally from their conversations.

The goal is to create a textbook that is exceptionally readable. We want *Talking About Ethics* to be their students' favorite textbook of the semester—at least! Of course, the use of dialogues is a venerable tradition in philosophy: they were used effectively by such great figures as Plato, George Berkeley, and David Hume. Now they are being brought to the contemporary study of ethics.

NOTE TO THE READER

This book is intended to be fun while at the same time being educational. The least entertaining chapter is, without a doubt, chapter one, which is an introduction to ethical theories. If you already have a basic understanding of theories like Virtue Ethics, Natural Law Theory, and Divine Command Theory, then you could skip it. However, if you aren't familiar with such theories, then it is important that you read chapter one before moving on. These theories are briefly described at various places in the subsequent chapters, but chapter one is the only place where they are explained in a systematic way. Furthermore, chapter one examines strengths and weaknesses of these theories. Hence it is an important chapter.

If you are researching a particular issue in applied ethics, you can profit from reading the chapter on that subject even if you have not yet read chapter one. You may not understand some of the theory behind what Bianca and her friends say, but you will benefit from reading their arguments anyway.

Please do not read these chapters expecting them to tell you what to believe or what the correct view is on the issues that they address. That's not the purpose of this book. The dialogues in this volume are intended to help you to understand issues more deeply, to expose you to a range of arguments supporting opposing perspectives on important issues, and most of all to spark your thinking about ethics. The chapters cannot possibly cover every argument that can be marshaled for or against the positions presented, but they do present important arguments that currently influence people's thinking on the subject. The authors suggest that you take the arguments presented as examples of the types of arguments that one could marshal in support of or opposition to some position. If you'd like to read additional arguments, you can find them in the "For Further Reading" section at the end of each chapter.

NOTE TO THE INSTRUCTOR

Talking About Ethics is intended as a theoretically informed introduction to applied ethics. It is an applied ethics book, not an ethical theory book. However, because the authors believe that applied ethics needs to be based upon theoretical ethics, chapter one introduces the ethical theories. By design this is a cursory introduction.

It is our opinion that the best way to use this book is in conjunction with a textbook on ethical theories. There are many good introductory textbooks on ethical theories, such as the following:

- Michael S. Jones, *Moral Reasoning: An Intentional Approach to Distinguishing Right from Wrong* (Dubuque, IA: Kendall Hunt, 2017).
- James P. Sterba, *What Is Ethics?* (Medford, MA: Polity, 2020).
- Steve Wilkens, *Beyond Bumper Sticker Ethics: An Introduction to Theories of Right and Wrong*, 2nd ed. (Downers Grove, IL: InterVarsity Press, 2011).

All three of these books provide an overview of the major ethical theories. The first and third are friendly toward religious perspectives while the second is critical of religious approaches to ethics.

As mentioned in our note to the reader, this book makes no attempt to present what the authors view as the correct position on the moral issues addressed. The purpose of this volume is to spur the reader's thinking on these issues rather than settling the issues for the reader. We leave it up to the instructor to provide further guidance, and we have confidence that a book that leaves this task in your competent hands is exactly what is needed in order to produce fruitful classroom discussions that will lead to transformative learning experiences.

ACKNOWLEDGEMENTS

While all three of the authors of this book had a hand in the production of each chapter, Michael S. Jones was the lead author of the preface and chapters one, two, four, twelve, thirteen, and fifteen. Mark J. Farnham was the lead author of the introduction, chapters six through ten, and compiled the bibliography. David L. Saxon was the lead author of chapters three, five, eleven, fourteen, sixteen, the conclusion, and compiled the index. Each of the coauthors expresses his gratitude to the others for the cordial and fruitful collaboration that they have enjoyed.

The authors extend their thanks to the good people at Kregel Academic. Their expertise in editing and publishing were invaluable to the production of this volume. The authors also acknowledge the very important role played by their wives—Adrienne Farnham, Jamie Saxon, and Laura Jones—who have supported them, advised them, and proofread their chapters as the book developed. Without our better halves, this book would not exist. Finally, their greatest gratitude is to God, whom they view as the ultimate source of morality and the succor of those who labor for a worthy cause. "They that wait upon the LORD shall renew their strength; they shall mount up with wings as eagles; they shall run, and not be weary; they shall walk, and not faint" (Isa. 40:31, KJV).

INTRODUCTION

I n 2015 the CEO of Turing Pharmaceuticals, Martin Shkreli, came under scrutiny when his company raised the price of Daraprim more than 5,000 percent, from $13.50 per dose to $750 per dose. Daraprim is used to treat toxoplasmosis, a potentially fatal parasitic infection. Toxoplasmosis afflicts some of the poorest and most vulnerable people on earth, including HIV/AIDS patients, cancer patients, transplant recipients, and pregnant mothers. It is contracted primarily from infected soil, food, and water. Daraprim is so important to the health of many afflicted by various diseases that it is on the World Health Organization's Model List of Essential Medicines.

When the media began to investigate the sudden price hike of this critical drug, Shkreli's flippant response earned him the frat-like nickname "Pharma Bro." The public was outraged that he didn't seem to care that the price hike would make the cost of Daraprim prohibitive for so many who depended on it to live. Shkreli responded that his ethical obligation was to the shareholders of Turing and that he had made them happy with increased profits. Many of the news outlets that reported on this development asked the question of the morality of the price hike.[1]

It soon became apparent, however, that Shkreli was not alone in his preference for shareholders over patients in the pharmaceutical industry. Nostrum Laboratories CEO Nirmal Mulye raised the price of the antibiotic nitrofurantoin 400 percent, from $475 to almost $2,400. The drug is very effective to treat bladder infections, and now it is cost-prohibitive for many

---

1. For example, Rachel Baldelomar, "Where Is the Line between Ethical and Legal?" *Forbes*, July 21, 2016, https://www.forbes.com/sites/raquelbaldelomar/2016/07/21/where-is-the-line-between-what-is-ethical-and-legal/#1186ebed250b.

people. Mulye defended this move, claiming that it was a moral requirement to sell his product at the highest price possible.[2] Finally, in 2015 Heather Bresch, CEO of Mylan Pharmaceuticals, oversaw a price hike of the life-saving EpiPen from $100 to $600. Schools required to stock the drug and parents of children susceptible to anaphylactic shock were incensed at the increased cost, especially since the expiration date on the drug is eighteen months after it is manufactured.[3]

Much of the outrage over the sudden rise of prices for critical medications centered on the ethics of profit versus social responsibility. Consumers and politicians saw these actions as immoral on the grounds that they harmed people. Business leaders saw the situation differently. They often defended such actions because of their responsibility to return to shareholders the highest possible profit. In addition, pharmaceutical industry leaders also defended price increases on the grounds that unless they have money to research and develop new drugs, people will continue to die of diseases that could be cured. Since it costs on average $2.6 billion to bring a drug to market,[4] companies must charge high prices for medications to keep the pipeline of developing drugs flowing.

What is the ethical solution to this thorny problem? As you can probably see, the situation is not as clear as we would like. Is it ethical to charge less for a medication, even if that means fewer drugs are developed in the future? What about those with diseases for which there is no cure or treatment and who are waiting for a drug to be developed? How would we decide which choice is ethical?

Ethical dilemmas often raise the question: What kind of society do we want to have? Should everyone who wants to come to the United States be

2. David Crow, "Pharma Chief Defends 400% Drug Price Rise as a 'Moral Require-ment,'" *Financial Times*, September 11, 2018, https://www.ft.com/content/48b-0ce2c-b544-11e8-bbc3-ccd7de085ffe.
3. Emily Willingham, "Why Did Mylan Hike EpiPen Prices 400%? Because They Could," *Forbes*, August 21, 2016, https://www.forbes.com/sites/emilywill-ingham/2016/08/21/why-did-mylan-hike-epipen-prices-400-because-they-could/#7bff191d280c.
4. Joseph A. DiMasi, Henry G. Grabowski, and Ronald W. Hansen, "Innovation in the Pharmaceutical Industry: New Estimates of R&D Costs," *Journal of Health Economics*, May 2016, 20–33.

allowed to immigrate without restriction? Should marijuana be legal in all forms like alcohol? Should the interests and rights of animals be on par with those of humans? What principles should guide our military when we enter a conflict or go to war? Is torture or enhanced interrogation moral or immoral? Should the death penalty be carried out for murder? Should people who are dying be allowed to take their own lives with the help of their doctors?

We also face ethical dilemmas in our personal lives. What if your boss tells you to lie on a report or he will lose his job and his health insurance, and as a result his wife won't be able to continue with chemotherapy? Do you do it? If your GPA falls below a certain number, do you cheat so you can stay in school, get your degree, and provide for your orphaned sister? When your mother tells you a secret, but then your father asks about it, do you lie or tell the truth? Is it really wrong to have sex with your fiancé two weeks before your wedding?

The reality is that we face ethical decisions often in our personal lives and in our relationships with others. Many people adopt an ethical system or philosophy that works for them, without often thinking about why they do what they do. On some issues average people have a rather sophisticated argument for or against, but on other issues their reasoning can be simplistic or naive. Part of intellectual and moral maturity is to develop an ethic that is consistent, coherent, and grounded in something beyond mere feelings and intuitions.

This book seeks to help readers sort through a number of common ethical issues to see the strengths and weaknesses of each view. It is an example of *applied ethics* as opposed to *metaethics*. The latter pertains to the use of language in our statements about ethics and other theoretical considerations prior to doing applied ethics. What do we mean by *good, moral,* and *evil*? Metaethics is often one of the first considerations when tackling the subject of ethics in a comprehensive manner. Applied ethics, on the other hand, proceeds with the understanding that basic concepts of right and wrong are assumed, and then applies those to concrete examples in real life. Applied ethics looks at actual experiences and situations and asks, "What is the right thing to do, given these conditions?"

As you can imagine, many ethical issues and countless scenarios could happen in real life. Consider for yourself a scenario that involves an ethical dilemma. What would be the right thing to do? Now, change one factor in the scenario. Does your position change—or at the least, does the change make your conclusion more difficult to hold with confidence? Now change another factor. And another. The variety your mind can conjure reflects the complexity of life. Every situation is different. Yet we intuitively believe that some things are right no matter the situation, and some things are wrong no matter the situation. This is what we are pursuing in a study of ethics. What is universally ethical for all people of all times, and what is wrong? What principles should guide the actions of all people, societies, cultures, and nations?

Because sorting out ethical issues is often difficult, it helps if we understand accurately the various positions on the issues. Sometimes we approach an ethical issue unaware of our presuppositions about it. We may not realize how much our family, culture, and experiences have shaped our thinking on the subject. We may also not have an accurate understanding of why those who disagree with us do so.

One of the most important ways we can ensure that we think clearly and truthfully about an issue is to listen to those who disagree with us. We may ultimately remain in disagreement with them, but by hearing their side of the issue we avoid the mistake of listening only to evidence and arguments that support our view. When we take the time to hear the best arguments for the other side, we often find ourselves learning facts we did not know before. We hear a different perspective from another living, breathing human being who is a person with interests, loves, and hopes. This humanizes the issue for us. Our minds on the issue may not change, but we benefit from hearing all the available data. This allows us to make informed conclusions, and to keep others in mind as we do so. This has only positive implications for public policy, life in a peaceful society, and neighborly talks across the back fence.

This book is unique, in that we, the authors, address many of the most important ethical issues of our day in a conversational manner. Each chapter after the first one addresses ethical issues as conversations between friends of very different persuasions. Three college students—Lauren, Micah, and Bianca—are introduced as they work their way through an ethics class at Lone Mountain University. Each of them approaches the ethical issues they encounter from a particular worldview, as do we all. Their conversations reflect both their growing understanding of each issue and the best arguments for each perspective. The chapters, then, provide the reader with the basic facts of the ethical issue, the intellectual and moral struggles of the friends as they process the issue, and the best arguments they can find to express their positions on the issue. As you read about their discussions on each issue, our hope is that you will reason through the issue with them.

Such is the goal of this book—a careful consideration of each ethical issue that is presented, an application of various ethical theories to help you see the issue more clearly, and a more informed conclusion about your position on the issue. Just as Lauren, Micah, and Bianca talk through each issue, our hope is that you too will engage in conversations with others about ethics and its application to everyday life. This will allow you to test your thoughts, sharpen your reasoning, and come to sound conclusions on the pressing issues of the day and in your life.

THEORETICAL
CONSIDERATIONS

ETHICAL THEORY

Synopsis: In this chapter we explain what ethics is and why it's important. Ethics is too important to leave up to chance, so we argue that people should be very intentional about how they approach ethics. We illustrate this by providing a sober discussion of the various theories about how to distinguish between moral and immoral actions. We largely reject ethical relativism in favor of ethical absolutism, but while we review the strengths and weaknesses of various other ethical theories, in the end we do not take sides for or against any of them, leaving the reader to make up his or her own mind about the best approach to ethics. We end by explaining how this first chapter of the book performs a very important function by setting the stage for the subsequent, more practical, and more fun chapters. Without this initial introduction to ethical theories, what follows would make much less sense, so please read this chapter carefully!

* * *

INTRODUCTION

Ethics is the systematic study of morality; it is the attempt to discern what is morally right from what is morally wrong. When we think about ethics, our minds probably turn immediately to important issues such as abortion, euthanasia, immigration, alcohol consumption, and gambling. These are very important issues: if a human fetus really is a person, as pro-life advocates argue, then aborting a human fetus ends a human life in a way that may be just as tragic and immoral as is ending the life of an adult. Immigration is a very contemporary issue that has significant practical implications: many people's lives could be greatly improved if they would be allowed to immigrate to wealthy nations such as Germany, France, and the United States; on the other hand, such immigrants might compete with the citizens of those countries for jobs and housing and could financially burden the health care and public education systems of those countries. What is the moral attitude toward the plight of such people? Should the needs of German and U.S. citizens eclipse the needs of noncitizens simply because of their citizenship status? Gambling has been seen as a way to infuse Native American reservations and other economically disadvantaged areas with jobs and new cash flow. Research, however, suggests that gambling addiction is just as serious a problem as drug addiction for those who suffer from it.[1] Is it right to take advantage of someone's addiction in order to help out someone else? Is it moral to take the money of a gambling addict in order to strengthen the economy of a disadvantaged region?

Such questions are complex and not easily answered. Nonetheless finding the right answer to them is extremely important, both because we want to do the right thing and because these problems (and many others like them) have serious consequences that affect the lives of many people. Hence answer them we must, difficult though it be.

Most people respond to such dilemmas by going with what "their gut" tells them. Sometimes this is described as appealing to "common sense." Such an appeal can be very helpful, for the dictates of common sense are often the result of wisdom that has been distilled from generations of experience. For example, regardless of what position you take on the morality of having a glass of wine with your supper or a bottle of beer while watching a game at the ball park, common sense tells us that it's not good to get plastered—or at the very least, it's not good to do so except on very special and rare occasions.

---

1. Ferris Jabr, "How the Brain Gets Addicted to Gambling," *Scientific American,* Nov. 1, 2013, https://www.scientificamerican.com/article/how-the-brain-gets-addicted-to-gambling.

Some people disagree with this—members of some college fraternities, for example—while others basically agree but choose to ignore this dictate. But society has learned that drinking to the point of losing control has many undesirable consequences for drinkers, for those near to them, and sometimes for those who are not so near. So society frowns upon heavy drinking, and this is beneficial to the drinkers, their families, and their neighbors, as long as the drinkers allow themselves to be guided by this piece of collective wisdom.

Common sense, however, is not a completely reliable guide to morality. Let me explain why. As illustrated in the example about drinking alcoholic beverages, the deliverances of common sense are, at least to an extent, social constructs. What this means is that they are beliefs that have been crafted by society over a period of time and that are often accepted by society without any conscious critical examination. Since different societies face different challenges and have different histories, societies sometimes arrive at different conclusions about what is moral and what is not.

For example, while Western societies have developed in a way that emphasizes the importance of individuals and encourages independence and self-reliance, some Eastern societies have developed in a way that emphasizes the interdependence of individuals and encourages willing submission to the family, village, and state hierarchy. In such societies arranged marriages make complete sense. But to those who grow up in the individualism of the Western world, arranged marriage seems horrific. Both sides can martial pragmatic arguments for their traditions, and both can appeal to "common sense," for what they take to be right is nearly universally accepted in their respective cultures. Thus in this situation the deliverance of common sense seems to lead to a contradiction: arranged marriage is moral and arranged marriage is immoral.

Of course, it could be the case that arranged marriage is moral in a communal society while at the same time it is immoral in an individualistic society. This is because there may not be anything inherently moral or immoral about whether marriages are arranged. Instead, it may be that what is morally important is whether the structures of each society are respected, or whether the rights of the individuals who make up a society are upheld, or something like that. But there could be issues that transcend societal differences, issues upon which all societies should agree, even if they don't. For example, all societies should respect human life. Hence even though some societies don't seem to respect human life as much as they should (cannibalistic societies, for example), it's still the case that those societies should respect it. But in a cannibalistic society, common sense says that under certain conditions it's OK to end the life of another human being in order to eat that person's body. At the same time, in most societies common sense says that it's wrong to end the life of a human being in order to eat that person's body. Here we have a clear contradiction of the dictates of common sense.

If common sense is not up to the task of guiding our moral inquiries, what should we do? Well, first of all, it's good that we realize that we need to do something. Some people assume that they are automatically going to do the right thing without even trying. If that were true of all of us, then we'd never do anything that's wrong. Since we all do things that are wrong from time to time (or more often), we know that it can't be the case that we automatically do whatever is right.[2]

What we need to do is find a reliable methodology for determining right and wrong. This requires that we be intentional about morality rather than just assuming or hoping that what we already believe is right or that what we're naturally inclined to do is moral. We need to think carefully about how to figure out what the moral action would be in any given circumstance. And we need to do this before we find ourselves confronted by moral dilemmas, for once we're embroiled in an ethical controversy, it will be very difficult for us to remain objective about what course of action we should take.

ETHICAL RELATIVISM

All of this assumes that there really are actions that are right and actions that are wrong. While many people make this assumption, some question it. Some people advocate **ethical relativism**, the view that nothing is morally right or wrong in itself, but instead actions are morally right or wrong only

---

2. This is a logical argument against the view that we automatically do what is right. The name for this particular type of argument is *reductio ad absurdum*, which means "reduction to absurdity." It shows that a belief must be mistaken because if you were to accept it and follow it to its logical conclusion you'd end up with an absurdity. In this case, the belief that we automatically do the right thing leads to the absurd conclusion that we never do anything that is morally wrong.

because of their relationship to something else. In other words, the morality of an action is relative.

The most common form of ethical relativism is **cultural relativism**. This is the view that what is right or wrong is determined by the culture in which you live. Strictly speaking, cultural relativism does not deny that actions are moral or immoral. Rather, it denies that actions are *inherently* moral or immoral and instead asserts that morality is assigned to actions by cultures: what is moral or immoral is decided for you by the culture in which you live. Hence a cultural relativist would have no problem affirming that arranged marriages are moral in some societies while at the same time they are immoral in others.

Typically cultural relativists expect to see significant differences between the mores[3] of different societies. But they don't stop there: they also say that having differences like this is the way things should be. They are convinced that what works in one society is right for that society, but if that same practice doesn't work in another society, then it is not right for that other society.

Here you should notice that cultural relativism is not simply a descriptive position; it's not simply describing the way things currently are. That there are differences between societies on moral issues isn't disputed. Cultural relativism goes beyond mere description to make a prescription: it affirms that there *should* be disagreements between societies, for what is good for one society sometimes really is bad for another.

Please note that this is a pretty radical position, one that is sharply at odds with the way most people have thought about morality. Most people throughout history have thought that some things are inherently wrong. Examples of things that are usually thought to be inherently wrong include murder, theft, lying, adultery, and the like. The cultural relativist says that these things are not inherently wrong and that if and when they are wrong, it is only because a specific society says so.

There are reasons that some people think that cultural relativism is right. One is that the opposite of relativism, which is called **ethical absolutism**, is

---

3. The English word "mores" comes from Latin and is usually pronounced "morays." It refers to the beliefs about etiquette and moral behavior that are commonly accepted in a given society.

often associated with intolerance. Ethical absolutism is the view that there are at least some timeless, unchanging moral principles ("absolutes") that all people should abide by. People who believe in ethical absolutes are often intolerant of those who do not comply with those absolutes. For example, people who believe that tattoos are immoral are often intolerant of those who have tattoos. Less trivially, people who believe that abortion is murder are often intolerant of abortion and those who support it. Relativists feel that such intolerance is a problem and therefore think that views that lead to intolerance, as absolutism sometimes does, should be avoided.

Of course you could respond to this by pointing out that sometimes it is good to be intolerant. For instance, almost no one thinks that we should tolerate rape, murder, racism, and things like that. When it comes to that sort of thing, nearly everyone seems to be an absolutist. And there's an even more potent response to the intolerance argument against absolutism: this objection to ethical absolutism fails because it makes tolerance a moral absolute. This is a bit of a catch-22: if tolerance is always a good thing, then it's an absolute, but if tolerance is not always a good thing, then it's sometimes okay to be intolerant, so why object to absolutism for being intolerant? Hence there seem to be at least two reasons for thinking that this argument is not a strong rebuttal of ethical absolutism.

An alternative reason for believing in cultural relativism is that it may accurately describe the way things actually are. We can see that moral beliefs vary from one culture to another. So we can see that what cultural relativism says *should be* the case actually *is* the case.

The problem with this argument is, perhaps, a little more subtle than the problem with the first one. It has to do with conflating the prescriptive and the descriptive. Conflation is the fallacy of treating two separate things as if they are one and the same. This argument conflates descriptive relativism with prescriptive relativism. It assumes that the way things currently are is the way that they should be. Currently each society forms its own mores, its own set of moral beliefs. This is a description of the way things are. But the prescriptive question asks whether things *should* be this way. Should each society make up its own ethical system, or should societies be searching for an objective set of moral absolutes that transcends culture and society? Is morality created or discovered? Cultural relativists often seem to overlook the fact that there are two distinct issues here. The fact that societies create their own systems of moral beliefs does not in any way prove that they *should* be doing that.

A third argument for cultural relativism is that if there really are moral absolutes, then there should be general agreement on what is moral and what is immoral. Just as the objective existence of the laws of nature has resulted in general agreement around the world on what those laws are, if there really were unchanging, objective moral laws, there would be widespread general agreement on what they are. But there isn't widespread agreement on what is moral. Therefore there probably aren't any moral absolutes.[4]

This objection seems to forget that the current consensus on the laws of nature is something that has taken millennia to develop and has appeared only recently in history.[5] Boyle's law was published late in the seventeenth century, Newton formulated the law of gravity late in the seventeenth century and his three laws of motion early in the eighteenth century, and Mendel's laws of inheritance were discovered in the middle of the nineteenth century, for example. So this argument for relativism could be turned on its head: we could argue that just as the existence of objective laws of nature didn't necessarily mean that people would be aware of or in agreement on what the laws were, so the existence of unchanging, objective moral laws, if true, does not necessarily mean that people will be aware of or in agreement on what they are.

There's another way to respond to this argument, though. C. S. Lewis has argued that while there is considerable diversity of opinion on many moral issues, there also appears to be a great deal of agreement on the fundamental principles of morality that underlie this diversity. We could view the diversity as a matter of diverse applications of underlying moral principles about which there really isn't a significant amount of disagreement. He specifically mentions courage and honor as moral ideals that surface in cultures around the world.[6]

---

4. The logical form of this argument is *modus tollens*, which is a valid argument form.
5. There is an interesting philosophical discussion about the nature of such laws, but it is neither appropriate nor necessary to broach such subjects here.
6. C. S. Lewis, *Mere Christianity* (New York: HarperOne, 2002), 19.

These arguments for ethical relativism don't seem very strong. But things get even worse for relativism, for there are some pretty strong arguments against it. To begin with, every person is a member of more than one cultural or societal group. Hannah, a college student from Ohio, is an American. Broadly speaking, she is part of the Western world. But more specifically, she's part of the Christian West rather than the Islamic West, since she grew up in a part of the Western world that has historically been more influenced by Christianity than by Islam. Within the Christian West she is part of the Anglo-American culture group. Within that group she comes from the American branch, and more specifically, from the Midwest. But within the Midwest there are cultural subgroups. Hannah is a Gen Zer, which sets her apart from previous generations in various ways. She's also a college student, which sets her apart from those who are less educated (and also from those who are more). And she's on the women's lacrosse team, which has a unique subculture all its own.

The problem is that although Hannah is part of each of these groups, value differences exist between them. The lacrosse team values physical fitness very highly; on the other hand, more than a third of Americans are overweight and out of shape.[7] College students value education, but many Americans tend toward anti-intellectualism. Surveys show that the majority of Millennial Americans don't see homosexuality as immoral, but other surveys show that most Midwesterners think that it is.[8] The Western tradition emphasizes individualism and autonomy, while some non-Western traditions emphasize social groups. So which of these many cultural subgroups to which Hannah belongs should determine her morality? There doesn't seem to be any clear answer to that question. This is called "the problem of specificity": there doesn't appear to be any clear way that we can determine to which specific culture group morality is relative.

---

7. Alexandra Sifferlin, "More Than Two Thirds of Americans Are Overweight or Obese," *Time*, June 22, 2015, http://time.com/3929990/americans-over-weight-obese.

8. See, for example, Robert P. Jones, Daniel Cox, and Juhem Navarro-Rivera, "A Shifting Landscape: A Decade of Change in American Attitudes about Same-sex Marriage and LGBT Issues," *PRRI*, February 26, 2014, http://www.prri.org/research/2014-lgbt-survey. See also Mary E. Kite and Kinsey Blue Bryant-Lees, "Historical and Contemporary Attitudes toward Homosexuality," *Teaching of Psychology* 43, no. 2, April 2016, 164–70, http://journals.sagepub.com/doi/abs/10.1177/0098628316636297?journalCode=topa.

That argument is a little abstract. Here's one that is a bit simpler. If relativism is true, then moral progress is impossible, because if relativism is true, then whatever your culture says is right actually is right. So there's no need to change, and any change from what your culture currently says would actually be apostasy rather than moral progress. But it seems absurd to say that moral progress isn't possible. Therefore it's absurd to say that morality is relative.

This is another *reductio ad absurdum*, one that attempts to show that embracing relativism leads to an absurdity. Let me illustrate it for you. In the antebellum South of the United States, most citizens thought that slavery was perfectly ethical. Defenders of slavery had come up with a range of convincing arguments in defense of its morality and had successfully convinced the majority. So Southern culture taught that slavery was moral. If cultural relativism is true, then slavery actually was moral in the antebellum South. That's a difficult pill to swallow, but it gets worse. If cultural relativism is true, then it follows that deviating from what your culture teaches is itself immoral. Today this seems like a very strange conclusion, for it seems obvious to us that slavery is immoral. And if we're right—if slavery really is immoral—then that cultural relativism justifies believing that it was moral in the antebellum South suggests that something is fundamentally wrong with cultural relativism.

Martin Luther King, Jr.
Courtesy of the Nobel
Foundation. Public domain.

A similar argument can be made from the ethical standing of moral reformers like William Wilberforce and Martin Luther King Jr. If the status quo is moral, then attempting to change the status quo is immoral. Moral reformers like Wilberforce and King attempt to change the status quo. Therefore their actions— and arguably they themselves—are immoral. This would be true of all moral reformers: those who are attempting to end the culturally entrenched practice of genital mutilation, those who are fighting sex trafficking in developing nations, and so on. All such people would be immoral if cultural relativism is true. But that seems absurd, doesn't it?

ETHICAL ABSOLUTISM

It seems that although cultural relativism is a widespread view, it is most likely mistaken. There don't seem to be strong arguments for it, and conversely there are strong arguments against it. So if cultural relativism is false, then what should take its place? The answer to this important question is the afore-mentioned ethical absolutism—the view that there are timeless, unchanging moral truths that apply equally to all people, everywhere, all the time.

Are there good reasons to believe that ethical absolutism is true? We believe there are. For starters, if cultural relativism is false, then morality is either a result of something other than culture, or morals are timeless, unchanging truths, as absolutism maintains. Could morality be the result of something other than culture? What other options are there?

One option is **nihilism**, the view that morality is an illusion, a crutch that the weak use to prop up their existence.[9] If nihilism is true, then there's nothing inherently wrong with adultery, lying, murder, rape, theft, and so on. This seems like a *reductio ad absurdum* just waiting to happen. So is there a better alternative? Some think there is: **subjectivism**. This is the view that moral judgments are individual evaluations that are relative to each person. For one person vegetarianism may be moral, while for another it may not be. For some people pacifism may be moral, while for others it's not. This view shares some ground with cultural relativism and nihilism, for it denies that there is anything inherently wrong with any act: acts aren't wrong in and of themselves, but rather are wrong for some people and not wrong for others.[10]

We might ask what it is that makes an act wrong for someone. The usual answer to this is that a person's culture determines what he or she takes to be moral and immoral. This, however, turns subjectivism into cultural relativism and renders it subject to the same counterarguments to which cultural relativism fell.

A more consistent response would be that the valuation of an act as moral or immoral is completely subjective, and therefore what makes an act immoral may differ from person to person, since each person is unique. This implies that there's nothing objective about morality: it's all subjective.

---

9.   Friedrich Nietzsche is the paradigmatic nihilist.
10.   David Hume and Bertrand Russell are examples of ethical subjectivists.

If this is correct, however, then it's just as true for subjectivism as it is for nihilism that "there's nothing inherently wrong with adultery, lying, murder, rape, theft, and so on." Once again this seems very implausible, as does the implication that for some people adultery, lying, murder, rape, and theft could be perfectly moral.

A final alternative to absolutism is **ethical contextualism**, better known as "**Situation Ethics**." This is the view that there is nothing that is moral or immoral when taken out of context: it's only when placed in specific contexts that actions become morally right or wrong.[11] For example, saying something that's not true is sometimes immoral, but not always. If you're telling a story, then you're probably saying many things that aren't literally true, but there's nothing immoral about that, for you're not expected to stick to historical facts when telling stories. On the other hand, if the police stop your car because you've been swerving all over the road and ask you if you've been drinking, you are expected to stick to the truth. If you don't, you're not just telling a story: you're lying.

Contextualists argue that this is true of all actions: their morality and immorality is determined by the context in which they take place. Killing someone is not immoral if it's the only way to stop him or her from killing your family; taking something from someone else without giving anything in exchange is perfectly moral when that thing is freely given and only becomes immoral when it is forcibly gained; sexual intercourse is moral within the bounds of marriage but immoral outside of those bounds.

That actually sounds pretty reasonable, don't you think? It seems like a sort of relativism, since it makes the morality of an action dependent on the context in which the action occurs. But it seems less susceptible to the criticisms that were leveled at the other forms of relativism: it doesn't tie morality to culture and thus it avoids the problem of specificity, and it doesn't make morality a matter of subjective opinion, and thus avoids the contradiction that murder could be morally wrong for one person and morally right for another. It's far from nihilism, for it affirms that there are moral truths.

Ethical contextualism naturally leads us to ask what it is that makes an action moral in some contexts and immoral in others. The quick answer to this seems to be that the crucial factor is how the action reflects or fails to

11. Joseph Fletcher was a leading proponent of contextualism/situation ethics.

reflect some underlying moral principle that's determinative of the morality of that kind of act. In the example of killing (given above), killing someone is moral if it is provoked and if it is done to save other lives, while it is immoral if it is unprovoked and not done in an effort to save lives. The underlying principles would be preservation of justice and of life. So in any context where killing falls on the preservation side of these principles, it is moral, while anytime it falls on the demolition side of these principles, it is immoral.

Many ethical absolutists would not find much here to disagree with. But they would object that this really isn't relativism at all: it's absolutism. This is because these underlying principles that make an act moral or immoral depending on the context are, they would argue, moral absolutes. And we think they would be right. Perhaps ethical contextualism is merely a nuanced form of ethical absolutism.

What we see here is an elimination of possibilities until there's only one left standing. If cultural relativism, moral subjectivism, and nihilism don't work, and if contextualism works but is actually a form of ethical absolutism, then it seems like ethical absolutism wins. But there is another argument for ethical absolutism that deserves mention.

There is a form of logical reasoning that's called *abduction* or *inference to the best explanation*. When reasoning abductively, a person is seeking an explanation for something. If there are several plausible explanations, then the one that has the most considerations in its favor and the least considerations against it is the best explanation. This sort of logic is often used in science, but it can be applied to many other areas of study too.[12]

In application to ethical relativism, what the ethicist needs to explain is the fact that all cultures seem to develop systems of ethics. In fact, as mentioned previously, there seem to be similar conclusions across cultures about certain underlying ethical values. How can we best account for this widespread appearance of ethical thinking and similar conclusions? Is it luck? Coincidence? Is there some other explanation?

---

12. The conclusions of abductive reasoning are always provisional: as new evidence surfaces, the strength of the competing explanations may change, and as a result, a view that was at one time the most justified may no longer be the most justified. Hence abductive arguments never lead to complete certainty. Nonetheless abduction is a valuable tool in the logician's toolbox.

While it's difficult to completely rule out the possibility that this is a result of mere coincidence, when we consider all the different moral principles that might conceivably underlie an ethical system, it seems very unlikely that nearly all of the world's cultures would end up in the same place by sheer chance. Some other explanation seems more likely, and several have been proposed by various thinkers.

Nihilists sometimes argue that systems of morality develop in order to protect the weak in society from the excesses of the strong. Hence the ethical similarities between societies are a result of the fact that all societies contain weak individuals, strong individuals, and the struggle between these two groups. Some nihilists see this as a criticism of morality: morality weakens society by handicapping the strong and thus enabling the weak to survive. It could be argued in response that if the strong can be thus handicapped, then those who are able to pull this off are the real "strong." Perhaps true strength comes from our social nature rather than from the abilities of individuals: we are strongest when we work well together. This seems like a cogent response. Hence the nihilist critique of ethics fails, but perhaps there's some truth to the suggestion that ethics serves to help the individually weak to be collectively strong.

Cultural relativists have a different theory. They sometimes argue that since all humans share the same basic nature, they may also share the same basic needs and wants. Then they suggest that ethical systems develop within societies in response to these requirements and desires. This accounts for the similarities underlying the ethical systems found in different societies around the world. But even though our basic needs and wants are universal, our cultural and historical contexts vary, which is why some things are deemed moral in one culture and immoral in another.

This too seems like a helpful insight. There do seem to be similarities and differences between the ethical systems that have developed in the world's many diverse societies. Those cultural relativists who begin their position by asserting that some morally relevant facts transcend cultural differences, however, seem to be advocating something that's in the final analysis closer to absolutism than to relativism, for they are saying that there is at least one thing that is in fact not relative, not a cultural construct. If human nature is universal and is the cornerstone of human ethics, the principle from which all other ethical principles flow, then fundamentally all human ethical systems are starting from the same point and only differ in the application of that point. Furthermore, if all humans share the same basic needs and desires, then those too are universal rather than constructs that differ from one culture to another.

As explained earlier, ethical absolutism is the theory that timeless, unchanging moral principles ("absolutes") underlie morality and apply to all people. Those who hold to absolutism are not necessarily committed to the belief that all moral views apply to all people in exactly the same way: that's a straw man of absolutism.[13] But they are opposed to the idea that morality is nothing more than a cultural creation, a social construct. Ethical absolutism provides a ready explanation for the fact that all human societies develop systems of ethics and that there are deep underlying similarities between these systems. The explanation offered is that the societal propensity to develop ethical systems is a response to a set of absolute moral principles that in one way or another form part of the fabric of reality. In their interactions with one another and the environment in which they live, people come into contact with these principles and therefore discover their existence. Then they seek to understand them, eventually attempting to develop a systematic framework for living in harmony with these principles.

An illustration of this comes from a child's discovery of the principle of truth-telling. Many children are instructed by their parents to always tell the truth. But even those who aren't so instructed often recognize this principle on their own. Sometimes it happens when they are lied to by a friend and experience feelings of bewilderment and betrayal as a result. Or it may happen when they begin to tell lies, eventually get caught in a web of their own inconsistency, and then discover for themselves that "honesty is the best policy." Either way, this can serve as a first step down the road to belief in ethical absolutes.

---

13. The straw man fallacy is committed when you inaccurately portray a position in a way that makes it easy to refute. Saying that ethical absolutism holds that all moral beliefs are binding for all people, or anything similar to that, would be a straw man, for ethical absolutists generally make a distinction between moral beliefs and moral absolutes, and they also recognize that the application of moral absolutes must take into consideration the context in which the application is occurring.

> ### A SHORT LIST OF VIRTUES
>
> | | |
> |---|---|
> | Pru- | Hope |
> | dence | Love |
> | Courage | |
> | Temper- | |
> | ance | |
> | Justice | |
> | Faith | |

The absolutist explanation is not completely at odds with the explanations offered by nihilism and cultural relativism. The relativistic insistence that human nature figures into morality is quite acceptable to absolutists, who affirm that moral absolutes are reflected in human nature and society. Absolutists also recognize that context is important when applying moral principles to concrete situations, and that different contexts sometimes call for different applications of the same underlying principle.

Finally, the nihilistic suggestion that ethics is a tool that the weak use to overcome the strong can be embraced by absolutists, who might argue that if it were not for the fact that something is inherently immoral about the strong imposing their will on others, it would be much more difficult for the weak to arouse the sympathy and support of society in order to mount a successful resistance.

To recap the abductive argument for absolutism: The theory that is best able to account for the fact that all cultures seem to develop ethical systems that share certain underlying moral values is the one that is most likely correct. Absolutism seems better able to account for these phenomena. Therefore absolutism is most likely correct.

ETHICAL THEORIES

We've argued that timeless moral truths exist, that they somehow form part of the very fabric of reality, and that these principles should be followed as closely as possible by all people. But in order to live by them, we need to be able to discover them. That's where ethical theories come into the picture. Over the last twenty-five hundred years, a number of strategies have been suggested for discovering ethical absolutes. Let's take a quick look at some of them. A basic understanding of the various ways that different people approach moral decision-making will enable you to better understand the dialogues that make up the rest of this book and will even help you to understand the way that you yourself approach ethical decision-making—and perhaps improve upon it!

One very old tradition dates all the way back to the ancient Greek philosopher Aristotle (fourth century BCE). It's called **Virtue Ethics**. This approach views ethics as primarily concerning a person's nature, believing that what you do follows naturally from the sort of person you are. The virtuous person will naturally do the right thing. Therefore Virtue Ethics advocates that ethics focus mainly on cultivating a virtuous character.

Naturally in order to cultivate a virtuous character, you need to know which traits are virtuous and which traits are not. Aristotle had a theory about how to identify virtuous character traits: we should look for those that evidence balance by falling midway between two extremes. An example of this is courage, which strikes a balance between rashness and cowardice. He called these balanced character traits "the **Golden Mean**."

There is much to like about this approach to ethics. For one thing, it prepares us to face ethical dilemmas by requiring us to cultivate a moral character ahead of the time when we find ourselves confronted by them. This is very useful, for once you are caught up in a moral crisis, you may have neither the time nor the patience to contemplate what character traits should be guiding your response. But it has at least one significant short-coming: while it does tell us how to identify virtuous character traits, it does not tell us how to accurately identify what course of action a virtuous person should take. In other words, it does not provide a method for determining what acts are moral. So in theory people who have successfully cultivated their inner virtue could, when confronted by a moral dilemma, find themselves unable to determine what to do.

Another approach that has roots in Aristotle—and was further developed by the medieval theologian Thomas Aquinas—is **Natural Law**

Aristotle. Courtesy of After Lysippos. Public domain.

Ethics. This approach is predicated on the belief that morality is woven into the very fabric of reality and can be discovered in a way that is similar to how the laws of nature are woven into the fabric of reality and can be discovered. Supporters of Natural Law Ethics argue that the basic principles of the moral life can be discovered through careful study of the natural world, human nature, and human social interactions.

Examples of such careful analysis abound. For example, comparison of truth-telling and lying shows the inherent superiority of truth-telling: lying frustrates communication, undermines trust, and can destroy relationships. Similarly through comparing monogamous and polygamous marriages, we can see that monogamy has inherent advantages: it is harmonious with the nearly even birth rate of male and female children, it prevents destructive rivalries between wives, it promotes the greatest intimacy between husband and wife, and so forth. Also, heavy consumption of alcoholic beverages compares very unfavorably with drinking unfermented juices: the former undermines good health while the latter supports it; the former deprives a person of self-control while the latter can be a result of exercising it; and in North America and many other parts of the world the former is more expensive than the latter.

These examples illustrate how the very nature of reality encourages certain paths in life, paths that are conducive to lives that flourish rather than lives that destroy. These are the choices that the Natural Law theorist views as moral. But it's not that they are moral because they produce flourishing lives: rather they produce flourishing lives because they are moral. Good actions naturally tend to produce a good life. Or so the Natural Law theorist argues.

There's a fly in the ointment, though. Often disagreements arise about what moral conclusions the examination of reality really supports. Take polygamy, for example: polygamous groups have long argued that polygamy actually has many more benefits than are generally acknowledged. Multiple wives are said to be able to share childcare and household responsibilities, which not only makes life easier for them but can also free them up to pursue education and career opportunities that are often difficult to combine with motherhood. They can also provide companionship to each other and more easily satisfy the romantic desires of their husband.

There are good arguments on both sides of many debates in applied ethics. Discerning the true Natural Law position on weighty issues, such as the death penalty and voluntary physician-assisted suicide, and on a very large number of less weighty issues, such as tattoos, body piercing, musical styles, and dietary choices, can be very difficult. This will become apparent as you read the dialogues that make up most of this book.

For this reason many ethicists have taken a different approach: they have sought moral principles that can be applied to issues in order to evaluate their moral status. For example, **Utilitarianism** argues for the principle of maximal utility: we should always do whatever will provide the most benefit to the greatest number of people.[14] For example, while the death penalty clearly involves a very significant loss for one person, if it can be shown to have an even greater benefit to the rest of society, perhaps as a deterrent or through some other means, than the death penalty would be moral. Conversely, if it can be shown that the death penalty harms more people than it helps, perhaps through undermining belief in the sanctity of life or something like that, then the death penalty would be immoral.

At first Utilitarianism seems like a very straightforward approach to ethics. But because it can be very difficult to predict the consequences of our actions, it's not always clear what action a Utilitarian analysis should prefer. Furthermore, it's not clear that having beneficial consequences always makes an action moral. For example, it would be possible for the government to tax the rich very highly and use the proceeds to help the needy. Perhaps this could even be done in such a way that the needy are helped far more than the rich are harmed. Many would object, however, that such a course of action would be unfair to the rich and thus immoral because it takes from the rich what is rightfully theirs.

Another moral principle comes from the eighteenth-century German philosopher Immanuel Kant. His approach to ethics focuses on fulfilling a person's moral obligations and is therefore called "**Duty Ethics.**" The central principle of Duty Ethics is the **categorical imperative**: act only according to that principle that you could consistently will to become a universal law.

---

14. Utilitarianism has been a major approach to ethics in the twentieth and early twenty-first centuries. The founders of Utilitarianism were the nineteenth-century philosophers Jeremy Bentham and John Stuart Mill. More recent Utilitarian thinkers include R. M. Hare and Peter Singer.

What this means is that you should live by only those principles that you wouldn't mind other people living by. Put even more simply, you should only do what you wouldn't mind others doing. This is similar to the Golden Rule: do unto others as you would have them do unto you.

Kant didn't conceive of the categorical imperative as an emotional test, as if what matters is what you would *prefer* to have done to you. Rather he conceived of it as a logical test: do only that which will not involve you in a logical contradiction. You contradict yourself if you say that what is acceptable for you to do would not also be acceptable for others to do. In effect, you are making yourself an exception to the rule.

Lying is a good example of this: if we would adopt as our guiding principle "I should lie when it's convenient for me," we would have to be willing for everyone else to live by that principle. But if everyone lives by that principle, then lying would become so commonplace that people would always be suspicious of what others are telling them. Effective communication would be significantly undermined. Therefore we probably do not want to universalize the principle that people should lie when it is convenient for them to do so. And if we wouldn't want others to live by that principle, then it would be hypocritical for us to live by it. Furthermore, Kant would say that we would

be involving ourselves in a contradiction by saying, on the one hand, that it is moral to lie (for us), and on the other hand that it's not (for others). In contrast if we would adopt as our guiding principle "always tell the truth," we would have to be willing for everyone else to always tell the truth. That's an outcome that we might consider to be desirable, and since we would be adopting the same principle for ourselves as we would want others to live by, we're not contradicting ourselves. Hence this is a principle that we might indeed want to universalize.

Immanuel Kant. By Gottlieb Doebler.
Public domain.

Duty Ethics sounds very promising. But there are difficulties. For example, like cultural relativism, Duty Ethics faces a "problem of specificity": How specific should our moral principles be? We may not want to universalize the principle that lying is good. But perhaps we should universalize the principle "lying is good when it saves a life." Here we can think of the familiar scenario of a family harboring Jews in Nazi Germany. If the Security Service knocked on the door and asked whether the family was harboring Jews, the family would face a difficult choice: Should they lie to protect the Jews, or should they tell the truth, with the very likely result that the Jews would be sent to a concentration camp? Surely in such a situation it is more moral to lie than to tell the truth. But then, haven't we abandoned our principled approach to ethics in favor of an approach that says that we should base our moral decisions on the consequences that we anticipate our actions will have? Haven't we traded Duty Ethics for contextualism?

There is one more ethical theory that must be mentioned: **Divine Command Theory**.[15] This is the idea that what is moral is so because a sovereign and omnipotent God declared it to be so and that what is immoral is so because God declared it to be immoral. Some people reason that if God is the creator of all things (other than himself), then he is the creator of the principles of morality too. Furthermore, they argue, since God is completely sovereign, he has the right to determine what counts as moral and what counts as immoral.

Understandably this view has a great deal of appeal for theists. There are, however, some serious objections to it. The most famous of these comes from the ancient Greek philosopher Plato and is called the **Euthyphro Dilemma**.[16] Cutting to the chase, Plato points out that if nothing is moral or immoral until God declares it to be so, then prior to God making this determination, everything is morally neutral. If that's the case, then there's no explanation for why God chooses what he chooses other than arbitrary free choice, and things like rape, murder, and lying are not inherently wrong. Similarly, love, compassion, and telling the truth are not inherently right. This is a powerful *reductio* against the thesis that God decides what is moral and immoral.

---

15. A contemporary proponent of Divine Command Theory is Robert Adams.
16. Plato's little book titled *Euthyphro* can be read online at http://classics.mit.edu/Plato/euthyfro.html.

Plato. Courtesy of the Louvre Museum. Public domain.

Of course, it could be the case that rape, murder, and lying are inherently immoral and that God proclaims that we should not do them because, being omniscient, he knows with complete accuracy their immoral nature. This view sees morality as something that exists separate from God's will and to which God's will conforms because he is both omniscient and perfectly holy. *Prima facie*[17] that sounds like a better theory. But with this theory, in order for God to be holy he would have to perfectly conform to this standard of morality that he did not create. This seems to impugn the sovereignty of God by asserting the existence of a moral authority higher than God himself. Many theists would find this to be a very problematic suggestion.

Perhaps a better solution would be to modify Divine Command Theory so that morality isn't tied to the will of God (his "commands") but rather to his nature. This has been variously called "modified divine command theory" and **"Divine Nature Theory."** The idea is that the standard of morality isn't something outside of God to which he must conform in order to be holy. Instead, the standard of morality is God himself. God, who is perfectly holy, loving, compassionate, and so forth, is the source of morality. The same morality that shines from God's nature is reflected in the fabric of his creation, so that love, compassion, and God's other positive attributes are the foundation of morality throughout the created order. What is immoral, then, is anything that is inconsistent with God's nature.

---

17. *Prima facie* means "at first appearance." It refers to our initial impression of an issue. *Ultima facie* means "on final analysis" and refers to the conclusion one arrives at via careful consideration.

Divine Nature Theory (hereafter DNT) has several advantages over the more traditional version of Divine Command Theory. First, it escapes the horn of the Euthyphro dilemma that makes morality arbitrary by anchoring morality to the nature of an eternal and unchanging being. Second, it provides an explanation of why God commands what he commands and prohibits what he prohibits. Third, it eludes the other horn of the Euthyphro dilemma by removing the need for a moral authority outside of and higher than God. Finally, it provides the basis for an explanation of why moral principles seem implicit in many aspects of the created order.

For theists, DNT seems like a reasonable choice. But as a methodology for evaluating the morality of an action, it leaves important questions unanswered. In fact, it is more an explanation of the underlying nature or source of morality than a theory about how morality can be discovered. Therefore more needs to be said about the epistemological aspects of DNT.[18]

Since DNT implies that God's moral nature will be reflected in the nature of his creation, there's a smooth segue from DNT to Natural Law Ethics. In fact, theologians speak about "general revelation," which is their term for what God has revealed about himself to all people through nature itself. If the truths of general revelation include truths about God's moral nature, then there's a possibility of pursuing a Natural Law approach to ethics while at the same time embracing DNT.

As noted in our earlier discussion of Natural Law Ethics, however, it's not easy to discern the true Natural Law position on many issues. As a result, theists often disagree about what moral conclusions our examination of God's creation really support. This comes as no surprise to theologians, who recognize the limitations of general revelation and advocate utilizing special revelation whenever possible. "Special revelation" is the theological term for God's revelations that communicate specific truths to specific people, such as when God speaks to Moses out of the burning bush, when God speaks to his people through a prophet, or when God inspires the writing of Scriptures.

The most prominent form of special revelation in the Christian tradition is the Bible. The Bible contains many moral commands, prohibitions,

---

18. *Epistemology* is the study of human cognition, of how we know things, what knowledge is, and related issues. Another term for it is "the theory of knowledge."

principles, and examples. It is a very rich resource for Christian ethics. Some of the principles that underlie the ethical theories examined earlier in this chapter (such as importance of cultivating a virtuous character, natural law, maximal utility, and the categorical imperative) can be found among the principles contained in the Bible (actions flow from the heart, general revelation, the impact of our actions on those around us, and the Golden Rule).

Of course, DNT is a theory that depends on the existence of God. If God does not exist, then DNT cannot get off the ground. Hence DNT presupposes theism. Investigation of the grounds for theism goes far beyond the scope of this book. There are many good books on the subject, though, and the reader is encouraged to make a study of that fascinating topic.

CONCLUSION

Ethics is a very important topic. A systematic approach to ethics is also very important. This chapter has been devoted to introducing a range of systematic approaches but has made little effort to guide the reader toward any particular approach. But determining or carefully developing how you will approach ethical issues is a worthy endeavor—more than just worthy, it's essential. The reader is urged to embark on this venture posthaste, for the approach to ethics that you adopt will often determine what conclusions you arrive at when you consider issues in applied ethics, big and small.

In addition to being important, ethics is fun. This chapter has been quite academic. No attempt has been made to lighten the mood. That is because the authors want to give to the reader a succinct but thorough introduction to ethical theories prior to diving into the chapters on applied ethics. But the authors also want the reader to enjoy doing ethics. The following chapters will be much more pleasurable to read. All of them are written as dialogues and address issues of contemporary importance. We sincerely hope that you like them. We do ask, though, that as you read, you keep in mind the various ethical theories introduced in this chapter. As you read the dialogues, you may find yourself trying to make up your mind about where you stand on the issues. That's a good thing, but please keep in mind that you can't really form a well-reasoned conclusion about what is right until you've come to a conclusion about what methodology you should be employing—what ethical theory should guide your decision and ultimately your life.

QUESTIONS TO PONDER

- What is the difference between a descriptive statement and a prescriptive one, and why does it matter?

- Which is correct, ethical relativism or ethical absolutism?

- What do you think is the most effective methodology for evaluating the morality of an action? What reasons lead you to this conclusion?

- How would you go about actually applying that methodology to a concrete issue in applied ethics—say, for example, the debate about what attitude Americans should have toward immigrants who are fleeing persecution and of necessity enter the United States illegally?

TERMS TO KNOW

- Ethics
- *Reductio ad absurdum*
- Ethical relativism
- Cultural relativism
- Ethical absolutism
- Nihilism
- Subjectivism
- Situation Ethics
- Ethical contextualism
- Abduction
- Straw Man Fallacy
- Virtue ethics
- The Golden Mean
- Natural Law Ethics
- Utilitarianism
- Duty Ethics
- Categorical Imperative
- Divine Command Theory
- Euthyphro dilemma
- Divine Nature Theory

FOR FURTHER READING

Two very readable introductions to ethical theories are:

Jones, Michael S. *Moral Reasoning: An Intentional Approach to Distinguishing Right from Wrong.* Dubuque, IA: Kendall Hunt, 2017.
This volume focuses on ethical theories and is written by one of the authors of the current volume.
Wilkens, Steve. *Beyond Bumper Sticker Ethics: An Introduction to Theories of Right and Wrong.* 2nd ed. Downers Grove, IL: InterVarsity Press, 2011.
Included are chapters on ethical theories and applied ethics.

For those desiring more advanced reading:

Baggett, David, and Jerry Walls. *Good God: The Theistic Foundations of Morality.* Oxford: Oxford University Press, 2011.
A detailed but readable book on Divine Nature Theory.
Becker, Lawrence C., and Charlotte B. Becker, eds. *Encyclopedia of Ethics,* 2nd ed. New York: Routledge, 2003.
Bourke, Vernon. *History of Ethics.* 2 vols. Edinburg, VA: Axios Press, 2007.
Feinber, John S., and Paul D. Feinberg. *Ethics for a Brave New World.* 2nd ed. Wheaton, IL: Crossway, 2010.
This book treats ethical theories and applied ethics. It's fairly advanced reading. It approaches ethics from a theistic perspective.

HUMANITARIAN
ISSUES

IMMIGRATION

Synopsis: Bianca, Lauren, and Micah are students at Lone Mountain University, who meet at a tea shop where they often discuss issues from Dr. Platt's ethics class. The class focuses on practical issues, what Dr. Platt calls *applied ethics*, although his introductory lecture includes a discussion of the presuppositions that underlie moral values, also called *metaethics*.[1] During this meeting, they end up discussing issues related to immigration, which had been the subject of that morning's class. Bianca is studying education and is the child of immigrants who worked their way up to middle-class status. She empathizes with other immigrants and doesn't understand why some Americans seem rather xenophobic. Her friend Lauren, a nursing student, grew up in a solidly middle-class family and has seen friends and neighbors experience job loss because of outsourcing the importation of inexpensive products. She argues that while xenophobia certainly isn't justified, strict immigration policies are in America's best

---

1. The academic study of ethics is often divided into two broad areas: *metaethics* and *applied ethics*. Metaethics is the study of the presuppositions that underlie someone's moral values. It is the more abstract, philosophical part of ethics. Applied ethics, on the other hand, is the study of concrete issues in order to attempt to determine what the moral stance is on any particular issue. It is the attempt to evaluate the morality of specific actions such as dancing, lying, abortion, and eating meat. As such it is the more practical part of ethics, but it cannot be approached systematically without first studying metaethics.

interest for a variety of reasons. Micah, who studies business, is aware that foreign workers in the United States—even those who are here legally— sometimes compete for jobs with American workers. He is also aware of the complexity of this situation: employers who benefit from affordable labor are able to retain a greater number of employees than would otherwise be possible, but Micah suspects low-paid immigrant labor could drive down wages for American workers.

He sees the arguments on both sides, including arguments that stem from his Christian faith.

* * *

"There they are," Bianca said, staring out the window. She was enjoying a hot cup of jasmine tea at The Grey Earl, a locally owned coffee-and-tea shop near campus. Lauren and Micah looked up. A group of Hispanic-looking construction workers was approaching from the direction of the university.

"Are those the men who are building the new School of Business?" Micah was looking forward to moving into the new facilities when they are completed.

"I wish our administration would do the right thing and hire American workers," Lauren stated flatly.

"What makes that 'the right thing'?" Bianca asked, her voice tight.

Lauren suddenly realized how insensitive her comment was. "I'm sorry, Bianca. I didn't mean anything offensive by that. There's nothing wrong with people from other countries coming to America and working to improve their lot in life. But America's first duty is to look out for her own citizens, and plenty of unemployed Americans could be doing the work that these Mexicans are doing on our campus."

"Maybe Americans didn't want those jobs. It looks like pretty hard work—and dirty too. I wonder how well it pays? Perhaps there aren't enough Americans who are willing to work that hard for the salary that a Mexican worker will accept." Bianca's voice relaxed, but she wasn't ready to concede the argument either.

"I recently read a *Washington Post* article about that," Micah noted. "It was based on a study of migrant agricultural workers in North Carolina. It turns out that even in times of high unemployment, Americans are unwilling to take on many jobs because of the combination of low wages and difficult work. Furthermore, when Americans do take such jobs, they frequently don't keep them very long. The article contrasted this with foreign workers, who it claimed often take such jobs, do them well, and stick to them until the job is done."[2]

"That doesn't reflect very positively on American workers," Bianca opined.

"Well," Micah responded, "it's not necessarily a poor reflection on American workers. Today many Americans graduate from college with at least a two-year degree and look for jobs that involve more technical expertise. There's nothing wrong with executing a life strategy that results in higher pay for doing less taxing work, is there?"

"Not in our opinion, obviously," affirmed Bianca. "Look at us. We've all chosen college over manual labor."

"But that study is about agricultural workers, right?" Lauren wasn't giving up just yet. "Agricultural labor is very low paying, isn't it? Contractors receive better wages, and a lot of immigrants are working in IT, engineering, medicine, and other well-paying fields. American workers must compete with immigrants for the limited number of jobs available in each of these fields, which sometimes makes it hard for Americans to find employment. That just doesn't seem right to me; after all, this is *our* country. It should provide for *our* needs first and foremost, and only help out others after the needs of Americans are met.

"Furthermore," she continued, "Isn't it the very existence of low-cost labor that enables farmers to pay so little for hired help? Doesn't the existence of low-cost foreign labor drag down the wages of all laborers in a given field?"

"That's a fair question, Lauren," Micah replied. "I think there could be some truth to that. The *Washington Post* article points out that if it wasn't for cheap migrant workers, farmers would indeed need to pay more. But it also points out that if the cost of labor goes up too much, farmers won't be able to afford it, and as a result they'll go out of business. I imagine the same thing would be true in any business: construction firms might be saving

---

2. Dylan Matthews, "North Carolina Needed 6,500 Farm Workers. Only 7 Americans Stuck It Out," *Washington Post*, May 15, 2013, https://www.washingtonpost.com/news/wonk/wp/2013/05/15/north-carolina-needed-6500-farm-workers-only-7-americans-stuck-it-out.

some money by using inexpensive foreign labor, and we might feel like that's just being cheap or padding the bottom line or something inappropriate like that. But if that labor wasn't available and they had to pay significantly more for domestic labor, that could threaten their viability as businesses. Furthermore, if labor costs go up, then the price of what those laborers pro-duce—whether peaches and apples or college buildings, computer software, or anything else—will go up too. At our university, that could result in the School of Business not finishing its new building, or alternately, the cost of tuition rising. As they say, 'There's no free lunch.'"

"So you think that immigrant workers are a good thing?" Lauren asked.

"Well, it's a complex issue," he responded.

"It sure is!" Bianca wanted back into the discussion. "Besides these eco-nomic considerations—we're not all business majors like you, Micah—there are historical concerns too. America is a nation of immigrants. No race originated in North America. The so-called Native Americans descended from people who immigrated from Siberia millennia ago. The Caucasian majority in the United States descended from European immigrants who came in waves starting in the sixteenth century; African Americans and Asian Americans began arriving shortly thereafter. Why should we start discriminating against people from other parts of the world at this late date in history? How could we possibly justify such xenophobia?"

"Hold on a minute, Bianca," Lauren objected. "Opposition to uncon-trolled immigration does not equal xenophobia. Do you really think I'm a xenophobe? We're friends, aren't we? I don't oppose your presence in America, nor the presence of your parents nor people from many other countries who are making positive contributions to American society. But not all immigrants are as honest and hard-working as you are. There are whole crime syndicates formed by immigrants from Latin America, and they are extremely violent. Many immigrants can't care for themselves and place a burden on America's social safety net. Then there's the concern about terrorists posing as refugees in order to enter America and set up terrorist cells right here on our soil. At the very least you must admit that we should try to prevent this kind of immigrant from entering the US, right?"

"Sure, Lauren," Bianca relented. "I completely agree with you there. But in my experience, the vast majority of immigrants are like my parents:

people who come to America because they see it as the land of promise. They have an extremely positive opinion of America, and so far from wanting to undermine America's legal and social systems, they want to support them and participate in them. Think about the immigrants you know. What kind of people are they? How do they view America?"[3]

"Well," responded Lauren, "I don't actually know many foreigners very well. I know you, but you've been in America your whole life. There really aren't any other foreigners whom I've gotten to know closely. I'm sure most immigrants are more like your parents than like the members of MS-13 and other violent gangs. My main argument is that America should prioritize caring for the needs of its own before it looks to the needs of others. There are more poor people here than we can care for already. And there's unemployment and our overburdened healthcare and criminal justice systems to think about. We've kind of got our hands full already. I'm not hesitant about allowing more immigration because I am afraid of foreigners—in fact, I think that having foreigners here makes America a more interesting place. I'm hesitant about immigration because I don't think we can care for immigrants and Americans both."

"I appreciate your concern for the well-being of other Americans, Lauren," Bianca assured her, "and I admire your compassion. I wonder if it's not a bit misplaced though. After all, America is the land of promise. It's a place where anyone who has the drive to succeed and a little bit of luck can get ahead. That's the beauty of American capitalism, isn't it? And it's not true of many parts of the world. Even developing countries that are trying to be like America don't offer the economic mobility that America offers."

"Sure, Bianca. America is the land of promise. But how is that relevant?" Lauren asked.

"It's relevant because there are people throughout the world who would love to have a chance to work long, hard hours in order to have

---

3. Bianca's response to the suggestion that immigrants are dangerous (in various ways) is very restrained. More direct denials of this allegation have been made by various immigration advocates, who point out that research shows generally lower levels of crime among immigrants than among American citizens. See, for instance, Alex Nowrasteh, "Immigration and Crime: What the Research Says," *Cato at Liberty* (blog), the Cato Institute, July 14, 2015, https://www.cato.org/blog/immigration-crime-what-research-says.

even the possibility of improving their lot in life, but they are trapped in political or economic situations that prevent it," Bianca explained. "But in America, those who are so inclined are rewarded with the opportunity to try. So why not afford this same opportunity to hard-working people from all over the world? Isn't basing this privilege on the location of one's birth rather arbitrary? Mexicans have the same needs and desires that Americans have—and Canadians, Europeans, Asians, and Africans do too, for that matter. It seems to me that the most consistent and most compassionate approach to the question of immigration is to allow in as many immigrants as possible within the constraints of a thorough system of criminal background checks."

"That seems a bit extreme to me, Bianca. I want to be a compassionate person, but I don't want to be foolhardy. Micah, what do you think about all of this? You haven't said anything for quite a while."

"I'm not sure where I stand on this issue, Lauren," he answered. "You know I'm a Christian. I want to stand where God wants me to stand—but I'm not sure where that is. On the one hand, I need to be compassionate. Jesus gives us that example: he was very compassionate, healing even people whom his disciples didn't consider to be worthy of his attention. He healed non-Jews even though he himself was a devout Jew, he showed compassion on harlots and tax collectors, and he treated the poor and uneducated with just as much respect as the wealthy and elite—perhaps even more. But that doesn't necessarily mean all Christians everywhere should advocate unlimited immigration into their countries. So the question I've been wrestling with is about the form that Christian compassion should take in the twenty-first-century American context. Should I view the responsibility of our government to be prioritizing the well-being of US citizens? Or should I view the responsibility of our government to be acting in such a way as to provide the greatest benefit to all people, regardless of their nationality? Most American Christians seem to take the former approach, but at the moment I'm not sure that's where Jesus would stand."

"I'm not sure it's a good idea to combine religion and politics, my friend," Lauren offered. "That violates the separation of church and state. And why should we look to a two-thousand-year-old book for guidance on twenty-first-century issues?"

"The Bible's not just an old book, Lauren. It's the inspired Word of God. What it says is relevant to all ages." Micah spoke with a somber tone that conveyed complete conviction.

"Micah, you know that I respect you a lot. You're intelligent, for one thing, but besides that, I really value your friendship. I just don't get why you hold so firmly to your Christian beliefs. To me, Christianity seems no more plausible than any other ancient religion. They all seem to be full of superstitions, outdated moral teachings, and useless rituals. What does a modern university student see in any of that?"

"I value your friendship too, Lauren. And I respect you. Let me ask you a question. Is every belief that has a long history automatically false?" Lauren looked puzzled at this question. Micah continued, "It's not because Hinduism and Confucianism are old that I reject them: it's because I think that their central teachings are not true. Conversely, while Christian beliefs are old, if they are true, we should accept them anyway, shouldn't we?"

"Of course," Lauren granted. "But that's a pretty big if. What reasons do you have for thinking that the central teachings of Christianity are true? Some Christian claims seem not just old but out of date, don't you think? Don't Christians believe that Mary was a virgin when she gave birth to Jesus and that Jesus walked on water? Those things seem highly improbable to me."

"I can understand that," he replied. "If they weren't improbable, they wouldn't be miracles, I guess. I mean, by definition miracles are improbable. They violate the very laws of nature, and that's got to make them about as improbable as anything ever could be.[4] But that doesn't make them *impossible*. Hence if we have good reasons for believing that they actually did happen, we should accept them as historical, don't you agree?"

"I don't know," she said, doubt and hesitation clear in her voice. "This may be an area that you've studied more than I have. If you're right, then we only accept things as historical if there's good evidence for them, right? So if there isn't good evidence, do we reject them?"

"Almost. I'd say that if the evidence for a miraculous occurrence is better than the evidence against it, then we should accept that it is historical, but if the

---

4. See David Hume, *An Inquiry Concerning Human Understanding*, ed. Charles W. Hendel (Indianapolis: Bobbs-Merrill, 1955), 122.

situation is the opposite then we should reject it. That's why I reject Buddhist claims that Siddhartha Gautama performed miracles—although there's some evidence that he did, there's better evidence that he didn't. But there's a third option, a sort of historian's middle ground. If the evidence for and against the historicity of an event is equal, then we should remain neutral toward the event until we have evidence that clearly points in one direction or the other."

"OK, that seems fair to me. So your opinion, I take it, is that there's better evidence for the virgin birth and Jesus walking on water than against it. What is this evidence?" Lauren's question seemed sincere, as if she was genuinely open minded about the possibility that Micah had some kind of evidence to offer.

"The Bible itself is the evidence, of course. The Bible accurately records many details about Jesus, including who his mother was and that, as unlikely as it sounds, she was a virgin when he was born. It also records that he walked on the Sea of Galilee without sinking."

On hearing this argument, Lauren's face took on a somewhat unconvinced expression. "If you say so, my friend. But don't a lot of scholars question the accuracy of the Bible?"

"Yes they do," he admitted. "But there are also a lot of scholars who affirm its accuracy, including Bible scholars, historians, and archeologists.[5] Besides, if the Bible is inspired by God, then it must necessarily be accurate, for God knows all things and he never lies."

"That's another very big if. I can't imagine what proof you have that the Bible is actually inspired by God. How would a historian go about proving that?" she asked.

"It can't actually be proved by historians," he granted. "It's more of a theological issue than a historical one. I believe the Bible is the inspired Word of God because it says it is."

"Wait a minute—that doesn't work," she objected. "If every book that says it's inspired is, then the Qur'an, the Hindu Vedas, and who knows what

---

5. See, for example, Yitzhak Meitlis, *Excavating the Bible: New Archaeological Evidence for the Historical Reliability of Scripture* (Savage, MD: Eshel, 2012); Craig L. Blomberg, *The Historical Reliability of the New Testament: Countering the Challenges to Evangelical Christian Beliefs* (Nashville: B&H Academic, 2016).

other books are all inspired. But since they contradict each other in a variety of ways, they can't really all be inspired, can they?"

Micah saw that he needed to be more careful about how he was phrasing his thoughts. "No, and I wouldn't want to argue that those books are inspired. I guess what I meant to say was that I believe the Bible is inspired because God said it's inspired. But he said that in the Bible, which I guess is why I initially responded the way that I did."

"But that doesn't really work either, does it?" Lauren was on a roll. "Aren't you essentially saying 'I know that the Bible is inspired by God because the Bible claims that God says that it's inspired by God'? How would that be different from saying 'I know that the Qur'an is inspired by Allah because the Qur'an claims that Allah said that the Qur'an is inspired by Allah'?"

"OK, Lauren, let me try again. Obviously I'm struggling to formulate my beliefs clearly, but if you'll bear with me, I really do believe I can provide good reasons to believe what the Bible says. What I should have said is only a little different from what I actually said. I should have said that I believe that the Bible is inspired because Jesus said it's inspired. And I believe that Jesus is correct about this because I believe that Jesus was God incarnate, and therefore everything that he said must be correct since God never makes any mistakes. Is that better?"

"Hold on a minute. Let me make sure that I've understood you." Lauren seemed to be enjoying this exchange, even though it was pretty intense. "You're saying that you know that Jesus was God incarnate, and that enables you to know that the Bible is inspired by God?"

"Yes, I think that's what I want to say." Micah didn't seem fully confident that he hadn't misstated himself again.

"How do you know that Jesus is God incarnate? You're not going to say 'Because the Bible says so,' are you?" Lauren's tone indicated she was trying to help her friend figure out what he believed and why.

"Um . . . I guess not. Would there be a problem with saying that?"

"I believe so," she confirmed. "That would be circular reasoning. You'd be arguing that the Bible is inspired because Jesus says it is and that Jesus is God because the Bible says that he is, in effect using Jesus to prove the Bible and the Bible to prove Jesus. The problem with circular reasoning is that it doesn't actually prove anything. If you use A to support B and B to support A, the result is that neither A nor B has any real support. It's just a juggling act."

"I think I see your point," Micah admitted. "But I don't think I meant it in quite the way that you think I did, and perhaps what I meant isn't circular. I see that it would be problematic to say 'I believe that Jesus is God because the inspired Bible says that he is, and I believe that the Bible is inspired because Jesus who is God says that it is.' That would be like me saying to you, 'We know that a college education is a good thing because it makes us better-educated people and we know that being better-educated people is a good thing because that is the reason people go to college.' Obviously this assumes that college education is good rather than proving it. But what I was trying to say was that I know that Jesus is God because the Bible provides historical evidence that supports belief in his divinity, and since he's God, his affirmation that the Bible is inspired shows us that it is. That's not circular as far as I can see. What do you think?"

"Oh brother," moaned Bianca. "You guys are getting more than a little carried away. Micah, you don't need to go through all of this careful formulation of arguments in order to know that Jesus is God incarnate. We Orthodox accept that by faith, and that's enough. No arguments are needed."[6]

"That's an interesting approach, Bianca," Micah replied.

"How does that work?" Lauren asked. "Can every belief system be justified by an appeal to faith? Can I claim that atheism is true because I accept it by faith?"

"Let's return to the question of immigration, shall we?" offered Micah. "We've gotten off on a rabbit trail—an interesting one, for sure, but immigration is interesting too."

"Perhaps we can have a discussion of atheism, religion, and faith some other time," Bianca suggested.

"Sure," the others replied in unison.

Reaching for his mug, Micah was disappointed to find it empty, but the thought-provoking discussion kept him from leaving to get a refill.

"Returning to my inner struggles over immigration," he said, "the Bible—"

"Can we return to my point about the separation of church and state?" an apologetic but insistent Lauren interjected. "It's distinct from the question

---

6. Bianca is Eastern Orthodox, an ancient branch of Christianity that is very common in Eastern Europe and has adherents throughout the world.

of the inspiration of the Bible, and I think it needs to be addressed before we go on."

"Sure," he responded. "Perhaps you think it's problematic for me to base my views on my religion. But if I were to in ways inconsistent with my faith, you'd rightly call me a hypocrite. Either way I lose. On the other hand, you probably think it's perfectly fine to adopt an attitude toward immigration that's consistent with your atheism (or your agnosticism, if that's what you'd prefer to call it). So you implicitly believe that it's more appropriate for irreligion to affect one's views than it is for religion to do so. How do you justify such unequal treatment?"

"Hmmm . . ." Lauren paused. "I see your point—or points. I guess I should be willing to allow your beliefs to guide your positions on this kind of issue just as I'd want you to allow me to base my positions on my beliefs—or disbeliefs. I wouldn't want to force someone to be hypocritical any more than I would want to be forced to adopt positions that are inconsistent with my own convictions."

"Right." Micah felt good about finally coming out on top of an argument. "We don't need to be in complete agreement about whose religion or philosophy or worldview is right in order to agree that people should have the liberty to determine their beliefs according to the dictates of their conscience. And if we adopt that approach, then we're respecting the separation of church and state, because no one is using the law to impose anyone's beliefs on anyone else.

"So as I was beginning to say," he continued, "the Bible has a lot to say that's relevant to the issue of immigration. In general, it seems to side with immigrants, just as it generally sides with the poor, oppressed, and needy. I don't have the various passages memorized, but we can begin by remembering that Jesus, when he was a baby, was an immigrant in Egypt: his whole family fled to Egypt when an angel warned his father that Herod would try to kill the baby.[7] This shows me that there's nothing inherently immoral about being an immigrant—a point that comes as no big surprise. But since the Bible indicates that Christians should obey the government as long as they can do so without disobeying God, it would generally be immoral for

---

7. Matt. 2:13–15.

Christians to become illegal immigrants.[8] Similarly I'm inclined to think that it would be immoral for Christians to help others to immigrate illegally. That does not mean that Christians should not help legal immigrants, though, nor that Christians in America should oppose immigrants from entering America legally. That's probably the main issue that we're talking about, isn't it—immigrants entering America legally?"

REFUGEE ARRIVALS

Fiscal Years 1980 to 2018

Year	Number	Year	Number
2018	22,405	1998	76,712
2017	53,691	1997	69,653
2016	84,988	1996	75,421
2015	69,920	1995	98,973
2014	69,975	1994	111,680
2013	69,909	1993	114,181
2012	58,179	1992	115,548
2011	56,384	1991	113,389
2010	73,293	1990	122,066
2009	74,602	1989	107,070
2008	60,107	1988	76,483
2007	48,218	1987	64,528
2006	41,094	1986	62,146
2005	53,738	1985	67,704
2004	52,840	1984	70,393
2003	28,286	1983	61,218
2002	26,785	1982	98,096
2001	68,920	1981	159,252
2000	72,165	1980	207,116
1999	85,285		

Department of Homeland Security,
https://www.dhs.gov/immigration-statistics/yearbook/2018/table13

"I think so," Bianca chimed in. "In the Hebrew Bible, although the Israelites were discouraged from fraternizing with the surrounding nations, they were commanded to treat foreigners justly and compassionately just as if they were Jews. In those days national boundaries were much more porous than they are today, so people passed freely from one region to another without much consideration other than to know which roads were the safest. The Jews were liable to encounter immigrants frequently, and the biblical mandate was to treat them well. The New Testament builds on this basic attitude, instructing us to be hospitable to strangers because in doing so we might unknowingly be playing host to angels.[9] The whole tenor of the Bible is positive toward foreigners."

"Well, I guess that settles the matter for you Christians, but I still have my concerns." Lauren was not going to be convinced by quotes from the Bible. "As a nursing student, I'm concerned about the burden that low-income or no-income immigrants place on our healthcare system. When people without health insurance come to America and do not have the means to pay for doctor's visits and prescription medicines, they often go to hospital emergency rooms for every medical need that arises. Emergency room personnel are not allowed to turn them away, so hospitals end up absorbing the cost of their treatment. This can be a huge financial burden for hospitals—who then must pass the costs on. Eventually the costs are spread out between their other patients, insurance companies, staff, local governments, and other benefactors. As you said, Micah, there's no free lunch. Someone's got to pay for all this free medicine."

"You're exactly right, Lauren. As a business student, I have to agree with you. The Christian approach to the issue needs to be holistic: we cannot simply say 'The Bible is pro-immigration' and then ignore the difficulties that could result from that position. We've got to have an approach that takes into account all of the data relevant to the issue—biblical and empirical."

"But this problem is not unique to immigrants," Bianca objected. "Lauren, you're a nursing student: don't low-income Americans do the same thing? Isn't this a problem that's endemic to the American healthcare system? It's one of the issues that has motivated Democrats to try to reform healthcare

---

9. Heb. 13:2.

over and over again. Poor people use the emergency room as if it's a family doctor's office whether or not they are immigrants. We can't blame this problem on immigrants alone. Maybe it's not right to blame it on poor people at all—who chooses to be poor? It's a problem with our society and the way we've set things up. If we'd fix the structure of our healthcare system, then immigrants wouldn't place a burden on it anymore."

"Well, someone would have to pay for their healthcare, Bianca. Are you suggesting that the cost of healthcare for those who can't afford it be passed on to the taxpayer?" As a business major, Micah was quick to see this implication.

"Sure, why not? That's the way many countries handle it. In fact, most developed nations have some form of universal health care. Even many developing nations do." Having relatives in the developing economies of Eastern Europe, Bianca knew what she was talking about.

"But is it fair to take money from middle-class families via taxation and redistribute it to low-income people for healthcare? Is it OK to play Robin Hood and 'rob from the rich and give to the poor'?" Micah was giving voice to one of the major objections to universal healthcare.

"Is it moral to turn a blind eye to the needs of the poor around us? You're a Christian: what does the Christian faith tell us about that?" Bianca asked, looking directly at Micah.

"Honestly, Bianca, I'm not completely sure. I see some arguments for both sides. Jesus clearly advocates caring for the poor, even at one's own expense. The Parable of the Good Samaritan is a clear example of his teaching on this subject. But that does not necessarily mandate the government take control of healthcare. And the apostle Paul's admonition that 'the one who is unwilling to work shall not eat' may also be relevant to this issue."[10]

"Slow down, guys," Lauren interjected. "I'm not all that interested in what the Bible says about this issue because I don't feel compelled to follow its teachings. I'm more concerned about the practical arguments, and from that perspective I can see both strengths and weaknesses to universal healthcare. But the healthcare problem is only one facet of my overall concern about opening the door to more immigration. How about the other concerns, such as our overburdened justice system and overcrowded prisons? And how

---

10. 2 Thess. 3:10.

about the impact on our schools, which must struggle to educate students who don't know English and whose parents make little contribution to the tax base that supports the public school system?"

"I think there may be some misconceptions at play here," Bianca answered. "For instance, you seem to be assuming that most immigrants will be low income. Perhaps you're also assuming that they'll be poorly educated and unskilled. I don't think those assumptions are warranted. I've read that most legal immigrants are actually better educated, on average, than are Americans,[11] and I heard on NPR the other day that immigrants tend to be among the most highly motivated members of society, and as a result account for a significant amount of American entrepreneurship."[12]

"Yeah, I read about that in one of my textbooks," Micah interjected.

Bianca continued. "Lauren, you mentioned immigrants being a burden on the public schools. Don't you think that having students from diverse backgrounds in a school is itself beneficial in a variety of ways? For example, it promotes tolerance and open-mindedness, it offers the teacher opportunities to discuss cultures and traditions from around the world, and it can expose American students to foreign languages. So the common belief that immigrants are an economic and educational burden on society seems to me to be mistaken. Even though they are often economically, linguistically, and culturally disadvantaged when they first arrive, many go on to become very successful. Just think for a minute, Lauren. How many medical doctors do you know who are immigrants?"

"It's a lot, I'll grant that," Lauren replied.

"You know," Micah reflected, "we seem to be making another very big assumption in this discussion."

---

11. A 2015 report from the Pew Research Center found that immigrants to the US are more than 10 percent ahead of those born in the US in earning bachelor's degrees. "Modern Immigration Wave Brings 59 Million to U.S., Driving Population Growth and Change Through 2065: Views of Immigration's Impact on U.S. Society Mixed," Washington, DC: Pew Research Center, September 2015, https://www.pewresearch. org/hispanic/2015/09/28/modern-immigration-wave-brings-59-million-to-u-s-driving-population-growth-and-change-through-2065.

12. A short but interesting study of this phenomenon is Peter Vandor and Nikolaus Franke, "Why Are Immigrants More Entrepreneurial?," *Harvard Business Review*, October 27, 2016, https://hbr.org/2016/10/why-are-immigrants-more-entrepreneurial.

"What?" the girls queried.

"I think we're assuming that the right attitude toward immigration can be determined by looking at the costs and benefits that immigration has for American society."

"Hah!" Bianca replied. "You're right!"

"Is that a problem?" Lauren asked.

"Well, it might be. It all depends on what you think is the right way to approach ethics. Do you remember how Dr. Platt began the semester talking about various ethical theories that subconsciously guide the way we approach moral issues?"

"Sure, I remember that," she affirmed. "It didn't interest me as much as what we're studying now, though, and I haven't given it much thought since then."

"Well, one of the theories that he explained was Utilitarianism, which is the view that the most moral action is the one that benefits the most people to the greatest extent and harms the fewest people to the least extent. That's exactly how we've been discussing this issue: we seem to be assuming that if immigration harms Americans more than it helps them, then it's bad. Or perhaps we're assuming that if, all told, it harms more people than it helps, Americans and immigrants included, it's bad. On the other hand, if it helps more people than it harms, we're assuming that it must be good.

"I think it's a very appealing theory," he continued. "It seems to fit well with democracy and a basic free-market approach to economics. But I remember that Dr. Platt had some concerns about it. For one thing, it might enable a country to justify taking advantage of a minority population in order to benefit the majority, as Germany did to numerous minority groups during World War II."

"Huh—I guess I *was* assuming Utilitarianism. It's odd how one can so completely assume some theoretical approach without even being aware of what the approach is." Lauren seemed rather concerned by this. "Are there other approaches to thinking about ethical issues that are better than Utilitarianism?"

"I myself am inclined to Divine Command Theory, but I don't imagine that would appeal to you very much," Micah responded with a laugh.

"No, I guess not!" she agreed, also laughing. "Aren't there any others?"

"There are," Bianca affirmed. "I myself find Virtue Ethics to be the most satisfying of the theories that we've studied. Perhaps that's in part because it's the closest to Eastern Orthodox moral theology. I like the focus on developing my character so that when I find myself faced by a moral dilemma I actually have some inner motivation to do the right thing. The other theories that Dr. Platt mentioned seem to be too disconnected from a person's heart. They're all about figuring out what the right answer is rather than actually becoming moral and doing the right thing in a moral crisis."

"I understand what you're saying, Bianca," Micah affirmed. "Nonetheless, in order to 'do the right thing,' as you put it, you need some sort of method for determining what the right thing actually is, don't you think?"

"I guess so," she granted. "I'm not really sure what would be the best way to approach that. A modified Divine Command Theory would be the easy choice for a Christian, but there are also aspects of Kant's Duty Ethics that I find appealing."

"Wow, you guys pay too much attention in class!" Lauren protested. "How is it that you remember all of these theories? I just barely understood them when they were explained to us, and I don't remember any of the details about them now."

"I took the theoretical aspect of this class very seriously precisely because I think that the applied aspects are important, Lauren," Bianca explained. "When Dr. Platt showed us that in order to come to any sort of firm conclusion in applied ethics we must first have a sound methodology for determining right and wrong, that made a lot of sense to me. As soon as I saw that point, I started to pay close attention to the theories that he was explaining to us."

"Yes, that's what got me interested in the theories too," Micah admitted. "I was sort of put off by the theoretical tone of the class at the beginning of the semester until I saw the important relationship between theory and practice. Then I started to see that practice without a theoretical foundation would be haphazard. I certainly don't remember all of the arguments for and against each theory that Dr. Platt mentioned, but I've tried to keep the basic theories in mind as we study each practical issue that comes up. Eventually though, I'll need to review the arguments. I'm sure they'll be on the exam."

"The exam—when's that?" Lauren asked. "I'm obviously going to need to do some serious studying!"

"It's not for a few weeks," Bianca replied. "Perhaps we should stop de-bating immigration and start studying our notes instead."

"I really can't stay much longer," Micah interjected. "I want to go to the gym before work this afternoon, and I have schoolwork to do too. Perhaps the three of us could form a study circle and set up a time to meet later this week."

Everyone liked this idea and agreed to meet at The Grey Earl on Thursday for the first official meeting of the "Applied Ethics Study Circle." Their debate over immigration hadn't radically altered anyone's opinion, but everyone had gained a more sympathetic understanding of the other viewpoints and a deeper understanding of the issues. Best of all, they managed to do all this without destroying their friendships—in fact, the polite and thoughtful exchange seemed to enhance each person's opinion of the others.

QUESTIONS TO PONDER

- What is the best way to go about determining one's position on issues like immigration?

- Should religious considerations play a role in determining the position that one takes on moral issues? Why or why not?

- Should religious considerations play a role in determining government policy on issues like immigration? Why or why not?

- Should a moral person give more weight to the welfare of Americans than to the welfare of non-Americans when the two come into conflict?

TERMS TO KNOW

- Ethics
- Applied ethics
- Metaethics
- Outsourcing
- Empathy
- Xenophobia
- Historicity
- Circular reasoning
- Atheism
- Agnosticism
- Utilitarianism
- Divine Command Theory
- Virtue Ethics
- Duty Ethics

FOR FURTHER READING

General works:

Carens, Joseph. *The Ethics of Immigration*. Oxford: Oxford University Press, 2013. Reprinted by Oxford, 2015.
    A scholarly, carefully argued treatment of the ethics of immigration.
Hoyt, Joanna Michal. *A Wary Welcome: The History of US Attitudes toward Immigration*. Athens: Skinny Bottle Publishing, 2017.
    This small book is an interesting study of the change in American attitudes toward immigration throughout the history of the United States.
Sager, Alex, ed. *The Ethics and Politics of Immigration: Core Issues and Emerging Trends*. New York: Rowman & Littlefield, 2016.
    A very nice collection of scholarly articles on a range of issues related to immigration ethics.

Christian perspectives:

Bauman, Stephan, Matthew Soerens, and Issam Smeir. *Seeking Refuge: On the Shores of the Global Refugee Crisis*. Chicago: Moody Press, 2016.
    This book combines biblical considerations with data from other sources such as economic studies and interviews to argue for a much more active Christian intercession on behalf of immigrants.

Hoffmeier, James K. *The Immigration Crisis: Immigrants, Aliens, and the Bible*. Wheaton, IL: Crossway, 2009.

This book studies the biblical injunctions to show compassion to immigrants and concludes that they do not apply to illegal immigrants.

Soerens, Matthew, Jenny Yang, and Leith Anderson. *Welcoming the Stranger: Justice, Compassion & Truth in the Immigration Debate*. Downers Grove, IL: InterVarsity Press, 2018.

This book argues from the Bible to the conclusion that Christians should welcome immigrants to America.

CAPITAL PUNISHMENT

Synopsis: Our three friends—Bianca, Lauren, and Micah—are back at their favorite tea shop to study for their upcoming ethics test. The focus of their conversation is capital punishment. Bianca is firmly opposed, both for religious and more general ethical reasons. Micah, for his own religious reasons, believes the death penalty is sometimes necessary. Lauren is inclined to agree with Micah but, because of her atheism, brings a very different perspective to the discussion.

* * *

"Hi, Lauren, you look nice today," Micah greeted, as Lauren found the semi-private area in the back of The Grey Earl that the friends had claimed for the first meeting of the Applied Ethics Study Circle. Micah was just trying to sound friendly, but he was slightly alarmed when Lauren blushed and looked a bit awkward. He made a mental note to compliment Bianca too when she arrived.

"Thank you, Micah," Lauren responded. "I brought notes for us to review today, especially on the latest topic, capital punishment. I found the classroom discussion on this topic really challenging. I had always assumed the death penalty was appropriate in some situations, but I'm not sure now."

"I agree," said Micah. "It's more complex than I initially thought. It will be interesting to see what Bianca thinks."

Just then, Bianca came bounding into the room. She was clearly agitated, and before Micah or Lauren could say anything, she exclaimed, "Did you guys see the news last night?"

Both shook their heads. Lauren had had a long day of nursing clinicals and gone to bed early. Micah was participating in a marketing project that had filled his evening.

Bianca continued, "One of the main stories was about a Mexican-American man named Jorge Esposito who was convicted of murder eighteen years ago. Three years ago he was executed by lethal injection, although he continued denying he had committed the crime right to the end. Well this week, DNA testing positively proved that he was innocent! Isn't that awful? That's one of the reasons I've always been opposed to the death penalty. I can't think of anything worse than executing an innocent man, can you?"

"It's certainly a terrible thing," Micah agreed.

"After I saw the news report," Bianca went on, "I did some checking. Did you know that scores of innocent people have been executed in the United States?[1] Some of the stories are absolutely heartbreaking. We've got to put an end to this barbaric practice!"

Lauren was also saddened by the news report, but then she asked, "I understand that what happened to Mr. Esposito is a very sad example, but do you really think examples like this prove that the death penalty is wrong?"

"Of course I do," responded Bianca.

"Please don't think I'm being cavalier about it, but consider an analogy. Almost every year, someone will leave buffet food out too long, people will get food poisoning, and sometimes someone dies of it. Should our response be to discontinue buffets? Shouldn't our response be to do our best not to allow a good thing to be done in the wrong way?"

"Those are hardly the same thing," Bianca replied. "How can you say the death penalty is a good thing? It's basically killing a person, the very same activity that we are punishing the murderer for. Why is it immoral for

---

1. For specific examples see "Eric," "8 People Who Were Executed and Later Found Innocent," *AVVO*, May 5, 2010, https://stories.avvo.com/crime/murder/8-people-who-were-executed-and-later-found-innocent.html.

a person to commit murder, but moral for the government to then kill the person? Shouldn't we value life?"

Micah weighed in, "That's certainly a legitimate question, and perhaps comparing capital punishment to buffets was not terribly helpful"—this earned a bit of a glare from Lauren—"but there seems to be a big difference between homicide, especially when it's premeditated and intentional, and execution after due process."[2]

"Yes," chimed in Lauren. "We talked in class about how motive enters into evaluating the morality of an action. Can I try another analogy, Micah?" She asked this question a bit sharply. He nodded. "If I give fifty dollars to a homeless shelter because I care about homeless people and want to help, that is a moral action. But if I donate the same fifty dollars because the action will look good on the résumé I'm compiling for a job application, most people wouldn't consider it a moral action. Rather it would be considered selfish."

"What Lauren is driving at, I think," interrupted Micah, "is that a person who kills another out of jealousy, for revenge, or for money has committed a deeply immoral act. But the motivation, presumably, for the government in punishing the crime is justice. Couldn't the act be considered moral, in that case?"

Bianca was unconvinced. Her branch of the Orthodox Church had condemned the death penalty some years before, and her family was firmly opposed to it. She argued, "Good motives can make an action moral only if the action is not intrinsically immoral. I believe it is intrinsically immoral to take another person's life."

"Do you really?" responded Lauren and Micah, almost simultaneously.

"You don't think a person could use lethal force to defend herself from harm?" asked Lauren.

Micah went on, "It's a different subject—hopefully, it will come up in Dr. Platt's class later—but what about a just war? Couldn't a country defend

---

2. Due process is "the observation of the proper legal procedures in a particular context. Now: spec. the administration of justice in accordance with the established rules and principles of the land, typically in the context of protecting the rights of the individual; the principle of guaranteeing that this is observed in the courts," *Oxford English Dictionary*, OED Online, June 2020, https://www.oed.com/view/Entry/268782.

itself from attack? In the process, surely its soldiers would have to take lives. Do you really believe killing in itself is always immoral?"[3]

Bianca was not a pacifist,[4] or at least she had never believed herself to be one, so she saw her mistake immediately. "Okay, I overstated my case. There are times when killing may be moral, but those times appear to be always in self-defense. Are you arguing that capital punishment is self-defense?"

"It could be, I suppose." Micah was clearly thinking out loud. "One of the reasons a government might put a criminal to death is to protect society."

"But life imprisonment would accomplish that, wouldn't it?" asked Bianca. "That is the maximum penalty in my parents' home country, and they have far fewer murders than we have here."

As Lauren and Micah tried to figure out how to respond to that, a friend of theirs who worked at The Grey Earl asked if they would like to order some drinks. They all decided to have tea. Lauren ordered first. "May I have an English breakfast tea?"

Bianca chimed in, "You do serve Earl Grey, right?"

Then Micah ordered. "Do you have honeysuckle ginger tea?" When the waitress said that they did, he continued, "Is it caffeine-free? Oh, and can you mix in some almond milk?"

Lauren smiled and said, "Seriously, Micah?"

Bianca rolled her eyes. "You eat four Pop Tarts every morning for breakfast, and you're drinking caffeine-free ginger tea with almond milk?"

"What?" Micah replied. "I like it!"

After the three had placed their orders, Bianca picked up the conversation: "Why would killing a criminal ever be necessary? We can protect society by locking him away, and that is so much more humane."

---

3. The conversation in this chapter will focus on homicide for simplicity's sake. Note that the government also employs the death penalty at times for those convicted of other crimes, such as treason, espionage, drug trafficking, and so forth. The common factor in all these crimes is that lives are taken or put at risk on a large scale. See the following for a list of federal laws providing for the death penalty: https://deathpenaltyinfo.org/federal-laws-providing-death-penalty.

4. There are many varieties of pacifism, as the chapter on just war theory will explain, but the usage here refers to someone who opposes war or any kind of violence.

"True, but protecting society isn't the only reason for punishing criminals, is it?" prompted Micah. He realized his self-defense argument wasn't holding up very well.

"The real issue is what the murderer deserves, right?" Lauren interjected.

Micah immediately agreed. Bianca nodded but looked like she might challenge this idea if it went in a direction she didn't like.

"When we studied Duty Ethics," Lauren went on, "I did some reading on Immanuel Kant, the guy who came up with the categorical imperative."

"I remember that vaguely," said Micah, "but could you go over it again with us?"

"Basically, he said we should always act in such a way that we would want everyone else to act the same way,"[5] Lauren explained.

"That sounds like the Golden Rule," Bianca chimed in.

"Now it's my turn," said Lauren. "That sounds vaguely familiar, but could you elaborate?"

Bianca replied, "In his Sermon on the Mount, Jesus gave a pithy summary of his ethical teachings: 'Do to others what you would have them do to you.' Isn't that exactly what Kant is saying?"

"I don't think Kant thought he was echoing Jesus," Lauren responded. "Kant thought reason was a sufficient guide in figuring out morality. It just makes sense to avoid activities that you wouldn't want others to do. How could you justify stealing, for instance, if you insisted that it was wrong for others to steal from you? That's not exactly what Jesus was saying, is it?"

"That's very helpful, Lauren," Micah said. "I believe Jesus is expressing a similar morality but with a very different motivation. The Golden Rule is based on love for others. We do for others what will make them happy because we know what makes us happy."

"Yes, even atheists like me appreciate Jesus's teachings that are like that," said Lauren.

---

5. Immanuel Kant (1724–1804) formulated the categorical imperative in his landmark work, *Groundwork of the Metaphysics of Morals* (1785). He stated it in various ways, but the one echoed by Lauren is this: "Act according to the maxim that you would wish all other rational people to follow, as if it were a universal law."

"Back to the categorical imperative, though," interjected Bianca. "How does it justify the death penalty?"

"Well, Kant thought it did," replied Lauren. "In fact, in his *Metaphysics of Morals*"—at this point, Lauren riffled through some of the notes she had brought to the meeting, finding the citation—"Kant said, 'Even if a civil society were to be dissolved by the consent of all its members (e.g., if a people inhabiting an island decided to separate and disperse throughout the world), the last murderer remaining in the prison would first have to be executed, so that each has done to him what his deeds deserve and blood guilt does not cling to the people for not having insisted upon this punishment; for otherwise the people can be regarded as collaborators in his public violation of justice.'"[6]

"Wow, that is strongly stated," exclaimed Micah. "So Kant thought that the common morality that binds all rational people together means that we are all responsible for meting out justice on a murderer. Is that a fair summary?"

Lauren replied, "I think that's what he meant."

Bianca was shaking her head vigorously and spoke up, "That doesn't make sense to me at all. It makes good sense that the categorical imperative, and the Golden Rule for that matter, would forbid murder. Obviously, society couldn't function if everybody thought murder was fine. But how does this principle justify the death penalty? Kant's claim that we would all be guilty of the murder only follows if execution is the sole appropriate penalty. And that's what we're arguing about! I think Dr. Platt would say he's begging the question."[7]

"Hmm," mumbled Lauren and Micah. They didn't know how to respond. Bianca seemed to have made a really good point.

Just at that point, their tea arrived, and they rested for a moment and sipped their drinks.

After this break, Micah decided to take a religious tack, which he thought more likely to convince Bianca.

---

6. Kant, *Metaphysics of Morals* (1797), quoted and critiqued by Nelson T. Potter in his article, "Kant and Capital Punishment Today." Potter makes a case that Kantian Duty Ethics can be used to argue against the death penalty rather than endorse it. See his argument at http://digitalcommons.unl.edu/cgi/viewcontent.cgi?article=1004&context=philosfacpub.

7. Begging the question is also known as arguing in a circle. It is assuming as a premise in one's argument what one is trying to prove.

"I don't personally depend on Duty Ethics for supporting capital punishment. I believe God commands that governments punish with capital punishment crimes that take lives."[8]

"What?" blurted out Bianca. "I hadn't brought up the Scriptures before now, but it's actually their teachings that cause me and my family to *reject* the death penalty. And it's not only us. Did you read about Pope Francis and how he recently declared the death penalty inadmissible and promised that the Roman Catholic Church would oppose it worldwide?[9] If the Pope doesn't think the Bible teaches capital punishment, how can you claim it does?"

Lauren was very interested to see that Micah and Bianca, both of whom claimed to be Christians, appeared to take opposite sides on the question.

Micah felt ready for this question, though, and responded, "The case for capital punishment begins all the way back in Genesis. When Noah got off the ark, God gave him instructions about how life was to function moving forward. In the sixth verse of the ninth chapter of Genesis, God says to Noah, 'Whoever sheds human blood, by humans shall their blood be shed; for in the image of God has God made mankind.' That clearly is referring to the death penalty."

"Wait," said Bianca. "You're appealing all the way back to Genesis?"

"Yes, God is giving instructions for human government. There's no reason to think this command was ever set aside. Also the ground for the command is the fact that humanity was made in God's image. That is still true."

Bianca pulled out her iPhone and asked Siri to show her the ninth chapter of the book of Genesis. Within a few seconds, she was checking the context of verse six. "How about verse four? Doesn't it say that people aren't allowed to eat raw meat? Is that still binding too?"

Micah, looking perplexed, said, "I don't know . . . no, I guess not. But when God established the nation of Israel under His rule, He instituted the death penalty in her laws. This is clear in a number of places.[10] So God must be in favor of it."

---

8.   In the previous chapter we learned that Micah espouses the Divine Nature ethic, which finds final authority for ethical decisions in the character of God.

9.   The following, which is a publication of the Society of Jesus, a Roman Catholic organization, explains Pope Francis's declaration on the death penalty: https://www.americamagazine.org/faith/2017/10/11/pope-francis-death-penalty-contrary-gospel.

10. See the next note for a list of some of these passages.

Lauren, who was listening carefully, interjected, "That certainly seems to demonstrate that God—if the Old Testament God is the same one you guys still worship—is not theoretically opposed to the death penalty. But do you follow everything else written in that law? Don't Jews avoid pork and worship on Saturday and stuff? I've seen you eat bacon, Micah . . ."

"Besides," Bianca chimed in, "in the Old Testament law, God commanded that they execute people for lots of things, including homosexuality, incest, teaching people to worship false gods, and the list goes on.[11] Do you think America should follow all that?" Micah began to look very uncomfortable.

He persevered though. "But the New Testament also speaks of the death penalty." He opened the New Testament on his phone and found the thirteenth chapter of Romans. "When the apostle Paul discusses the role of government in his letter to the Romans, he says, 'If you do wrong, be afraid, for rulers do not bear the sword for no reason. They are God's servants, agents of wrath to bring punishment on the wrongdoer.'[12] In this verse the word 'rulers' is referring to the Roman government, and the sword is a symbol that indicates execution, a penalty often carried out by the Romans."

"The fact that Paul says Romans executed people does not prove that he approved of it or thought we should execute people," retorted Bianca.

"But look at the context. In chapter 12 Paul urges believers not to seek vengeance against those who harm them. God will bring those people to justice. Then in chapter 13, immediately after that, Paul says God has raised up government with just that purpose, to punish wrongdoers and reward those who obey the law. Even if I can't prove that Genesis 9:6 and the Old Testament law directly apply, they establish the principle that God thinks some crimes deserve death. And here the New Testament endorses this punishment." Micah looked positively triumphant.

---

11. "The Law, as given to Moses on Mt. Sinai, ordained execution for several offenses: murder (but not accidental killings), striking or cursing a parent, kidnapping, adultery, incest, bestiality, sodomy, rape of a betrothed virgin, witchcraft, incorrigible delinquency, breaking the Sabbath, blasphemy, sacrificing to false gods, oppressing the weak, and other transgressions. (See Exod. 21, 22, 35; Lev. 20 & 24; Deut. 21–24.)." This is part of a helpful, brief discussion of the death penalty at the Prison Fellowship website: https://www.prisonfellowship.org/resources/advocacy/sentencing/the-death-penalty.

12. Rom. 13:4.

Bianca shook her head. "I'm unconvinced. There's much stronger scriptural evidence against the death penalty. For instance, Jesus said to turn the other cheek when people hurt us[13] and to love our enemies and forgive them.[14] He told Peter to put away his sword because those who live by the sword die by it,[15] and the death penalty leaves no opportunity for repentance and change. Micah, I think you're being very selective with your use of Scripture."

Micah didn't usually get heated in these discussions—they were great friends, after all—but he actually raised his voice a bit. "*I'm* being selective! The whole point of government dealing with murderers is so that private people like us *can* turn our cheek, love and forgive our enemies, and pray for their repentance and change. But it's the government's job to establish justice!"

Lauren motioned with both hands for Bianca and Micah to stand down. "Obviously, Christians are not in complete agreement on this issue. In any event, your debate doesn't help me resolve the issue. Let's take another approach. What is the purpose of punishment in general?"

"We've already talked about the protection of society. I think that's one of the purposes," replied Micah, who was feeling a bit embarrassed by his outburst. He had admitted at the very beginning of their session that this was a challenging topic, but now he was arguing in a way that demeaned his friend's opinion. One doesn't have to believe there is more than one right answer to respect those who disagree.

"Punishment should rehabilitate the person being punished, shouldn't it?"[16] added Bianca. "Prisoners are given opportunities to learn skills and get education that will help them cope when they get out. I think that is very important and the main reason we punish criminals."

"Granted that rehabilitation is important," replied Lauren, "can it be the main purpose?"

"Why not?" asked Bianca, as she took another sip of her Earl Grey.

"I'm going to try another analogy." Lauren glanced at Micah as she said this. "Suppose a town instituted a policy where they would cut off one finger

---

13. Matt. 5:39.
14. Matt. 5:44.
15. Matt. 26:52: "for all who draw the sword will die by the sword."
16. Rehabilitation is the restoration of someone to proper functionality, in this case, of a convicted criminal to proper function in society.

of anyone caught shoplifting. Do you suppose a person who lost a finger because he stole from a convenience store would ever try that again?"

"That's a really gross analogy," said Micah, but then he added, "but very effective."

"I see where you're going," said Bianca. "Even though the punishment would successfully rehabilitate shoplifters, it would not be just. The punishment doesn't fit the crime, as they say."

"Exactly," responded Lauren, relieved that one of her analogies had finally paid off. "So rehabilitation is important, but it can't be the sole reason for punishment."

"Another reason for punishment is that it warns others not to do the same crime," added Micah. "I believe this is called the deterrence effect, because people are deterred from committing the crime when they see how bad the punishment is."

Bianca saw where this was going and said, "I'm sure you're going to claim now that capital punishment deters murders."

Micah replied, "Isn't that common sense? But anyway, a number of studies have shown that the death penalty does in fact deter murders."[17]

Lauren flipped through her notes and found an article on that subject. "The simplest studies show the number of murders graphed against the number of executions. There does seem to be a decrease in murders over the last forty years or so as the number of executions has increased."[18]

Even though this supported Micah's point, he was enough of a numbers guy to know something was not quite right with that argument. "When two things are graphed against each other like that, it doesn't really prove that one of them is causing the other. At best, it shows correlation between the two, but there could be many other factors involved, such as increased law enforcement." Bianca appreciated Micah's honesty in pointing this out.

After downing some of her English Breakfast tea, Lauren went on. "Other studies are much more sophisticated and claim that capital punishment does

17. See a number of studies at the website of the Criminal Justice Legal Foundation: https://www.cjlf.org/deathpenalty/dpdeterrencefull.htm.

18. See, for example, Roy D. Adler and Michael Summers, "Capital Punishment Works," *Wall Street Journal*, Nov. 2, 2007, http://online.wsj.com/article/ SB119397079767680173.html.

CHAPTER 3—CAPITAL PUNISHMENT

deter murders. For every one of those studies, though, there is rebuttal from other studies. It's very hard to determine *why* someone commits a crime, and it's even more difficult to determine why someone *does not* commit a crime. When murder numbers go down, how can we know for certain that capital punishment is the main deterrent?"[19]

"Let's suppose, for the sake of argument, that capital punishment does deter murders," said Bianca, surprising Lauren and Micah. "Wouldn't your argument against rehabilitation apply here as well?"

"Oh, I see what you're getting at," replied Lauren. "If mutilating shoplifters completely stamped out shoplifting in the town because no one else would risk it, that still wouldn't justify the punishment."

"If it did," Micah added, "one could justify all kinds of injustices as long as the results were beneficial. I think Dr. Platt would say this is another example of the failure of Consequentialist Ethics.[20] Something isn't right just because it turns out well." Micah had inadvertently illustrated this principle. He was thoroughly enjoying his almond milk ginger tea, although both girls thought there was nothing right or reasonable about his ordering health food.

Lauren summarized, "So punishment has the purposes of protecting society, rehabilitating the perpetrator, and deterring others from committing the same crime. But none of these purposes can be the main reason government punishes criminals. What is the main reason?"

"We've mentioned justice at a number of points in our discussion," responded Micah. "Isn't that the answer? Shouldn't we punish people because they *deserve* to be punished?"

Checking her notes again, Lauren said, "I believe this approach is called retributivism. The Retribution Principle says that a people who perform harmful actions should be punished in proportion to the gravity of their

---

19. For articles that question the validity of the deterrence studies, see articles at the Death Penalty Information Center: https://deathpenaltyinfo.org/policy-issues/deterrence. Feinberg and Feinberg write, "No one has figured out how to determine how many are deterred from homicide by the death penalty. However, if it cannot be shown that those who don't kill were deterred by fear of capital punishment, we must drop talk (pro or con) of capital punishment as a deterrent" (*Ethics for a Brave New World*, 236).

20. Consequentialist Ethics systems aver that an action is moral if it leads to desirable consequences.

offenses. Justice is served when moral people are proportionally rewarded and immoral people are proportionally punished.[21] That seems right, doesn't it?"

Micah seized on this, "Yes, as we saw earlier, the Old Testament Law embodies that principle as well. You might say that it's divinely sanctioned."

"A lot of legal codes throughout history have done so, Micah, not just biblical law," responded Lauren.

Bianca spoke up, "That principle seems self-evident, but does it really solve our problem regarding capital punishment? How do governments determine what is the appropriate penalty for various crimes? For instance, some municipalities give a $200 fine for reckless driving, but others may fine only $150. Which is proportional? Aren't these punishments somewhat arbitrary?"

"Maybe each political unit determines what the penalties should be," Lauren offered. "So as long as the Retribution Principle is the foundation, there is no right or wrong answer. If one society decides to execute murderers or traitors and another society decides against it, we have no right to criticize either one."

"So you're saying the murderer deserves death if he lives in one region, but he doesn't deserve death if he lives in another? How does that work?" questioned Micah. Before he could get the answer, though, he excused himself to answer his phone. It had been buzzing for several minutes, and he couldn't ignore it any longer. It was Mom.

"I think Micah has raised an interesting objection, Lauren," Bianca added. "Remember when Dr. Platt critiqued Cultural Relativism, the idea that morality is relative to each culture that defines it?"

"Yes, I do. One of the key problems he pointed out is that it makes a culture's morality not liable to either criticism or reform."

"Exactly," agreed Bianca. "If the morality of a culture is right simply because the culture affirms it, then how could anyone outside the culture ever criticize it, and how could anyone inside the culture ever fix it?"

"In our case, if a culture executed everyone who failed to pay his taxes, it would be right simply because the culture agreed to do it. That can't be the right answer!" concluded Lauren.

---

21. For an interesting but technical statement of this definition of justice, see Louis Pojman, "Justice as Desert," http://www.austlii.edu.au/au/journals/QUTLawJJl/2001/7.html.

At this point, Micah returned to the discussion. "What'd I miss?"

"We refuted Cultural Relativism and decided that there must be a firmer basis for retribution than just various legal codes," answered Bianca.

"Good. That's exactly what I thought," replied Micah, with a slightly smug expression. Conclusions are always easier than discussions.

"Perhaps," suggested Lauren, "Natural Law can help us sort this out.[22] If someone steals, it seems natural for him to restore what he took and to pay a price commensurate with the crime. Using this logic, if a person murders someone, he or she should forfeit the right to live."

"Whoa! Hold your horses." Bianca was clearly uncomfortable with the direction this had taken. "The problem with Natural Law, as Dr. Platt pointed out in class, is that it is not self-interpreting. Who's to say that losing one's life is the only appropriate penalty for taking a life? If a murderer were locked away for the rest of his life, that would surely be a losing of his life to a similar degree, wouldn't it?"

"Maybe," Micah weighed in, "but societies around the world throughout history have utilized the death penalty for various serious crimes, and the basis for most of these legal codes has been the Natural Law principle of death corresponding to death. You can't deny centuries of jurisprudence, can you?"

"Have you ever heard of progress, Micah?" responded Bianca. "This is the twenty-first century. Perhaps a more enlightened interpretation of Natural Law is called for today. None of your arguments have convinced me that capital punishment is humane. And there's another factor we haven't even considered."

"What's that?" asked Lauren and Micah.

Looking at Lauren, Bianca asked, "Don't your notes on capital punishment have anything to say about the disparity between African Americans and other races in the legal system of the United States?"

Lauren looked through her notes for a moment. Bianca and Micah took the opportunity to return to their half-forgotten teas.

---

22. Natural Law, in this context, may be defined as "The law as it is naturally or immediately interpreted; the principles of morality, held to be discernible by reason as belonging to human nature or implicit in the nature of rational thought and action; such principles as the basis for man-made laws," *Oxford English Dictionary*, OED Online, June 2020, https://www.oed.com/view/Entry/255255.

"Indeed, there is," admitted Lauren. "I think we need to dig a little deeper into the processes involved in capital punishment. How does a person get from crime to punishment in the American system?"

"Obviously, the person is arrested," began Micah. "If the crime is sufficient to possibly warrant execution, the person will receive a trial before a jury of his peers."

"The presiding judge then issues a sentence for the crime," added Bianca. "In America, I'm pretty sure the judge cannot sentence a person to be executed unless the jury brought back a unanimous recommendation to do so."[23]

"Lawyers undoubtedly will appeal the sentence, especially if the result is the death penalty," said Micah. "I'm pretty sure most people on death row stay there for years and years."[24]

Lauren concluded, "If there is no stay of execution the sentence is eventually carried out."[25] Those somber words caused all three to think about real people rather than just statistics and theory.

"At each stage we just mentioned," continued Bianca after the brief pause, "there has been a disproportionate number of minorities—especially African Americans. More African Americans are arrested per capita than white or Hispanic people; more are sentenced to death; and more are actually executed. According to these notes"—Bianca glanced at one of the pages Lauren had brought—"12.3 percent of the American population consists of black people. But since 1977, 34 percent of all executions have been of African Americans."

"Wow, that's disturbing." Micah was genuinely shocked by these disparities.

Lauren added, "Another study says that blacks are 3.9 times more likely to receive the death sentence for comparable crimes than other ethnicities. That's just wrong!"[26]

"These facts show that the death penalty is morally indefensible and should be abolished!" stated Bianca passionately.

---

23. As of 2018, this is true in every state except Alabama.
24. The average time on death row in America is 178 months, or nearly fifteen years.
25. The word "stay" in this expression means "to stop or halt." The president of the United States and state governors have the power to stop execution proceedings against murderers sentenced to capital punishment.
26. See the statistics at the Death Penalty Information Center: https://deathpenaltyinfo.org.

**Percentage of Executions since 1976
Compared to Percentage of the US Population[27]**

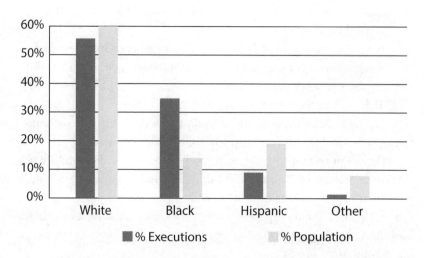

"Here we go again," muttered Micah. Out loud he said, "Actually these facts show that the justice system is far from perfect, and we should not rest until all such injustices are a thing of the past."

"They do not, however," chimed in Lauren, "prove that capital punishment itself is immoral. They simply show that it can be done immorally."

Bianca looked stubborn, but she had to acknowledge once again that her conclusion was a non sequitur.[27]

"So where are we now?" Lauren asked. She had taken it upon herself to be the summarizer of their discussion. Micah and Bianca seemed okay with that. "Someone who commits murder should receive punishment that is proportional to the crime. That is the Retribution Principle. Whether one bases it on Natural Law, Duty Ethics, or even the Bible," she added, acknowledging her two religious friends, "the only reasonable basis for punishing people is that they deserve it. Of course, punishment may also serve as a deterrent, it may rehabilitate criminals, and it may protect society from repeat offenders. Is that a fair summary?"

"Absolutely," said both Bianca and Micah, who finally agreed on something.

---

27. A non sequitur is a conclusion that does not logically follow from the premises.

"The hard question," Lauren went on, "is whether or not someone ever deserves death."

Micah spoke up, "That's where specific cases can be helpful, I think."

"What do you mean?" Bianca asked.

"Have you ever heard of Ted Bundy?" he asked her. Of course she had. "He was convicted of raping and killing over thirty women, and many think the number was closer to one hundred. What do you think he deserved?"

"That's not an argument, Micah," interrupted Lauren.

"Maybe not exactly, but isn't the point that we are trying to determine appropriate retribution? Seriously, what did Ted Bundy deserve?"

"Okay, I'm willing to grant that Bundy deserved to die," said Bianca, surprising Micah and Lauren. "But I think it's God's business to exact that penalty in his time and in his way. Not the government's. The government can lock people like Bundy away where they can't hurt anyone else. In the meantime, we should ask God to give us the grace to forgive even people like Ted Bundy."

Both Lauren and Micah were moved by that sentiment.

"Bianca, you are absolutely right," Micah responded. "Even when somebody does things as horrible as what Bundy did, we are supposed to leave the vengeance to God. Forgiveness is a key part of the gospel, and nothing is more God-like than forgiving terrible acts. But—"

"I don't particularly see the necessity to extend or even feel forgiveness for a serial killer like Bundy," said Bianca. "But I think I know where Micah is headed. Personal vendettas are for the action movies. To maintain an ordered society, it is the government's role to maintain justice. We couldn't live peacefully if the government made a habit of forgiving people's crimes without punishing them."

"That was sort of where I was going," agreed Micah. "A person can simultaneously forgive a person for the personal aspect of the crime while applauding the execution of justice against the public aspect of it."

"What?" asked Bianca.

"Sorry. I know that wasn't stated well. Let me try an example. Suppose someone broke into my home and stole my television. If I simply said: 'I guess I'll just forgive the person, whoever he is, because I can get another TV, and Jesus wouldn't want me to get the person in trouble,' isn't it likely that the person is going to break into other homes and steal other stuff? Isn't my over-looking the person's crime actually doing harm to my innocent neighbors?"

"Yes, I see that," answered Bianca.

"So," continued Micah, "I should both personally forgive the guy who stole my TV and ask the police to find him, punish him, and restore my TV to me, if possible. These attitudes are not inconsistent with each other."

"Okay," both girls granted.

"Then too, I can be glad the rightful authority is executing justice against a killer like Bundy even though I hope his victims can find grace to forgive him for his crimes or, better, that he will repent and seek forgiveness," concluded Micah.

Bianca then asked, "If Bundy had repented and sought forgiveness, would you still have wanted him executed?"

Lauren answered as Micah pondered the question. "His repentance wouldn't bring back those scores of girls he murdered."

"But his death wouldn't bring them back either," responded Bianca.

Micah observed, "I guess we're back to what Bundy deserved for his crimes."

"And I'm convinced," Bianca concluded, "that life imprisonment is a sufficient penalty regardless of the crime. It gives the most chance for repentance and maintains the most hope. I believe it is the most humane. Thank you, though, for the helpful conversation."

Lauren smiled and gave her own conclusion, "Given the many injustices in the American court system, it seems that the death penalty should be the last resort. But I'm inclined to agree with Micah that some crimes just deserve execution, as horrible as that is."

Micah nodded, but didn't think he needed to say anything else.

Suddenly remembering the beginning of the meeting, Micah added, "Oh, Bianca? You look really nice tonight."

Both girls looked at him as if he'd completely lost his mind.

QUESTIONS TO PONDER

- Which arguments regarding capital punishment do you find the most convincing? Why?

- Do you think capital punishment deters murder and other violent crimes? Why or why not?

- One of the issues the students did not bring up is the economic impact of punishing convicted murderers (or others who have broken laws that might entail the death penalty). In most cases capital punishment, because of the lengthy appeals process, is considerably more expensive than life imprisonment. Does that fact have a bearing on this discussion?

- Did this discussion spend too little time talking about the *victims* of violent crime? How does their perspective (i.e., the viewpoint of relatives and friends of the murdered persons) enter into your thinking on capital punishment?

TERMS TO KNOW

- Capital punishment
- Death penalty
- Due process
- Duty Ethics
- Categorical imperative
- Begging the question
- Rehabilitation
- Deterrence
- Consequentialist Ethics
- Retributivism/Retribution Principle
- Cultural Relativism
- Natural Law
- Stay of execution
- Non sequitur
- Justice

FOR FURTHER READING

Baird, Robert M., and Stuart E. Rosenbaum, eds. *Punishment and the Death Penalty: The Current Debate*. Amherst, NY: Prometheus Books, 1995.

Feinberg, John S. and Paul D. Feinberg. *Ethics for a Brave New World*. Wheaton, IL: Crossway, 2010.

Geisler, Norman L. *Christian Ethics: Contemporary Issues & Options*. Grand Rapids: Baker Academic, 2010.

Pojman, Louis P., and Jeffrey Reiman. *The Death Penalty: For and Against*. Lanham, MD: Rowman & Littlefield, 1997.

Rae, Scott B. *Moral Choices: An Introduction to Ethics*. Grand Rapids: Zondervan, 2009.

4

TORTURE

Synopsis: In this chapter we follow our three friends into their ethics class, where the topic for the day is torture. We discover that Dr. Platt uses a very interactive teaching style. The professor is a big fan of the Socratic method—the approach to teaching employed by Socrates, the ancient Greek philosopher. Socrates was famous—or infamous, depending on your perspective—for teaching by asking questions and instigating debates. So Dr. Platt's teaching frequently takes the form of posing questions that provoke students into thinking through issues together. Many of the students are involved in the discussion, and a wide range of perspectives on the issue are considered. The assigned reading is from one of the course texts, a book exploring issues in applied ethics through the stratagem of presenting opposing sides of an issue via articles that took contrasting stances. Each article was written by an author who had a strong conviction for the position he or she was defending. The result is that readers are exposed to convincing arguments for both sides, which sometimes leaves them a bit bewildered about which position is correct.

* * *

"Good morning, class. Today's topic for discussion is a torturous one." Dr. Platt's announcement was met by slight grins and soft groans.

"Today's reading was about torture," he continued. "What did you think of it?" No one seemed to be in a hurry to begin the discussion; perhaps their heads were still spinning from the intense reading.

After waiting patiently, Dr. Platt saw that he'd have to work a little harder at getting the discussion going. "OK, what exactly are we talking about here? How did the reading define *torture*?"

Dr. Platt nodded his head at a student in the front row who raised her hand. "It said that torture is inflicting pain on someone in order to pressure that person into doing what you want," she explained.

"That's correct, Summer. Thank you." This was a beginning, but Dr. Platt felt the need to nudge the discussion along. "So what do you think of this definition, class? Is it accurate?"

A student sitting near the middle of the room raised her hand. "Yes, Bianca?"

"I think Summer's definition is correct as far as it goes, but it leaves out some details from the textbook's definition. For example, the textbook mentioned that there can be motives for torture other than getting someone to do what you want."

"You have a good memory! That broadens our definition. Can you remember any of the other possible motives that the textbook mentioned?"

"Well," she responded, "Summer focused on coercion or compliance, but torture could also be used as a form of punishment."

"The book also mentioned torture as a deterrent," the boy next to her offered.

"That's correct, Micah. Thank you. Did the book mention any other motives?"

"No, I don't think so," Micah replied.

A girl across the room spoke up. "I think it mentioned doing it for fun and for revenge, didn't it?"

"I believe you're right, Shakira," Dr. Platt agreed. "And I'm glad you brought these up, for now we have a whole range of motives, from the most selfish to the least selfish, that we can examine.[1] Let's talk about them in that

---

1. Article 2 section 2 of the United Nations' *Convention against Torture and Other Cruel, Inhuman, or Degrading Treatment or Punishment* states that "no exceptional circumstances whatsoever, whether a state of war or a threat of war, internal political instability or any other public emergency, may be invoked as a justification of torture." This strongly implies that the UN views torture as immoral, which raises two questions: (1) What are

order. Is there anyone who thinks that torturing someone for the fun of it is morally defensible?"

The room was silent. After giving the class time to speak up, Dr. Platt remarked, "Good—I'm glad. But apparently some people do think it's okay. Or at least that's the impression that I get from movies and TV shows."

"The people in the movies who think it's okay to torture for fun are generally portrayed as the bad guys," Shakira remarked. "Doesn't that suggest that even Hollywood realizes that torture for fun is immoral?"

"That's an astute question," he replied. "We may be able to find a few exceptions to this rule—perhaps a father whose family has been killed finding some pleasure in torturing their murderer or something like that—but they would be rare. So what does that prove?"

"That we intuitively know that torturing for fun is wrong?" she offered.

"Perhaps," he granted. "Is that the only possible answer?" Again the class was silent. "What would a cultural relativist say?" he prompted.

Bianca raised her hand again, and when Dr. Platt nodded to her, she said, "I think a cultural relativist would say that we think it's immoral because that is what our culture tells us. Furthermore, they'd say that since Hollywood shares the values that are basic to our culture, Hollywood's depiction of such people as bad guys reflects our culture's influence on Hollywood. But that doesn't necessarily mean that there's anything inherently wrong with torturing for fun. It's only wrong because our culture tells us that it's wrong."

"I think you're right, Bianca. Well done again!" Dr. Platt was pleased. "A few minutes ago all of you seemed to think that torture for fun is immoral. But if Cultural Relativism is true, then it's likely that torture is neither moral nor immoral in itself, and if our culture tells us that it's moral under certain circumstances, then in fact it is. What do you think about that?"

---

the grounds of this conviction (why does the UN believe that all torture is immoral?); and (2) Is this conviction correct (is it true that all torture is immoral?). The discussion of torture in this chapter is an exploration of these two questions. The reader should not take it as an endorsement of torture but rather as a discussion between people who are still trying to formulate their own positions on this important contemporary issue. *United Nations Treaty Collection: Convention against Torture and Other Cruel, Inhuman, or Degrading Treatment or Punishment* (New York: United Nations, 1984), https://treaties.un.org/doc/Treaties/1987/06/19870626%2002-38%20AM/Ch_IV_9p.pdf.

Lauren was sitting on the other side of Micah. Now she spoke up. "Dr. Platt, I found your arguments against relativism pretty convincing. At least, they seem much stronger than the arguments for it. So if relativism is false, then it doesn't really matter what relativism says about torture, does it?"

"No, Lauren, I guess not. If we know that relativism is false, then we don't have to concern ourselves very much with the relativist position on torture except to the degree that it might be useful to be familiar with the position in order to respond to their arguments. And I'm inclined to agree with you that the arguments against relativism considerably outweigh the arguments for it.

"Furthermore," he continued, "I think you've illustrated a very important methodological point: we need to decide what approach to morality—what ethical theory—we should employ before we begin to tackle issues in applied ethics. To put it another way, metaethics needs to precede applied ethics. Do you see that? Do you understand why this would be important?"

"I think I do," she replied. "If we haven't decided what theory should guide our thinking, then we could end up thinking like a relativist, a Utilitarian, an Aristotelian, or something else without even realizing it, and how we think is going to determine what conclusion we draw. So if we hadn't already decided that relativism is mistaken, then today our discussion might end up by concluding that torturing people for the fun of it can be perfectly acceptable depending on what our culture says."

ETHICAL THEORIES ON TORTURE	
Theory	**View of Torture**
Utilitarianism	Likely to approve
Natural Law	Likely to disapprove
Duty Ethics	Disapproves
Divine Command Theory	Unclear—depends on theological factors
Virtue Theory	Likely to disapprove in connection with Natural Law or DCT

"Does everyone understand what she's saying?" Dr. Platt asked the class. "Lauren is absolutely right, and it's a very important point. Even though this class focuses on applied ethics, a foundation in theoretical ethics is absolutely necessary to making solid progress toward recognizing the correct moral position on the issues that we're studying. Thank you, Lauren, for pointing this out." At this praise she looked down a little sheepishly. Abstract theories were not her strongest area, so it felt very good to be publicly praised for making an important theoretical contribution to the discussion.

"There is another approach to ethics that could perhaps justify torture for pleasure: Ethical Egoism. But I suggest that we move our discussion on to the next motive for torturing someone: revenge. How many of you think that torturing someone for revenge would be moral?"

Students shifted in their seats as they stole furtive glances at each other. A student on the left side of the room raised his hand. "Yes, Miguel?"

"I don't really think that revenge is ever right, but I can understand someone wanting to get revenge if something really bad is done to someone he loves. I'm not saying it would be right, but I might feel the same way if I were in his shoes."

"I appreciate your honesty, Miguel," Dr. Platt replied. "And I think that most of us can probably empathize with the desire for revenge. But that doesn't necessarily make it right. And when we add to that the element of torture, it's perhaps even harder to justify. After all, revenge doesn't necessarily have to involve torture, so when we combine revenge and torture together, we're talking about an act that has at least two aspects of it that are morally questionable. But the question of the morality of revenge is separate from the question of the morality of torture. If we try to handle both at the same time, not only do we make our task twice as difficult, but we also run the risk of conflating separate issues. So for the sake of the argument, let's assume that revenge is sometimes morally permissible—an assumption that may well be wrong, but one that I think we need to make for a few minutes just so that we can focus on one issue at a time. Does that make sense to everyone?"

The class was in agreement with this approach, so Dr. Platt continued. "If we provisionally grant that revenge is sometimes permissible, then the question of the morality of torture as a means of getting revenge doesn't seem to be distinct from the question of whether torture itself is sometimes moral. So how should we approach the question of whether torture is ever moral?" he asked.

Summer raised her hand, ready to rejoin the discussion. "I guess you want us to say that we need to choose an ethical theory so that our thinking will have a guiding principle, rather than just shooting from the hip. Is that the answer you're looking for?"

"Yes it is! This is why summer is my favorite season of the year." Dr. Platt's attempts at humor were not always successful. "I wasn't fishing for exactly that answer, but it's exactly the one that I *should* have been fishing for. It shows us that we're at a fork in the road: we must decide how the class is going to proceed. Either we can ask ourselves how each of the ethical theories that we discussed at the beginning of the semester would approach the issue, or we can try to figure out, together, which ethical theory really is the best and then apply that to this issue. Either of these is a large project, of course. The latter option may not even be possible, for in my experience it's rarely possible to get everyone in a class to adopt the same ethical theory. So let's give the other approach a try, shall we? What ethical theories have we discussed in addition to Cultural Relativism and Egoism?"

"Utilitarianism?" Bianca offered.

"Good," he replied. "Do you remember the central principle of Utilitarianism?"

"That we should always do whatever would bring the most benefit to the most people?"

"Exactly right!" Dr. Platt beamed with approval.

"We've been studying," she said with a grin.

"Being a consistent Utilitarian, are you, Bianca? Studying because that will result in the greatest amount of good for you and your classmates?" Dr. Platt was smiling as he said this, but he didn't give her a chance to respond. Instead he directed a question to the whole class. "Well, everyone, what position do you think a Utilitarian would take regarding torture?"

Many hands shot up in response to this. Dr. Platt took the opportunity to call on a large, athletic-looking student who didn't often participate in the discussions. "Tyrone, what do you think?"

"Our textbook described a really interesting scenario that I haven't been able to stop thinking about. It was the one where the Department of

Homeland Security uncovered a plot to detonate a powerful bomb in a large city. It would have injured and killed a lot of people, but the DHS also captured a member of the terrorist cell that had planted the bomb. They hadn't been able to get him to reveal the location of the bomb, so they were considering whether it would be a good idea to try torturing him. I don't like the idea of torture, but if we're comparing the temporary pain of a terrorist to the death of thousands of innocent people, a cost-benefit analysis would indicate that torture is justified in such situations, wouldn't it? I mean, isn't that how a Utilitarian would look at it?"

The whole class seemed moved by this scenario. Hands were raised all over the room. Rather than answer Tyrone's question himself, Dr. Platt chose to let the discussion play out for a while. "Zach, what do you think?"

"Dr. Platt, I think I need some guidance on how to apply Utilitarianism. I understand why Tyrone thinks that a Utilitarian would advocate torturing the terrorist, but couldn't it be argued that treating torture as moral would be contributing to the undermining of human rights and as a result would actually be bad for humanity? And for this reason wouldn't Utilitarians oppose torture?"

This was some subtle thinking, to be sure. Some of Zach's classmates looked a little puzzled, so Dr. Platt restated Zach's question for them. "Are you saying, Zach, that there's more than one possible way that a Utilitarian could evaluate the morality of torture? It could be positively evaluated due to its potential to save many lives, or negatively evaluated due to its potential to undermine respect for human rights?"

"Yes, that sounds right," Zach responded. "How do we know which way a Utilitarian would go?"

"Well, Zach, I'm not sure that we can be 100 percent certain which way a Utilitarian would go. In fact, Utilitarians don't always agree with each other on how the principle of maximal utility should be applied. The best we can do may be to think through the various costs and benefits for ourselves and try to figure out what course of action would probably have the most benefit while involving the least negative impact. That can be a difficult calculation at times—but no one said that ethics was going to be easy!"

Here Tyrone spoke up without waiting to be called on: "But in this situation the Utilitarian position seems pretty clear, don't you think? I mean, if DHS doesn't torture the terrorist, then thousands of people are certain to die, while the possibility that torturing him would contribute in some way to decreasing respect for human rights is much less certain. Don't you think a Utilitarian would see the certainty of thousands of deaths as outweighing the mere possibility of a decrease in people's attitudes toward some belief?"

Tyrone's question seemed to be directed to Dr. Platt, but Dr. Platt looked at Zach as if to redirect the question to him. "Well, I guess so," Zach responded. "Not that human rights aren't important, but I guess the relative degrees of certainty and uncertainty do tip the scales in favor of torture."

During this exchange a lot of arms must have gotten tired, for most of the students had put their hands down. Bianca still had hers up, though, so Dr. Platt called on her again. "Bianca?"

"I see that this is the direction that a Utilitarian analysis would go, Professor," she said, "but should we even approach this issue from a Utilitarian perspective? There are a lot of problems with Utilitarianism, aren't there?"

"Well, there are at least a great many *concerns* about Utilitarianism, Bianca. You're right about that. Whether or not these concerns are actual problems or whether they are merely aspects of Utilitarianism that need to be approached in a carefully nuanced way is an issue that ethicists debate. As I stated in our unit on ethical theories, quite a few ethicists still think Utilitarianism is a very useful way to approach moral dilemmas, while some other ethicists think it's not."

"Professor," Miguel called out, while simultaneously raising his hand. Dr. Platt looked at him, and he continued with his question. "What position do most Utilitarian ethicists take on the morality of torture?"

"I don't know," Dr. Platt admitted. "I've never seen any figures published on that. Perhaps someone has actually surveyed Utilitarian ethicists to determine this, but I haven't seen such data. I've seen quite a few articles arguing for torture from a Utilitarian perspective, though. Of course, they are usually very careful to specify that torture is only justified in extreme circumstances where the benefits will clearly outweigh any detriments. In fact, nearly all the arguments I've seen favoring torture have come from a Utilitarian perspective."

Another student raised her hand. "Leah?" Dr. Platt said, glad to have her participation.

"You said that nearly all the arguments favoring torture are Utilitarian. Some of them aren't?" she asked.

"Yes, I've seen a few arguments for torture from a Natural Law perspective, actually," he explained. "It kind of surprises me, since Natural Law ethicists tend to be Christians and Christians tend to oppose torture, but then again, there was plenty of torture going on during the Inquisition. So let's talk about Natural Law Theory and torture. For starters, would someone please remind us how Natural Law Theory approaches ethics?"

Bianca raised her hand again. "Thank you, Bianca. I appreciate your class participation, but let's see if someone else can help us this time."

Micah raised his hand, and Dr. Platt called on him. "Natural Law Theory says that morality is built into the very nature of reality and that we can discover moral principles in a way similar to how we discover the laws of nature. In essence, we study the world, human nature, and moral dilemmas to infer what the right action would be in a given situation."

"Very good, Micah!" Dr. Platt exclaimed. "I can see that you've been studying too."

"Yes, we've a little study circle going on. Actually, we're all a little puzzled about how Natural Law Theory works. It seems like just about any possible position can be justified using Natural Law Theory. How do we determine what position nature actually supports?"

"That's a very good observation and concomitantly a very good question. In fact, critics of Natural Law Ethics have often pointed this out. But perhaps it's not very different from the situation of natural science. Every observation of a natural event is open to multiple scientific interpretations. That's why there are competing scientific theories. Ideally the theory that wins widest acceptance will be the one that best accounts for all the relevant observational data and enables scientists to accurately predict the results of experiments. But sometimes it takes a lot of work to figure out which theory is best.

"Something similar pertains in ethics: regardless of what theory you adopt, figuring out which action is the right one, the most moral one, is going to take work. It's true of Natural Law Ethics, but it's true of Utilitarianism, Duty Ethics, and all the rest." Dr. Platt was taking Micah's question seriously and giving him a very philosophical response. "So when we think about human nature, the world in which we live, and the various situations in which one might be considering the possibility of torturing a fellow human being, what sorts of considerations might guide us one way or another regarding whether or not we should torture someone?"

"As a nursing student, the first thing that comes to my mind is the negative impact that torture will have on the health of the one being tortured," Lauren volunteered. "Although we haven't said just what kind of torture we're talking about, and I guess there are some that would be more psychological than physical, what first comes to my mind are the kinds of torture that involve physical pain like beatings and stuff. Even waterboarding can endanger someone's health—some people have died from it."

"Great, Lauren. That's one very solid Natural Law consideration: torture imperils a person's physical well-being and thus goes against the natural design. Class, can you think of any others?"

Shakira raised her hand, and Dr. Platt called on her. "Couldn't the fact that the terrorist is endangering the lives of thousands of people be the basis of a Natural Law argument *for* torture? I know you just said that since torture imperils a person's well-being it's not natural, but that bomb that we were talking about is going to imperil a whole lot of people's well-being!"

"That's a very good question, Shakira. Class, how should we answer her?"

"Her argument sounds a lot like Utilitarianism to me," Lauren answered. "I can see why she thinks it would also be Natural Law, though. Can it be both?"

"I don't think so, Lauren," Dr. Platt replied. "Let me explain why. While it's true that killing thousands of people would go against the natural order, that it would undermine rather than support life, that's looking at the consequences of the action rather than the action itself. The action under consideration is torture. If we focus on torture and whether it fits with the natural order, we're doing Natural Law Ethics. If, on the other hand, we focus on the consequences of torture, then we're doing some kind of consequentialism, whether it be Utilitarianism or Ethical Egoism.[2] If we say that an action is wrong not

---

2. "Consequentialism" is an approach to ethics that says that the morality of an action is determined by its consequences. According to consequentialism, a morally right action is one that has desirable consequences and a morally wrong action is one that has undesirable consequences. There are two major divisions of consequentialism: Ethical Egoism and Utilitarianism. Ethical Egoism says that good actions have desirable consequences for the one performing the action, while Utilitarianism,

because it's bad but because it would lead to something else that is bad, or that it's good because it would lead to something else that is good, we're thinking consequentially. So if we say that torture is moral when it is done to prevent the loss of thousands of lives, we're reasoning consequentially. On the other hand, if we say that torture is immoral because its very nature is to damage a living being, that's based on the act itself. Does that make sense to you? I know it's a bit of a fine line to draw, but I think a legitimate distinction is being made."

"OK, I think I understand. So then is it right to say that Utilitarianism supports torture and Natural Law Theory opposes it?" Lauren seemed to be puzzling through the pieces pretty well.

"Well, perhaps, but we should bear in mind that there are some Utilitarian ethicists who don't support torture. Let's look at the issue from a new perspective. How would someone working from within the Kantian tradition of Duty Ethics view the issue? Can anyone tell me?"

Micah, Lauren, and Bianca all raised their hands. Dr. Platt smiled to himself; he had a pretty good idea of who was in their study circle. Instead of calling on one of them, he called on Summer, who hadn't spoken for a while. "Kant's central principle is the categorical imperative, which is similar to Jesus's Golden Rule. It basically says that you should only do what you wouldn't mind someone else doing to you in return. Therefore since I wouldn't want to be tortured, I shouldn't torture anyone else, right?"

"That's good, Summer. It's basically correct, though it's actually a little closer to the Golden Rule than to the categorical imperative. But let me introduce a lesser-known version of the categorical imperative. When I told you about the categorical imperative at the beginning of the semester, I gave you Kant's most famous articulation of it: 'I should never act except in such a way that I can also will that my maxim should become a universal law.'[3] However, we could debate how this should be applied to torture: Should we say that torture is never moral because I can't consistently universalize the principle that people who are a threat to society should be tortured? Or should we say

---

roughly speaking, says that good actions produce the greatest number of desirable consequences for the largest number of people.

3. Immanuel Kant, *Groundwork for the Metaphysics of Morals, with On a Supposed Right to Lie because of Philanthropic Concerns*, trans. James W. Ellington, 2nd ed. (Indianapolis: Hackett, 1981), 14.

that torture is moral in specific situations such as the time-bomb scenario because we could consistently universalize the principle that in situations where a culpable person can be forced to do something that would save the lives of many innocent people, that person should be tortured if that is the only way to get that person to do what is required to save those innocent lives? This is the problem of specificity that we talked about.

"The basic idea behind the categorical imperative, however, shows up in another of Kant's moral principles: the practical imperative. This tells us that we should never treat people only as means to ends, but rather we should always treat people as ends in themselves.[4] In other words, you should never treat someone as if he or she is merely a tool that you are going to use to get something done. You should always keep in mind that a person is a person, not a thing. People are not tools.

"Maybe an illustration would help. If you befriend someone because you genuinely like her, then you're reflecting a positive valuation of her worth as a person. If you befriend her because you see that she needs a friend, you're likewise treating her as a person who is valuable just because she's a person, regardless of whether she's popular, pretty, or anything else. But if you befriend someone because you know that she has a car and you know that at the end of the week you're going to need someone to drop you off at the train station so that you can go home for the weekend, then you're not really interested in her. You're just using her as a means to an end. According to Kant, that isn't moral. You should always bear in mind that she is just as much a person as you are. And that is where we can see the connection between the practical imperative and the categorical imperative—and the Golden Rule for that matter. Since you don't want to be treated as a tool, as merely a means to an end, you cannot consistently universalize the principle that it's okay to treat someone else as a tool. You must treat others as you would want them to treat you.

"So tell me, how does this apply to torture?" Dr. Platt looked around the room and was pleased to see a number of hands raised. His explanation seems to have succeeded. "Miguel?"

---

4. The exact quote is, "Act in such a way that you treat humanity, whether in your own person or in the person of another, always at the same time as an end and never simply as a means." Kant, *Groundwork for the Metaphysic of Morals*, 36.

"I don't think anyone in his right mind wants to be tortured, so I don't think torture can be universalized. Therefore Kant would be against it."

"I think you're right. Thank you. But let me press this a little harder, just to see if you can defend your position. Couldn't someone argue that a different principle could be universalized—the principle that we should torture whenever doing so is the only way to save innocent lives?"

"Sure, I guess so," Miguel granted. "I guess the correct application of the categorical imperative isn't all that clear."

"Does everyone agree with him? Is the categorical imperative inherently ambiguous?"

Bianca raised her hand. "I think the second formulation—the practical imperative—makes it pretty clear where Kant would stand. There's no way to torture someone without ignoring his personhood and treating him as a means to an end. Therefore I don't think Kant could ever sanction torture."

"You state that with real conviction, Bianca, as if you strongly agree with Kant." Dr. Platt seemed just a little bit surprised—perhaps because previously she hadn't shown an attraction to Duty Ethics.

"No—sorry—I didn't mean to give the impression that I'm joining Kant's camp. I only meant to argue that Kant wouldn't condone torture. I don't want to make Kant out to be some immoral person when his practical imperative seems so clearly opposed to torture. To me that seems like it would be a misreading or misrepresentation of Kant."

"I see," he relented. "That's a good distinction—well said. I think you've interpreted Kant correctly. It seems to me that there's no way Kant could condone torture." Turning to the whole class, he summarized their progress so far. "Our tally so far is two theories against torture and one theory at least provisionally in favor of it. What other ethical theories have we learned about, class?"

Micah raised his hand. "Divine Command Theory?"

"Good, Micah. Do you have an opinion about what position the advocates of Divine Command Theory would take on the issue?"

"Until a couple of minutes ago I would have said that the Golden Rule is clearly against torture and that because of this a Christian who holds to Divine Command Theory would be against it. I still think that the Divine Command theorist should be against it, but I'll need to think about what biblical passages or principles should be applied."

"Okay, fair enough. No one has all of the answers right at his fingertips at all times. Does anyone else have any ideas?"

Lauren raised her hand, and Dr. Platt called on her. "I don't want to lock horns with my dear friend Micah, so I'll try to put this tactfully. It's not clear to me that Divine Command Theory clearly stands on either side in this debate. To me it seems like DCT could go either way. The reason that I say this is that there have been a lot of theists from various religions who have had no trouble justifying horrific violence in the name of God. They range from contemporary Muslim terrorists all the way back to the religious violence recorded in the Hebrew Bible. You yourself mentioned the Inquisition, Dr. Platt. I don't know how common torture was or how consciously any of these people appealed to the commands of God, but from what I understand, Muslim terrorists appeal to Allah to justify many of the things that they do. So it seems pretty likely that Divine Command Theory can be used to support the morality of torture.[5]

"On the other hand, there are sweet Christians like Micah here," she continued, elbowing him as she spoke, "and there are Christian pacifists like the Amish, Mennonites, and Quakers, who probably oppose torture very strongly on some theological basis or other. At the least, I think we can see empirically that theists are on both sides of this issue."

"True enough," Dr. Platt granted. "I don't think anyone would disagree with that. The fact that theists might disagree on whether God's commands condone or prohibit torture doesn't necessarily mean that there isn't a correct answer to the question, of course, but since none of us are theologians—am I right, or is there a theologian in the room?—we're probably not going to be able to come to a conclusive decision about what position Divine Command Theory should take regarding torture. For one thing, different religious traditions have different views on the issue, and adjudicating which tradition is most correct—if any of

---

5. This paragraph should not be interpreted as implying that all or even most Muslims are terrorists, condone terrorism, or anything to that effect. Most Muslims oppose such tactics. See John Esposito and Dalia Mogahed, *Who Speaks for Islam? What a Billion Muslims Really Think* (New York: Gallup, 2007). See also Willa Frej, "How 70,000 Muslim Clerics Are Standing Up to Terrorism," *Huffington Post*, December 11, 2015, https://www.huffingtonpost.com/entry/muslim-clerics-condemn-terrorism_us_566adfa1e4b009377b249dea.

them is—goes well beyond the scope of this class. This is Ethics, after all, not World Religions. So let's consider one of the other metaethical theories that we talked about at the beginning of the semester: Virtue Ethics. Would anyone care to refresh our minds about the nature of Virtue Ethics?"

Again Bianca, Lauren, and Micah raised their hands. Since no one else had a hand raised, Dr. Platt's options were limited. He called on Bianca. "Virtue Ethics is an Aristotelian ethical tradition that focuses primarily on the development of a person's character and arguing that a virtuous person should seek to base his or her character on the Golden Mean."

"Well done!" he commended her. "That's a solid definition. Can you complete it by reminding us what the Golden Mean is?"

"Sure," she replied. "The Golden Mean is the balance point between two extremes of character. For example, courage is the mean between cowardice and foolhardiness. A person who is a coward is at the extreme of excessive fear; a person who is foolhardy in the face of danger has a deficiency of healthy fear; a person who is courageous has an appropriate amount of fear in the face of danger so that he doesn't throw his life away but at the same time is not terrified to the point of not being able to act rationally to protect himself or others."

"That's a well-chosen illustration in light of today's topic. Nicely done, Bianca. Thank you for a thorough and very appropriate explanation. Now, class, how do you think someone who adheres to Virtue Ethics would view torture?" Dr. Platt looked around the room expectantly. Not a single hand went up. He waited, still looking around. The students all looked back at him, waiting for him to give them a clue about what the Virtue ethicist would do. Eventually he returned to Bianca.

"No one want's to take a stab at this? Bianca, you seem to have a good handle on Virtue Ethics. What do you think a Virtue ethicist would say about torture?"

"I'd like to think that he or she would be against it, Dr. Platt, but I'm really not sure. It doesn't seem like being courageous or just or disciplined would necessarily compel a person to be either for or against torture. I mean, a brave person could be either for or against it and still be brave, right?"

Another student raised his hand. "Yes, Nate?" Dr. Platt said.

"In my notes I have written down that one of the weaknesses of Virtue Ethics is that because of its focus on developing character and on virtuous character traits, it doesn't provide a clear way to determine what actions are moral and immoral. Could that be why it's not easy to see how to apply Virtue Ethics to torture?"

"You could be right, Nate. What are you seeing—can you give us a little more detail about what you think the problem is?" Even though the class was struggling a bit with the application of Virtue Ethics to the problem of torture, Dr. Platt was happy to have so many students involved in the day's discussion.

"I guess I can try. Virtue Ethics gives us a way to determine which character traits are good and which are bad. That's the Golden Mean that Bianca was talking about. But it doesn't give us a way to determine which *actions* are good and which are bad. Maybe the Golden Mean could be applied to actions, but I'm not sure that would work. Think about torture. What would the extremes be—lots of really painful torture and no torture at all? Then the mean would be a moderate amount of mildly painful torture. But what good would that do? It wouldn't get a terrorist to reveal where a bomb is hidden, that's for sure."

Here Bianca had an idea. "I think I see the problem. Virtue Ethics prepares the person to do the right thing once he or she knows what the right thing is, but Virtue Ethics can't tell him or her what the right thing is. As a result, there is no Virtue Ethics position on the morality of torture. Is that correct, Professor?"

"I think it is, Bianca. You and Nate have figured it out. Some Virtue ethicists have argued that the Virtue Ethics concern for the type of person you are becoming leads Virtue Ethics to disavow torture because torturing someone would be likely to produce in the torturer a whole range of unvirtuous character traits. A possible counter to this is that torturing a culpable person in order to save many innocents, as in the time-bomb scenario, might actually be a result of having a virtuous character, one that is empathetic, has compassion for innocent people, and so on. I don't see a way to choose between these competing claims, and as a result it seems to me that Virtue Ethics is unable to answer the problem of torture. In fact, in the history of Virtue Ethics, it has often been paired up with other theories—Natural Law or Divine Command Theory, much of the time—precisely because of this shortcoming in what is otherwise a very helpful approach to ethics.

"OK, we've considered torture from the perspectives of Cultural Relativism, Utilitarianism, Natural Law Theory, Divine Command Theory, and Virtue Ethics. That covers most of the theories that we've learned—good work! But now our time is running out, so let's return to some unfinished business from the beginning of our class: motives for torture. We talked about two possible motives: the pleasure of torturing someone and torturing for revenge. I think we're probably in agreement that neither of these is a justifiable motive for torture, regardless of what metaethical approach one adopts. Let's talk about the other three motives that were mentioned. Is it ever right to torture someone as a form of punishment?"

Shakira raised her hand and, after Dr. Platt called on her, said, "In a way all punishment is torture, isn't it?"

"I think we'll need you to explain what you mean, Shakira," Dr. Platt replied. "Would you care to elaborate?"

"Sure. I remember being punished when I was a little child. Punishment came in a variety of forms depending on my offense: sometimes I was spanked, sometimes, I was given time out, sometimes I lost some privilege or had a toy taken away, and so forth. All of these were traumatic to me: for some reason, no matter what the punishment was, it caused me to feel real anguish. Even when there wasn't physical pain involved, the emotional pain was real. It felt like torture. I'm sure that not all people are as sensitive as I was, but deep down, everyone feels some sort of pain in response to punishment, otherwise it wouldn't be punishment, would it?"

"I guess you have a point there. If we take the term *torture* to mean any causing of unwelcome pain inflicted on one person by another, then perhaps all—or at least most—punishment would qualify as torture. But I'm not sure that we should construe the term that broadly. For one thing, a doctor or nurse sometimes has to inflict unwanted pain on a child as part of a necessary medical treatment that's being done for the child's own good. We wouldn't want to classify that as torture, would we?" He paused to let the class think about this. "Similarly," he continued, "when we send a criminal to jail, that's punishment, but it's not the same as waterboarding him or forcing bamboo under his fingernails, right? In the ordinary use of the English language we do make a distinction between *punishment* and *torture*, reserving the latter term for something considerably harsher than many common forms of punishment. That makes sense to me. So I'm inclined to think that the distinction between torture and punishment is legitimate. Don't you agree, Shakira?"

She nodded her head in agreement. "OK," he said, "then the question remains: is it okay to torture as a form of punishment?"

Summer raised her hand. "I guess we've kind of addressed this already, haven't we? The only school of thought that seems to strongly support torture is Utilitarianism, with the possible addition of Divine Command Theory depending on whose god is the true God. So torture is only moral if Utilitarianism is true and if the circumstances are such that torture will bring about the greatest good for the largest number of people, or if some religion that condones torture is true and the conditions for torture that it stipulates are in effect."

"Excellent! That's an A+ answer!" Dr. Platt responded, his pleasure at her answer written all over his face.

"So do I get any bonus points?" she asked.

"At the very least I'll refrain from torturing you," he replied, laughing.

"Couldn't the final exam be considered a form of torture?" she shot back.

"I think the final is actually more like the needed medical procedure that I mentioned earlier," he replied. "But your approach to my question is exactly what I wanted to hear. I was trying to see if I could trick the class into thinking about the issue as if it can be handled separately from our discussion of ethical theories, but you saw right through me. We cannot evaluate the motives of our actions from some supposedly theory-neutral perspective: any such evaluation will always be from the perspective of some theory or other, even if it's not a carefully formulated philosophical one. Therefore the answer to the question 'Is torture a moral form of punishment' is 'Moral according to whom?' To a Utilitarian it could be, but to a Natural Law theorist or a Kantian it wouldn't be.

"However—and this is very important—I don't want you to get the impression that torture could actually be moral for a Utilitarian ethicist and immoral for a Natural Law theorist. In fact, I believe that it's going to be just as moral or immoral for a Utilitarian to torture as it is for the Natural Law person. But one or the other of them is going to think that it's moral even if it's not—or vice versa. Let's not forget that we're talking about two different things here: what a person *thinks* is moral because of his or her approach to morality, and what *actually is* moral. There are moral truths that exist independently of our opinions. Our job is to discover what these moral truths are."

Micah raised his hand. "Yes, Micah?"

"What you just said is implied by your rejection of relativism, isn't it? That's why you believe that there are moral truths that are distinct from our opinions about what's right and wrong."

"That's right, Micah. I'm glad you can see that. There are other arguments for the existence of moral absolutes, of course, but the repudiation of moral relativism is one motive for my belief in absolutism.[6]

"Now if all of this is true about torture as a form of punishment, what does that suggest about torture as a deterrent or for the purpose of information gathering? Would either of those motives justify torture, perhaps in extreme cases like the time-bomb scenario?"

This time Dr. Platt called on Miguel. "The same thing would be true for both of those motives as is true for punishment; how they would be seen will depend on the person's moral theory. So they might be seen as moral if the person is a Utilitarian, or they might not be if the person holds to some other theory."

"Correct, Miguel. Now you're seeing why we began the course with a discussion of ethical theories. They form the foundation for all well-formed opinions in ethics.

"OK, class," he finished, "our time is up. This has been an interesting discussion, hasn't it? I don't know if we've settled the question of torture in your minds, but I think we've at least accomplished one important goal: we've gotten you to see that you really need a systematic approach to moral issues before you can judge something as right or wrong. And today's class was a handy impromptu review session for the upcoming exam. Please be studying for that, and have a great afternoon!"

---

6. *Moral absolutes* are timeless moral truths that apply to all people. *Absolutism* is the belief that moral absolutes exist.

QUESTIONS TO PONDER

- Do you think it is necessary to choose or develop a moral theory (such as Ethical Relativism, Utilitarianism, Duty Ethics) in order to have a good reason for your moral beliefs?

- Do you think it is ever moral to torture someone? Why or why not?

- If you think it would not be right to torture a terrorist in order to save the lives of thousands of people, do you think that allowing those people to die when you could possibly have saved their lives is moral? In other words, is the choice to not save their lives moral?

- If you were the terrorist captured by the Department of Homeland Security, would you want to be tortured? (Some might answer yes—please give this some careful thought before answering.)

TERMS TO KNOW

- Socratic method
- Torture
- Coercion
- Deterrence
- Conflation
- Problem of specificity
- Categorical imperative
- Practical imperative

FOR FURTHER READING

Greenberg, Karen J. *The Torture Debate in America.* New York: Cambridge University Press, 2005.

Levinson, Sanford. *Torture: A Collection.* Oxford: Oxford University Press, 2006.

Taylor, Justin. "Torture and Ticking Time Bombs: A Christian Ethics Symposium." The Gospel Coalition. https://www.thegospelcoalition.org/blogs/justin-taylor/torture-and-ticking-timebombs-a-christian-ethics-symposium (accessed 5/18/2020).

United Nations Treaty Collection: Convention against Torture and other Cruel, Inhuman, or Degrading Treatment or Punishment. New York: United Nations, 1984. https://treaties.un.org/doc/Treaties/1987/06/19870626%2002-38%20AM/Ch_IV_9p.pdf.

5

ANIMAL RIGHTS

Synopsis: Bianca, Lauren, and Micah have decided to do an extra-credit report on animal rights, a subject about which none of them has given much thought. They initially meet at a park to plan how they are going to address the issue, thinking it will probably not be very difficult. They are in for a few surprises.

* * *

"I love this park! It's so quiet and peaceful here," said Bianca, as she, Lauren, and Micah found a good spot in the middle of Cedar Bluff County Park to talk over the extra-credit assignment Dr. Platt had made available in ethics class. It was unusually warm in the sunshine, so all three were sipping iced coffees they'd picked up on the way.

Dr. Platt had provided a list of topics that he did not plan to cover in class; students could do a paper on one of the topics to earn extra credit in the class. After the last test, all three friends felt like extra credit was a good idea. The teacher had also assured the class that working together on a topic was acceptable and, in fact, recommended. He was a big believer in collaborative learning.

"Are you still thinking we should choose animal rights?" asked Micah. He was a little dubious about the topic, having little interest in animals himself.

Almost in unison both girls said, "Absolutely!" Lauren added, "It's a lot more interesting than gambling, and surely you don't want to get into business ethics—that would be so boring!"

"Hey, I'm a business major!" retorted Micah. "But whatever. How are we going to get started?"

"I brought an article from Dr. Platt's suggested reading list. Maybe we could go through it and see what we think," suggested Lauren.

"Sounds good," Bianca and Micah agreed. Bianca then asked, "Which article did you bring?"

"'Equality for Animals,' an excerpt from a book by Peter Singer, a really famous guy who teaches at Princeton. It says here that this section is from a book called *Practical Ethics*, which he wrote in 1979," replied Lauren.[1]

"Is he still teaching?" asked Bianca. "He must be really old now!"

"Yeah, Siri says he's seventy-two and still going," replied Lauren. Fortunately, no senior citizens were nearby to be offended at what the three friends thought constituted "really old."

Micah suggested, "Let's go through his arguments and see why Dr. Platt recommended his writings."

Bianca took out a pad to take notes, and Lauren began reading and summarizing.

"Singer says the key to the whole issue is what he calls the 'fundamental principle of equality,' which means the interests of all parties in a transaction must be equally considered."

"What in the world does that mean?" queried Micah.

"He gives some examples," replied Lauren. "Slavery is immoral because the interests of the slaves are just as important as the interests of the masters."

"I certainly agree with that," chimed in Bianca.

"Harming another human is immoral for the same reason. No one wants to be harmed, and everyone has equal right to have that interest respected," continued Lauren. "This is making sense! Who said Ivy League professors are hard to understand?"

---

1. Peter Singer, *Practical Ethics*, 2nd ed. (Cambridge: Cambridge University Press, 1993), 55–82.

Lauren then drew Singer's conclusion: "So this principle also applies to 'non-human animals.'"

"Whoa! Wait a minute," interrupted Micah. "What did he mean by that?"

"Just what it sounds like, I think. If animals have interests, those interests should be respected," replied Lauren.

"What kind of interests?" asked Bianca.

"They want to live; they want to be free of pain; they don't want to be confined—"

Micah interrupted Lauren again, "Is Singer saying ants don't like to be stepped on? That seems ridiculous. Ants don't even know they're being stepped on, and there's no evidence they feel pain if they're injured or loss if grandma gets stepped on."

"I think you're jumping the gun," said Bianca. Addressing Lauren, Bianca asked, "Does he talk about different levels of animal?"

"Yes, he does, Bianca," replied Lauren. "He says that there is a 'precondition' for having interests. Namely, the being must be able to experience pain or its opposite, pleasure.[2] This excludes rocks, trees, and a lot of lower levels of animals from the discussion including, presumably, ants, Micah."

Micah nodded his head.

Lauren explained further, "Professor Singer makes a big point about comparing our treatment of animals to our treatment of other people. For instance, he says that racism is regarding one's own race as having interests that override those of other races. It is immoral to give one's own race preference over another's, when they feel the same pain and desire the same pleasure as you do. Similarly, it would be wrong for a more intelligent person to ignore the needs of a less intelligent person just because of the difference in their IQs."

"I think I see where this is going," said Micah. Bianca nodded, also seeing the implication Singer was going to draw out.

Lauren stated it anyway: "Non-human animals and human animals belong to different species, and humans are typically more intelligent than animals. By animals, remember, he means higher-order animals that can

---

2. Note that ethical decisions based on the pain or pleasure produced is fundamental to Utilitarianism. Singer is a modern Utilitarian ethicist.

experience pain and pleasure. These facts do not give humans the right to deny the interests of non-human animals. If they do, it is 'speciesism.'"

"Speciesism?" echoed both Micah and Bianca. The term made sense to them, but they had never heard it before.

"Yes, favoring one's own species over others for arbitrary reasons," explained Lauren, still referring to the article.

"I think there are reasons for favoring humans over animals that are not arbitrary," asserted Micah.

"Maybe, Micah, but let's finish going through Singer's arguments before we start trying to refute them, shall we?" suggested Lauren.

"Okay, but I'm having a little trouble with an expression he keeps using," responded Micah.

"Me too," said Bianca, feeling pretty sure she knew what Micah meant. "He keeps referring to 'non-human animals' as though people are just animals too."

"Exactly," said Micah, giving Bianca an approving glance. Oddly, she blushed. "People aren't just animals, Lauren."

Lauren replied, "Professor Singer is basing his discussion on science. Biologists, zoologists, anthropologists, and everybody else in science who studies humans categorize us as advanced animals. You Christians may not like it, but that's the way it is. Can we agree to disagree on that for the moment?"

"I suppose so," answered Bianca, "but I think that's going to be a really important point later." Bianca was very pleased to note Micah's vigorous agreement.

"Then let's continue," Lauren went on. "Singer says there are several ramifications of this view of speciesism. First, it is not right for modern Westerners to use such animals as food."

"What? No steak or pork chops or fried shrimp?" cried Micah.

"Obviously, eating shrimp would be fine," corrected Bianca. "But I think he is ruling out steak and pork chops. Bummer."

"The reason Singer says 'Westerners' is because certain cultures have eaten animals of necessity. Hunter cultures, for instance, lived on eating animals. Singer argues that modern Westerners by no means need to eat animals to survive. I suppose he's right about that," Lauren argued.

"I know being a vegetarian is a healthy way to live, and all that," said Micah, "but I never thought of that as the only moral choice. What Singer is saying would completely change how Western society operates!"

"He's not done," replied Lauren. "Most animal experimentation is based on speciesism. What right do humans have to kill thousands of mammals a year in order to develop medicines or even cosmetics?"

"Once again," responded Micah, "animals aren't like humans. That's what makes it okay."

"Singer replies to that," said Lauren. "If rats weren't like humans, then tests done on them couldn't help humans."

Bianca argued, "Surely the benefit to medical research justifies the harm done to animals. It's often the only way to test medicines and to determine effective remedies."

Lauren nodded. "The article acknowledges that some animal testing might be justifiable on that basis. The harm to the animals' interests might be justified because the human interest sufficiently outweighed it. Certainly, Singer recognizes that humans experience their pains and pleasures in a different way than non-human animals. A person doesn't just die of cancer. He or she dreads the cancer and experiences emotional and mental suffering that animals are not capable of. But he claims that a lot of experimentation on animals does not save human lives; it is simply for scientific advance or for human convenience. He concludes that all such animal suffering is immoral."[3]

Micah and Bianca were uncomfortable thinking about animals being made to suffer for human convenience, but they were also uncomfortable with how Singer's arguments seemed to undercut how society had always functioned. They were wondering if mankind could have been this wrong about the treatment of animals throughout all of history.

Before leaving this point, Lauren brought out another aspect of Singer's argument: "The professor brings up 'orphaned humans with severe and irreversible brain damage.'"

"Oh, no, he's not going there, is he?" asked Bianca, with a look bordering on horror.

"Don't reject his argument without thinking it through," responded Lauren. "We would not do experiments on such people, would we? But

---

3. The Utilitarian underpinnings of Singer's argument should once again be apparent. The morality of experimentation on animals is being evaluated in terms of its beneficial or harmful results to the "interests" of the animals and humans.

apes, monkeys, dogs, cats, and even rats and mice are more sensitive to pain, more intelligent, and more aware of their suffering than many humans in this situation. How, then, can we justify experimenting on the animals?"

"But the mentally damaged person is still a person! How can he make such a comparison?" cried Bianca.

Micah surprisingly replied, "I don't think Professor Singer is arguing that we should do such experiments on brain-damaged people. He's just saying we shouldn't do them on animals. I don't agree with equating *any* humans with animals, no matter how damaged, but we need to be fair to him."

"Exactly," responded Lauren. "He says as much in this article. The analogies are not intended to teach that certain humans have no value, but rather that some animals have just as much value." Micah and Bianca made eye contact and raised their eyebrows at that. Lauren continued, "He gives a final ramification, but it's kind of a catchall. I'll read it to you: 'There are many other areas which raise similar issues, including the fur trade, hunting in all its different forms, circuses, rodeos, zoos, and the pet business. Since the philosophical questions raised by these issues are not very different from those raised by the use of animals as food and in research, I shall leave it to the reader to apply the appropriate ethical principles to them.'"

"He's saying I'm being immoral because I have two pet cats," bemoaned Bianca. "My cats love me!"

"But did they choose to be your pets, or did you choose them?" asked Micah. "I think Singer would say you don't have the right to make this decision for your cats. They should be free to go where they wish."

"I think that's a bad example," Lauren interjected. "Bianca's cats may be perfectly happy living with Bianca. But what if she was caring for them only so she could fatten them up for Thanksgiving dinner? Would that be moral?"

"It would be gross!" exclaimed Bianca.

"Maybe, but in most of the states in our country, it is perfectly legal to kill and eat your pets, even dogs and cats," stated Lauren. "When Singer mentions the 'pet business,' he's not talking about the loving relationship that may exist between an owner and her pets, but rather he's thinking of businesses that treat animals like commodities, keep them in cages until someone chooses them, and then sell them without consulting in any way the interests of the animal."

"You almost sound like you agree with this guy, Lauren," stated Micah.

"I'm playing the devil's advocate a little bit, Micah, but I do want to read with an open mind if we're going to write a good paper on animal rights."

"Okay, fair enough," Micah replied. "Does the article say any more?"

Lauren scanned the article for a couple of moments. All three took advantage of the break to return to their coffees, which were rapidly warming up in the hot conditions.

"He finishes the article by anticipating various objections to his position. I think he realized his position was controversial," surmised Lauren.

Bianca nodded. "Back in 1979 it must have been shocking to a lot of people."

"I can think of some objections," said Micah. "Which ones does he anticipate?"

Lauren began listing them. "First, are we sure animals can feel pain like humans?"

"My cat sure can," replied Bianca. "I was trimming her nails the other night, and I accidentally got down into the quick. You should have heard her howl!"

"That is one of Singer's points," Lauren agreed. "Animals respond to painful stimuli much as humans do. Many of them have nervous systems like those of humans, so you would expect similar responses."

"Granted. Animals feel pain. I think we can all agree on that," answered Micah. "What's next?"

"Second, if animals kill and eat each other, why isn't it moral for us to kill and eat them?"

Micah spoke up, "That seems like a good question. How does he answer that?"

Lauren replied, "Animals who kill and eat other animals do so in order to survive. Humans don't have to. Also—and here I think he gets a little sarcastic—why would we seek moral guidance from the animals we are killing and eating? That is, if we really believe they are so far below humans that we have a right to use them as food, how can we dare argue that their behavior is a pattern for ours? That's an interesting point, isn't it?"

"Yeah, maybe," Micah mumbled.

"Third, animals don't know that eating other animals is unethical, but humans should know that. We're accountable for that knowledge, but we can't hold animals accountable for it," Lauren concluded.

Bianca responded, "It seems like Singer makes animals and humans equal whenever it suits his argument, and then he makes animals less than human when *that* suits his argument. Am I the only one bothered by that?"

"I see your point," responded Lauren, "but let's keep going. In fact," she said as she scanned the next section of the article, "it looks like Singer responds to the idea that humans should be considered superior to animals because of the differences between them. For instance, some people say humans are distinct because we make tools, use tools, and communicate. The article says that science has shown that some animals do all of these things."

"Yeah," chimed in Micah, "I saw a National Geographic special on TV a couple of months ago that showed porpoises talking to each other and stuff like that. I suppose he's got a point."

Bianca arched her eyebrows at Micah. "Thank you for that scientific confirmation, Micah. Very helpful." He apparently missed the sarcasm.

Lauren continued, ignoring their banter, "Others point to humans' self-consciousness as their distinguishing characteristic."

Bianca spoke up, "That does seem like a big deal. We're the only species that not only feels pain but is aware that it is feeling pain."

Lauren responded, "Singer answers that it is hard to see how having self-consciousness somehow makes humans more valuable. Furthermore, if that's the reason we have value, what about unfortunate humans who, for one reason or another, lack self-consciousness—say, someone in a coma. Would that person be less valuable than other people?"

Bianca, after taking this in, said, "So he acknowledges differences between humans and what he calls non-human animals, but he doesn't think those differences give humans the right to do what they want with animals. Is that essentially correct?"

Lauren nodded in agreement. "If I'm reading him correctly, I believe so." After a pause, Lauren went on. "He addresses one more objection. Some people have argued that animals do not and cannot reciprocate good behavior."

"What does that mean?" Micah interjected.

"I think it means that if you feed a wild animal, he won't say thank you or bring you food in return. In fact, given the chance, he might kill and eat you. He's not bound by the Golden Rule or Kant's categorical imperative."[4]

"I see that," responded Micah. "What's the point?"

"These people are arguing that we don't owe moral behavior to animals because they can't respond with moral behavior to us," Lauren replied.

Bianca spoke up, "From the rest of the article, I think I can see how Singer is going to shoot that down."

"How?" asked Lauren and Micah, almost simultaneously.

"Babies, people in comas, and other unfortunate people can't reciprocate our good deeds to them either, can they?" asked Bianca.

"Not only them," added Lauren, "but he mentions people not living yet. Future generations can't do anything to benefit us, so why do we worry about nuclear waste? He is rejecting a view of ethics that he calls 'contractualism,' that the basis of moral behavior is an unwritten contract between equals.[5] Contractualism clearly doesn't work."

"No, it doesn't," agreed Micah. "It appears that he has successfully rebutted all the objections . . . if the foundations of his argument are sound. I think we should explore those some more."

"I do too," agreed Bianca, "but I've got to run. I've got an appointment across town in about an hour."

"How about we all do some reading on the topic and get back together tomorrow afternoon? Does that work for you guys?" asked Lauren.

As Bianca was nodding, Micah suggested, "In honor of our topic, let's meet at River Bend Zoological Park. I've never been there, but I've heard it's a pretty good zoo." Both girls thought that was a great idea.

---

4. The Golden Rule, as taught by Jesus, is found in Matthew 7:12: "So in everything, do to others what you would have them do to you." The categorical imperative as taught by Kant is found in *Groundwork of the Metaphysics of Morals*: "Act according to the maxim that you would wish all other rational people to follow, as if it were a universal law."

5. T. M. Scanlon popularized the concept of Contractualism in *What We Owe to Each Other* (Cambridge, MA: Harvard University Press, 1998). This is his definition of the concept: "An act is wrong if its performance under the circumstances would be disallowed by any set of principles for the general regulation of behaviour that no one could reasonably reject as a basis for informed, unforced, general agreement" (153). For a thorough discussion of this principle, see https://plato.stanford.edu/entries/contractualism.

***

The next day as Micah made his way through the River Bend Zoo, he saw Lauren and Bianca sitting in a nice pavilion that offered an excellent view of the giraffe and zebra exhibits.

"Hi, guys," greeted Micah. "Sorry I'm late, but I've got a good reason. I stopped at the convenience store on the way and got you each an Icee. I've got lemon-flavored, orange, and cola. Which would you like? I like them all."

"Thank you, Micah. I'll take the lemon, if that's alright," responded Bianca.

"Sounds good," said Lauren. "I'd like the orange."

"Excellent," responded Micah cheerfully. "I really wanted the cola." Both girls smiled, clearly aware that that was what he wanted.

"Did you guys find more articles on our subject?" asked Lauren.

"Yes," replied Bianca. "I found an organization called Vegan Outreach that has accepted Singer's idea of speciesism and is trying to get Americans to become vegetarians."[6]

"I read an article by Stephen Wise, who is involved in the Nonhuman Rights Project, which is advocating for animal rights," answered Micah.[7]

"Very good," said Lauren. "I decided to read some Christian perspectives, since I figured you guys wouldn't want to introduce your faith-based arguments at first. Who wants to go first?"

"I will," Micah promptly responded. "I think my research connects closely to what we read yesterday in Singer's article. Wise is just as strange as Singer is."

"Wait, Micah," interrupted Lauren. "Why are you calling their positions 'strange'? Aren't you prejudging them?"

"Humans have been interacting with animals for thousands of years on the basis of people being essentially superior to animals and, therefore, having the right to own or use animals in reasonable ways to meet human

---

6. Vegan Outreach, https://veganoutreach.org.
7. Steven Wise, "Animal Rights, Animal Wrongs: The Case for Nonhuman Personhood," *Foreign Affairs,* April 28, 2015, https://www.foreignaffairs.com/articles/2015-04-28/animal-rights-animal-wrongs.

needs. It seems to me that Singer, Wise, and others have come along in the last few decades and are claiming that 99.9 percent of humans have been wrong throughout world history," responded Micah.

"Micah," interjected Bianca. "Do you remember when we studied Jeremy Bentham in class?"

"I think so. Wasn't he a Pragmatist or a Utilitarian or something?"

"He was one of the developers of Utilitarian Ethics back in nineteenth-century England. Vegan Outreach quoted his book *An Introduction to the Principles of Morals and Legislation*, which he wrote way back in 1823. He said concerning animals, 'The question is not *Can they reason?* or *Can they talk?* but *Can they suffer?*' So the ideas Singer and your guy are talking about may not be all that recent," explained Bianca.

"So let's avoid calling any of the positions strange until we sort this out. Okay, Micah?" suggested Lauren.

"Fair enough," replied Micah. "Wise begins his discussion by acknowledging that animal welfare became a concern in the Western world in the nineteenth century and that Western governments have issued a fair amount of legislation since that time that seeks to prevent unnecessary pain and suffering for animals, especially animals involved in human life, like farm livestock."

Lauren interjected, "But the tricky word there is 'unnecessary,' isn't it?"

"Given how much suffering slaughterhouse animals go through," responded Bianca, "it seems obvious that food-producing industries can justify a lot of animal suffering as necessary."

"Wise doesn't get sidetracked by discussing those issues," said Micah. "His thesis is more fundamental. Let me quote what he says about the more advanced animals, 'Great apes, cetaceans (whales, dolphins, and porpoises), and elephants . . . possess a complex consciousness and self-consciousness, exquisite sentience, robust general intelligence, and a powerful sense of autonomy.'"[8]

"Wow," Bianca spoke up. "He makes them sound almost human."

"Exactly!" cried Micah. "Wise argues that animal welfare should not be the issue today. Instead, the argument should be over animal rights."

---

8. Wise, "Animal Rights, Animal Wrongs."

"We haven't solved the many human rights issues that face us today," responded Lauren, "and Wise is trying to get us to think in terms of animal rights?"

"Actually, Lauren, Wise is trying to get us to think of both subjects as essentially the same issue. Here is, I think," Micah went on, "the philosophical center of his article: 'The roots of the animal rights movement do not lie in the anticruelty legislation of the nineteenth century; they reach deeper into the worldwide antislavery movements that began in the eighteenth century and flowered into the broad international human rights movement of the twentieth century.'"[9]

"That's basically what Singer was saying too, wasn't it?" asked Bianca.

"I think so," answered Micah. "Wise and his group link human rights and animal rights by arguing that animals ought to be regarded as persons."

"Does he think animals should have the same rights as humans because animals are persons just like us?" asked Lauren.

"No, he doesn't go that far," responded Micah. "Because animals are at various levels of awareness and intelligence, we should give them rights accordingly. He speaks of 'chimpanzee rights,' 'elephant rights,' etc. Presumably, an elephant would deserve more rights than, say, a garter snake."

Lauren asked, "He would want to give rights to a garter snake?"

"Well, that was my example. But presumably we would want to pass legislation to protect their habitats, not restrict their freedom, and that sort of thing. Elephants would need more rights, because they have greater intelligence and self-awareness," explained Micah.

"That's really interesting," observed Bianca, "but who would decide what the rights should be for each animal species? That sounds like a simple thing to explain but a hard thing to do."

"Yeah, Wise and his group just want to make a little progress here and there. A few years ago, they sued some people in New England who owned chimpanzees as pets, arguing that chimpanzees, as persons, could not be owned. I don't think they won."

"Is that all, Micah?" asked Lauren.

"He makes one more connection that I find interesting. Wise argues that denying rights to animals in proportion to their cognitive abilities undermines the advances over the last couple of centuries in granting rights to all

---

9. Wise, "Animal Rights, Animal Wrongs."

different kinds of people. If we can deny rights to horses, for instance, just because we want to, then why couldn't we deny rights to Australian aborigines or Asian immigrants or blonds or short people? He thinks the foundations of a free society are at risk," concluded Micah.

"Fascinating," answered Bianca. "That's pretty sweeping!"

Lauren added, "I don't think he'd like that we're sitting in a zoo, enjoying the captive animals. If animals really are persons, I don't guess persons should use other persons for recreation."

Micah nodded his head. After a brief pause, he asked, "What about your studies, Bianca? What have you turned up?"

"The organization I studied also thinks speciesism is behind all human mistreatment of animals," replied Bianca. "Their main goal is to inform the American public about the horrors of slaughterhouses and in this way convince people to give up eating meat, or as they say, animal flesh."

"That's a tall order," replied Micah.

"We know you like steak," answered Lauren, "but we should make our decisions on a rational basis, not just out of convenience or emotion."

"I actually think it is very intelligent to eat steak, no matter how inconvenient or sad."

"Very funny."

"If you two are finished," said Bianca, "they quote Paul McCartney—"

"Wait," interrupted Lauren. "You mean *the* Paul McCartney, of the Beatles?"

"One and the same," replied Bianca. "Apparently McCartney said, 'If slaughterhouses had glass walls, everyone would be vegetarian.'[10] What I've read about these places supports his claim. Chickens and pigs are sometimes burned or skinned alive; cows and their calves are separated shortly after birth; milk-producing cows are kept in tight spaces, unable even to turn around, for months. . . ."

"Stop, already!" blurted out Micah, accidentally spewing cola Icee on his shirt. "I thought this discussion was going to be rational rather than emotional. We have to decide what kinds of rights animals have philosophically before we allow ourselves to be swayed by stuff like this."

---

10.   "What Is Speciesism? And How You Can Make a Difference," VeganOutreach.org.

"Is that true, Micah?" asked Lauren. "If the treatment of animals is so horrific that we can't even talk about it, doesn't that weigh in as an argument against treating them that way?"

"Not necessarily," Micah responded. "Mistreatment implies some standard of appropriate treatment. I don't mistreat a rock by throwing it in the lake or mistreat my lawn by mowing it. So if killing animals for food is appropriate, it may be right to do so in the most efficient way possible, even if that involves some suffering for the animal before it dies. That makes sense, doesn't it?"

"Maybe," the two girls allowed, although they sounded skeptical.

"Be that as it may," Bianca went on, "Vegan Outreach argues that most humans—especially Westerners—don't need to eat animals. There are healthier ways to eat that do not involve any animal suffering."

"I bet they then offer a whole line of veggie products," suggested Micah, sounding a bit sarcastic.

"Yes, of course," countered Bianca, "but that doesn't mean their arguments against animal cruelty are insincere."

"Did you check out any other organizations that argue for animal rights or welfare, Bianca?" asked Lauren.

"There are quite a few of them, actually," replied Bianca. "I made a list of several of the most significant ones. Do you two want to see if you can guess my list?"

"Okay," Lauren and Micah agreed.

"Everyone knows about PETA," offered Micah first. "People Eating Tasty Animals."

"That's not funny and is in really poor taste," said Bianca. Micah winced. "People for the Ethical Treatment of Animals is the largest animal rights group in the world, and they stand for a lot of the things we've been talking about."

"How about the Humane Society?" asked Lauren.

"Correct," said Bianca. "That organization has been lobbying on behalf of animals for over sixty years, first in America and now around the world."

"I've heard of one more," said Micah. "The ASPCA, which, I think, means the American Society for Prevention of Cruelty to Animals. By the way, I *am* against being cruel to animals."

"That's reassuring, Micah," Bianca added. "That's one of the oldest organizations that has argued for animal welfare. William Wilberforce was involved in founding the British SPCA back in the 1820s, and the American organization started right after the American Civil War. Any more?"

Lauren and Micah shook their heads.

Bianca responded, "There are hundreds of such organizations, some of which defend animals in general and many that focus on specific animals or particular areas where animals are exploited. This is a major movement worldwide nowadays."

SELECTED ANIMAL RIGHTS ORGANIZATIONS	
Organization	**Website**
ASPCA	https://www.aspca.org
Animal Equality	https://animalequality.org
Animal Legal Defense Fund	https://aldf.org
Farm Animal Rights Movement	https://farmusa.org
Friends of Animals	https://www.friendsofanimals.org
Humane Society	https://www.humanesociety.org
People for the Ethical Treatment of Animals	https://www.peta.org

"Okay, I think we've got a pretty good picture of the case against animal exploitation," concluded Lauren. "Would you like me to share some of my research into Christian animal ethicists?"

"Please do," replied Bianca, as Micah nodded.

"As you know, I'm not up on a lot of Christian terminology," started Lauren, "so you guys may have to help me sort some of this out."

"We'll help if we can," replied Bianca. Once again, Micah nodded his agreement.

Lauren spoke up, "I found an article by a Christian writer who argues *for* animal welfare but from a Christian viewpoint.[11] He acknowledges that

---

11. Dan Story, "Is 'Animal Rights' a Biblical Concern? A Christian Response to the Modern Animal Rights Movement," *Christian Research Journal,* 37, no. 2 (2014).

Christians have often treated animals as a resource no differently from plants or inorganic materials. In another article, by the way, I found this quotation from the early church theologian St. Augustine: 'By a most just ordinance of the Creator, both their [animals'] life and their death are subject to our use.'[12] So for a long time, most Christians haven't given much thought to animal suffering."

"In fairness," responded Micah, "wouldn't you agree that that was true of almost all people until the nineteenth century?"

"Granted," said Lauren. "I guess the point is that people of your religion did not see implications in their faith for treating animals better than the cultures to which they belonged."

"That's too bad," said Bianca. "Even today, I doubt that most of the leaders in these various animal welfare groups are known for their Christianity, although, of course, I could be wrong."

Lauren continued, "This author—his name is Dan Story, by the way—says that Christians need to face up to three questions. 'Do animal rights activists have a just cause? Do animals have value to God beyond their usefulness to people? Do humans have a moral responsibility to nonhuman life?' He takes up each question."

"I'm guessing," interjected Micah, "that he thinks animal rights activists do have a just cause, or he wouldn't be writing the article."

"Correct," responded Lauren. "He cites the same kind of evidence we've seen in the other sources. The number of animals used in laboratory experiments is almost unbelievable. Granted, these stats are from 2001, but he says scientists in that one year experimented on '690,800 guinea pigs, rabbits, and hamsters, in addition to 161,700 farm animals, 70,000 dogs, 49,400 primates, 22,800 cats, and 80 million mice and rats.'"

"You're kidding," exclaimed Bianca. Even Micah looked stunned.

"Most of these animals are killed, and many die in very painful ways," Lauren explained. "To justify the claim that these animals experience painful deaths, he confirms what we've read before: animals 'not only feel pain but also stress, fear, anxiety, grief, loneliness, despair, and other humanlike

12. "Animal Rights," BBC editorial, http://www.bbc.co.uk/ethics/animals/rights/rights_1.shtml.

characteristics. These attributes have been well documented by numerous studies in animal behavior during the past few decades.'"

"So far," Micah observed, "he sounds like Singer, Wise, and the PETA people."

"He's answering the first question," responded Lauren. "As a self-professed Christian, the author believes animal rights advocates have a point."

"What was the second question, Lauren?" prodded Bianca. As a cat lover, she was finding all this talk of suffering animals quite distressing, especially as she looked across at the beautiful zebras and giraffes munching grass contentedly.

"This will make more sense to you guys, since you're Christians," answered Lauren, "but he asks whether or not animals have value to God beyond their usefulness to people."

"That's a good question," added Micah. "In Genesis 2 God brings all the animals before Adam to name them,[13] and I'm told that naming something in the Bible usually means having authority over it."

"The Bible says Adam named all the animals?" exclaimed Lauren, sounding a bit incredulous.

"That's what it says," answered Bianca. "I think Micah would agree that it probably doesn't mean God brought every insect, fish, and bird. The point is, as Micah said, God showed Adam that he was in charge of the animal kingdom." Micah nodded in agreement at Bianca's observation.

"That explains why the author felt like he needed to address this issue," responded Lauren. "Apparently, some Christians have felt that this means that animals exist solely to serve human needs."

"I can see how people might draw that conclusion," said Micah.

"But the author gives some good pushback to that idea," Lauren went on. "If animals are only for human needs, why did God—supposedly—create so many animal species that don't benefit man in any known way? Further, there are many animals that are positively harmful to humans and make life more difficult. Those seem like good points."

"I like where he's going with this," Micah interjected.

"You do?" asked Lauren.

---

13. Gen. 2:19–20.

"One of the foundational stones of our faith is that everything God does is ultimately for his own glory. So the author is probably arguing that God created animals for himself, not finally for humans. That's a really cool idea."

"He cites some verses in the Scriptures to prove this," Lauren continued. "I visited my Grandma last night and looked up these verses with her in her Bible."

"Your grandmother is a Christian?" asked Bianca.

"Yes. She's a Presbyterian and goes to her church pretty often. My dad went against those teachings when he went to college, so I've grown up in an atheistic family. But grandma talks to me about her faith sometimes."

"What Scripture passages did he use?" prompted Micah.

"There's a section in the fiftieth psalm that talks about God creating and owning all the animals.[14] And there's kind of a strange passage in Job, near the end, where God says He sees things in the animal kingdom that humans don't even know about,"[15] answered Lauren.

"Did he mention the verse in Proverbs about people being kind to their farm animals?" Bianca asked.

"Yes, I think so." Lauren consulted her notes. "Do you mean the tenth verse of the twelfth chapter of Proverbs?"

"I'm pretty sure that's it," responded Bianca.

"I'd forgotten about that verse," exclaimed Micah. He pulled out his phone, opened the Bible app on it, and looked up Proverbs 12:10. He then read aloud, "'The righteous care for the needs of their animals, but the kindest acts of the wicked are cruel.' That verse deals directly with what we've been discussing!"

"So far," Lauren brought them back to the argument, "the author has argued that animals do suffer at the hands of humans—animal rights activists have a point—and that God made animals for himself, not just for us. As an atheist, I can land at the same basic place by agreeing that humans do make animals suffer a lot for our needs or conveniences, and animals did not evolve so that they would one day serve human needs. At this point, though, the article gets more theological, and I got lost. I'll tell you what he says, but you'll have to explain it to me."

---

14. Ps. 50:10–12.
15. Job 39:1–30.

"Sure," said Micah. "Can you remind us of the third question?"

Lauren answered, "Do humans have a moral responsibility to nonhuman life?"

"The verse we just read sure makes it sound like we do," answered Bianca.[16]

"That verse seems to be talking about farm animals, though," Micah observed. "Does the author make a more general point?"

"Yes. He appeals to two theological ideas. First, he says that only man is made in 'the image of God.' It seems that he gets that idea from the creation account in Genesis, but what does that mean? The author apparently thought his readers would already understand it."

Micah looked at Bianca. "Do you want to try to answer that, or do you want me to?" She nodded to Micah.

"Okay. I'll try. But I'm no theologian."[17] Micah began, "The Bible teaches that God created people to be like him in various ways. We know right from wrong, for instance. Animals don't. We can communicate in ways animals can't."

"Some animals communicate, Micah," affirmed Lauren.

"I know, but you've got to admit their communication is much more primitive than that of humans. Also, we seem to have self-awareness that animals lack. There's probably other stuff, but in various ways humans stand out from the rest of creation. In those ways we are able to show others what God is like, at least to some extent."

"Couldn't this idea that humans are godlike and animals are not be used to justify exploiting animals or using them irresponsibly?" asked Bianca.

"The author goes in the opposite direction," responded Lauren. "He says that God cares for and loves animals. Therefore, to be godlike, humans ought to care for animals too."

"Nice. What's the second idea?" asked Micah.

"Excuse me, Micah. But before we move on, I have another question." Bianca pressed on. "It seems like Singer would bring up infants and mentally

---

16. Note that Bianca is endorsing Divine Command Theory in her assumption that a verse of Scripture could prescribe appropriate ethical conduct.

17. For explanation of the concept by a theologian, see Anthony Hoekema, *Created in God's Image* (Grand Rapids: Eerdmans, 1986).

handicapped people at this point. When a person lacks self-awareness and advanced communication skills, is he or she still in God's image? How are such people different from adult mammals?"

Lauren looked at her notes and then replied, "I don't see this author addressing that idea, Bianca. That's a good question."

Micah said, "I think Christians respond something like this: God's image is what man is, not just what he does or can do. So even though not all humans at any given moment enjoy all the benefits of being in God's image, as a group they reflect God as Creator. On the flip side, even though some mammals can seem almost human at times, as a group they are not created in God's image."

Bianca smiled and said, "That was pretty good for being a nontheologian, Micah."

Micah blushed a little. "We just studied this in Sunday school last week," he admitted.

Lauren processed Micah's answer and replied, "So it's a matter of just believing what the Bible says about man being in God's image, regardless of the characteristics a particular human may have."

"Exactly," replied Micah.

"I like that answer," Bianca offered. "With that idea in place, we will treat all people with the same dignity, no matter where they are currently in life."

A young couple walked by, pushing a stroller and talking excitedly in what sounded like an Eastern European language.

"People in God's image," observed Micah quietly.

"Yes," replied Bianca. "We're all fellow humans."

"I don't buy all this theology, of course," Lauren weighed in. "But regarding all people as having equal dignity is a lovely thought."

Getting back on track, Bianca said, "What is the author's second theological idea, Lauren?"

"Okay. Apparently, after God created man, he ordered man to take care of the world, which includes the animal kingdom,"[18] answered Lauren.

"So the Bible does place man over animals," Bianca observed, "but not to exploit or harm them but rather as a responsibility to care for them, since they ultimately belong to God."

---

18. Gen. 1:28.

Micah added, "I think that's how most Christians have interacted with animals throughout history. Abusing an animal has never been considered Christian behavior. Nowadays, though, we don't get our food from farm animals that we care for. We go to the grocery store and get eggs, steak, and bacon that may have come from factories that mistreat animals terribly. I guess I need to think about that."

"Me too," agreed Bianca.

"This discussion was enlightening for me," said Lauren. "But these conclusions obviously come from a certain view of God and man that I don't share. Most non-Christians eat bacon and eggs without much concern, and they go to zoos and own pets, and they support laboratory experiments on test animals. If they believe in evolution, like I do, why don't they agree with Singer and PETA that such things are wrong? I guess I'm asking, why don't most people oppose speciesism?"

"Let's talk to the zoo management and see what they think," suggested Bianca. "If we find out they are not using biblical ethics, that is, Divine Command Theory, for handling their animals, maybe they can tell us *their* reasons for treating animals well."

"Great idea, Bianca!" exclaimed Lauren. "Let's go see someone at the main office, and maybe we can set up an interview for later in the week."

Two days later the three friends gathered at the zoo again. They were excited to learn that the zoo employed a zoologist, who also taught part-time at Lone Mountain University. Ms. Lazeile had she graciously agreed to help them with their school project.

As they waited for her to free up from a meeting with other zoo personnel, they decided to summarize their findings from the previous two discussions.

Lauren began, "Let's make sure we have our facts straight before we meet with Ms. Lazeile. By the way, how do you think her name is pronounced?"

Micah offered, "It's probably pronounced La-*zeel*," emphasizing the second syllable.

"But it's spelled like a French word," countered Bianca. "I bet she pronounces it La-zay."

"I didn't know you knew French," remarked Lauren.

"Well, I don't. But—"

"So really you have no idea," interrupted a smirking Micah. Bianca was just about to punch him when the door opened and they were invited in. So much for reviewing their notes.

"Good morning, and welcome to the River Bend Zoological Park. I'm Amah Lazeile. How may I help you?" greeted Ms. Lazeile (who pronounced her name *La*-zi-lay, with the emphasis on the first syllable). Bianca and Micah looked at each other and shrugged.

After the three friends introduced themselves, Lauren said, "As I mentioned on the phone, we are doing a project on the ethics of animal rights. We've discovered a lot of people who think zoos, medical experiments on animals, mass production of animal food, and even owning pets are unethical. My two friends here are Christians and distinguish people from animals using various theological concepts. On that basis, they think people should be able to do those things as long as they treat animals humanely. I, not to mention many Christians who think differently from my friends, believe animals and people have evolved from lower life-forms. My struggle is to see a rationale for many of the human uses of animals, like zoos, that does not depend on speciesism. Can you help us sort this out?"

"Excellent question. Of course I'm familiar with the concept of speciesism, but I don't agree with a basic presupposition that it depends on."

"What is that?" asked Bianca.

"First, before I jump to the heart of the matter, let me confess that I too am a Christian. I have personal, religious reasons both for treating animals humanely and for thinking human rights should usually take precedence over animal rights. But because I work here at the zoo, I interact extensively with representatives of the Humane Society here in town, I hear periodically from other animal rights activists, and occasionally the government will ask me to represent the interests of animals when they are being abused in industrial settings. So I think I understand the issue from a perspective that does not depend entirely on a Christian perspective."

Micah blurted out, "We came to the right place!"

Ms. Lazeile smiled. "Before I address speciesism, though, let me assure you that we maintain the highest level of humane care for our animals. Zookeepers love animals and do not believe they should be treated cruelly. Nevertheless, the assumption in speciesism is that humans do not have the right to assume superiority over animals. Most people disagree with that assumption."

Lauren asked, "Isn't it Professor Singer's point that the only reason we assume ourselves superior to animals is because we prefer our own species to others?"

"It is," answered Ms. Lazeile. "Professor Singer considers and rejects an argument that most people find compelling. It is the argument that humans, and only humans, form a moral community."

"I think I can guess what a moral community is, but can you spell that out some?" queried Bianca.

"A moral community is a group of persons who live in relationship with each other in accordance with moral rules. They respect each other as moral persons, and in particular, they acknowledge each other's autonomy."

"What do you mean by *autonomy* in this context?" asked Bianca.

"Within the framework of the moral rules established in the community, each individual has freedom to act in a variety of ways. For instance if stealing is wrong in our community—and stealing is one of those things that communities almost always view as wrong—then you are unethical if you steal. But you may purchase something for less than it's worth, as long as you don't cheat the other person. Or you may choose to give something away, even if other members of the community think it odd for you to do so. That's what is meant by autonomy: freedom to act within the rules," Ms. Lazeile explained.

"The point is, I presume, that animals simply don't live in moral communities," Micah interjected.

"Precisely. Animals may have intelligence, some communication skills, and sensitivity to pain. But they do not form moral communities and hold one another accountable to moral rules. No one criticizes a lion for wanting to eat a weak or injured wildebeest. Much less do other lions criticize him if he *fails* to kill a wildebeest needed by the pride. Humans have always recognized this about animals. When a dog attacks someone, we do not put it down as a punishment for immoral behavior. If we do so, it is to protect other humans."

"Why does that give humans the right to own or use animals?" asked Lauren.

Ms. Lazeile responded, "The argument is that only members of a moral community have rights at all. It makes no sense to speak of the rights of a creature that neither knows it has rights, respects the rights of others, or is concerned that others are violating its rights. Let me illustrate from something that occasionally happens at zoos—thankfully, we haven't had this happen here. Suppose a person ignored the safety signs and climbed over a wall into the bear habitat. If one does not follow the argument I've laid out here, one could argue that the bear has the right to his space and even to defend his space. So the bear would be within his rights to kill and eat the person. Zoos, to my knowledge, do not operate that way. We would—with great sadness and regret but without delay or second thought—shoot a bear before it had the chance to kill a human. The bear is unable to view his actions toward the person as ethical or moral. It simply acts on instinct. The person is, therefore, more valuable."

"I don't think Professor Singer would agree with that conclusion," Lauren commented. "He would view it as begging the question."[19]

"Unless he wandered into a bear habitat," quipped Micah. Lauren and Bianca narrowed their eyes at him.

Ms. Lazeile smiled and responded, "Yes, the professor would probably say that we are drawing that conclusion only because we favor our own species. But the fact that we can draw such a conclusion, that we can favor our species, that we play by moral rules at all—all of these facts suggest that humans—whether by creation or by evolution—have a status on this earth that entitles them to manage animals for their benefit. I would add that only humans have the intellectual or moral capacity to establish rules for proper treatment of animals, so that we can share this planet profitably. Only they can establish 'moral communities.'"

"This seems to be an appeal to Natural Law Ethics,"[20] suggested Bianca. "Is that what you intend?"

"Yes, indeed," replied Ms. Lazeile. "Mr. Singer's ethics is Utilitarian but does not take seriously enough the nature of man and animals as we find them, once again through creation, or evolution, or both."

---

19. Recall that begging the question is arguing in a circle. It is assuming as a premise in one's argument what one is trying to prove. In this case Ms. Lazeile is trying to prove that humans are more valuable, but her illustration seems to assume that humans are more valuable.

20. Recall that Natural Law is "the belief that morality is woven into the very fabric of reality and can be discovered in a way that is similar to how the laws of nature are woven into the fabric of reality and can be discovered" (chap. 1).

Lauren asked, "What about babies and intellectually disabled persons? Are they parts of the moral community?"

"I see you've done your homework," responded Ms. Lazeile. "Singer tries to argue that the moral community argument fails because certain humans are unable to participate in the community. He even suggests that treating mammals in certain ways would justify treating babies or intellectually disabled people in those ways, since the mammals are just as advanced relative to intelligence, self-awareness, and so forth. Is that what your research indicated?"

"Just about exactly," Lauren answered.

"I suppose he would call it a prejudice, but humans throughout history have embraced such persons as full members of the community and have acted morally toward them despite their inability to reciprocate. In fact most people recoil almost instinctively from the idea that the same dignity should be given a chimpanzee as an infant. Embracing and caring for the weakest among us is a key part of what makes us a *moral* community."

Bianca summarized, "So you would be comfortable with most of the normal ways humans have used—for lack of a better word—animals throughout history: zoos, personal pets, food production, and laboratory experiments for human need?"

Ms. Lazeile nodded but said, "I cannot endorse all the ways these things are done. We should constantly be seeking more humane ways to interact with the animal kingdom. But, overall, yes, I think these basic activities are consistent with a high standard of ethical treatment of animals."

The three friends rose and said almost in unison, "Thank you so much! That was very helpful."

Once outside, they laid plans for getting together one last time to actually write the extra-credit essay.

"But how in the world are we going to summarize all that in two thousand words?" Bianca moaned.

Micah responded, "I don't know. But we better. When evaluating essays that are too short or way too long, I've heard that Dr. Platt can be pretty inhumane."

QUESTIONS TO PONDER

- What is the distinction between animal welfare and animal rights? What is the relevance of this distinction for the discussion in this chapter?

- What do you think of animals being regarded as persons?

- Should humane treatment of animals be a significant matter of governmental regulation? To what extent would you support legislation that requires the humane treatment of animals if the result were higher food prices or loss of human employment?

- Do you think the Christian doctrines of the image of God and the Dominion Mandate lead to better or worse treatment of animals? Why?

- What do you think of the moral community argument? What arguments can you think of that support or contradict this argument?

- How would Virtue Ethics impact this discussion? How is a person's character related to how she treats animals?

TERMS TO KNOW

- Animal welfare
- Animal rights
- Principle of equality
- Moral interests
- Speciesism
- Reciprocal behavior
- Contractualism
- Personhood
- Image of God
- Dominion Mandate
- Self-awareness
- Moral community

FOR FURTHER READING

Geisler, Norman L. *Christian Ethics: Contemporary Issues & Options.* Grand Rapids: Baker Academic, 2010, chapter 19: 335–58.

Rollin, Bernard E. *Animal Rights & Human Morality.* Amherst, NY: Prometheus Books, 1981.

_____. *A New Basis for Animal Ethics: Telos and Common Sense.* Columbia: University of Missouri Press, 2016.

Singer, Peter. *Animal Liberation: The Definitive Classic of the Animal Movement.* New York: Harper Perennial Modern Classics, reissue, 2009.

MEDICAL
ETHICS

6

LEGALIZING NARCOTICS

Synopsis: Bianca just returned from Colorado, where recreational use of marijuana is legal. She was quite surprised at the casual nature of pot use among the people she met there, both young and old. She wasn't sure how she felt about it, so she asks Micah and Lauren what they think over a cup of tea at The Grey Earl.

* * *

"I just returned from Denver, and let me tell you there are cannabis stores *everywhere!*" Bianca was sharing the details of her recent ski trip to Colorado. "They were more common than regular pharmacies in some places, and it just seemed so natural, like it was no big deal. That seems so odd to me."

"It's not a big deal," replied Lauren. "At least it shouldn't be. Marijuana is not addictive, doesn't cause any serious health problems, and is no more destructive than alcohol. There are bars and liquor stores everywhere, and we don't think twice about it. I wouldn't be surprised if more states don't legalize recreational use in the next few years."

Bianca looked surprised at Lauren's response, but Micah wasn't. "I'm not sure I disagree with Lauren. It seems that the war on drugs in America that began in the 1970s has failed and that other countries that legalize drugs seem to have much lower rates of addiction. I don't think I would ever smoke pot, but it seems that prison time for marijuana is a waste of our law-enforcement resources. Maybe we ought to legalize pot and see what happens as a test case to legalizing other drugs too."

Bianca's surprise morphed into shock. "Micah! I am so surprised to hear you say that. I thought that as a Christian you would be dead set against legalizing drugs."

Micah crinkled his nose and had a pained expression on his face. "Yeah, I surprise myself sometimes. I guess I am looking at it from a Utilitarian point of view. What good has it done to criminalize soft drugs like marijuana? I don't see much difference between pot and alcohol. I know it can be abused, like alcohol, but we don't criminalize alcohol. We only arrest people who abuse it."

Bianca looked slightly agitated. "I hear what you both are saying, but I am not sure all your facts are straight. I have heard statistics that indicate recreational marijuana can be addictive and does have serious health consequences. I think we ought to look into this topic more carefully before we arrive at conclusions. I know there are passionate defenders and detractors of marijuana, so the more factual information we can get, the more confident we can be that our conclusions are not merely based on what we want to be true but on what is actually true."

They decided to bring up the topic in the next class with Dr. Platt.

"That's a great question," Dr. Platt said a couple of days later. He seemed amused at Bianca's request for his opinion on the topic. He turned to the class. "Just out of curiosity, how many of you approve of medical marijuana for people with seizures, chronic pain, and other such ailments?" About two-thirds of the class raised their hands. "What about recreational use?" About half the hands went down. "I am somewhat surprised that there was such a drop-off with that second question," said Dr. Platt. "For those of you who support the medical use of marijuana but not recreational use, would you be willing to share your reasons?"

Summer's hand shot up. "I'm against recreational use because I saw how it ruined my cousin. He received a full ride scholarship to the University of Illinois, but in his senior year of high school he got into the pot scene and decided not to go to college. He lost all drive to do anything with his life and now just works at a restaurant washing dishes. All he does in his spare time is smoke pot. I hate what it did to him! He had so much potential and just wasted it." Summer was visibly upset, and her cheeks flushed bright red.

Tyrone raised his hand. Dr. Platt called on him. "I agree with Summer. I have seen how pot has affected my family and friends, and it hasn't been good. My concern as a business student, however, is about the regulation of the market. The demand for pot is skyrocketing, and I wonder how well the whole industry is being handled. How do we know quality control is being practiced? Will the tax benefits be worth the medical problems of users if that becomes an issue? There seem to be all kinds of unanswered questions from a business and regulatory standpoint. I'm not even sure this is being managed in the medical marijuana scenario."

Micah's ears perked up at this. He hadn't thought too much about the business side of marijuana legalization, but Tyrone's statement suddenly flooded his mind with questions.

"On the other hand, since marijuana has been illegal all these years, yet people use it, maybe legalizing recreational use would result in huge tax revenue." Several heads turned as other students looked at Micah with surprise. His commitment as a Christian was well known. He blushed a bit at all the attention but continued. "I'm not saying that I agree with smoking pot, but since it is going to happen anyway, shouldn't the government regulate it and benefit from it? I mean, we already do that with gambling and alcohol."

"You have jumped ahead, Micah," commented Dr. Platt. "We will get there eventually. But I want to stay focused on the difference between medical use and recreational use for right now."

Weston chipped in. "I've heard that in places where medical marijuana is legalized, sometimes there's been a marked increase in cases of unspecified 'severe pain' that allows a person to get a doctor's prescription. In his TEDx talk, one of the largest marijuana growers in Colorado, Josh Stanley, talked about the epidemic of back pain that swept through college campuses when medical marijuana was legalized in Colorado."[1]

The class gave a collective groan.

"On the other hand," continued Weston, "Josh Stanley and his brother developed a nonpsychotropic strain of cannabis for epileptics that has been shown to greatly reduce seizures."

---

1. Josh Stanley, "The Surprising Story of Medical Marijuana and Pediatric Epilepsy," TEDx Talks, October 2013, http://www.youtube.com/watch?v=ciQ4ErmhO7g.

"Ooh, I heard about that little girl, Charlotte Figi, who was having hundreds of seizures a week and was not expected to live long," jumped in Marta. "Her condition was so bad that her parents signed a DNR—Do Not Resuscitate order—and took her home from the hospital with the expectation that she would die. This strain, which was high in CBD and low in THC, was turned into oil, and after the first application she went from having four hundred seizures a week to only zero or one per week. It was so effective that Stanley renamed the strain from the Hippie's Disappointment to Charlotte's Web. So for some people the medical use is life-saving."

"Yes," said Dr. Platt, "Charlotte Figi is one of the most well-known beneficiaries of CBD, or cannabinoids, which are compounds found in cannabis. THC is the most well-known compound because it is what makes people high when they smoke pot. Because the Charlotte's Web strain is low in THC it is not desirable for people wanting to get high. So there certainly can be a difference between the medical use of marijuana and recreational use. Of course as Weston pointed out, that is abused quite a bit. Some people are willing to claim pain and other medical needs to get pot when it is illegal otherwise, and plenty of doctors are willing to write a prescription for those who ask."

"Are we going to discuss why smoking pot recreationally is an issue to begin with?" Ralph looked impatient. "We keep talking as if we are assuming everyone agrees that getting high is wrong, but I don't see what the big deal is." Several students murmured their agreement.

Ralph continued. "I mean, how many people on this campus get wasted every weekend, and the college does nothing about it. Every weekend people get rushed to the hospital for alcohol poisoning, and sometimes they die. I would think getting stoned in a dorm room or off-campus apartment would be far preferable."

Dr. Platt tried to be fair without communicating sympathy for Ralph's position. "You are certainly correct that light pot smoking can have fewer health consequences in the short run than binge drinking. Chronic use of either, however, has serious implications for long-term health. Besides health consequences, there are a number of serious social and intellectual consequences that come with regular pot smoking. The fact that we are not handling the alcohol issue well in our society makes me wonder why we would remove obstacles to marijuana use on top of that. What if by legalizing recreational use we create another major health crisis like alcohol abuse? Once we legalize recreational use, it will not be easy to reverse course and make it illegal again if it develops into a health crisis."

Dr. Platt continued. "There is also a great amount of misinformation spread about the health implications of marijuana use. Like gambling and pornography, the industry is so profitable that those involved are more than willing to spread disinformation about consequences to keep the money rolling in. That may sound jaded, but it has been seen many times before, most notably by cigarette manufacturers. Look how long it took for them to admit that smoking cigarettes had any serious health implications. So if anyone wants to do some investigative digging into the real science of the health impact of cannabis, I would be happy to see it."

Dr. Platt began to hear the low rustling of laptops closing and notebooks being stowed in backpacks. He glanced at the clock and noticed the class was about to end, so he waved his hand and said, "Have a great day!"

Lauren, Micah, and Bianca gathered as the class let out, as was their usual custom.

"Let's take Dr. Platt up on his challenge," said Lauren excitedly. "I've already thought this out. I'll take the medical and scientific side of the health consequences. Bianca, you study the financial and social impact of legalization. And Micah, why don't you figure out the religious angle, since you are getting us all concerned with your unusual lack of clarity on ethical issues as a Christian."

Lauren smiled, knowing she was walking a fine line between being bossy and taking initiative. Micah and Bianca both laughed, because they could see Lauren walking that line and found it amusing rather than annoying.

"Well, okay," replied Micah with a grin. "That will save us time getting organized. One quick question, though. Why did you assign Bianca the financial side of the issue when I am the business major?"

Lauren was ready. "I did it because you are usually very decided on the ethical issues we study. I think that comes from your belief in the authority of the Bible for all of life. I admire that, even though sometimes it seems a little closed-minded to me. I am coming to see that in regard to many ethical issues, people often seem to hold their views with little rational justification for what they believe. Many seem to just pick a side of an issue because they like it or want it to be so, without solid reasons. That doesn't seem to be very reasonable for me. So I respect your usual conviction because I know you are trying to be consistent and provide good reasons for your positions. The fact that you seem to be unsure on the topic of legalization of drugs amuses me, and I want to see where it goes."

Micah looked a little chagrined at Lauren's words but tried not to take them too much to heart. "Well, I am glad I can provide some entertainment for you," he said, feigning hurt. "Maybe you're right. Maybe this is a good opportunity for me to see if I have a conviction about this issue, which doesn't seem as black-and-white as many of the others we have talked about this semester."

The three friends agreed to not go overboard on their research for this issue, so they set a limit of two days of research before meeting together at The Grey Earl.

A couple of days later, the three friends gathered at their usual table, but something was different. While Bianca and Lauren got their usual drinks, Micah uncharacteristically brought a little espresso cup to his seat. The girls looked at him, waiting for an explanation. "It will make sense in a little while," he said with a mischievous smile.

As they settled in and began to sip their brews, Lauren volunteered to start.

"I was somewhat surprised at how scarce the scientific and medical studies on long-term effects of cannabis use were," she began. "It wasn't until the late 1990s that intensive scientific study began to be carried out, largely due to the push for legalization.[2] The results of those studies are highly disputed too. Depending on the source of the articles I read, the story varies widely. Some sources claimed that marijuana has little to no side effects, is not addictive, and actually has positive health benefits. Other sources list dozens of long-term consequences and warn of the addictive nature of pot and its role as a gateway drug to harder and more addictive substances. My

---

2. Alice G. Walton, "What 20 Years of Research Has Taught Us About the Chronic Effects of Marijuana," *Forbes,* October 7, 2014, https://www.forbes.com/sites/alice-gwalton/2014/10/07/what-20-years-of-research-has-taught-us-about-the-chronic-effects-of-marijuana/#4748e36117be.

mind has been somewhat changed from when we first started talking about this when you got back from Colorado, Bianca. It seems that there are more serious consequences to marijuana use than I thought."

She continued. "All the major medical and government sources are quite clear that there are a number of side effects and long-term consequences. The American Medical Association says that, 'cannabis is a dangerous drug and as such is a serious public health concern.'[3] The National Institute on Drug Abuse reports that chronic use of marijuana can cause permanent memory and cognitive problems, such as lower IQs, short-term memory loss, 'diminished ability to carry out long-term plans, a sense of apathy, decreased attention to appearance and behavior, and decreased ability to concentrate for long periods of time.'[4] This obviously has significant impact on a person's ability to succeed in school, and the younger a person begins marijuana use, the worse the impact."

"That sounds like a lot of the stories I have heard from people who have smoked pot or from their family and friends," said Bianca. "One of the things that confuses me is the different terms used for cannabis products. Did you gain any clarity on that?"

"Do you mean like the different slang terms and strains of pot?" asked Micah with a laugh. "I have heard it referred to as grass, ganja, reefer, herb, dank, and chronic. And the different varieties have hilarious names, like Bubba Kush, Granddaddy Purple, Nine Pound Hammer, Chernobyl, and Red Headed Stranger."

"No, that is not what I meant," replied Bianca with a frown as she gave Micah a chastening look. His smile quickly faded. "I was referring to the difference between terms like cannabinoids, tetrahydrocannabinol, and marijuana. What is the difference between them?"

"Good question," replied Lauren. "Yes, I learned those distinctions. Cannabinoids are chemical compounds that bind to receptors in the human body. The two most common cannabinoids are CBD and THC. When a cannabis

---

3. Cannabis Legalization for Recreational Use H-95.924.
4. "Brain Power: Grades 6-9," National Institute on Drug Abuse, https://www.dru-gabuse.gov/publications/brain-power/grades-6-9/weeding-out-grass-module-4/background.

product is consumed, they bind to naturally occurring endocannabinoids in our bodies to produce effects in our bodies and brains. Marijuana refers to the dried leaves and flowers of the cannabis plant that can be smoked, cooked, or vaporized to extract the cannabinoids. The problem is there are hundreds of compounds in cannabis, and while some, like CBD and THC, have been studied and may have some health benefits, the impacts of many of the other compounds are unknown. Tetrahydrocannabinol, or THC, is the primary psychoactive compound in cannabis and is what gives the high that most people think of.[5] Cannabidiol, commonly known as CBD, generally refers to the active compound in a wide array of products that promise health benefits without the high of THC, although some cannabidiols have small doses of THC in them."

Common Terms	Explanation
Cannabis	The plant from which all marijuana, THC, and CBD products are derived
Marijuana	The dried leaves and flowers of the cannabis plant that can be smoked, cooked, or vaporized to extract the cannabinoids
Cannabinoids	Chemical compounds found in cannabis that bind to receptors in the human body
THC	Abbreviation for tetrahydrocannabinol, the primary psychoactive compound in cannabis that gives a high
CBD	Abbreviation for cannabidiol, the active compound in a wide array of products that promise health benefits without the high of THC

"That clears it up a bit," said Micah. "It seems that the different terms are used rather casually and interchangeably, when in reality there can be significant differences between them. Is CBD pretty tame and mostly harmless, then?"

---

5. Seth Ammerman, Sheryl Ryan, and William P. Adelman, "The Impact of Marijuana Policies on Youth: Clinical, Research, and Legal Update," *Pediatrics* 135, no. 3 (March 2015): e769–e785, https://pediatrics.aappublications.org/content/135/3/e769.

"That's what I thought until I came across the FDA website," answered Lauren. "I was surprised at the strong tone of warning regarding CBD products. The FDA has approved only one CBD medication used to treat two rare and severe forms of epilepsy. So many of the products on the shelves of CBD stores make claims that have not been scientifically proven, and contrary to the expectations of many, there is no evidence that taking CBD products can't hurt. The FDA site lists the following potential risks associated with CBD use: liver injury, adverse interactions with other drugs, male reproductive toxicity, and lesser risks such as sleepiness, insomnia, decreased appetite, abdominal pain, and changes in mood.[6]

"On the other hand," Lauren continued, "THC has been shown to help some people with chronic pain, anxiety, depression, nausea, and vomiting. The effectiveness of THC is one of the primary arguments for medical use of marijuana. I mean, who wouldn't want to be able to find relief from these symptoms? Why would we deny suffering people relief just because others misuse cannabis?"

Bianca chimed in, "I agree with you, but it seems that wherever medical marijuana is legalized, general use rises too. As Weston mentioned in class, people can easily fake illnesses in order to obtain medical marijuana. The other question we have to ask is whether the legalization of medical marijuana is often a half-measure to obtain legalization for recreational use. Do advocates for medical use have a greater agenda in mind? Or maybe advocates for medical use are used by and/or supported and funded by those seeking full recreational use? The social side of this issue is very difficult to sort out." Bianca seemed a bit exasperated.

"What other social and financial implications did you find, Bianca?" Micah was itching to get to his part of the conversation but didn't want to interrupt.

"Well, several social issues overlap with medical issues. For example, the National Safety Council has issued a strong warning about driving under

---

6. "What You Need to Know (And What We're Working to Find Out) about Products Containing Cannabis or Cannabis-derived Compounds, including CBD," https://www.fda.gov/consumers/consumer-updates/what-you-need-know-and-what-were-working-find-out-about-products-containing-cannabis-or-cannabis.

the influence of marijuana. It concluded that 'it is unsafe to operate a vehicle or other complex equipment while under the influence of cannabis, due to the increased risk of death or injury to the operator and the public,' and that due to rapid changes in blood THC concentrations over time, there is no minimum safe threshold blood concentration below which a driver can be considered to have been unaffected while driving following recent cannabis use.' This conclusion is based on the cognitive and psychomotor effects of THC, such as coordination and reaction time.[7] So, at the very least, driving high ought to be considered as dangerous as driving drunk.

"There is also great concern for the impact on younger minds and bodies and pregnant women. The younger people are when they begin to smoke pot or ingest THC, the more damaging it can be to intellectual and cognitive development. THC can pass from a pregnant woman to her baby, or even through breast milk after the baby is born. Cannabis exposure during pregnancy can cause neurological impairment, hyperactivity, and poor cognitive function.[8] So, clearly, marijuana has some serious health and social concerns that ought to be considered when making public policy.

"Finally, we have to ask the question if there are benefits to legalizing marijuana completely, and for that matter, ending the war on drugs. What would happen if we treated all drugs like alcohol and simply regulated it?"

"I don't know," pondered Lauren out loud. "As someone who is going to be a nurse, that sounds like a nightmare scenario for a hospital. It is bad enough when I go to clinicals and see overdoses of heroin or meth or opioids. Legalizing marijuana is one thing, but legalizing all drugs seems scary. It seems we would have to move all the money we invest in law enforcement to addiction recovery facilities and mental health hospitals. It could devastate society."

"Perhaps," replied Bianca, "but keep in mind I am focusing on the social and economic side of the issue. Whenever a society outlaws something when there is demand, it creates a black market usually filled by organized crime.

---

7. "Marijuana and Driving," National Safety Council (September 2017), https://www. nsc.org/Portals/0/Documents/NSCDocuments_Advocacy/Divisions/ADID/Position-on-Cannabis-and-Driving.pdf.

8. Catherine Dong, et al., "Cannabinoid Exposure During Pregnancy and Its Impact on Immune Function," *Cellular and Molecular Life Sciences* 76, no. 4 (Feb 2019): 729–43.

That requires massive amounts of spending on law enforcement. Organized crime becomes more aggressive and violent now that it has to contend with law enforcement. This cycle perpetuates itself, and the price rises, organized crime has a monopoly, and the federal government has to spend more than $3 billion annually to combat drugs, with states spending another $7 billion annually. The Center for American Progress predicts that legalizing marijuana would save more than $7 billion annually and raise more than $6 billion in tax revenue."[9]

Micah whistled. "That is a perfect example of a Utilitarian ethic if ever I heard one," he said. "The question, however, is whose good is of most concern? Utilitarianism seeks the greatest good for the greatest number of people, so do we prioritize the economic benefit or the impact on people who would never take drugs if they were illegal?"

"Precisely," agreed Bianca. "But it is hard to tell if legalization would increase use. Conflicting reports of legalization in other countries abound, and there is no way to predict accurately what would happen here. One thing that is probably certain is that the government would get a new revenue stream of taxes, but is that a good thing? I don't know that it is, considering the track record of government spending, the national debt, and the deficit."

"Well, this is all more complicated than I thought it would be," sighed Lauren. "I was hoping this would be a simple issue, but it seems that it is as complex as many of the other ethical topics we have tackled. Micah, please tell me your study has produced something with clarity!"

"Yes it has, at least for me. I feel more conviction about this issue now than I did a few days ago. First let me say that beginning with a Divine Command Theory provides a starting point for dealing with thorny issues that seem difficult to sort out otherwise. If all we have is Utilitarianism, we have to argue about whose good is most important. We run into a similar problem with Natural Law Theory, I believe. On the one hand, Natural Law could argue that there should be no restrictions on personal choices of human behavior, such as drugs or alcohol. You could argue that human nature thrives best

---

9. Betsy Pearl, "Ending the War on Drugs: By the Numbers," The Center for American Progress, June 27, 2018, https://www.americanprogress.org/issues/criminal-justice/reports/2018/06/27/452819/ending-war-drugs-numbers.

when there is freedom, and therefore people should have the right to freely choose behavior that is not destructive to others.

"The problem, though, is that we already restrict behavior for the good of society in other areas. We don't let people drive on public roads however they want, even though it could be argued that people will naturally be concerned for their safety and drive accordingly. We already have rather lax rules about alcohol use in our country. We don't limit how much alcohol people purchase or consume in their own homes. We set a minimum age limit, but that is ignored more as a rule than an exception. The same goes for cigarettes. Yet some sources estimate that the government spends almost $140 billion annually to treat alcohol and nicotine addiction.[10] Natural Law Theory could also be used to conclude that allowing people the freedom to drink and smoke, and by extension take drugs, is detrimental to human flourishing. In other words, it doesn't seem that Natural Law Theory settles on a position in regard to legalization."

Micah looked up to make sure that Bianca and Lauren were still listening. They were.

"A Divine Command perspective doesn't solve all the problems we have been talking about either, but it does set some boundaries that I find helpful. First, God tells Adam and Eve in Genesis 1:29, 'I give you every seed-bearing plant on the face of the whole earth, and every tree that has fruit with seed in it. They will be yours for food.' In other words, God gave a creation full of potential for food, medicine, industry, and more with the intent that people would cultivate it for good. Now, I'm not sure that includes smoking the plants God made, but we can come back to that.

"Second, God did put in nature chemicals that enhance or alter our experiences." He lifted his empty espresso cup and offered a salute to the girls.

"Is that why you got espresso today?" asked Bianca incredulously. "Just to make that point?"

"Really, Micah," said Lauren rolling her eyes. "I didn't think you were so dramatic to order a drink you probably didn't even like just to make a point an hour after you finished it." Lauren almost laughed at the thought.

---

10. "What America Spends on Drug Addictions," The American Addiction Centers Resource, https://addiction-treatment.com/in-depth/what-america-spends-on-drug-addictions.

"Hey, I do like espresso—once in a while. Anyway, I made my point, didn't I?"

"Please continue," laughed Bianca, with mock impatience.

Micah cleared his throat. "As I was saying, there are many things in nature that alter our perception or affect our physical and cognitive states. Sugar, for example, is a powerful substance. Caffeine is too. Many naturally occurring plants can be treated in such a way to change or enhance these effects. Take grapes, for example. When fermented they make the juice into something that can intoxicate when consumed in large enough quantities. The Bible doesn't forbid all consumption of wine. If you consider all the references to wine in Scripture, you end up with warnings about its danger and praise for its refreshment. What is uniformly forbidden, however, is intoxication."

"Micah, get to the point and just be clear," said Lauren impatiently.

"Sorry," said Micah, looking down. "I am trying to frame this in a way that seems rational to you both, even though you may not agree. What I am trying to say is that the Bible puts a high premium on sobriety and self-control.[11] The Bible takes seriously the impact of alcoholism on the family and in society. It places drunkards in the same category as thieves, the greedy, people who swindle others, and the sexually immoral.[12] When you look at how alcohol is often involved in everything from automobile accidents, to abuse, to adultery and divorce, and to crime, it makes sense there are such strong warnings against getting intoxicated."

"So you are against all alcohol too?" asked Lauren abruptly.

"I am getting to my point," replied Micah. "A person can drink a certain amount of alcohol without getting drunk. In fact, many more mature people drink alcohol with no intention of getting even tipsy. The National Institute on Alcohol Abuse and Alcoholism states that the legally defined level of intoxication typically occurs after four drinks for an average-sized woman or five for an average-sized man, depending on how quickly the drinks are consumed over a period of hours.[13] What makes marijuana consumption

---

11. See Gal. 5:21; Eph. 5:18; 1 Pet. 5:8.

12. 1 Cor. 5:11; 6:10.

13. "Drinking Levels Defined," The National Institute on Alcohol Abuse and Alcoholism, https://www.niaaa.nih.gov/alcohol-health/overview-alcohol-consumption/moderate-binge-drinking, as summarized in Joe Carter, "Is Recreational Marijuana

different than alcohol consumption, then, is that the intent is always to get high. It also takes far less intake to achieve a high—approximately four puffs of a joint. When we recall the cognitive and physical impact of cannabis on people that your research revealed, smoking pot would be a violation of the command to remain sober and self-controlled.

"I know many people in our world see no harm in getting drunk or high as long as they don't hurt somebody, but that approach can often minimize the definition of harm. Is a father who tells his children that he loves them only when he is drunk or high really doing harm? Some might minimize that and say that such behavior is minimally harmful compared to abusing his kids, but the alcohol or drugs still play a primary part in the situation. While harm can certainly be done without any substance abuse, there is no doubt that drugs and alcohol exacerbate situations when they are present."

Bianca could see Micah was very passionate about his conclusions. "So have you come to more conviction about this topic, Micah?"

"Yes, reluctantly at first, but I have become more firmly resolved that as a Christian I need to be self-controlled, and so any substance that would make me lose control of myself or reduce my ability to do something like drive a car safely should be avoided."

"So, epileptics and other sick people who only get relief from cannabis products are out of luck?" Lauren's eyes blazed at the thought.

Micah quickly answered. "No, when it comes to medical marijuana, I do see that there are legitimate reasons for CBD or THC if nothing else works. It just seems to me that there is not much settled science or regulation yet to make sure the idea is not abused. Recreational use, however, seems to me to be a real problem for society."

"It sounds like your reason for opposing legalization of recreational use of marijuana is a combination of Divine Command and Utilitarianism," noted Bianca. "It is not just that the Bible condemns intoxication as intrinsically wrong, but it also emphasizes the extrinsic consequences."

"Hmm. I think you are right," mused Micah. "I think my position against legalization does involve both. Many people would probably disagree with

Use a Sin?," The Gospel Coalition (blog), January 6, 2014, https://www.thegospel-coalition.org/article/is-recreational-marijuana-use-a-sin.

me that getting high or drunk is necessarily wrong in itself, but it is hard to deny that the social and financial consequences are immense."

"I'm still not convinced that some form of legalized recreational use isn't possible without widespread social harm, but I don't think I have any definitive answer for what that would look like." Lauren was trying hard to balance her libertarianism with her great concern for health and medicine.

"I can appreciate Micah's points, and I am so glad he is demonstrating his usual robust conviction about ethical issues again," said Bianca with a big grin as she punched him in the shoulder. "I might be stuck between you both, but maybe that is a good place for me to be."

QUESTIONS TO PONDER

- How much freedom should people in a society have to consume what they want?

- How would a society make legally enforceable distinctions between medical and recreational uses of marijuana?

- What should be the limits of medical use of marijuana products?

- Is it wrong to become intoxicated by alcohol, drugs, or other substances? Why or why not?

- How does a society determine when an issue negatively impacts human flourishing enough to regulate or criminalize it?

TERMS TO KNOW

- Cannabis
- Cannabinoids
- Cannabidiols
- Medical marijuana
- THC
- CBD
- Controlled substances
- Intrinsic
- Extrinsic
- Utilitarianism
- Divine Command Theory

FOR FURTHER READING

Breeden, Tom and Mark L. Ward Jr. *Can I Smoke Pot? Marijuana in Light of Scripture.* Hudson, OH: Cruciform, 2016.

Caulkins, Jonathan P., Beau Kilmer, and Mark A. R. Kleimann. *Marijuana Legalization: What Everyone Needs to Know.* New York: Oxford University Press, 2016.

Derrickson, Jason, ed. *Marijuana Legalization: State Initiatives, Implications, and Initiatives.* New York: Nova Science Publishers, 2014.

Hill, Kevin P. *Marijuana: The Unbiased Truth about the World's Most Popular Weed.* Center City, MN: Hazelden, 2015.

Skinner, Daniel. *Medical Necessity: Health Care Access and the Politics of Decision Making.* Minneapolis: University of Minnesota Press, 2019.

Vasquez, Margie, ed. *Marijuana: Medical Uses, Regulations, and Legal Issues.* New York: Nova Science Publishers, 2014.

7

ABORTION

Synopsis: Micah, Bianca, and Lauren go for a walk and pass the local Planned Parenthood office in their city. They see pro-life personnel gathered around the front gates, but seemingly separated into two groups. Near the entrance to the parking lot stand several people holding signs and poster-sized pictures of aborted babies. Some of them shout to the cars as they drive into the parking lot. Closer to the fence stands a slightly larger group of people attempting to talk to the women who drive into the parking lot to seek the services within. They are talking calmly to women as they exit their vehicles. The three students decide to watch for a while and see what unfolds. While they do so, they begin to talk about the ethics of abortion.

* * *

"I have never walked past here before," said Bianca.

"Neither have I," added Lauren.

"I have," chipped in Micah. "My church sets aside a service in January every year for Sanctity of Life Sunday. The pastor has talked about different ways to get involved in defending the lives of the unborn. One of the things he recommends is coming down here and just praying that the women who come here would change their minds."

Lauren turned to the other two and said somewhat abruptly, "I don't see how it's anyone's business what women do with their bodies. This is a private matter between a woman and her doctor. Why don't these people respect that decision and leave them alone?"

Bianca saw that Lauren felt strongly about this issue that they had never discussed before in any depth, so she responded cautiously. "Abortion is not just about a woman and her body. It has to do with the life she is carrying inside her. There is a baby growing in her womb, and abortion ends its life. I think these groups outside the clinic are trying to stop what they believe is the taking of an innocent life."

Micah looked a bit uneasy. "I think we ought to talk more about this, but one of my concerns is whether you both think a man is allowed to weigh in on this issue."

Bianca was surprised at Micah's statement. "Why would you say that, Micah?"

"Well, I have heard some women in this debate say that men shouldn't have a say because it is not their bodies in question. This is a woman's issue, so men should stay out of the debate."

Lauren quickly disagreed. "I have heard that too, but it takes two to make a baby, and the father of the baby should have some say. That is one place I disagree with the pro-choice side of this issue."

"I agree," added Bianca. "This is an issue in which everyone should have a voice."

"So how should we go about studying the issue of abortion then?" asked Micah.

Bianca voiced what they were all thinking. "Well, we definitely want to get credit for our work, so let's ask Dr. Platt. I believe we are scheduled to address this topic in a few weeks in class. Maybe we can get a head start on the research."

Lauren liked the idea. "I think it would be quite revealing to try to interview the different groups that we are observing. As much as I don't like the protestors with their signs, I would like to ask them in person why they do what they do. The group gathered by the fence looks more approachable, so I don't think that would be a problem. Do you think the clinic would let us interview someone about their services and why they support abortion?"

Bianca replied, "I think it would be great to let each group speak for itself. Let's go get contact information from the two groups, and then we can call the clinic and set up a time to interview them."

They walked over to the group gathered by the fence. Micah spoke up. "Is there someone in charge of your group? We would like to ask some questions about what you are doing here."

Several heads turned and a slight twenty-something woman, looking not much older than the three friends spoke up. "I am Brittany Sellars," she said cheerfully. "What do you want to know?"

They chatted briefly with Brittany and got her cell number, with a promise to call within the week.

"What do you know about that group?" asked Lauren, as she pointed to the small crowd holding signs by the entrance to the clinic parking lot.

"You should talk to them," said Brittany. "Max is their leader, and he's very nice."

"Why don't you work together?" queried Bianca.

"We share many of the same beliefs and goals, but we disagree about how best to accomplish them," answered Brittany. "I am sure Max would be happy to explain."

"I'll take this one," braved Bianca. She walked over to Max, a tall, dark-haired man in his forties with glasses. He was holding a sign that implored women not to enter the clinic.

"Excuse me, could I ask you a question?"

Max turned and smiled. "Of course. What can I do for you?"

"My friends and I are students taking an ethics class at Lone Mountain University, and we would like to hear from each side of this issue of abortion. Brittany thought you might be willing to let us interview you about why you are doing what you are doing here."

"I would be happy to," said Max, "as long as you commit to representing us fairly. We have done several interviews for the local papers and news shows, and we are often portrayed as extremists, which we are not. Can you promise to be objective?"

Bianca smiled and nodded. "Yes, I promise. My friends and I have learned that we truly want to know all the facts regarding the ethical issues we research, even if that means changing our views. And this is not for an article or news story, just classwork."

"OK then," replied Max, "I would be happy to talk."

Bianca returned to the group, and they divvied up the interviews. They were about to each take the interview that fit with their own positions on abortion when Bianca spoke up. "Maybe I should call the clinic, and you should speak to the protestors, Lauren. It would be good for us to talk with people with whom we disagree to get a more objective viewpoint. Micah can interview Brittany."

Lauren nodded. "OK, let's do that. But let's be thorough in our questions and honest in our summaries. I know this issue is deeply emotional to every person, regardless of her stance, so we have to be sure to ruthlessly pursue the truth."

"Agreed," confirmed Micah.

"Absolutely," responded Bianca.

They decided to interview their assigned people within the week and gather at The Grey Earl to share what they had learned. In the meantime, they all agreed to learn the basic facts of abortion on their own so they could conduct the interviews knowledgeably.

When they met again the following week, they began to make a list of the facts of abortion. By drawing straws Micah was tasked with writing the list.[1]

- Somewhere between 15 and 20 percent of pregnancies in America end in abortion.
- More than 85 percent of abortions happen in the first trimester (thirteen weeks) of pregnancy.
- The number of abortions in America has been in steady decline since the 1980s.
- About one in four women in the United States will have an abortion by age forty-five.
- Black women are four to five times as likely as white women to have an abortion, and Latina women are two to three times more likely than white women to have an abortion.

---

1. Sources for this information come primarily from the Centers for Disease Control's report, *Abortion Surveillance—United States, 2015*, https://www.cdc.gov/mmwr/volumes/67/ss/ss6713a1.htm; and the Guttmacher Institute, *Induced Abortion in the United States*, https://www.guttmacher.org/fact-sheet/induced-abortion-united-states.

- Among women who have abortions, 75 percent are considered low-income or below the federal poverty line.
- Abortions occur because of rape or incest in 1 percent of cases.
- Abortion in the first trimester was legalized in all fifty states in 1973 with the Supreme Court case *Roe v. Wade*. In the second trimester, states may regulate abortion, and in the third trimester states may regulate or prohibit abortion, except in cases necessary to preserve the life or health of the mother.
- The same day *Roe v. Wade* was decided, the court ruled in *Doe v. Bolton* that a law that expanded what was meant by the life or health of the mother to include her emotional and psychological health was constitutional. This essentially established a constitutional right to abortion on demand at almost any point in the pregnancy.
- Abortion is performed in three primary methods:
  - Medication
  - Saline
  - D&C

"There are so many facts and statistics that this could go on forever," remarked Bianca. "Some of these are sociological facts, some medical, and some are legal. Why don't we focus on the act itself and discuss that?"

"That sounds good," said Micah.

"Here is a definition I found," said Lauren. "*Encyclopedia Britannica* defines abortion as 'the expulsion of a fetus from the uterus before it has reached the stage of viability (in human beings, usually about the 20th week of gestation).'"[2]

"That is a strange definition," interjected Bianca. "Some abortions happen late in the pregnancy when the baby could easily survive outside the womb with care. How about this one from Merriam-Webster: 'The termination of a pregnancy after, accompanied by, resulting in, or closely followed by the death of the embryo or fetus.'"[3]

"Wait," blurted Micah. "What is the difference between a fetus and an embryo again?"

---

2. https://www.britannica.com/science/abortion-pregnancy.
3. https://www.merriam-webster.com/dictionary/abortion.

"An embryo is the early stage of development after the sperm fertilizes the egg. Between the ninth and eleventh weeks of development the term 'fetus' is introduced," clarified Bianca. "Practically, though, the terms are sometimes used interchangeably in the first trimester."

"Thanks for clarifying that," said Micah. "That definition was a bit complicated. I found a definition that is a little simpler: 'Abortion is essentially the intentional cause of death and removal from the womb of an unborn child.'[4] So it is not the same as birth control, which prevents an egg and sperm from fertilizing. Nor is it the same as a miscarriage, where the body naturally expels an embryo."

"I don't care for the term 'unborn child' in that definition," objected Lauren. "The other definitions use the terms 'fetus' or 'embryo.' 'Unborn child' seems like an anti-abortion term."

"But the word 'fetus' means 'unborn child' when it is referring to humans," replied Micah.

"It seems you are playing language games," said Lauren, "Let's stick with the common usage of the term."

"Let's talk about the methods of abortion," suggested Bianca.

"Do we have to?" asked Lauren. "What does it matter how it's done?"

"We absolutely have to talk about it," said Bianca. "That is part of what makes this issue such a hot topic."

"We don't have to know the details of cancer surgery or the procedure for removing a ruptured appendix in order to discuss the good of medical intervention. It's all so gruesome. I mean, I am in nursing school, but I don't want to see surgical procedures if I can help it."

"That is one of the main ethical questions, though," countered Bianca. "Abortion is very different from surgery to remove a tumor or fix a ruptured organ. What is being removed is a *person*."

The discussion had suddenly gotten heated, and Micah wisely felt the need to get a refill. "Before we get to the ethical issue of personhood, let's finish the discussion on the methods of abortion. After I get some more tea, that is."

When Micah returned, Bianca volunteered to summarize the methods of abortion.

---

4. Wayne Grudem, *Christian Ethics* (Wheaton, IL: Crossway, 2018), 566.

"First, there is the option for an abortion pill that does not require a surgical procedure. The proper name is mifepristone, and it is taken along with another medication, misoprostol. It can be taken until a woman is about ten weeks pregnant, and it stops the growth of an embryo and causes the body to expel it.

"In the first trimester two primary methods are used to perform a surgical abortion in a clinic. First, Dilation and Curettage, also known as D&C, is when the mother's cervix is dilated, and the surgeon inserts an instrument (curette) to scrape the wall of the uterus, cutting the embryo's body to pieces and removing the placenta from its place in the uterine wall. The second method is known as vacuum curettage, vacuum aspiration, or suction and is often used in combination with D&C. A machine tears both the embryo and placenta from the uterus into a jar with a force twenty-eight times that of a vacuum cleaner. The doctor then reassembles all the pieces of the embryo to ensure that nothing is left behind in the uterus."

Bianca stopped and the three friends looked at one another soberly.

"How does the doctor reassemble the pieces of the embryo if it is just a blob of tissue as the pro-choice side argues?" asked Micah. "What is there to reassemble?"

Lauren and Bianca looked at one another in surprise.

"The embryo could only be perceived to be a blob of tissue for maybe the first three weeks, but even then, it is not tissue, but a rapidly forming human." Bianca went on. "By the end of the second week, the brain and heart are beginning to form, and by the fourth week blood circulation begins, many organs have begun forming, and the heart begins to beat. By the seventh week the hands and feet move and the embryo can develop hiccups. Well before the end of the first trimester, the fetus is yawning, sucking its thumb, squinting, and has fingerprints."[5]

Micah's mouth dropped open in wonder. "I never knew any of this!" he exclaimed. "How is it possible to know all this detail?"

"There is actually way more detail regarding the stages of formation than what I mentioned," said Bianca with a smile. "Ever since the invention

---

5. "Interactive Prenatal Development Timeline," The Endowment for Human Development, https://www.ehd.org/science_main.php?level=i#fh5.

of ultrasound machines, we have been able to see in incredible detail the day-by-day formation of the baby's body from conception to birth. This is one of the parts of nursing school I loved."

"Can we get back to that later?" asked Bianca. "I would love to learn more, but we need to get through the rest of the methods of abortion before we share what we learned in our interviews."

"Sure," the others said, and Bianca continued.

"In the second trimester a saline injection is often used. A needle is inserted through the mother's abdomen into the amniotic sac, and some of the fluid is removed and replaced with a solution of concentrated salt. The fetus breathes in and swallows the salt and is poisoned. The outer layer of skin is burned off and the brain hemorrhages. It takes the fetus one hour to die. The next day the mother goes into labor and delivers the dead fetus. Alternately potassium chloride or digoxin is injected directly into the heart of the fetus. This is more than 95 percent effective to end the life of the fetus."[6]

Bianca blinked back tears as she continued. "In the third trimester a number of methods are used. In a procedure called a hysterotomy, the baby is delivered alive via C-section and allowed to die of neglect or a traumatic injury at the discretion of a doctor. A hysterotomy can also be induced by administering to the mother a powerful drug known as a prostaglandin, which induces labor. In this case the baby is delivered vaginally and also allowed to die of neglect or traumatic injury."

"I don't want to hear any more," said Lauren abruptly. "I am in nursing school and have never heard about the saline method. That disturbs me."

"There is just one more," replied Bianca. "Let's just finish this. Dilation and extraction (D&X) and dilation and evacuation (D&E) are methods used in what is sometimes called 'partial birth abortions.' These procedures are also used with miscarriages, but in an abortion they are used on an intact baby, or one that would survive outside the womb if given care. The intact baby is delivered feet first until all but the head is outside the womb. A doctor then punctures the skull and scrambles the brains. Alternately, the mother's cervix is dilated, and the doctor pulls the viable baby apart piece by piece."

---

6. M. Moleai et al., "Effectiveness and Safety of Digoxin to Induce Fetal Demise Prior to Second-Trimester Abortion," *Contraception* 77, no. 3 (March 2008): 223–25.

"Stop!" Lauren stood up suddenly and pushed her chair back. "I can't listen to any more of that. I support a woman's choice, but I do *not* agree with that last one. That cannot be happening in the United States!"

"It doesn't happen in every state, but it is not universally banned," said Bianca. "And you are not alone. Many people who are pro-choice are opposed to partial birth abortions. Congress enacted the Partial-Birth Abortion Ban Act in 2003, but it was challenged immediately. The Supreme Court upheld the law in 2007, but it is still performed in some states, primarily by Planned Parenthood."[7]

Lauren slowly sat down. "Surely there must be a reason that such a procedure exists at all. Maybe it is medically necessary," she said, her eyes pleading for some reassurance from Bianca.

"Sometimes D&E or D&X are performed if the fetus has an enlarged head due to a deformity, but those aren't the only times they are used on an intact fetus," Bianca stated.

"See!" Lauren said. "There are some medically necessary uses of these procedures."

"That may be true," said Bianca, "but even the question of 'medically necessary' is open to debate. Some of the babies who are aborted this way have physical or mental disabilities, but does that mean they should be killed?"

Trimester	Common Methods of Abortion Used
First	Medical abortion using drugs or chemicals, such as methotrexate, misoprotol, and mifepristone, often in combination Surgical abortion using suction or vacuum aspirator, or alternately dilation and curettage (D&C)
Second	Saline injection Dilation and evacuation (D&E)
Third	Dilation and evacuation (D&E) Dilation and extraction (D&X)

---

7. "Special Report: Partial Birth Abortion at Planned Parenthood," *The Center for Medical Progress*, https://www.centerformedicalprogress.org/human-capital/special-report-partial-birth-abortion-at-planned-parenthood.

Everyone was silent for a moment. The gravity of the topic was weighing heavily on all of them. Micah finally spoke up. "This has been an exhausting discussion. Why don't we change gears and share what we learned in our interviews?"

"Good idea," said Bianca. "Why don't you go first, Micah?"

"Okay," he replied. "So I visited Brittany at her clinic's offices. I didn't realize she runs her own clinic around the corner from the Planned Parenthood clinic we saw. It's called Valley Pregnancy Center (VPC), and she is the director. I asked her about the purpose of the clinic and also why they go to the Planned Parenthood clinic to talk to women going in for an abortion. She said VPC exists to provide resources and support for pregnant women in crisis. They offer health screenings, free ultrasounds, and consultations with a nurse practitioner. One day a week a local ob-gyn provides free OB exams for pregnant women. The clinic also works with social services to help women with housing, food, and public services. They have a resource store where women can get maternity clothes, baby clothes, car seats, diapers, formula, and other necessities. Everything in the store is available for about 90 percent off the retail price.

"Brittany said that the fence ministry, as they call it, started when a woman came to VPC after two abortions and told her that if someone had just talked to her the morning of her last abortion, she would have changed her mind. The law prohibits them from stepping onto the property at the Planned Parenthood clinic, but there is nothing preventing them from standing at the fence and trying to talk to women as they get out of their cars. I asked her what they say to the women, and she said they start by asking their names and if they would be willing to talk for a few minutes before they go into the clinic. They ask the women if they need assistance in any way and if they would like to keep their baby but feel they cannot. They ask them if they have seen an ultrasound image of their baby and offer the free services of VPC. They also offer to pray for them if they want prayer for any specific needs. I asked Brittany if they ever get anyone to change her mind and she said that once or twice a week a woman will get back into her car and leave or drive over to the VPC. I also asked her *why* they try to stop women from getting abortions, and she said that the primary reason is that they believe every fetus from conception onward is a human being made in God's image and therefore precious and deserving protection. She believes women going into Planned Parenthood know this, but for whatever reason feel the only way out of their predicament is an abortion."

"She seems nice," said Bianca. "What about you, Lauren? How was your talk with Max?"

"It was disturbing and surprising all at once," replied Lauren. "I met Max at The Grey Earl, and I can tell you I was very nervous to be seen with him in public. I don't know how many people know what he and his group do, but I was afraid someone might start yelling at him. Part of me wanted to yell at him too for trying to deny women their rights, but I tried to be cool and rational about it.

"Max told me his group is made up of men and women of all ages and backgrounds who believe that abortion is murder. His organization is called RUN, or Rescue the Unborn Now. Because they believe, like Brittany, that everyone is a person from conception, abortion is the murder of a human being. He said RUN wants everybody to know what abortion is, and he believes if people knew the truth about the procedure, the vast majority would rise up and abolish abortion. I have to admit that even though Max was very nice and calm, his words made me very agitated. He started to show me some of the signs they hold up when they gather at the entrance to the driveway of Planned Parenthood. Some of them just have words, and they weren't as bad as I was expecting. None of them accuse the women of murder or anything like that. What really bothered me was the signs that were poster-sized photos of aborted fetuses. I told him how offended I was by the graphic pictures of the fetuses all cut to pieces and reassembled like you described earlier, Bianca. Max didn't seem upset by my reaction. Instead he leaned in and said, 'That is exactly why we do this, Lauren. Your reaction shows that the abortion is easy to defend as long as it remains abstract as a surgical procedure, but when you actually see what it does to the unborn in the womb, you are repulsed.' He said that they try to educate people about the reality of abortion in the hopes that people will be so repulsed that they will change their minds."

"Did he say if it works?" wondered Micah.

"He said that people have varying reactions. He thought that about 20 percent of people who claim to be pro-choice change their mind at least somewhat if they are willing to look at the pictures. He is not sure how many women at Planned Parenthood change their minds as they are driving in.

He thinks that the combination of RUN and VPC does cause some of the women to keep their babies."

"What did you think about all that, Lauren?" asked Bianca.

"Well, he was right that I didn't want to see what an abortion really does to a fetus. After seeing a few of his pictures, I couldn't take it anymore. That is probably why I reacted the way I did a little while ago. I was hoping that your description of the methods of abortion would show that his pictures had been exaggerated or photoshopped. But the description matches the pictures to a T. He hasn't changed my mind about a woman's choice, but I have to admit that the reality is more concerning that I had thought.

"Regardless of the method of abortion, however, I think it is important to keep in mind the most important issue in abortion is the woman's choice. You may think that is unfeeling in light of the methods of abortion, but I cannot imagine anything much worse than a woman having to carry a fetus to term that she doesn't want and then spending the next eighteen years caring for the child. I think we forget all the situations where this would be completely unfair. Think of a woman whose boyfriend leaves her because she is pregnant, and she is left to raise the child alone. Think of an abusive husband or boyfriend. Think of grinding poverty many women are subject to, and then add another child to the mix. Think of a pregnancy where the amniocentesis shows a disability or defect.

"It is easy to be pro-life when your only concern is the life of the fetus, but the entire life of the woman is affected when she is carrying a baby she doesn't want. Nothing disempowers a woman more, I believe, than having to upend her whole life for a baby she doesn't want. And all this has to do with her own body. I mean, if you can't have rights of self-determination with your own body, how can you ever feel safe? So I am sorry for the fetuses that are aborted, but their lives, if you want to call them that, are over quickly. I am more concerned with the ongoing life of the woman." Lauren heaved a big sigh, indicating she was finished.

Bianca looked at Lauren wide-eyed for a moment, then reported about her interview. "I called Planned Parenthood and made an appointment with the director, Missy Walker, for an interview. She was very kind and answered all my questions. She even encouraged me to consider becoming a volunteer. I didn't have the heart to tell her I am pro-life. Anyway, I asked her what the mission of Planned Parenthood is and why they do so many abortions. She informed me that Planned Parenthood is a family planning and women's health organization committed to giving women the choice of when and how to become pregnant. She also said that one of the core beliefs is that a woman's right to make choices about her body is hers and hers alone. The pro-choice movement is committed to keeping men out of the decision-making process of women's health and believes that for too long restrictions on abortion have been driven by religious interests that should not be allowed to influence public policy and legislate morality.

"Missy stressed the educational side of Planned Parenthood. She said that they are committed to providing sex education, information on contraceptives, and health screenings. Many people only think of abortion when Planned Parenthood is mentioned, but she emphasized that abortion is only 3 percent of what they do. She started to go off on all the other services that they provide, but I reminded her that our group was specifically studying abortion and that I wanted to ask more about that. She told me that there are many reasons a woman might have an abortion, and that regardless of the reason, a woman ought to have the right to have one because it is her body. A woman may not be ready to have a baby, or it may not be a good time in her life. She may already have other children and feel another would jeopardize her ability to care for the children she has. She may be in a relationship with someone with whom she doesn't want to have a baby, sometimes because of abuse or a destructive lifestyle. She may have been sexually assaulted. Regardless of the reason, a woman ought to have the right to choose.

"I asked her to tell me what exactly an abortion is, and she explained that it is simply the termination of a pregnancy. I asked her about the methods of abortion, such as vacuum curettage, and she said that method 'gently sucked the pregnancy from the uterus.'[8] I asked her why she doesn't use the word 'fetus' instead of 'pregnancy.' She smiled and said they don't use that term because, while it is a fetus inside a woman, the point of abortion is to end the pregnancy.

---

8. "What Facts about Abortion Do I Need to Know?" Planned Parenthood, https://www.plannedparenthood.org/learn/abortion/considering-abortion/what-facts-about-abortion-do-i-need-know.

"I have to tell you that I was getting very frustrated by the fact that she would not talk specifically about the baby in the womb and kept calling it a pregnancy and not a baby. I think she sensed my exasperation and by that time could tell I was not neutral about abortion. The interview started to fall apart, so I thanked her for her time and left. She kept emphasizing all the good that Planned Parenthood does for women, but all I could wonder was which room down the hallway was the one where babies were being killed."

"That is a little one-sided," objected Lauren. "You are completely ignoring all the good she just told you that they do there."

"I'm not ignoring it," replied Bianca, "but doing good does not negate the evil of ending innocent human life. No amount of good could justify that."

"And that is what we need to move on to discuss in order to come to some ethical conclusions," reminded Micah. "Let's try applying the ethical theories we learned in class to this topic. Let's start with Utilitarianism. Does that help us sort out whether abortion is a good thing or bad?"

"With that theory of morality, I guess it would depend on how we view the outcome," offered Lauren. "From the mother's point of view, if she doesn't want to carry the baby to term, then an abortion would be good for her for several reasons. First, it would prevent an unwanted child from coming into this world. That is one of the values of the pro-choice movement—'every child a wanted child.' Second, for those who think that overpopulation is a major environmental issue, it would at least limit babies being born to those who were wanted. Third, it would probably decrease financial pressures on the mother, which would alleviate social services that would otherwise be needed. We could go on and on."

"Of course, from the fetus's perspective, there is no way to see good in it since it would be dead," objected Bianca. "Why is a healthy fetus's good never considered in this issue?"

"Before you told me all those details about the development of the fetus in the womb, I would have said because it is not a baby, just an embryo or fetus," replied Lauren. "But now I don't think I can honestly believe that anymore. I'm not sure what to make of the whole identity of the thing in the womb yet."

"I am glad that you are wrestling with that issue still," said Micah. "That seems to be one of the key issues in this whole debate."

"There are a few more Utilitarian arguments against abortion," continued Bianca. "We have to believe that with the almost one million abortions in the United States every year and fifty million worldwide, among those babies being killed are people who would have been valuable members of society—doctors, scientists, artists, and humanitarians—not to mention good, upstanding citizens of all kinds. Finally, we have to ask what the impact is on the culture and soul of the nation that kills its most vulnerable members."

"Wouldn't that number also include a certain percentage of criminals? You know, murderers, rapists, and terrorists? You make it sound as though only productive members of society would come from that number. I think that is called the fallacy of suppressed evidence. It seems, then, that Utilitarianism doesn't really help us decide whether abortion is right or wrong," concluded Lauren. "What about Kant's categorical imperative?"

Micah jumped in. "It seems that we are left with the same problem. If we view it from the mother's standpoint, allowing people to make their own decisions about their bodies would be what we would want to be universal law. But again, from the fetus's position, it's the opposite. In that case if the fetus is a person, we should not kill it because we would not want to be killed if we were vulnerable."

"Ditto for Virtue Ethics," added Bianca. "The pro-choice position says it is a good and virtuous thing to bring a baby into this world only if it is wanted. In addition, a virtuous person will not want a woman to suffer unnecessary hardships in carrying a baby to term, and so will support the right of a woman to abort her baby if she feels it is best for her. The pro-life side will say similar things with the baby's best interests in mind."

Micah groaned. "Ugh! This is such a complex and highly charged topic. Maybe we should ask Dr. Pratt to provide some direction so we can arrive at some ethical conclusions."

"That sounds like a good idea," agreed Lauren, and Bianca nodded her assent. They decided to approach him after class the following day.

***

In class the next day, Dr. Pratt was introducing some philosophical concepts before beginning a new set of lectures on medical ethics. The concept that most intrigued the three friends was that of *personhood*.

"Many ethical issues assume a theory of personhood without necessarily arguing for it," he stated. "In other words, advocates of a position assume some form of belief in the dignity or rights of an individual without presenting a sound argument for why this is so or from where dignity and rights arise. This leads some, such as Peter Singer at Princeton University, to argue that animals ought to have the same rights as human beings,[9] or others to argue that some supercomputers ought to have more rights than mentally disabled humans."

"Whaaaaat?" interrupted Sam, one of their classmates. "Are you serious, Professor?"

"Yes, I am," replied Dr. Platt. "In philosophical and scientific discussions of abortion and other issues, being a human being and being a person are not the same thing. In those discussions the term 'human being' describes your species. 'Personhood' is reserved for those who qualify for rights, dignity, and protection. Increasingly there is pressure to apply the term 'person' to nonhuman entities such as highly intelligent animals and aspects of nature. In 2008 the Swiss Parliament declared that plants had to be handled and harvested ethically because they very well may have self-interest and be able to experience something as good or bad.[10] In 2017 the New Zealand Parliament declared the Whanganui River and a nearby forest to be a person, with all the rights, powers, duties, and liabilities that come with that status.[11]

"This has significant implications for issues such as abortion, euthanasia, and infanticide, among others. The question becomes: If being human doesn't automatically make one a person with all the accompanying rights and protections, what does? One philosopher, Mary Anne Warren, proposed five criteria for determining personhood:[12] consciousness of things external and internal to oneself, especially the ability to feel pain; reasoning, the capacity to solve new and relatively complex problems; self-motivated activity, activity that is

---

9. Peter Singer, *Animal Liberation* (New York: Harper, 2009).

10. "The Dignity of Living Beings with Regard to Plants," https://www.ekah.admin.ch/inhalte/_migrated/content_uploads/e-Broschure-Wurde-Pflanze-2008.pdf.

11. Kennedy Warne, "A Voice for Nature," *National Geographic* (April 2019), https://www.nationalgeographic.com/culture/2019/04/maori-river-in-new-zealand-is-a-legal-person.

12. Mary Anne Warren, "On the Moral and Legal Status of Abortion," *The Monist* 57, no. 1 (1973): 43–61.

not determined by genetics or external control; the capacity to communicate messages of an indefinite variety of types on indefinitely many topics; and the presence of self-concepts and self-awareness."

Dr. Platt looked up and asked, "Now can any of you spot problems with these criteria?"

Immediately a number of hands shot up. "Josh, what do you see?"

Josh was almost incensed. "What in the world does 'communicate messages of an indefinite variety of types on indefinitely many topics' even mean? If they are indefinite, how would we ever know when they were enough for Mary Anne Warren?" He was incredulous. "Those criteria sound so vague and arbitrary!"

"Good," said Dr. Platt with a smile. "Who would determine these indefinite tests? Do we suppose that scientists or doctors could give an objective opinion on something indefinite? Couldn't that kind of ambiguity be easily misused ?"

Sarah spoke up with a gleam in her eyes. "How would an unconscious person meet these criteria? What about someone in a coma or in surgery? What about when we sleep? Don't we lack some of these, such as the ability to solve problems?"

"I do calculus in my sleep, so I am always a person," cracked Javier. The class laughed roundly at this.

Dr. Platt chuckled and said. "Great point, Sarah. Warren is adamant that to be a person one must meet all of these criteria. Even the loss of one would disqualify an individual."

"But couldn't we say with Warren that these are only temporary losses of ability?" Lauren was thoughtful as usual.

"Some of them might be temporary, but some are not, such as dementia. Also, if the condition is temporary, then an embryo would eventually meet these criteria, and would therefore qualify as a person."

The class nodded in thought.

"Besides," Dr. Platt continued, "when it comes to the abortion question, not only do babies in the womb fail this test, but so do babies outside the womb, and for many weeks or months. This is why philosophers such as Peter Singer and Helga Kuhse argue that parents ought to have the right to kill their newborn babies within the first month or so after they are born if they are not wanted for any reason. They argue this on the basis of their belief that a newborn does not meet the criteria of personhood and therefore has no rights to protection."[13]

The class broke into chaos, and it took Dr. Platt three minutes to calm everyone down. Several students were visibly upset. He explained that Singer's and Kuhse's views were widely rejected, but he did note that they were consistent with the criteria Mary Anne Warren had proposed. "This is why we must think critically and challenge criteria like these that are not rooted in any philosophical or religious foundation, but are merely arbitrary proposals."

Dr. Platt dismissed the class, and the students streamed out of the room, talking intently. Micah, Lauren, and Bianca waited around until almost everyone was gone. They shared with him all that they had learned about abortion through their research, as well as what their interviews had taught them. When they had finished summarizing their research, Micah spoke up.

"It seems that this idea of personhood is key to this whole issue," he said.

"It certainly lies at the heart of the issue," replied Dr. Platt. "Every position on abortion assumes certain things about the personhood of the unborn, and sometimes those assumptions are unexamined."

"What do you mean? asked Lauren.

"An unexamined assumption is a basic belief one has without realizing it. For example, if I were to randomly pick on a student and embarrass him in front of the entire class until he broke down crying, you would probably object, correct?"

"That would be horrible!" agreed Lauren.

"That is my greatest fear every time I go to class," Micah said, half joking.

"You say it is horrible, but what if I asked you *why* it was horrible?" Dr. Platt was back in professor mode and enjoying it.

"Because you should never treat another person that way," answered Lauren.

"But why not?" he rebutted.

"It's just wrong." Lauren knew that Dr. Platt was using the Socratic method on her, but she still felt awkward about the exchange.

---

13. Helga Kuhse and Peter Singer, *Should the Baby Live?* (Oxford: Oxford University Press, 1986).

"Let me help you," he continued. "Ultimately if I kept pushing you would probably say that every person deserves to be treated with dignity and respect, which I believe. But if I asked *why* you believe that, you would have to ground your belief either in a deity who revealed that such treatment is wrong, or in a legal declaration formulated by people, or in evolutionary biology. All the other theories rely on a universally held idea of Natural Law, Utilitarianism, or categorical imperative that people regularly deny or fail to practice. That leaves only three choices for grounding the ethic of human dignity: a deity, a particular entity enforcing such a law, or the result of evolutionary forces so far. Each of these justifications for morals has implications that are often unforeseen."

"I think I understand," said Lauren with an uncertain glance.

"When it comes to abortion, those for and against abortion argue these two positions. Pro-life groups argue that, from the moment of conception, that entity is a human being with all the rights and protections of a person. Those on the pro-choice side argue that the fertilized egg does not obtain the status of personhood until it reaches a particular point in the pregnancy."

"Or after the live birth, if Peter Singer and Helga Kuhse have anything to say about it," chimed in Bianca, who had been listening intently.

"Yes, or until the mother or both parents expressed a desire to let the baby live," added Dr. Platt.

"So the issue is not just personhood, but also the status of the baby as wanted or not wanted," concluded Bianca.

"Yes, that seems to be how many people who approve of abortion judge whether to call what is in the mother's womb a baby or merely a fetus, and whether it is moral to abort it." Dr. Platt was finished packing his laptop away and was walking to the door. "I have another class soon, so I have to get going. I think the way to wrap up your topic will require a little more work on this issue of personhood and whether the baby is wanted or not. You have an excellent start on this issue, so use these elements to finish it up."

***

"Wow, if I had missed this class I would not have been prepared to come to a knowledgeable conclusion about abortion," remarked Bianca as the three friends walked out onto the quad together.

"We need to talk through personhood and *wantedness*, for the lack of a better term," said Lauren. "Do you both have time to go to The Grey Earl now? I would really like to wrap up this topic today if possible."

"Let's do it," replied Micah, turning to Bianca with raised eyebrows. Bianca nodded and off they went.

As they settled in with their steaming mugs, Lauren spoke first. "So where does personhood come from?"

Micah answered first. "As a Christian I believe God has created every person in his image since the first couple, Adam and Eve. All their descendants, including us, carry that image, and that's what gives us dignity and humanity. A fertilized human egg, if it develops normally, can only ever result in a human being, as opposed to an animal or plant of some kind. So I would argue that the personhood is there from the beginning. Being human is the equivalent of being a person."

Lauren countered. "And because I don't believe in the creation story, I have to figure out at what stage an embryo or fetus becomes a person, with all the rights and protections of the law."

"Or baby outside the womb," interjected Bianca.

"I just cannot agree with infanticide," said Lauren insistently. "And I don't think most pro-choice people do either. The views of Singer and Kuhse have to be on the fringe."

"Not in places around the world where babies are still abandoned or exposed to get rid of them," said Bianca. "In China the one-child policy resulted in the death of millions of babies for decades as women who gave birth to a second child either willingly or unwillingly had their babies taken from them and many babies were tossed on the side of the road.[14] There are other countries where that still happens. And besides, when an abortion is botched and the baby is born alive, the person performing the abortion does have the right to kill it in some way. So we have to ask when personhood begins even for a baby born alive."

---

14. "China's One-Child Policy: The Government's Massive Crime against Women and Unborn Babies," House Hearing of the 112th Congress of the United States, September 22, 2011, https://www.govinfo.gov/content/pkg/CHRG-112hhrg68446/html/CHRG-112hhrg68446.htm. See also the documentary, *One-Child Nation* (Amazon Studios, 2019).

"OK, so yes, I have to consider that too." Lauren looked glum. She knew her support for abortion was facing serious challenges with the issue of personhood.

"It seems that the pro-choice view determines personhood entirely on whether the baby is wanted by the mother," said Micah.

"Well, shouldn't a baby be wanted? What do you think happens to a baby who is not wanted by its mother? Think about the abuse or neglect that baby will probably experience. The pro-choice movement has a motto, 'Every mother a willing mother, every child a wanted child.' I think that's a pretty good mantra for this issue." Lauren seemed to regain some of her old confidence in her support of abortion.

"But Lauren, think about what you are saying," cautioned Micah. "If the determination of personhood is whether a baby is wanted or not, what if the mother's desire for the child in the womb or outside the womb changes day by day or minute by minute? Does the baby gain and lose its dignity, right to life, and protections entirely by the mother's desire for it? If that is the test, then it should apply to babies who have been born too.

"Add to that the question of whether the father of a baby in or out of the womb has a voice in the decision to keep a child. The child is half his genetically, so shouldn't he have a say? And there is the option of giving the baby up for adoption if the mother decides she doesn't want to keep the baby," Micah said.

"Ugh!" Lauren groaned. "This issue of personhood is a major problem for the pro-choice view, isn't it? It seems like the only choice I have is to say that the medical community or the government or some other authority has to determine when personhood begins. But who does so and on what grounds? I am so confused. And I don't want to allow any kind of infanticide. Once a baby has made it out of the womb, I believe it should be protected and provided with medical care to keep it alive. Maybe personhood should be reserved for when a fetus becomes viable—when it could survive outside the womb with only minimal medical attention."

"I appreciate the fact that you oppose infanticide, Lauren, but consider the real differences between a baby outside the womb and one still in it," said Bianca. "There is an acronym to show that the differences are not significant at all. It is called SLED. The differences are size, level of development, environment, and degree of dependency. We don't grant more personhood to a professional basketball player who is seven feet tall and weighs three hundred pounds. So size doesn't matter. The baby in the womb is smaller than a four-year-old, but that is only a size difference. A four-year-old is more developed than a two-year-old, but that doesn't mean it has greater dignity and rights, and neither should the developmental differences between a child that is born and an embryo in the womb confer a difference in status. The environment in which one lives doesn't determine personhood outside the womb, so why should it in the womb? Finally, the degree of dependency should not affect personhood, because all through life we have varying degrees of dependency on others, whether at birth, through serious illness, and even old age."

Lauren was silent for a moment. "I see what you're saying," she said quietly, "but there is still the fact that you argue a woman should have to carry this baby in her body for nine months whether she wants to or not. That seems like a violation of her rights as a person. So whose rights should win in these situations?"

"That's a real consideration, Lauren," answered Micah. "I don't want to minimize the fact that the woman endures all the discomforts and even dangers of pregnancy and birth. But the question still arises whether she has the right to end what is another human being's life in her body. If we are talking about inconvenience and difficulty versus death, it seems we should give priority to protecting the life of the baby over protecting a woman from discomfort as she carries the baby to term."

"What about a pregnancy in the event of rape or incest? Think about the added trauma of having to carry a baby to term because you were raped or because your uncle molested you when you were twelve?" Lauren again seemed to regain her commitment to her views. "That does happen, you know. What about a woman who is being trafficked by a pimp or who has an abusive boyfriend or husband? Should any of these girls or women have to carry the baby of men who do such horrible things?"

Bianca gulped and said, "Those are horrible scenarios, Lauren, and I know they happen in real life. I don't imagine any of those situations would be anything but traumatic and devastating. I understand your desire to leave abortion as an option for situations like that. However, abortions because of rape or incest in the U.S. account for less than 2 percent of all abortions.[15] And it is unknown whether having an abortion after trauma like these increases or decreases the trauma. In some cases women who have endured these kinds of evils have additionally regretted aborting the baby."[16]

A silence descended on the friends. They were spent. The discussion and research over the last few weeks had been emotionally exhausting. They looked at each other and sighed.

"Nothing else we have discussed in this class has been so emotionally difficult," said Bianca somberly.

"I never realized how serious this ethical issue was," agreed Lauren. "No matter which position you take, there are such difficult factors to consider. I don't think I am as convinced as I was regarding my position."

"I feel drained in a way that no amount of coffee or tea would help. This seems to have serious emotional and spiritual weight to it," added Micah. "I think we should wrap up our research and get it ready for Dr. Platt. I don't know that there is much more to discuss at this point."

The girls agreed, and the study group gathered up their belongings with heavy hearts. They would bring this topic to a close for now, but they would not stop thinking about it for a long time.

15. Lawrence B. Finer, et al., "Reasons U.S. Women Have Abortions: Quantitative and Qualitative Perspectives," *Perspectives on Sexual and Reproductive Health* 37, no. 3 (2005): 110–18, https://www.guttmacher.org/sites/default/files/pdfs/pubs/psrh/full/3711005.pdf. See also https://abort73.com/abortion_facts/us_abortion_statistics.

16. David C. Reardon, Julie Makimaa, and Amy Sobie, eds. *Victims and Victors: Speaking Out about Their Pregnancies, Abortions, and Children Resulting from Sexual Assault* (Springfield, IL: Acorn, 2000).

QUESTIONS TO PONDER

- When does a human life begin?

- How does a woman's right to choose conflict with the right of the fetus to live?

- How does abortion differ from the removal of an organ?

- What qualifies a human being at any stage to possess personhood?

- Should a woman impregnated by rape or incest be required to carry the baby to term?

TERMS TO KNOW

- Abortion
- Embryo
- Fetus
- Dilation and extraction
- Dilation and evacuation
- Vacuum curettage
- Categorical imperative
- Virtue Ethics

FOR FURTHER READING

Alcorn, Randy. *Pro-Life Answers to Pro-Choice Questions*. New York: Multnomah, 2000.

Beckwith, Francis J. *Defending Life: A Moral and Legal Case against Abortion Choice*. Cambridge: Cambridge University Press, 2007.

Greasley, Kate. *Arguments about Abortion: Personhood, Morality, and Law*. New York: Oxford University Press, 2017.

Greasley, Kate and Christopher Kaczor. *Abortion Rights: For and Against*. Cambridge: Cambridge University Press, 2017.

Klusendorf, Scott. *The Case for Life: Equipping Christians to Engage the Culture*. Wheaton, IL: Crossway, 2009.

Manninen, Bertha A. and Jack Mulder Jr. *Civil Dialogue on Abortion*. New York: Routledge, 2018.

EUTHANASIA AND PHYSICIAN-ASSISTED SUICIDE

Synopsis: Micah's grandfather is suddenly diagnosed with terminal cancer. Micah has been close to Pops since childhood and is devastated. He misses class without warning, and Bianca and Lauren's attempts to reach him are met with silence. He finally replies to their texts and asks to meet at The Grey Earl the next day. He is troubled by the thought of his grandfather suffering as the pancreatic cancer takes his life. He wonders if it is moral to ease someone's suffering by hastening his death before he has to suffer the worst of the pains of dying.

* * *

"Micah, what is it? Why haven't you returned our texts and calls?" Bianca voiced the concerns she and Lauren had felt with increasing urgency over the last week.

Micah struggled to find his voice. He was still very broken up about his grandfather's recent diagnosis of pancreatic cancer. As he shared the details with his friends, he had to pause several times to keep from crying.

"I am so sorry, Micah!" Lauren could see how upset he was and felt deeply for him.

"That is awful news," Bianca agreed. "I cannot imagine what you are going through. I will be sure to offer prayers for him." She made a mental note to include Micah's grandfather in her prayers the next time she was at church.

Micah was encouraged by their sympathy and found his heart strengthened. "I think my biggest concern is that I don't want to see Pops suffer. I have heard that some cancers cause suffering at the end that cannot be helped much by pain medication. It has made me wonder how much suffering a person should be required to endure, or if there is a way to allow a person to choose to end his life to end the suffering."

Lauren and Bianca were surprised at Micah's words but didn't know how to respond.

"I'm not saying that I would want Pops to take his life or have a doctor take his life. I just wonder what the right thing is for someone in great pain. It may be selfish, but I don't want that to happen to him."

"It sounds like you are wrestling with that topic that Dr. Platt covered in class earlier in the semester—physician-assisted death. When we were discussing it, I never thought it would be personal to any of us." Lauren was remembering the heated debate in class that day.

"I probably shouldn't be wondering about it," said Micah sadly. "Most likely, Pops would ask what in the world I was thinking." He smiled. "You would have to know my Pops to understand how ridiculous he would think I am for bringing it up. He would playfully smack me in the back of my head and say something like, 'Grandson, have you lost your mind? I am not afraid to die.' He is the strong one here, not me."

Micah heaved a heavy sigh. He looked at Lauren and Bianca and said, "I'm probably way out of line to ask you this, but would you be willing to look into this issue with me and help me find some clarity? Our ethics class has really made me want to be knowledgeable and discerning about ethical issues, but I am afraid my own situation may cloud my study of it."

Lauren jumped in. "Of course, Micah. We can study end-of-life issues together and see if we can arrive at some conclusions. Let's find a few key sources and read them, and then we can talk through them."

"That sounds like a great idea," agreed Bianca. "Do some research and send your top choices in a group email. We can meet back here in a few days and discuss them."

Four days later the group gathered. Micah still seemed burdened, so the girls began by encouraging him. Micah admitted that his talk with his grandfather the night before had lifted his spirits somewhat, but he was still plagued by fears of what Pops might have to endure.

"Okay, enough about me and my situation," he said. "Let's talk about the issue. That will help me get my mind off my own fears for a little while."

"Let's start with the principles embodied in the Hippocratic Oath regarding a physician's duties to his patients. The essay, 'Is Physician-Assisted Suicide Wrong?'[1] summarized it well." Lauren was always good for getting a conversation started in a focused manner.

"The first is the Principle of Autonomy, which states that as moral agents, patients should be able to make their own decisions regarding their health care. This starts with the recognition that people are more than objects or things but have inherent rights as human beings. This means that health care professionals are obligated to provide full and truthful information so the patient can make a decision based on a full understanding of the facts. That is called 'informed consent.'"

"What happens when a patient is unconscious or not mentally competent?" asked Bianca.

Lauren answered, "In such cases a proxy, such as a family member, would help to make a decision. Absent that, a doctor must act in the best interest of the patient, to the best of his ability to discern it." It was times like these that Micah and Bianca were thankful that Lauren knew some of the tricky medical questions that arose in ethical discussions.

"I'll take the second principle," offered Bianca. "The Principle of Nonmaleficence forbids physicians from exposing their patients to the 'unnecessary risk of needless harm.' No unnecessary action should be taken in the course of treatment. Sometimes painful procedures are necessary to cure or relieve greater pain, but anything careless or negligent should be avoided at all costs."

Micah joined the discussion. "The third principle is the Principle of Beneficence, which obligates doctors to help their patients whenever they

---

1. Owen M. Smith and Anne Collins Smith, "Is Physician-Assisted Suicide Wrong?," in *Taking Sides: Clashing Views on Moral Issues*, eds. Owen M. Smith and Anne Collins Smith, 14th ed. (Dubuque, IA: McGraw Hill, 2016), 197–99.

can. Patients depend on their doctors, nurses, therapists, and social workers to know what they are doing and to possess the knowledge, skill, and experience to do them good. If a health care provider does not know what she is doing or needs to consult a specialist, she is obligated to do that for the good of the patient."

Micah continued, "If these principles guide doctors, then how could physician-assisted death (PAD) ever happen? How could a doctor ever help someone die if these are the guidelines they follow?"

Lauren answered. "The conflict of interest enters when ending a patient's suffering seems like a greater good than prolonging her life. That's the crux of the issue. Is dying when one wants to die more dignified than suffering a slow death? If someone is in severe pain and cannot be helped, isn't it more merciful to put him out of his misery? I have heard the comparison to shooting someone who is trapped in a burning car so he doesn't have to burn to death."

"These are such awful things to think about," said Bianca with a grimace.

"I know," agreed Lauren, "but in medicine these are the realities that doctors and nurses face all the time. My cousin is a nurse in a medical intensive care unit, which represents a hospital's last attempt to save someone who is dying. Most of the patients die because they are too sick or injured to recover. She has seen patients wither away to nothing in terrible pain, helped only by massive doses of opioids that basically put them in a coma at the end."

"Why don't they go to hospice if they are dying?" asked Micah.

"Some do, but many times families don't want to give up hope. Sometimes they insist on procedures and medications to keep their loved one alive, even though it causes the dying patient more pain. The dying person may just want to die and stop the suffering."

"I see now why some people might want to end their lives to avoid more pain as they are dying." Bianca leaned back and looked at the ceiling as she contemplated this idea.

"That was a helpful introduction to the issues at hand," said Micah. "Let's move on to the book we found, L. W. Sumner's *Physician-Assisted Death: What Everyone Needs to Know.*[2] I didn't get to read the entire book in

---

2. L. W. Sumner, *Physician-Assisted Death: What Everyone Needs to Know* (Oxford: Oxford University Press, 2017).

depth, but I did read enough to get a much better understanding of PAD. I am glad he chose the title he did instead of the other commonly used term, 'physician-assisted suicide' (PAS)."

"Yes, what is the difference between PAD and PAS? And do those differ from the term 'euthanasia'?" Bianca was flipping through her notes to see if she had answered her own question in the previous few days of study.

"Good question," affirmed Lauren. "Proper vocabulary is important in every ethical issue, but especially in this one. Sumner says that PAD 'refers to one particular way in which a doctor may help to hasten a patient's death: by providing the patient with medication (typically a barbiturate) at a dose level that is intended to cause death and that does in fact cause death.'[3] This can occur when a doctor prescribes the medication to the patient who then takes the drug herself. This is called 'physician-assisted suicide.' When the doctor administers the medication directly, however, the proper term is 'physician-administered suicide' or 'euthanasia.' PAD is an umbrella term with each of these scenarios as a distinct type of PAD."

"So, the difference is who administers the deadly medication," summarized Micah.

"Precisely," confirmed Lauren.

"What about when a patient refuses or asks to withdraw life-sustaining treatment? Is that considered suicide or PAD too?" Bianca's mind was swirling with a dozen possible scenarios.

"No, refusing or voluntarily ending life-saving treatment is not considered suicide," Lauren explained. "Patients have the right to refuse any treatment. The distinction of PAD is that it is a more active choice to end a life by receiving an injection."

"I do have one point of disagreement with you," said Micah. "I have heard stories of minors who wanted to refuse chemotherapy but were forced by state courts to continue receiving it.[4] So, it seems that you have to be at least eighteen to refuse life-saving treatment."

---

3. Sumner, *Physician-Assisted Death*, 34.
4. See the cases of Danny Hauser and Cassandra Callender: "Judge Rules Family Can't Refuse Chemo for Boy," NBC News, May 19, 2009, http://www.nbcnews. com/id/30763438/ns/health-childrens_health/t/judge-rules-family-cant-refuse- chemo-boy/#.Xk2IBi3MzUo; Amanda MacMillan, "A 17-Year-Old Forced to Get

"I didn't know that," replied Lauren, "but let's focus on adults for now. One of the arguments for PAD is that suffering is intrinsically bad and is something to be prevented or relieved at all costs. Sometimes people die peacefully, but with the advance of modern medicine, people live longer and die more often of degenerative diseases such as cancer and organ failure. As a result, dying may be accompanied by awful things like pain, shortness of breath, nausea, dizziness, agitation, or delirium. The aim of pain management is to provide the minimum dose of medicine sufficient to control the pain, but no more than is necessary. When someone is dying and her pain becomes intolerable, the decision may be made to permanently sedate the patient. This is called *palliative sedation* or *terminal sedation*."

"I remember reading about terminal sedation," added Bianca. "It happens when the only solution to intractable pain is to give opioids in doses that put the patient into a state of deep and continuous unconsciousness until the point of death."[5]

"It doesn't sound like any of that would be classified as PAD, though," observed Micah. "I am beginning to see that in all the complexity of end-of-life issues, one of the key factors is *intent*. None of what we have talked about so far regarding relieving pain has the intent to end a life, but simply to manage pain for those dying."

"That is correct," affirmed Lauren. "One of the arguments for PAD is that people have a right not to suffer, because it is intrinsically bad."

"You said that already," said Micah with a mischievous smile.

Lauren glared at Micah for a moment and then smiled. "I know that. I was just bringing the discussion back to that point. Such a position against suffering can easily become consequentialist, arguing that PAD is a moral choice because of the desirable consequences it produces. But desirable for whom? If we only think of the patient, then perhaps an argument could be made, but what about others such as family and friends? In addition, this argument against suffering includes not just physical pain but psychological too."

Chemo Takes Her State to Court," *Health*, January 7, 2015, https://www.health.com/mind-body/a-17-year-old-forced-to-get-chemo-takes-her-state-to-court; see also Christopher M. O'Connor, "What Rights Do Minors Have to Refuse Medical Treatment?" *The Journal of Lancaster General Hospital* 4, no. 2 (2009): 63–65.

5.   Sumner, *Physician-Assisted Death*, 32–33.

"I was fascinated by the list of forms of psychological suffering Sumner included," added Bianca. "He mentions anxiety, depression, despair, hopelessness, abandonment, rejection, humiliation, and indignity. That list made me sad. How many people in the world experience these things? I don't simply mean once in a while or slightly, but chronically and severely. On the other hand, the book seems to imply that these forms of suffering could conceivably justify PAD even when the person is physically healthy. That greatly concerns me."

"Yeah," agreed Micah. "If this principle holds, it seems that anyone who could demonstrate severe enough psychological trauma would be eligible for PAD."

Bianca spoke. "Actually, that has happened in places like the Netherlands. A twenty-nine-year-old woman was euthanized for depression, and it is legal in that country for children as young as twelve to be euthanized as long as they have parental consent."[6]

"That seems to blend into the next argument for PAD—autonomy. Just like the principle from the Hippocratic oath, the right of a person to determine his desired goals and medical treatment must be respected." Micah paused. "But the crux of the matter seems to be that there is a limit to this right. Does a person have the moral right to take his own life, especially if a physician must be involved to obtain the right medications?"

"It seems that the argument from autonomy lies at the heart of the matter," said Lauren. "We have talked about this before. Is it good for a society to make suicide safe and easy? We could ask the same question about drug use or gambling or cigarettes. In each of these cases, however, there seems to be a consensus that there should be limits imposed by government and taxes to discourage a certain amount of use. I think PAD is even more serious because the intent of those other things is not to die or end someone's life, even though that does sometimes happen."

---

6. Simon Caldwell, "Dutch Doctors Euthanize 29-Year-Old Woman with Depression," *Catholic Herald*, February 1, 2018, https://catholicherald.co.uk/news/2018/02/01/dutch-doctors-euthanise-29-year-old-woman-with-depression. See also Scott Kim, "How Dutch Law Got a Little Too Comfortable with Euthanasia," *The Atlantic*, June 8, 2019, https://www.theatlantic.com/ideas/archive/2019/06/noa-pothoven-and-dutch-euthanasia-system/591262.

THE HIPPOCRATIC OATH[7]	
Classical Version	**Modern Version**
I swear by Apollo Physician and Asclepius and Hygieia and Panaceia and all the gods and goddesses, making them my witnesses, that I will fulfill according to my ability and judgment this oath and this covenant:	I swear to fulfill, to the best of my ability and judgment, this covenant:
To hold him who has taught me this art as equal to my parents and to live my life in partnership with him, and if he is in need of money to give him a share of mine, and to regard his offspring as equal to my brothers in male lineage and to teach them this art—if they desire to learn it—without fee and covenant; to give a share of precepts and oral instruction and all the other learning to my sons and to the sons of him who has instructed me and to pupils who have signed the covenant and have taken an oath according to the medical law, but no one else.	I will respect the hard-won scientific gains of those physicians in whose steps I walk, and gladly share such knowledge as is mine with those who are to follow.
	I will apply, for the benefit of the sick, all measures [that] are required, avoiding those twin traps of overtreatment and therapeutic nihilism.
	I will remember that there is art to medicine as well as science, and that warmth, sympathy, and understanding may outweigh the surgeon's knife or the chemist's drug.
I will apply dietetic measures for the benefit of the sick according to my ability and judgment; I will keep them from harm and injustice.	I will not be ashamed to say "I know not," nor will I fail to call in my colleagues when the skills of another are needed for a patient's recovery.
	I will respect the privacy of my patients, for their problems are not disclosed to me that the world may know. Most especially must I tread with care in matters of life and death. If it is given me to save a life, all thanks. But it may also be within my power to take a life; this awesome responsibility must be faced with great humbleness and awareness of my own frailty. Above all, I must not play at God.

---

7. https://www.pbs.org/wgbh/nova/article/hippocratic-oath-today.

THE HIPPOCRATIC OATH[7]

Classical Version	Modern Version
I will neither give a deadly drug to anybody who asked for it, nor will I make a suggestion to this effect. Similarly I will not give to a woman an abortive remedy. In purity and holiness I will guard my life and my art.	I will remember that I do not treat a fever chart, a cancerous growth, but a sick human being, whose illness may affect the person's family and economic stability. My responsibility includes these related problems, if I am to care adequately for the sick.
I will not use the knife, not even on sufferers from stone, but will withdraw in favor of such men as are engaged in this work.	I will prevent disease whenever I can, for prevention is preferable to cure.
Whatever houses I may visit, I will come for the benefit of the sick, remaining free of all intentional injustice, of all mischief and in particular of sexual relations with both female and male persons, be they free or slaves.	I will remember that I remain a member of society, with special obligations to all my fellow human beings, those sound of mind and body as well as the infirm.
What I may see or hear in the course of the treatment or even outside of the treatment in regard to the life of men, which on no account one must spread abroad,	If I do not violate this oath, may I enjoy life and art, respected while I live and remembered with affection thereafter. May I always act so as to preserve the finest traditions of my calling and may I long experience the joy of healing those who seek my help.
I will keep to myself, holding such things shameful to be spoken about.	
If I fulfill this oath and do not violate it, may it be granted to me to enjoy life and art, being honored with fame among all men for all time to come; if I transgress it and swear falsely, may the opposite of all this be my lot.	—Written in 1964 by Louis Lasagna, Academic Dean of the School of Medicine at Tufts University, and used in many medical schools today.
—Translation from the Greek by Ludwig Edelstein. From *The Hippocratic Oath: Text, Translation, and Interpretation*, by Ludwig Edelstein. Baltimore: Johns Hopkins Press, 1943.	

"Does this get into Natural Law Theory?" asked Bianca. "Does the issue of PAD bother us so much because nature seems to teach us that the desire to live and flourish is built into us by nature and anything that threatens that is wrong?"

"I think you're right about that," replied Micah. "I think that goes hand-in-hand with the idea of the sanctity of life. When life functions normally, we have a desire to live, and we value actions that safeguard life."

"That seems to fit with a deontological approach to life. Life is valuable in and of itself," continued Bianca. "The book talks about the Thomistic and Kantian views as applied to PAD. Aquinas would argue that PAD is a violation of the respect we owe to the 'fundamental goods that constitute a person's well-being or human fulfillment.' Kant argues in a slightly different direction when he says that the respect is owed to the person himself."[8]

"What does Aquinas mean by 'the fundamental goods that constitute a person's well-being?" asked Micah. "I didn't understand what he meant when I read that."

"It refers to a number of things that Aquinas considered intrinsically good—knowledge, aesthetic experience, and friendship, for example." Bianca explained even as she was trying to comprehend the information. "Basically, he argues that we should never choose to destroy, damage, or impede one of these basic goods."

"That makes sense. It is basically an argument that assumes human life is valuable and argues that we should reject anything that intentionally would end it." Micah was starting to understand the argument.

"Yes, but keep in mind the issue of PAD addresses the situation when people are in intractable pain or are facing a deadly diagnosis," Lauren reminded them. "In such cases PAD would argue that the suffering such a person faces will do greater harm to his dignity and personhood than would death. Considering some of the ways people suffer, I can understand why they would make that argument."

"I certainly don't want Pops to suffer intractable pain at the end of his battle with cancer," said Micah somberly.

"Don't forget, though, that we have the ability to alleviate most pain at the end of life," reminded Lauren.

---

8.   Sumner, *Physician-Assisted Death*, 48–50.

"So what is the difference between giving someone so much pain medication that his heart slows down and he dies, and putting him into a coma to reduce pain?" Bianca was turning over scenarios in her head.

"It seems to me that the difference is in the intent behind the actions," mused Micah.

"I agree," said Lauren. "What makes PAD so controversial is that the intention is to end the life, not primarily to alleviate suffering. While terminal sedation may result in death, the cause of death is the disease or injury, not the sedation."

"That seems like a fine line of distinction," said Bianca thoughtfully. "It also would qualify as an example of an ethical principle Dr. Pratt mentioned in class once—the Principle of Double Effect. This principle is used to determine if an act that has both positive and negative, or good and evil effects, is ethical. When this is the case, an act must satisfy four conditions to be acceptable. First, the act in itself cannot be morally wrong or intrinsically evil. Second, the bad effect cannot cause the good effect. Third, the agent performing the act cannot intend the bad effect. Finally, the bad effect cannot outweigh the good effect. The reasoning is that if all four criteria are met, then the act is indirect and morally acceptable. If, however, these conditions are not met, then the act is direct and therefore evil.[9] This is why intent in alleviating suffering and the proportional risk of death are critical to determining the morality of pain relief."

"I'm sure it is a very fine line when it comes to actual situations in a hospital," agreed Lauren. "I am learning in my clinicals that actual medical cases are much more complex than I had expected, and each case is different in some way. That is why those who support PAD seek to pass laws to spell out the details of what is allowed and what is not."

"It still comes down to whether an individual ought to have the right to end her life." Bianca was trying to keep the core ethical issue at the forefront.

"That's correct," agreed Lauren.

---

9. Nicholas J. Kockler, "The Principle of Double Effect and Proportionate Reason," *Virtual Mentor: AMA Journal of Ethics* 9, no. 5 (May 2007): 369–74, https://journalofethics.ama-assn.org/article/principle-double-effect-and-proportionate-reason/2007-05.

"I found the article by Richard Doerflinger helpful," offered Micah. "He emphasized a number of factors in this issue that I hadn't thought of before. He argues against PAD by saying that a free act that destroys life destroys all the individual's future earthly freedom and so is immoral. He then argues that if PAD becomes socially acceptable it may jeopardize more than just the terminally ill because of how it will change thinking in a society."[10]

"I know the part to which you are referring, Micah," said Bianca. "He mentions the psychological vulnerability of the elderly and dying. If PAD becomes socially acceptable, older people may see themselves as useless burdens on younger generations and may feel a subtle pressure to get out of the way because no one has a strong interest in their survival."

"That is almost too sad to think about," said Lauren. "I love my grandma and could never think of her as useless. She is so wise!"

"Same with my Pops," agreed Micah.

"But think of how this would be if even a small percentage of elderly and sick people chose to end their lives. Doerflinger is right, I believe, that there could grow an expectation in society that an elderly person who was a bother should be noble and end her life." Bianca shuddered at the thought.

"Another point he mentions is the crisis in healthcare costs," said Micah.

Bianca nodded. "It is true that as people live longer, their medical care becomes very expensive. A conscientious older person may feel guilty for incurring such expenses."

"This factor is somewhat like the first one," said Micah. "It shows how acceptance of PAD could change expectations in a society. If the elderly consume significant amounts of healthcare and are not going to live long anyway, I could see the attitude developing that there should be a limit to what certain age groups could receive in healthcare dollars. There could develop the idea that great effort to sustain life should only be made for the young."

"Doerflinger also talks about how this attitude could extend to people with disabilities. It wouldn't be only the elderly and dying who feel the pressure." Bianca pressed on. "I read somewhere that many people would rather

10. Richard Doerflinger, "Assisted Suicide: Pro-Choice or Anti-Life?," in Smith and Smith, eds., *Taking Sides: Clashing Views on Moral Issues*, 200–203.

be dead than live in a severely disabled state. That already sounds like there exists in society a subtle view that disabled people have lives not worth living. If PAD were to become normal, how many other types of people would be perceived as candidates for it?"

"What about babies born with disabilities, like Down Syndrome or spina bifida?" Micah was thinking of his neighbor, an eight-year-old boy with Down Syndrome who was the happiest child he'd ever met.

"What about people in a permanent vegetative state or long-term coma?" offered Lauren.

"That also brings up the question of those who cannot communicate their desire to live or die," said Micah. "That is the difference between voluntary, involuntary, and nonvoluntary PAD."

"Can you remind me what those distinctions are again?" asked Bianca.

Micah continued. "Voluntary PAD is when a patient who is fully informed of the ramifications of his decision chooses to die with the help of a doctor. Nonvoluntary PAD is kind of the middle ground when the patient is unable to communicate a will to live or die but is euthanized because someone considers it in his best interest. This happens in the case of a person in a coma, a persistent vegetative state, or severely disabled and unable to communicate a will to live. Finally, involuntary PAD is essentially euthanasia against the person's wishes. One source I found said that based on physicians' own reporting in the Netherlands, for every three or four cases of PAD, one occurs without consent."[11]

Lauren's mouth dropped open, and Bianca felt tears spring to her eyes. "That is shocking and terrifying and infuriating all at once," said Bianca emphatically.

"That is part of the slippery slope that Doerflinger warns about," said Micah. "It seems in the countries that have legalized PAD, the slippery slope is hard to stop."

"That reminds me of another troubling statistic I read," added Lauren. "In 2002 in Oregon fifty-eight people were given prescriptions to end their

---

11. Neil Gorsuch, *The Future of Assisted Suicide* (Princeton, NJ: Princeton University Press, 2006), 159; cited in Scott Rae, *Moral Choices: An Introduction to Ethics*, 4th ed. (Grand Rapids: Zondervan, 2018), 256.

lives. Very few of them were requesting PAD for unrelenting pain, however. Of the fifty-eight individuals requesting drugs, 84 percent did so because of concern that they would not be able to participate in enjoyable activities; 47 percent were afraid they would lose bodily functions; and only 26 percent because of fear of pain."[12]

"I think we can all agree that involuntary PAD is very troubling," said Micah. "It seems to put too much power in the hands of the physician, whose worldview may not consider certain lives worth living."

"Did you read the end of his essay?" asked Bianca. "He says some shocking things about how once a physician ends one life, it becomes progressively easier to end more. It seems the history of PAD in Belgium and the Netherlands shows this to be the case."

The friends felt exhausted by the discussion.

"Do you ever feel that when you dive deep into a topic for so long you start to lose perspective on it and the ability to arrive at any solid conclusion?" Bianca didn't know how accurately she was voicing the feelings of the others.

"Totally!" said Micah and Lauren simultaneously, followed by (in unison), "Jinx! Double jinx! Knock on wood!"

All three burst into laughter. "I don't even know where that came from," said Lauren.

"My siblings and I used to say it all the time when we were little," smiled Micah.

"Anyway," said Bianca, "let's ask in class if anyone can help us with an ethical theory that could guide us to some kind of conclusion."

"That sounds good," agreed Micah. "I'll bring it up, because I would like to set it in the context of what's going on with Pops. I think ethical issues as serious as this one are taken much more seriously when they are tied to a real-life situation."

In the following week's class Micah waited for the end of class when Dr. Platt sometimes opened the floor for questions on any topic. He was ready and beat several other students on the draw to ask his question first. After explaining Pops' diagnosis and his own concerns about suffering, he briefly

12. John S. Feinberg and Paul D. Feinberg, *Ethics for a Brave New World,* 2nd ed. (Wheaton, IL: Crossway, 2010), 171.

recapped what the three friends had discussed at The Grey Earl. Dr. Platt was about to ask Micah to get to the point when Micah wrapped it up.

"So my question is, what ethical theories would help us make a decision on such an important issue?"

"Hmm, that is a good question for the class," said Dr. Platt with a smile and a twinkle in his eye. "On a more serious note, I am sorry to hear about your grandfather's diagnosis. That makes this dilemma very personal. Class, I hope we can approach this in a serious manner since it is not merely a theoretical question."

"It seems that Virtue Ethics always comes into a play in an ethical situation," offered Tyrone. "However, I don't know that it can ever be a deciding factor on its own. It always has to be combined with another theory to be helpful."

"Can you explain what you mean?" asked Dr. Platt.

"Well in this case Virtue Ethics would be most concerned about the character of a sick person. Or it could apply to the physician involved. Is the patient virtuous in his experience of dying? Is the physician virtuous in assisting the patient in dying? Before we can discuss that, however, we have to define what we mean by *life* and *death*. Otherwise we don't know whether PAD is wrong."

"Life is life, death is death," replied Barry. "What do you mean by defining life and death?"

Everyone smiled at this unintentional occasion of humor.

"I have done some reading on the medical and ethical definitions of life and death," replied Tyrone. "Some ethicists distinguish between *biological death* and *personal death*. Biological death is usually determined by the cessation of brain function or the absence of a heartbeat and breathing. Personal death, however, is often defined as the loss of permanent consciousness or the ability to function as a normal person with autonomy and the ability to pursue happiness. Personal death, then, sometimes happens before biological death. If that is what makes us human, then PAD would not be wrong, because even though a person would be alive biologically, he would have already lost his humanity."

There was a collective sucking in of air in the room and someone let out a low whistle.

"That is very deep, Tyrone," said Bianca. "I guess we need to hold onto Virtue Ethics but ground it in another theory, so we know what is virtuous."

"Great discussion so far," interjected Dr. Platt. "Does someone else have another theory of ethics that they think would help us here?"

"I would offer Utilitarianism," suggested Megan, "but I am afraid of where that might take this issue."

"Please explain," encouraged Dr. Platt.

"Well, it seems that PAD would be determined by a particular society's valuation of those in terrible pain at the end of their lives. If they are considered to be a drain on resources, then PAD would seem to be a way to reduce their use of money and medical costs. In a society where those who are suffering are valued and cared for, however, it would best serve society to provide care to reinforce the ethic."

"Yes, we considered that," said Micah. "Obviously healthcare at the end of life or for those with severe disabilities is very expensive. If a major cultural value is saving money and reserving resources for those who may live longer and fulfill a productive role in society, then PAD could easily go from an option to an expectation. It could create societal pressure to 'do your duty to die and get out of the way,' as the former governor of Colorado, Richard Lamm, once said."

"Oh, that is horrible," whispered Megan.

"I tend to lean toward Divine Command or Divine Nature Theory," said Kirk. "The sixth commandment forbids murder, so it would eliminate PAD. Just because people are very old or very ill doesn't mean that their death can be hastened, even by a physician. When God says, 'Thou shalt not kill,' he is forbidding any kind of premeditated killing.[13] The only exceptions to that rule would be war, self-defense, or in my opinion, capital punishment. The point is that life has been given by God, and we do not have the right to take it into our own hands. So any form of suicide or intent to end one's life would be considered wrong."

"Thank you, Kirk. Are there any other thoughts on ethical theory that could provide guidance?" Dr. Platt didn't want to end the discussion before the class was finished working through it.

---

13. Exod. 20:13.

Alisha raised her hand. "I think I may be coming at it from a different perspective because my uncle died of sepsis a few years ago and he suffered quite a bit at the end. All these theories may help us eliminate some of the cases that arise because of the slippery slope, like people who are merely depressed, fear the loss of health toward the end of their lives, or who don't want to live with a disability anymore. My concern, however, is the person who will most likely suffer great pain at the end of her life and doesn't want to have to endure it. I don't want to speak for Micah, but I was tormented by my uncle's pain, and I wondered why PAD wasn't an option since he was going to die anyway."

Micah nodded. "I feel the same way, even though I know my Pops would not want PAD. What about others who would? I can only imagine the fear of what you will face with a terminal diagnosis. And I cannot even imagine being in unrelenting pain. Yet Bianca and Lauren and I learned that with modern medicine, the vast majority of cases of that kind of suffering can be alleviated. I know my Pops will face his death with dignity, even if he has to be put into terminal sedation at the end."

"I guess the question comes down to autonomy then," concluded Alisha. "The real questions here seem to be whether a person has the right to make a decision for himself that includes death, and whether a society wants to make that legal."

"That seems to be the crux of the matter," agreed Dr. Platt. "All the other issues flow from that. And that also seems to be the end of our class time," he said, looking at the clock.

He looked at Micah. "Thank you for being willing to share this difficult personal situation with the class. It has caused us all to think hard about a very important issue."

QUESTIONS TO PONDER

- Should people have the right to legally end their lives?

- For what reasons should people be able to end their lives to avoid suffering?

- Compare the classical and modern versions of the Hippocratic oath. What significance do the changes have for the issue of PAD?

- Should physicians be legally allowed to help people end their lives?

- Is terminal sedation a form of physician-assisted death?

- What defines death?

TERMS TO KNOW

- Principle of Autonomy
- Principle of Nonmaleficence
- Principle of Beneficence
- Principle of Double Effect
- Physician-Assisted Death (PAD)
- Physician-Administered Suicide (PAS)
- Euthanasia
- Palliative (terminal) sedation
- Voluntary PAD
- Involuntary PAD
- Nonvoluntary PAD
- Biological death
- Personal death

FOR FURTHER READING

General:

Dworkin, Gerald, R. G. Frey, and Sissela Bok. *Euthanasia and Physician-Assisted Suicide.* Cambridge: Cambridge University Press, 1998.

Gorsuch, Neil. *The Future of Assisted Suicide.* Princeton, NJ: Princeton University Press, 2006.

Sumner, L. W. *Physician-Assisted Death: What Everyone Needs to Know.* New York: Oxford University Press, 2017.

Christian Sources:

Feinberg, John S. and Paul D. Feinberg. *Ethics for a Brave New World,* 2nd ed. Wheaton, IL: Crossway, 2010.

Foreman, Mark W. *Christianity and Bioethics: Confronting Clinical Issues.* Eugene, OR: Wipf and Stock, 2011.

Rae, Scott. *Moral Choices: An Introduction to Ethics,* 4th ed. Grand Rapids: Zondervan, 2018.

9

ORGAN TRANSPLANTATION

Synopsis: Our three friends are prompted to consider the ethics of organ transplantation after encountering organ donation advocates at the college health fair. This prompts Bianca to share with her friends her concern that her cousin, who lives abroad, is considering selling one of his kidneys.

* * *

Bianca, Lauren, and Micah were just walking out of Dr. Platt's lecture on medical ethics when they noticed some booths being set up on the campus quad. As they approached, a banner was being stretched between two light poles in a rather precarious fashion. Beneath one pole a very short girl stood on tiptoes on a chair and held onto one end of the banner while an ambitious male student shimmied up the second pole, grasping the other end of the banner. When the two students finally had everything in place, the banner was pulled taut, displaying the words "Health Fair" emblazoned in bright green.

"Ooh," said Micah, "I wonder if any of the booths will shed light on that bewildering lecture we just heard."

"What do you mean, bewildering? replied Bianca.

"Are you kidding me?" Lauren shot back. "There was so much involved I could hardly keep up. Genetic engineering, reproductive technology, insurance coverage, do-not-resuscitate orders—it was a lot to take in."

"Maybe it's because I have a cousin who is a doctor and an aunt who is a nurse," said Bianca. "We discuss health care issues all the time. I have heard at least a little bit about most of what Dr. Platt was saying."

Just then they approached a booth that was already set up. A man and woman were standing in front of the booth, ready to talk with students, and a display featured enlarged pictures of a driver's license and of a smiling kidney.

"Hi there," the woman said cheerfully. "Have you designated yourselves as organ donors on your driver's license?"

The three looked at each other in curiosity. "That's a good question," said Micah, reaching for his wallet.

"I have," piped Lauren quickly.

"Um, no," said Bianca somewhat reluctantly, looking sideways.

Micah looked at his wallet, then looked up and asked the woman, "How would I know?"

Lauren rolled her eyes. "How could you not know, Micah?" She snatched his license out of his hand and scanned it. "Nope, you're not a donor," she said to him with a slight smirk.

The woman introduced herself as Julia and her companion as Kevin. "We are not here to pressure you, but to educate people about the opportunity to save the lives of others."

Micah liked the sound of that. "Sign me up," he said to the woman.

"Well, dear, why don't you read this pamphlet about organ donation before you make the choice. You should understand what you're volunteering for before making the commitment."

"Like 'informed consent'?" asked Lauren. "We learned a little about that in our ethics class today. One of the foundational principles of medical ethics is making sure that patients are fully informed of the nature of a procedure without coercion, understand the risks and implications, and are in a state to make a decision."

"Yes!" said the woman, brightening. "That's exactly right. There is a lot involved in organ transplantation, and you should only designate yourself a donor if you fully understand to what you are committing."

"Okay, I'll read it, but I know I want to donate all my organs if I die," concluded Micah.

"That's great," said Kevin, speaking for the first time. "There are so many lives that can be saved by organ donation, and we believe that if more people were better informed, then the number of donors would rise."

Lauren noticed that Bianca hadn't said anything for a while. "You're pretty quiet, Bianca. Aren't you interested in becoming a donor?"

Bianca looked up tentatively and cleared her throat. "I'm not sure. It scares me. What if I wasn't dying but they tried to take my organs anyway? What if I could be revived but someone important needed my heart or lungs?"

Micah's mouth dropped open. "They wouldn't do that, would they?" he asked, whirling around to look at Julia. "They *couldn't* do that, could they? We just came from a lecture on medical ethics, but the professor never said anything about this."

Julia moved closer to Bianca. "Honey, that's not how it works. Very strict guidelines stipulate when and how organs are harvested from donors. The primary concern of doctors is to save a patient's life, not to give away her organs."

Kevin spoke again. "Why don't you three take some literature and our contact numbers and research this topic before you decide? Maybe your professor would even count it as a class assignment."

The three looked at each other and could instantly see that this would be a project that would keep them interested. They decided to speak with Dr. Platt after the next ethics class and ask him to give them credit for their research. They thanked Julia and Kevin and parted ways after making plans to get together at The Grey Earl that weekend to work on their strategy.

Saturday morning at ten found the three sitting together over hot drinks with their laptops churning out search results. Dr. Platt had approved the project and seemed genuinely interested in the topic. To help them get started, he encouraged them to focus on two of the most significant ethical issues surrounding organ transplantation—procurement and allocation.

"Just to clarify," said Micah, "procurement is . . . what?"

Lauren responded, "Organ procurement is the process of finding and obtaining organs for transplant."

Bianca jumped in, "And allocation is about the criteria or process of deciding who gets the organs."

"OK, then let's get started," said Micah.

Pretty soon the sounds of the three researching filled the air.

"It says here that the primary ethical challenge in organ transplantation is the shortage of organs," remarked Bianca. "If enough organs were available for everyone who needed them, there wouldn't be much of an ethical dilemma. The United Network for Organ Sharing (UNOS) website says that about 114,000 people in the United States are waiting for an organ—60 percent for kidneys, 20 percent for livers, and the rest for about ten other organs or tissues."[1]

Not looking up from her computer, Lauren remarked, "In some countries people can sell their organs, but in most countries, it isn't allowed. They must be talking about kidneys and the lobe of your liver, because other organs can't be donated until after death. Why can't people sell their organs?"

Organ	Average Wait Time[2]	Number of Transplants in 2019[3]	Number of People on the Waiting List[4]
Kidney	5 years	23,401	94,400
Liver	11 months	8,896	12,681
Heart	4 months	3,552	3,577
Lung	4 months	2,714	1,200
Pancreas	2 years	143	882
Kidney-Pancreas	1.5 years	872	1,767
Intestine	No information	81	246

1. https://unos.org.
2. https://www.donors1.org/patients/resources-for-transplant-patients/the-waiting-list.
3. https://www.organdonor.gov/statistics-stories/statistics.html.
4. As of May 13, 2020. The Organ Procurement and Transplantation Network (OPTN) updates these figures daily at https://optn.transplant.hrsa.gov/data.

"I think they ought to be able to," said Bianca casually. "My cousin lives overseas, and while it is not legal, he is planning to sell a kidney to be able to afford to go to college."

Micah and Lauren looked up from their laptops and stared at Bianca with their mouths open. "Are you serious?" asked Lauren.

"Yes, I am," said Bianca somewhat defensively. "Why, do you think that's wrong?"

"I don't know," replied Lauren. "I never thought about it before. How much will he get for his kidney?"

"He is not sure yet, but they told him that it could be anywhere from $3000 to $10,000. The kidneys are a redundant system in the body, so you only need one. That's why people can donate a kidney, because if one is removed, it just does the job that both kidneys shared before."

"Isn't that dangerous?" Micah finally rejoined the conversation. "I mean surgery always carries risks. And who is the 'they' your cousin is talking to? Are they doctors? Will he have this surgery at a hospital, and how can he if the procedure is not legal? Does he sign a contract? Will he get proper medical care after surgery?" Micah had a hundred questions.

"I don't know, Micah. Now that you ask those questions, I realize I hadn't thought about the details."

"Why don't we research this for the next hour and see what we find," suggested Lauren.

The others thought that was a good idea, so they each began to search the topic of buying and selling human organs. When they began to talk about their findings, they came to realize that the issue required a moral framework to make sense. They decided to run the issue through the grid of the various theories they had been discussing.

"From a Utilitarian perspective, selling your organs might be a good idea because it could conceivably solve the problem of people waiting for organs." Micah began the discussion. "Twenty people die every day in the US, waiting for an organ. That's more than seven thousand people a year."

"Wow," said Bianca, "I had no idea it was so many. Just think what would happen if people in the US were allowed to sell their organs. It would be good for everybody."

"It sounds like a good idea for a number of reasons," returned Lauren, "but my research shows that such a practice tends to exploit the poor. The rich won't take the risk of surgery because they don't need the money. Poor people, however, may see organ donation as a path out of poverty, or they may be in a desperate situation and feel they have no other choice."

"Hey look what I found!" exclaimed Micah. He pointed out two documentaries on the international organ market: *Tales from the Organ Trade*[5] and *Human Harvest*.[6] "Before we go any further, let's watch these documentaries. I need to leave soon anyway, so we could watch them in our spare time over the weekend and talk about them next week. They both seem to address critical ethical issues surrounding procurement and allocation."

Bianca and Lauren agreed, as it was getting late, and they determined to pick up the discussion the following week.

***

The next week in class Dr. Platt finished his lecture on genetic engineering early and asked if there were any questions on the topic. Crickets. So he asked if there were any questions on medical ethics in general. Bianca raised her hand and Lauren noticed that her face was a bit ashen.

"Dr. Platt, our group has been researching organ transplantation, and over the weekend I watched the documentary *Tales from the Organ Trade.* It showed how the poor are exploited in many places around the world by organ brokers who promise them significant money for a kidney, but then charge them for the surgery and post-op care. Sometimes the person walks away with only a few hundred dollars and the results of substandard care." Her voice trembled. "Does this really happen?"

Dr. Platt noticed the look on Bianca's face and spoke in a kind tone. "Yes, I saw that video too. The men of a whole village were exploited by a smooth-talking organ broker, and almost none of them attained a better life from their donation. The brokers turn around and sell these organs for tens of thousands and even hundreds of thousands of dollars to wealthy people.

---

5.   https://www.talesfromtheorgantrade.com.
6.   https://www.humanharvestmovie.com.

This is one of the major concerns of organ procurement—how to ethically obtain organs for those who need them."

The bell rang in the classroom to signal the end of the hour. Lauren approached Bianca.

"You were thinking of your cousin, weren't you?"

"Yes," she replied with a lump in her throat. "I don't think he knows that this kind of thing happens. Fortunately, he hasn't done it yet, but I need to talk to him."

Micah joined them. He looked at Lauren to get her take on the situation.

Lauren turned to Bianca and asked, "Is it too much to meet today? Do you want to take a break for a few days?"

Bianca shook her head and gathered herself. She looked up and smiled bravely. "No, I want to keep at it. The more I learn, the better equipped I feel to talk to my cousin. Let's meet in half an hour."

***

That afternoon, the three resumed their discussion at The Grey Earl.

"Obviously, Utilitarianism doesn't provide enough guidance for the procurement of organs," Micah stated. "The greatest good would probably allow for organs to be sold for the good that they would do, but that leaves individuals, especially the poor, in a vulnerable position because they are probably the only ones who would be motivated by gaining money."

"And when the poor are exploited in this way, it sounds like organ traffickers are following Ethical Egoism. They obviously don't care about these people, only the profit that they make from them," Lauren added.

"Wouldn't those who knowingly receive organs that were donated by the poor by economic coercion also exhibit Ethical Egoism?" Bianca asked.

"Ooh, I didn't think of that," replied Lauren, "but yeah. How could people live with themselves knowing that the organs they received were taken from people who were poor and powerless and possibly paid next to nothing? You would have to have a cold, icy heart to do that."

"I imagine that organ traffickers and brokers probably hide the origin of the organs," suggested Bianca. "I also watched the documentary on the organ trade in China, *Human Harvest*. China has been under investigation for years for their practice of selling the organs of prisoners against their will. They interviewed some people who felt bad once they were informed that they had received organs that had been stolen from prisoners. But surprisingly, some said they would do it again despite that fact. That seems like Ethical Egoism at its finest."

Lauren grimaced. "Ugh, the thought of some of this stuff is almost too much to bear. I never knew this kind of thing happened. Now I'm glad that the US doesn't allow people to get paid for their organs."

"Wait," interjected Micah. "Does a person who donates her kidney have to pay for the medical costs of the surgery? How does a person who wants to be a live donor afford it?"

"No, Micah," replied Lauren. "I read that in a live donation the recipient's insurance pays for both surgeries and all the medical testing. It even pays for the donor's travel expenses to and from the hospital, meals on the road, follow-up visits, and any other expenses."

"Remind me again what you mean by live donor," Micah requested.

"A live donor is someone who donates a kidney or part of her liver to someone else while alive and healthy. Her liver will grow back, and her body can function on just one kidney. A cadaver kidney or liver is one given by someone who has died. A donation after death has a whole other set of ethical issues."

"Guys, we are getting off the topic of ethical theories," reminded Bianca. "Let's explore that more before we get into other ethical issues related to procurement."

"What about Kantian duty?" suggested Micah. "Is it the duty of every person to be an organ donor? Shouldn't more people donate a kidney or liver lobe while alive if they can live without them? It seems that the Kantian ethic would erase a waiting list for organs if people took it more seriously."

"That sounds ideal, but other duties might conflict with that one." Bianca's mind was racing through the possibilities. "For example, even though transplant surgeries are 95 to 98 percent safe for donors, there are still risks because it's surgery. Think of all the situations in life where the risk may be too high."

"Like what?" asked Micah.

"Well, think about anyone who has children. If anything should go wrong in surgery, those children may not be cared for. Or anyone who cannot get paid time off of work. They could lose their job or go without a paycheck for a few months."

"Are you saying that donors don't automatically get time off work? And they don't get reimbursed for the pay they miss for not working?"

"No they don't—unless their employer is particularly gracious. Remember, donors in the US can't receive any compensation beyond medical care and travel expenses. Donors typically require two to three months to recover, and some take longer. This is one of the factors that keeps people from donating."

Lauren posed a question: "What would it hurt if live donors were reimbursed for verified time missed from work so they could at least take the time off and not miss their pay?"

They all agreed that this sounded like a reasonable idea. Such a policy would not be the same as paying someone for the organ and might increase the number of people willing to act as donors.

"But think about how much bureaucracy would be required to track and verify all that information," Lauren interjected. "That would add considerably to the cost of a transplant."

"How much does a kidney transplant cost right now?" asked Bianca.

"The cost is around $400,000,"[7] Lauren replied.

Micah gave a low whistle. "Wow, I did not expect it to be that high."

They paused. "I need more tea and some fresh air," said Lauren. "Let's take a short break. But when we return let's talk about some of the rules about who can and cannot donate. There must be some ethical issues related to that."

They all agreed to reconvene in fifteen minutes. Bianca walked outside with her phone and began to text.

***

When they gathered again and were ready to resume their work, Bianca seemed especially cheerful. "I texted my cousin during our break and shared

---

7. T. Scott Bentley and Nick J. Ortner, "2020 U.S. Organ and Tissue Transplants: Cost Estimates, Discussion, and Emerging Issues," *Milliman Research Report*, https://milli-man-cdn.azureedge.net/-/media/milliman/pdfs/articles/2020-us-organ-tissue-trans-plants.ashx.

some concerns with him based on what we have been learning. He was glad I contacted him because he had been looking further into selling one of his kidneys and was getting an unsettled feeling from the agents. They were putting pressure on him and wouldn't provide any details. They kept telling him that they would explain everything when he arrived for the surgery. He wasn't sure if his hesitation was just his own nerves, but while we were talking, he realized that he had good reason to be suspicious. Then he confessed that he hadn't even told my aunt about his plans yet. I begged him not to go any further with this plan because it could be very dangerous. He promised that he would not move forward unless he could get more information and until he confided in his older brother. That way if he proceeded with his plan, he would at least have someone to drive him to the airport."

"Drive him?" asked Micah with a puzzled look. "How old is your cousin, anyway?"

"Fifteen," answered Bianca.

"Fifteen?" exclaimed Lauren. "I thought we were talking about an adult!"

"Now you know why I was so concerned about him."

"Can teenagers donate organs in the United States?" queried Micah.

"I don't know. Let's look it up," replied Lauren.

Within minutes they had their answer. "Legal minors are not allowed to donate organs," Bianca informed them. "You have to be at least eighteen and have passed rigorous physical and mental health examinations."

"Why a mental health exam?" wondered Lauren.

"Well think about it," Micah said, summarizing what he was reading on his laptop. "If people do not have the cognitive ability to make intelligent decisions, they can be easily manipulated into donating without realizing to what they are committing. Or if they are donating for a motive that is less than noble, it wouldn't be a good idea."

"What do you mean?" asked Bianca.

"Well, what if someone donates because he wants the recipient to be indebted to him for the rest of her life—a kind of 'now you owe me' mentality? That would be very unhealthy. Or maybe the potential donor is seeking the admiration and praise of other people. That doesn't seem like a healthy situation, either."

"Aha!" exclaimed Lauren. "I found it. I knew that I had heard of people donating organs when they were younger than eighteen. It seems that in

California teenagers as young as fifteen can donate in some cases with the consent of a parent or guardian. But generally minors are not allowed to donate because they cannot legally consent, due to their inability to fully understand the issue and the implications of it."

"What parent would do that, though?" asked Micah.

"It says here that sometimes when an adolescent needs an organ, like a kidney or liver, the best matches come from siblings because they have a higher chance of being a match, and they may be of similar size, which makes the organ fit better. In a couple of rare cases, children as young as toddlers have provided a kidney for a twin, since they were such good matches." Lauren shared this information while experiencing a sense of amazement about all that they were learning.

"Isn't that a case of Situation Ethics?" asked Bianca. "How can a child consent to that kind of surgery? It seems that the hospital or doctors or whoever is in charge is bending the rules because of the situation."

"Well, Situation Ethics does place love as the highest good, and who wouldn't want to save the life of a sibling, even as a child?" Lauren's question resonated with them, but they also felt a little uneasy.

Bianca pushed back a bit. "There's still the issue of consent. What if the child felt pressured by her family to give an organ, even though she was scared to do it? Would she be able to say no or change her mind on the day of the surgery? How would the principle of love in Situation Ethics provide any guidance in such a context?"

Micah had been reading about informed consent and privacy while the girls talked. "There are very strict guidelines about privacy and patients' rights when it comes to transplants. A hospital will not inform the recipient of the identity of the donor. The donor has to do that himself if he wants. The hospital also sequesters potential family donors for a time of questioning to make sure that the potential donor is not being coerced. The potential donor has the right up until the moment of surgery to change his mind, and the hospital will cover for him by telling the recipient that the donor became ineligible for the surgery. So it looks like quite a few protections have been established for potential donors."

Micah continued. "And then there is the issue of informed consent. The hospital must fully explain all the risks of the surgery, both physical and emotional, so the potential donor can make his decision without being manipulated or coerced in any way."

"That's what concerns me about minors donating," Bianca interjected. "How *can* they give consent, even for donating to a sibling?"

"But Bianca, think of how sad you would be if you lost a brother or sister when you were young and then later discovered that you could have saved her life if you had been allowed to donate an organ." Lauren proposed this scenario in a way that made them all stop and think.

"That would be awful," whispered Bianca. "But still, do we just throw away the issue of consent in certain cases, but not in others?"

"My brain hurts," said Micah with a long sigh. "We haven't even touched on donations by people who have died or the issue of allocation."

Lauren gasped, "You're right, Micah. We're not even halfway there. Maybe we ought to jump right to allocation before we run out of time. This is a far more complex issue than I ever imagined."

The three decided to call it quits and reconvene another day. They agreed that they needed time to think about what they had learned already before moving on to the question of who should get organs in the donation process.

***

When the friends next saw each other, it was in Dr. Platt's class the following week. Bianca arrived early and began chatting with the professor about what they had discovered. He became so engrossed in their discoveries that he didn't notice the room fill up and the class hour begin. Finally, he saw that all the students were in their seats and were straining to hear his conversation with Bianca.

"Welcome, everybody. Since we have a lighter lecture today, let's start by discussing an ethical issue that not many people have considered before but that is becoming increasingly complex and important. Bianca, can you give us a quick summary of some of the ethical dilemmas surrounding organ transplantation?"

Bianca looked at Lauren and Micah to see if they wanted to join her in front of the class, but their facial expressions encouraged her to take the lead.

"My interest in this is somewhat personal," Bianca began. "I have a family member in another country who is—was—considering selling one of his kidneys to earn money for college."

"We can do that?" Zach spoke up in a light-hearted manner. "That means that I could make my first student loan payment!" Everybody laughed, even Dr. Platt.

Bianca took it in stride and kept going. She quickly reviewed the various ethical dilemmas surrounding the procurement of organs, and the more she explained, the more the rest of the class was drawn into the topic.

When she was finished, Dr. Platt thanked her for her summary and turned to the class. "As you can see, obtaining enough organs for the need out there is difficult enough, but what principles should guide the allocation of those organs to those who need them?"

Megan raised her hand quickly. "Dr. Platt, since many of us probably don't know anything about how organs are distributed, can you give us a general idea of how this works in the US, so we know which questions to ask?"

"Good thinking," replied the professor. "Bianca, does your group have any information that would get us started?"

Micah raised his hand. "I can share the general procedures. When a patient falls below a certain threshold of health, her doctor will perform several blood tests to determine blood type and tissue type among other tests to determine her compatibility with a donor. She is placed on the waiting list and gets in line behind others who need the same type. When an organ that matches that type becomes available, the person who has been on the list the longest is given first consideration. But the donated organ has to be a compatible size to the recipient. For example, a petite woman could not donate a kidney to a large man because it would not be able to perform the filtering function that he would need with his body size.

"Also, when the organ comes available, the potential recipient must be able to get to the hospital within a few hours or the organ will become unusable. If a potential donor happens to have a fever or even a cold, that also renders the organ unusable. Anything that hinders the transplantation for the person at the top of the list means that the next person on the list is contacted. So staying healthy and in the region where she is registered is critical for someone waiting for an organ."

"Thank you, Micah," said Dr. Platt. "So, class, what are some potential ethical issues that arise in regard to allocation"—several hands shot up—"and what ethical principles would guide us as we seek a resolution to the dilemma?"

Several hands went down, but Diego's remained up. "Do doctors ever give organs to people based on their importance? It seems that if a member of Congress or the governor of a state needs an organ they should be given preference over someone whose job was less important. What if a prisoner is next in line? Would he get an organ before the governor of his own state?"

"Wait, prisoners get organ transplants too?" Megan was stunned.

"Yes, they sometimes do get transplants," answered Dr. Platt. "Just because someone is in prison doesn't mean that they are not given adequate medical care."

"The answer to your question, Diego, is that no one is supposed to be able to move up the waiting list for any reason. In the medical community right now, however, there is discussion about that rule." Bianca was glad that she had discovered these facts during her research.

Dr. Platt reminded the class, "Don't forget to address the ethical systems in these comments. What system would guide the principle regarding waiting your turn on the transplant list?"

Diego responded, "Utilitarianism would prioritize the greatest good and rank people according to their importance, I would think. What is good for the greatest number of people would be prioritizing the health of the people who contribute the most to society, so they should get an organ sooner. That sounds cold, but if a janitor or cashier dies for lack of a transplant, that would have very little impact compared to a political leader or a researcher on the verge of a breakthrough. Would it be worth losing a brilliant scientist who is working on a cure for cancer so a janitor could live?"

Everyone sat silently, wrestling with the picture Diego had painted.

Micah spoke up. "But who would decide the value of a person? An elected leader? A council of medical personnel? That would be impossible to determine. And think about how that would relativize the value of human life. We would be right back to the world before Christianity arose, when every person's value was dependent on their social status at birth. It was Christianity that spread the idea that every person possessed inherent dignity and rights simply because they are created in God's image."

"Hmph," grunted Scott, who was an agnostic. "Where did you get that idea from?"

Micah responded quickly. "Luc Ferry, the French atheistic philosopher, makes that claim."[8]

Dr. Platt stepped in. "Micah is correct. Many philosophers acknowledge this fact about the impact of Christianity. But back to the issue at hand."

Alisha got the class back on track. "I would think that any favoritism would create problems for the public's confidence in the transplant enterprise. If the public lost faith in the integrity of allocation guidelines, it might significantly affect the number of people willing to donate."

"You're right about that, Alisha." Bianca shuffled some papers on her lap before pulling out one sheet and holding it up. "This is an article in the UK *Guardian* newspaper from 2013 that reports a massive fraud in Germany where doctors falsified medical records to move their patients up the waiting list. The motive seems to have been to increase the prestige of certain hospitals because the more transplants they performed, the higher their ratings rose. The result was a 20 to 40 percent decline in Germans registering to be donors."[9]

"Didn't Steve Jobs do something similar?" asked Diego, referring to the founder of Apple computers.

Dr. Platt answered. "Yes and no. There was no falsification of records, but because he had the resources, he was able to register in multiple transplant regions and therefore get his name on multiple waiting lists. California, where he lived, had a waiting period for a liver of a few years, but he registered in Tennessee where the waiting list was a few months. He was able to get a liver faster because he had the financial resources. That raises the question of whether wealthy people should be able to do things like that. Should anyone have an advantage over anyone else when it comes to their position on the waiting list?"

While other students contemplated these issues, Alisha spoke. "What Steve Jobs did sounds like Ethical Egoism to me," she said. "He essentially put himself first and was able to skip the line. If everyone acted that way, the rich would win and the poor would lose. That would bring us right back to the

8. Luc Ferry, *A Brief History of Thought* (New York: Harper, 2011).
9. https://www.theguardian.com/world/2013/jan/09/mass-donor-organ-fraud-germany.

inequality of society where a person's value would be practically determined by his wealth or power."

Ralph spoke up, which surprised everyone because he rarely said anything in class. "How is that any different from other ways people try to get an organ faster by finding a live donor. I have seen billboards, yard signs, and Facebook campaigns for people looking for a donor."

"I heard of three sisters who found a kidney for their father on Craigslist!"[10] said Alisha excitedly. "I had no idea people did things like that."

Micah responded, "Yes, but they didn't buy those organs. They were trying to appeal to the goodness of humanity. Many times, the people that respond to these advertisements and public pleas are strangers. This could be an example of Virtue Ethics, couldn't it, Dr. Platt?"

"How so, Micah?" Dr. Platt wanted to force the class to think.

Micah closed his eyes to aid his concentration. "Such attempts don't appeal to duty, so they don't fall into the category of Duty Ethics, and there is no focus on the most good for the most people. It seems that these actions appeal to certain individuals who have a strong sense of kindness and sacrifice for others, even strangers. They donate a kidney or part of their liver because the habits of their life are rooted in giving to others. They often explain that they couldn't sit by when they had a perfectly good organ they weren't using while someone else suffers needlessly."

"I think you are on to something, Micah," said Dr. Platt.

Micah opened his eyes, relieved that he hadn't embarrassed himself in front of the class.

Dr. Platt glanced at the clock. The brief discussion he had expected had blossomed into a discussion that had taken almost the entire hour. "We only have a few more minutes, but are there other ethical issues related to allocation of organs that we should discuss?"

Lauren addressed Bianca. "Why don't you ask Dr. Platt about the issue you mentioned to Julia at the Health Fair?"

As soon as the words came out of Lauren's mouth, she wished she hadn't said them. She didn't know how Bianca would respond, since at the time it was a very personal question for her friend.

---

10.   https://www.health.com/health/article/0,,20411621,00.html.

But Bianca had become emboldened by her research. "Good idea! Dr. Platt, in the case of organ donation by someone who has died, how do they know when a person is truly dead? If the person is already in the hospital and is dying, how do they determine death? Do the doctors who are going to harvest the organs determine that? Are they in the room waiting? How do they know when to start? If organs only have a short window of time where they are viable for transplant, would the medical team keep them alive just to buy more time for a recipient to get to the hospital? Would the medical team ever hasten death to get organs into a very sick person needing a transplant?"

Bianca's questions trailed off as the bell rang and the class began to gather up their notebooks and coffee cups. Micah and Lauren moved up to Bianca's side as the disappointment spread across her face.

Dr. Platt smiled broadly at the three and said with a twinkle in his eye, "It looks like you three are going to be working on this topic for a long time!"

They looked at each other and smiled. Bianca spoke first, "Anyone up for some tea?"

QUESTIONS TO PONDER

- What are the primary ethical issues surrounding the procurement of organs? Can you think of other potential ethical issues or dilemmas?

- Does any particular ethical theory help solve the ethical dilemmas of procurement and allocation?

- What are the pros and cons of allowing people to buy and sell organs? What are the limits of compensation a donor ought to be entitled to when he gives an organ?

- Do any biblical principles guide the procurement and allocation of organs?

- Have you designated yourself as an organ donor in your state? Why or why not? Should people have to choose to be a donor, or should that be automatic when you get your license, so that someone who doesn't want to be a donor has to decline the choice (presumed consent)?

TERMS TO KNOW

- Procurement
- Allocation
- UNOS
- Cadaver kidney
- Live donor
- Utilitarianism
- Duty Ethics
- Situation Ethics
- Ethical Egoism
- Virtue Ethics

FOR FURTHER READING

Caplan, Arthur L., James J. McCartney, and Daniel P. Reid. *Replacement Parts: The Ethics of Procuring and Replacing Organs in Humans.* Washington, DC: Georgetown University Press, 2015.

Jensen, Steven J. *The Ethics of Organ Transplantation.* Washington, DC: Catholic University of America Press, 2011.

Sharp, Lesley. *The Transplant Imaginary.* Berkeley: University of California Press, 2014.

Thobaben, James. *Health Care Ethics.* Downers Grove, IL: InterVarsity Press, 2009.

Documentaries:

Human Harvest: https://www.humanharvestmovie.com
Tales from the Organ Trade: https://www.talesfromtheorgantrade.com

REPRODUCTIVE TECHNOLOGY/HUMAN CLONING

Synopsis: Lauren is excited about all she has learned in Health Ethics class in her nursing program. She wants to share it with Micah and Bianca because she has some concerns about the advances in reproductive technology and genetic engineering. Based on their other discussions she knows that there may be some underlying ethical concerns that are overshadowed by the push for progress. The three friends meet at The Grey Earl on a gray morning.

* * *

"So, what is all the excitement?" Micah and Bianca were eager to hear what had gotten Lauren so motivated for yet another ethics discussion.

"My Health Ethics class, that's what!" Lauren knew they were teasing her with feigned overexcitement, but she was too fascinated by what she was learning to care. "This week in class we began to look at bioethics and all the amazing discoveries and advancements going on in medical technology. It's really quite breathtaking," she concluded loudly in a mock English accent.

Micah and Bianca laughed at her outburst as people seated around them glanced curiously in their direction.

"Seriously, though," she continued, "the whole field of bioethics for someone like me is a nerd's paradise. You would not believe the kinds of things that can be done these days!"

"Tell us," said Bianca, growing more interested by the minute. Lauren loved her nursing program, but this enthusiasm was beyond her norm.

"Take DNA for example. Since the Human Genome Project finished mapping the gene in 2001 or so, scientists increasingly have been able to see how genetics are related to certain diseases. Sometimes there are direct, causal links between genes and diseases like cystic fibrosis, sickle-cell anemia, Huntington's disease, and Down Syndrome. In that case, if a person has the gene, he will definitely get the disease. This increased understanding of genetics will someday allow earlier treatment and a better prognosis."

"What do you mean, 'someday'?" asked Micah.

"Well, the ability to identify if someone has a disease is way ahead of being able to treat the disease at this point," answered Lauren.

"Wow, I am not sure I would want to live with the knowledge that I was going to get a serious disease years before there was any treatment," mused Bianca. "That would likely cast a shadow over my life."

"Hmm," mused Lauren. "I never thought about it that way. When I heard this, I assumed it would necessarily be a good thing, but maybe not."

"Anyway, continue," encouraged Bianca.

"Even more, DNA informs us of *predispositions* to many diseases, including heart disease, cancers, and diabetes. Being predisposed doesn't mean that you will necessarily develop the disease, but it does allow you to change your lifestyle to reduce the chances of getting it."

"I've heard about this." Bianca's interest was beginning to match Lauren's. "I have a friend whose mom and aunt both had breast cancer and tested positive for the mutation that increases a woman's chance to have that cancer. She got tested and has the mutation too, and now she is wondering if she should have a mastectomy in her twenties so she doesn't get breast cancer."

"Yes, that is one of the biggest ethical questions related to genetic screening," agreed Lauren. "How far do we go to forestall diseases to which we may be predisposed, and at what point does that become a surrender to fear and extreme measures that may not be necessary?"

Micah let out a low whistle. "This is heavy stuff. I'm glad to be too young right now to think about it. What part of all this were you excited about, Lauren?" He made a face to show he was trying to understand but was pained by the implications.

"Certainly there are many serious aspects to genetic engineering and biotechnology, but there are inspiring aspects also. For example, *gene editing* technologies, such as CRISPR, snip DNA at precise points in order to modify or insert genes. This opens up new possibilities for treating diseases caused by genetic mutation, creating cheaper diagnostic tests, and hopefully engineering cells to kill cancer."[1]

"Now we're talking," said Micah. "That sounds amazing."

"One aspect of biotechnology I am especially interested in is reproductive technology," said Bianca. "I have a cousin who's been trying to get pregnant for years and hasn't been able to. But I do have some concerns about the advances in this field. It seems that all kinds of things can be done to help a woman have a baby as long as no one minds that embryos are destroyed in the process. Surrogacy is intriguing, but I wonder about some of the things that can go wrong there too."

"You're going to have to explain more about that," said Micah. "I have a general idea of in vitro fertilization and surrogate mothers, but I don't quite understand the details."

"You've come to the right place then," said Lauren, happy to put her growing medical knowledge to use once more.

"First, let's start with in vitro fertilization or IVF. It can happen several ways. In *intrauterine insemination*, a woman's egg is fertilized with her husband's sperm artificially in conjunction with powerful fertility drugs. This creates a better chance for conception. At other times this is done with donor sperm when the man's sperm is incapable of facilitating conception. The fertility drugs cause a woman to hyperovulate, producing many eggs instead of just one. In the usual scenario, a physician will implant between one and three embryos into the woman's uterus in hopes of a successful pregnancy."

---

1. Ellie Kincaid and Michela Tindera, "Gene Hackers," *Forbes*, May 31, 2019, 34. CRISPR stands for "clustered regularly interspaced short palindromic repeats."

"This is where I have a question," interrupted Bianca. "Don't they typically test and screen the embryos, looking for the best ones?"

"Yes, because IVF can cost between $10,000 and $15,000, all measures are taken to implant embryos that are optimal. That would mean screening out those with genetic defects. The embryos are graded according to their likelihood of successfully implanting, from low grade to high grade." Lauren stopped to make sure the others were still listening.

"Concern for the likelihood of implanting in the uterus is understand-able," said Bianca. "What concerns me is the potential that genetic screening could lead to designer babies. Physicians could list the genetic features of each embryo and allow the parents to pick the child they most desired. This comes dangerously close to the ideals of the eugenics movement in the early twentieth century. In a history class I took, they talked about contests held in the 1920s and 1930s for what they called Fitter Families, who were praised for fewer instances of physical disabilities. The whole eugenics movement had a goal of 'better humans through breeding.'[2] Imagine what we could do now."

"That sounds like a sci-fi movie or a dystopian novel," interjected Micah. "I have seen several movies where that kind of thing happens, and it never ends well. Can you imagine if we lived in a world where some people were designed to have certain attributes and other people were born in the old-fashioned, natural way? That could easily result in a class distinction that would favor the designed. That kind of thing is already happening on campus with people who enhance their cognitive abilities with certain medications."

Lauren and Bianca stared at Micah.

He continued. "What, are you unaware of people that use ADHD medications like Adderall and Ritalin so they can concentrate for excessive amounts of time or forego the need to sleep? And what about athletes that enhance their performance with human growth hormones or painkillers? I could go on, but the question remains: How far will we go to enhance humanity?"

"I am impressed, Micah," said Bianca with genuine admiration.

---

2. Charles W. Colson and Nigel M. de S. Cameron, eds., *Human Dignity in the Biotech Century* (Downers Grove, IL: InterVarsity Press, 2004), 68–69. See also http://www. eugenicsarchive.org/eugenics/list3.pl.

"Well, I have thought quite a bit about the ethics of enhancement ever since a friend told me his secret for testing so well." Micah grimaced. "He offered me what he was taking, but I just couldn't go down that road."

"Good for you," said Lauren, meaning it. "But I think we have strayed far from the topic of reproductive technology. Your ethical concern is duly noted, however, Bianca. The important point is that couples who cannot have children any other way are often helped by IVF."

"I can only imagine the joy that a couple feels when IVF is successful," said Bianca. "I have heard of other concerns about IVF, however. For example, if all the embryos implant in the uterus, what happens if the couple only wants one baby, instead of twins or triplets? And what happens to the embryos that are not implanted? Are they destroyed, or do they remain frozen indefinitely?"

"That is where you and I differ," observed Lauren, remembering their previous discussion about abortion and their disagreement about when an embryo becomes a baby deserving of the rights of personhood. "For me, destroying or keeping embryos is not a problem, but for you, IVF becomes a real ethical landmine."

"It certainly does," agreed Bianca. "I believe the embryo is a person, so destroying it would not be an option, nor would keeping it permanently frozen. If I was going to have IVF, I would feel the need to bring to term all the embryos I had fertilized."

"That would not be very realistic," countered Lauren. "The cost of IVF is already so high, and if you only implanted one or two embryos at a time, the cost would rise. Also, if you did not fertilize a maximum number of eggs, usually two to three, you might not get any embryos and you would have to pay the entire fee again to start over. That is why physicians like to get as many eggs from the fertility drugs as possible. It's a numbers game."

"How successful is IVF anyway?" asked Micah.

"Success depends largely on the age of the woman," answered Lauren as she pulled her Health Ethics notes from her bag. "Many factors are involved, depending on whether you count implantations or only live births, the method of IVF used, single or multiple-infant births, and more. IVF is more successful when women are younger, but the younger a woman is, the more fertile she is, and so younger women don't need IVF as often. As a result, the majority of women trying IVF are over thirty years old. Once a woman reaches forty, her chance of having a live birth from IVF is only 10 to 15 percent."[3]

"Wow, those are interesting statistics," said Micah with wonder. "So the younger a couple is seeking IVF, the better chance they have to conceive a baby and carry it to term. Even then it sounds like it is not a guarantee."

"No, certainly not," agreed Lauren.

"I have some questions similar to Bianca's," continued Micah. "What happens to the embryos that are left unused if a couple doesn't want any more babies? Do they remain frozen forever? How long can they remain frozen and still produce a live birth when thawed? How much does it cost to keep them frozen? Does the couple own them, or do they sign over rights to the clinic that keeps them frozen? What if the couple separates or divorces? Whose are they then? What if one of the couple wants to bring the embryos to term and the other doesn't? What if the man dies and his parents want to use the embryo to have grandchildren with a surrogate?"

Micah looked up to see the surprise in Lauren and Bianca's eyes as he peppered them with questions. "I could go on," he said with a smile. "My fertile mind is like a machine." He tapped the side of his head like he was a genius.

Lauren and Bianca laughed.

"You do have a fertile mind," agreed Lauren, "maybe too fertile."

"You have a point, though," chimed in Bianca. "Those are all questions with real consequences. This is why I am not against IVF per se, but the complications that can arise are serious and have implications that many people don't consider, I'm afraid."

"All joking aside," said Micah, "I agree. I read an article where these types of scenarios were considered and in some cases reflected real situations. As much as I am for progress and using technology and medicine to benefit people, when human embryos are involved, I can't ignore the realities."

"But think of the benefits," countered Lauren. "Isn't it a good thing that conception is happening? With all the emphasis on family and children in the Bible, I would think that technology used to bring that about would be appreciated."

---

3. Figures from the 2016 Assisted Reproductive Technology National Summary Report of the Centers for Disease Control, https://www.cdc.gov/art/pdf/2016-national-summary-slides/art_2016_graphs_and_charts.pdf#page=6.

"Christians do greatly value children," agreed Micah, "but you are presenting a consequentialist ethic that places the value of the few IVF embryos resulting in live births over the many that are destroyed or left frozen. It goes back to the inherent personhood of the fetus from conception. To add to that concern is the question of surrogate mothers. Although I don't know all the details of how that works, I do know there are at least legal concerns when one woman bears another woman's baby."

"Oh, Micah," said Bianca earnestly, "I think surrogacy is one of the most beautiful things about reproductive technology. To think that a woman's sister or mother or friend would offer to carry her baby to term when she can't is the height of love!"

Lauren looked pained. "I agree, Bianca, but as Micah said, there are legal concerns about the practice. On top of that are emotional and social concerns."

Bianca looked at Lauren, surprised but waiting to hear more. "Don't get me wrong," Lauren continued, "I am all for this incredible option to avoid infertility. I think it's amazing how common it is becoming for women to work together to bring children into the world for those who can't. What surprised me, however, was some of the real-world implications of surrogacy that my professor in Health Ethics class shared. He has been so forward-thinking and progressive in many of the issues we discussed, but he presented quite a few cautions when we got to the subject of surrogacy."

"What was he cautious about?" asked Micah.

"Do you mean, 'about what was he cautious'?" corrected Bianca with a smile.

"English is spoken by people, not grammarians," retorted Micah with feigned disgust. He had loved that response ever since he first heard it.

"Whatever," replied Bianca, waving her hand in mock dismissal.

Lauren cleared her throat to bring the conversation back to focus. "Well, first of all, to help Micah get clarity, surrogacy refers to the gestation of a baby by a woman who is not its biological mother.[4] It can happen any number of ways. A husband's sperm can be combined with his wife's egg

---

4. John S. Feinberg and Paul D. Feinberg, *Ethics for a Brave New World*, 2nd ed. (Wheaton, IL: Crossway, 2010), 433.

and the embryo can be carried to term in the womb of another woman. Alternately, the sperm could come from a donor, as could the egg, or both. A woman can even conceive a child naturally and transfer the embryo to another woman if she is unable to bring babies to term. Many arrangements involve either artificial insemination or IVF. Then there is the whole issue of whether financial compensation is given to the surrogate."

"I would think that compensation would be a real dilemma," interjected Bianca. "It is probably not an issue when a family member is a surrogate or maybe even a close friend, but compensation for surrogacy could easily run into the same problem as compensation for organ donation."

Lauren nodded. "It it's legal to compensate someone for surrogacy, we face the danger of exploiting the poor because they would be more likely to be willing to volunteer. The economic incentive could force a woman to be a surrogate out of desperation, even if she didn't really want to do it. So the most vulnerable women could be exploited by the practice. Additionally, the poor usually do not have access to the same kind of healthcare that the wealthy do. As a result, the surrogate may not receive adequate care if complications develop after the pregnancy."

"I would think compensation would also raise the issue of the commodification of the fetus." Micah was recalling some of the first lectures Dr. Platt had given in class. "Any time human life is tied to an economic incentive, we have to ask if the so-called progress could lead to treating people like things to be bought and sold. In a sense, when surrogacy involves compensation, the baby itself is essentially what is being bought and sold. That seems to violate Kant's principle of never treating people simply as a means, but also as ends in themselves."

"I understand your concerns Micah," said Bianca, "but pregnancy and childbirth are expensive. You cannot expect a surrogate mother to foot the bill for all those expenses."

Lauren replied. "The parallels with organ transplantation are helpful. Medical expenses are not considered financial compensation, so a surrogate's checkups, doctor's visits, and the cost of delivery are all paid by the couple who contracted with the surrogate mother. Unlike organ transplantation, lost wages and other expenses can be paid. And it is legal to also pay the surrogate a lump sum for carrying the baby to term. Sometimes the payment is in the tens of thousands of dollars."

"What other concerns with surrogacy did your professor mention, Lauren?" asked Micah. "I would think that emotional and social issues could arise with such an arrangement."

"He talked a lot about well-known legal cases with surrogacy. In the famous 'Marriage of Moschetta' case in 1994 while the surrogate was pregnant the intended couple separated, and the surrogate sued them, claiming that she had agreed to give the baby only to a stable married couple. The judge in the case agreed and granted the surrogate and the father custody, because it was his sperm and her egg that made the baby." [5]

"What about the intended mother?" asked Bianca.

"She was denied custody because the baby was not biologically hers."

"Yikes!" exclaimed Micah.

"I know," said Lauren. "It is hard to imagine how the intended mother felt. And how did the intended father and the surrogate share custody? Even though that scenario is less likely to happen, the first nationally known case pertaining to surrogacy happened in 1985. The surrogate, Mary Beth Whitehead, was paid $10,000 by William and Elizabeth Stern to conceive a child with the intended father's sperm. When the baby was born, Whitehead refused to give her up and fled to Florida, attempting to hide from authorities. Four months later Whitehead was caught and forced to return the baby to the Sterns. Even though the Sterns were eventually declared the legal parents of the baby, known as Baby M, the case showed the emotional ties that can easily grow between a woman and the baby she is carrying." [6]

"That kind of thing doesn't happen in most cases of surrogacy, though," said Bianca.

"No, most cases of surrogacy end with all parties apparently happy," agreed Lauren. "Much of it depends on the nature of the relationship between the couple and the surrogate."

---

5. Elie Stiz, "Through Her I Too Shall Bear a Child: Birth Surrogates in Jewish Law," *Journal of Religious Ethics* 24 (1996): 70. See also "In re Marriage of Moschetta (1994)," https://law.justia.com/cases/california/court-of-appeal/4th/25/1218.html.

6. Henry M. Butzel, "The Essential Facts of the Baby M Case," in *On the Problem of Surrogate Parenthood: Analyzing the Baby M Case*, ed. Herbert Richardson (Lewiston, NY: Edwin Mellen, 1987).

"I don't know," said Micah skeptically, rubbing his cheek in thought. "It seems to me that bringing a third party into the conception and birth of the baby violates the sanctity of the marriage and the child's sense of where she belongs. I have to wonder how the woman raising the child doesn't feel a sense of inadequacy that she couldn't bear the child herself, or a sense of jealousy if the surrogate is still in the picture. Also, if the child knows that his aunt or grandmother or some other woman bore him, I would think that could cause confusion or conflict. You might think I'm being overly analytical, but those are my concerns. As a Christian, I believe God intended children to be born to one man and one woman, so adding a third person to that seems to breed problems. No pun intended."

"Maybe you're right that the emotional and social aspects of surrogacy are more complex than they appear," said Bianca, "but I don't think the Bible says anything about this situation, does it?"

"Well, there is the example of Abraham and Sarah," replied Micah. "God promised them a son and when they felt they couldn't wait any longer for God to fulfill his promise, Sarah provided her handmaid Hagar as a surrogate. Abraham got her pregnant, and it caused all kinds of problems. Jealousy and conflict developed between the women and between Ishmael, the child born to Hagar, and Isaac, the son eventually born to Sarah."[7]

"That seems like a very different scenario," objected Bianca. "Sarah made Abraham have sex with Hagar. That is not how modern surrogacy works."

"I am aware of that," answered Micah, "but the principle of conflict between the three adults does have some application to the situation. It was by involving someone else in the act of procreation that the problems began. All I'm saying is that it's easy to downplay the personal and emotional factors involved in surrogacy because it all seems so virtuous and altruistic. The reality of human emotions, however, may be more complex than a simple exchange of a baby after it is born."

"I hate to agree, even partially, with Micah on this," remarked Lauren, "but as I said my professor was unusually hesitant about surrogacy. I think he had read enough articles about the emotional and social implications to be reluctant to praise it."

---

7. The story is told in Genesis 16 and 21.

"Whew," sighed Micah, looking around The Grey Earl. "I need a break. I'm going to walk around the block to clear my head and then come back for a refill. Anybody want to join me?"

"I'm going to stay," said Lauren. "I need to text my mom."

"In that case, I'll go with you," said Bianca. "I could use some fresh air."

After their walk, Bianca and Micah settled down again at the table with fresh cups of their favorite drinks.

"So, Micah," began Bianca, "it seems that many of your views on reproductive technology and genetic engineering are centered on the inherent value of the embryo and the foundational principle that once an egg is fertilized, it is a human being and should not be destroyed."

"That's right," agreed Micah. "It seems to me that attributing personhood to a fetus or baby at any time other than conception is to do so arbitrarily, because no other point of development is so definitive. As a result, I believe any procedure that destroys an embryo is wrong."

"I agree with you in principle," said Bianca, "but I don't know if you can be so dogmatic in every situation."

"It just seems to me that valuing embryos in that way puts the whole promise of reproductive technology in jeopardy," objected Lauren. "Such a position could quash the progress in other areas of biotechnology as well, like cloning."

"That isn't real," said Micah with a smirk.

"Of course it is!" countered Bianca before Lauren could reply.

"What she said," agreed Lauren, who was tempted to stick out her tongue at Micah.

"Are you telling me that someone could take a hair from my head and produce a genetically identical copy of me? That is science fiction and nothing more." Micah was holding his ground but sensed he was about to be refuted.

"If you were an animal, possibly, but cloning is not limited to just that scenario," said Bianca. "Even I know that. It can, however, reproduce human embryos with identical genetic code, even if they only live for a few days."

Lauren looked at Bianca. "I'm impressed you know that!"

"I loved my biology class last year and remember the lecture on cloning very well. I was surprised at what is being done in this field."

"So, what can scientists do in the area of cloning, if you don't mind my asking?" Micah hated not possessing the medical knowledge that Lauren made seem so easy. And with Bianca knowing facts about cloning, he felt like the odd man out.

Lauren pulled out her notes and began to summarize. "Well first of all, while scientists have been able to clone plants and certain animals, they have not been able to clone a human being in the form of a baby brought to full term. Have you heard of Dolly the sheep, the first animal ever successfully cloned? Dolly was born in 1996 in Scotland and was an identical twin of her mother. Dolly was plagued by health problems and died from joint and lung problems typical of old age when she was only six. But four clones from the same line lived much longer.[8] So far scientists have been able to clone cows, sheep, cats, deer, dogs, horses, mules, oxen, rabbits, rats, and a rhesus monkey.[9] Surprisingly, cloned animals do not look exactly like their genetic original because factors besides genetics play a part in appearance."

"Oh," said Micah, with feigned sadness. "I guess that means that if they ever do develop the technology to clone me, there will still be only one me with such dashing looks."

"Oh brother," exclaimed Bianca. "Let's hope your clone doesn't have as big a head as you do!"

Bianca and Lauren high-fived, and Micah was duly put in his place. He laughed at their synchronous reactions.

"The process of cloning is highly technical, so we won't get into it," continued Lauren. "Needless to say, there has never been a successful attempt to clone a human with the intent to bring a baby to term. That is known as *procreative* cloning, and it's illegal in many countries. Some have claimed to accomplish it, but every time the report has turned out to be a fraud. Apparently, complexities in cloning human beings are beyond what scientists can overcome at this point."

"That's a good thing, I believe," said Micah. "The ethical concerns would be endless."

"Like what?" asked Bianca.

---

8. Rachel Feltman, "Dolly the Sheep Died Young—But Her Clones Seem Perfectly Healthy as They Turn 9," *Washington Post*, July 26, 2016.

9. "Cloning Fact Sheet," National Human Genome Research Institute, https://www.genome.gov/about-genomics/fact-sheets/Cloning-Fact-Sheet#al-7.

"Yeah, let's hear the type of questions your fertile mind could think up on this issue," prodded Lauren with a smile.

Micah began. "Well, so many things come to mind. First are the legal questions about the process. What if the scientist producing the clone made an error in the process and the clone turned out to be a defective copy of the DNA donor of whom it is a copy? Would the scientist be liable to medical malpractice suits? Would the clone have legal rights of inheritance from the DNA donor? After all, the clone would be genetically the same person as the donor. Would the clone have its own legal identity? How could it if it was an exact copy of the donor? Since the clone would be younger and healthier, could it conceivably take the job of the donor? If a wife was cloned, would a man divorce his donor wife to marry the younger version of herself? Would a clone have to pay royalties to its donor? Writers receive royalties for their works, so why wouldn't a donor receive royalties, especially if he was cloned for his intelligence, athleticism, or attractiveness? Such a person might be cloned many times over, and then we are right back to the question of enhancement and the unfair advantage that might create."

Lauren and Bianca watched Micah in amused wonder as his mind raced and the questions continued to flow.

"Then there are moral and philosophical questions," Micah continued without missing a beat. "Would a clone even be human? Would it have a soul? We don't know because no one has ever been born into the world in this way. If it was human, would a clone have its own identity? How could it when there was someone with the same exact DNA out there? How would a clone feel about the fact that he was made without his consent? That is different from a child born in a normal way because the child is not an exact replica of either parent, but of both together. What if a great athlete, scientist, or musician were cloned to reproduce his talent, but the differences in environmental factors and experiences caused the clone to show no interest in the field for which he was made? Finally, would clones be produced expressly for the purpose of harvesting their organs? Since a clone is genetically identical to the donor, the damaging immunosuppressant drugs typically required of an organ recipient wouldn't be needed. Clones could easily become walking organ banks, existing only to replace parts as the original person needs them."

Micah took a deep breath and smiled. "I could go on, you know. So many movies have been produced and novels written that explore these scenarios. They almost all end in disaster or some dystopian future."

"Fortunately, we don't have to worry about any of those questions now," said Lauren. "The only kind of human cloning that is successful now is research cloning, also known as *therapeutic cloning*. Scientists clone humans through a complicated process for the purpose of extracting embryonic stem cells. These stem cells appear five to seven days after conception and are valued for their ability to be used to create almost any kind of cell and tissue the body produces."

"Can you explain stem cells in more detail?" asked Bianca.

"I'll try," replied Lauren looking more intently at her notes. "Scientists fertilize an egg, and as it begins to divide in the first few days, they can extract these cells to be used for various reasons. Embryonic stem cells are greatly valued because they have the potential to become any number of specific cells of the body, depending on when they are harvested. For example, in animals, scientists can take stem cells and manipulate them into becoming cells that will build tissues, like organs or blood cells. By editing the genes, they can manipulate the stem cell to become what they want. In laboratory animals, promising advances for treating spinal cord injuries, regenerating bone, and creating organs have appeared. Unfortunately, we don't have many major breakthroughs for humans. One research journal stated, 'Despite many reports of putative stem-cell-based treatments in genetic and degenerative disorders or severe injuries, the number of proven stem cell therapies has remained small.'"[10]

"I remember my father telling me that embryonic stem cell research was a major issue in the 2000 US presidential election," said Bianca.

"Yes, that was right around the time the Human Genome Project was finishing its efforts to map the gene, and new therapies for disease were already being discovered. People hoped that stem cells might be able to treat Alzheimer's Disease, muscular dystrophy, diabetes, and Parkinson's disease. The presidential candidates were divided on whether they would allow unrestricted

10.   Michele Deluca, et al., "Advances in Stem Cell Research and Therapeutic Development," *Nature Cell Biology* 21, no. 7 (2019): 810–11.

use of aborted embryos, abandoned IVF embryos, and cloned embryos, or whether they would restrict government-funded research to the stem cell lines already created. Private companies were not restricted by the laws, but the hype about the issue led many people to believe the choices were either no research on what could be a miracle cure, or unrestricted research. In reality, over the next few administrations, the law changed several times, but all the grand promises have failed to produce significant cures for those diseases."

"It seems this issue always comes back to the personhood of the embryo," observed Micah.

"In a way, you're right," agreed Lauren. "Extracting embryonic stem cells destroys the embryo every time, although there are new advances that may change that."

"Are embryos the only source of stem cells?" asked Micah.

"Actually no," replied Lauren, "although some scientists prefer them because of their ability to become any type of cell or tissue a person might need. Additionally, there seems to be an almost a limitless supply of them because of the ability to clone. But there are other sources. Bone marrow stem cells are highly valued because of their ability to regrow bone marrow after chemotherapy. The umbilical cord of a newborn baby contains blood that is rich in stem cells, as is the placenta and amniotic fluid. Finally, adult skin cells are showing promise as a source for stem cells.[11] All these additional sources are not as plentiful as embryonic stem cells, but they do have the advantage of not destroying an embryo, if that is an ethical concern."

"I am glad to hear that," said Micah. "I am all for research and advancements in science and medicine, but they shouldn't come at the expense of human embryos. I know that can be a difficult limitation for some to consider, but I believe it is a limitation that helps preserve our humanity."

"What do you mean?" asked Bianca.

"I think of it in terms of Virtue Ethics," Micah replied. "In all our pursuits of progress, we must remain virtuous people. Some lines we don't cross, and the taking of innocent life seems like an important one. If we violate that, we open up doors to do things that we wouldn't want to consider, but we would have no reason to stop."

---

11. Feinberg and Feinberg, *Ethics for a Brave New World*, 541–48.

"Can you give me an example?" asked Lauren somewhat skeptically.

"Well, I liken the refusal to destroy embryos in the pursuit of new treatments to a scenario where you have people in need of organs and a potential donor who is dying. Would we hasten the death of the potential donor, or kill him if he was a convicted murderer, in order to obtain his organs for upstanding or important citizens? Most people and most ethics panels would consider such an act to be immoral because it would be elevating the worth of one life over another. In the same way, if the embryo is a human, we shouldn't devalue it because of the potential to create a cure or treatment from it for someone else. In some ways, that's even worse because there's no guarantee that the death of the embryo would save another life, as it would in the case of organ donation. So I think this brings the issue back to the virtue of a society that values one life over another."

The girls were impacted by Micah's usual sense of conviction and his stirring speech.

"I still have a problem considering an embryo a human being in its full capacity, Micah," said Lauren, "but as always, I respect the clarity of your convictions. One objection that I would offer is that without cloning and testing on embryonic stem cells for the last few decades, we would have missed out on all the advances that have been made. Even though the inflated promises of stem cell research haven't been fulfilled, the progress that has been made has helped many people and probably extended or saved many thousands of lives."

"I am sure you are correct about that," added Bianca, "but that raises the question of whether the ends justify the means. I know the appeal to Hitler and to Nazi scientists can be overdone, but would we justify the horrors of Nazi experimentation on innocent children and adults by saying that what they learned from it helped advance science and medicine? Such a consequentialist ethic brings us right back to the foundations of ethics. Just because we *can* do it doesn't mean we *should* do it."

"That is the issue for me," agreed Micah. "History seems to demonstrate that without virtue in science and medicine, some in power will exploit others for some supposed benefit. The British philosopher and converted atheist C. S. Lewis once said, 'What we call Man's power over Nature turns out to be a power exercised by some men over other men with Nature as its instrument.'[12] Any time an embryo is used and destroyed, it is done without its consent."

"I hear what you're saying," said Lauren. "It comes back to the question of whether an embryo is a full human being with all the rights and protections of the law. We agree scientific advances should proceed if they can be done ethically. Maybe someday soon these other sources of stem cells will replace the need for using embryos."

The friends were weary from the discussion. They looked at each other, looked outside at the day, which had become bright and sunny, and began packing up their belongings.

"Who's up for some Frisbee?" asked Micah with a smile.

12.   C. S. Lewis, *The Abolition of Man* (New York: Harper Collins, 2002), 719.

QUESTIONS TO PONDER

- Is an embryo a human being?

- How far should we go to bring about conception?

- Is it right to do everything technologically possible, or should there be moral constraints that limit what we do?

- How far should we go to enhance or alter our abilities?

- Should people take radical medical steps to prevent a disease for which they merely have a disposition?

- Is it right to clone a human being, and if so, for what purposes?

TERMS TO KNOW

- Predisposition
- Eugenics
- Gene editing
- In vitro fertilization
- Surrogacy
- Commodification
- Cloning
- CRISPR

FOR FURTHER READING

General:

Glover, Jonathan. *Choosing Children: Genes, Disability and Design*. New York: Oxford University Press, 2008.

Marsh, Margaret and Wanda Ronner. *The Pursuit of Parenthood: Reproductive Technology from Test Tube Babies to Uterus Transplants*. Baltimore: Johns Hopkins University Press, 2019.

Sandel, Michael. *The Case against Perfection: Ethics in an Age of Genetic Engineering*. Cambridge, MA: Belknap, 2007.

Weikart, Richard. *The Death of Humanity: And the Case for Life*. Washington, DC: Regnery, 2016.

Christian:

Colson, Charles W. and Nigel M. de S. Cameron, eds. *Human Dignity in the Biotech Century*. Downers Grove, IL: InterVarsity Press, 2004.

Feinberg, John S. and Paul D. Feinberg. *Ethics for a Brave New World*, 2nd ed. Wheaton, IL: Crossway, 2010.

Foreman, Mark W. *Christianity and Bioethics: Confronting Clinical Issues*. Eugene, OR: Wipf and Stock, 2011.

Kilner, John F. *Dignity and Destiny: Humanity in the Image of God*. Grand Rapids: Eerdmans, 2015.

Rae, Scott. *Moral Choices: An Introduction to Ethics*, 4th ed. Grand Rapids: Zondervan, 2018.

Thobaben, James R. *Health-Care Ethics: A Comprehensive Christian Resource*. Downers Grove, IL: InterVarsity Press, 2009.

MARRIAGE
AND SEX

PREMARITAL SEX

Synopsis: After *The Lone Mountain Perspective*, the student news-paper, publishes survey results regarding sexual mores on campus, Professor Platt asks the Ethics class study groups to select aspects of the survey results and analyze them in terms of ethical theory. The Applied Ethics Study Circle—Lauren, Bianca, and Micah—meet in the Student Center to do so.

* * *

"So which topic do you think we should analyze?" asked Bianca, as the three friends settled in with milkshakes and french fries. "The survey asks questions about premarital sex, extramarital sex, homosexual relations, and transgenderism. Do you guys have a preference?"

Lauren responded first, "I think premarital sex is the most relevant for our age group, so it would be most interesting."

"I can go with that," chimed in Micah.

"Good. That was my preference too," agreed Bianca. "This survey is great. It not only gathered statistics, but it also asked the respondents to rank various reasons for their answers. I think we'll have a lot to analyze. I was so sure you guys would pick that one, I collected a few articles on the issue and brought them with me."

"Excellent. This may be obvious," offered Micah, "but let's define exactly what we mean by *premarital sex*. My understanding is that it is any sexual activity between persons who are unmarried. Correct?"

"The survey defines terms," responded Bianca, "and that is pretty much correct, as long as we specify that it is consensual."

Micah nodded. "Sure, that's what I meant."

"So what does our student body think about this topic?" asked Lauren.

"Well first, the survey simply asked the respondents whether or not they had ever participated in sexual activity while unmarried. And 87 percent said they had."

"Eighty-seven percent!" blurted out Micah. "Does that seem high to you guys?"

"The survey includes some comparative data," responded Bianca. "In 2016 the US Center for Disease Control and Prevention administered a National Survey of Family Growth, which also asked about premarital sex. Nationally, ninety percent of men and eighty-nine percent of women between 2011 and 2015 affirmed that they had participated in premarital sex.[1] So our campus results are actually a little under the national average, probably because the national survey included many people beyond college age."

"So nine out of ten people believe premarital sex is ethical," concluded Micah.

"Actually, that's the strange thing about our college data. Although 87 percent claimed to have participated in sexual activity while unmarried, only 76 percent said they thought premarital sex was morally appropriate," Bianca explained.[2]

---

1. The survey included men ages twenty to forty-four and women ages fifteen to forty-four. For precise results, see https://www.cdc.gov/nchs/nsfg/key_statistics/p.htm#premarital.

2. Survey information on national attitudes toward premarital sex takes in a wider demographic than the CDC study of actual behavior cited in n1. It is not easy to make direct connections between the data as Bianca is doing with the campus study. See the Pew Research study here: https://www.pewresearch.org/fact-tank/2014/04/15/whats-morally-acceptable-it-depends-on-where-in-the-world-you-live. It shows 30 percent disapproval, 29 percent approval, and 36 percent neutrality. Effectively, this would lead to 65 percent of Americans finding premarital sex unobjectionable morally. The statistics cited by Bianca from the campus survey are hypothetical.

"Interesting," replied Lauren. "That means about eleven percent of the campus has had premarital sex but thinks they were wrong to do so."

"It would be interesting to know if they thought it was wrong at the time they were doing it," Micah commented.

Bianca replied, "The survey doesn't address that kind of question. But we're trying to assess the reasons people think premarital sex is right or wrong, so we don't really have to address how consistently people live by their own principles."

"What kind of arguments do advocates of premarital sex make for their position?" asked Micah.

"Here are copies of the survey results, so each of us can study them for ourselves," said Bianca, as she distributed copies to Lauren and Micah. "I've also included an article by Jill Filipovic, which she wrote for the *Guardian* in 2012, in which she makes a case for premarital sex being moral.[3] I think a lot of students have read her article or various summaries of her article that have appeared since she wrote it. A number of the survey responses allude to her arguments. And just for good measure, I've thrown in a couple of articles that share other points of view." Bianca smiled at her friends, knowing they'd be impressed.

"Great job, Bianca! Thank you," Micah and Lauren responded.

"Let's take a few moments to review the data before we continue," suggested Lauren.

For the next forty-five minutes or so, the three pored over the data in the reports and familiarized themselves with Filipovic's arguments and the other articles in the collection.

"The first thing I notice," Lauren began, "is that people argue that sex is a natural need like eating and drinking, so it shouldn't be tied to a social convention like marriage. In short, if sex wasn't good for people, whether or not they are married, they wouldn't want to do it so badly."

"That sounds like a Natural Law argument," surmised Micah. "By considering their natural feelings, people think they can determine what is ethical for them."

"It's certainly true that most people *want* to have sex once they reach puberty, and they don't have sex either because they can't find a willing

---

3. https://www.theguardian.com/commentisfree/2012/sep/24/moral-case-for-sex-before-marriage.

partner or because they think it's ethically wrong for them to give in to their natural desires. If nature determines our morality, it would seem to suggest that premarital sex is moral," concluded Bianca.

"Is that the only message nature sends?" asked Micah. "We've all seen the warning signs posted around campus about sexually transmitted diseases. People in stable, marital relationships have very low risk of STDs, but they are a plague among those who are sexually active outside marriage. One study in these notes says that about 25 percent of sexually active adolescents is infected with an STD every year. Sexually active people are much more likely to get Human Papilloma Virus and Hepatitis B, both of which make them more likely to get cancer. And we haven't even mentioned the danger of AIDS. It seems to me that nature is sending a lot of messages that argue against premarital sex."

"It looks like Filipovic and others admit the danger of STDs but argue that embracing premarital sex as a morally good option would lead to safer, more informed decisions about sex and thus less health risk," replied Lauren. "Filipovic writes 'Instead of fooling ourselves into thinking that waiting until marriage makes sex 'good,' we should focus on how ethical, responsible sexual practices—taking precautions to protect the physical and mental health of yourself and your partner; having sex that is fully consensual and focused on mutual pleasure—are part of being an ethical, responsible human being.'"

"Let me get this straight," responded Micah. "Nature teaches us that sex is good, anytime, anywhere, with anyone, if we feel like it. But all the signals that nature sends that sex is incredibly risky outside stable relationships must be overcome through education and other unnatural interventions. That doesn't seem very consistent. Couldn't the stronger argument from nature be that lifelong, covenanted faithfulness to a single partner is the safest and healthiest context for sexual relations?"

Lauren countered, "Micah, I don't think Filipovic says any time with anyone we feel like—or whatever it is you just said. You are caricaturing her position. Instead, she speaks of 'ethical, responsible sexual practices.'"

"I'm sorry if I was unfair to her position," responded Micah. "My point was that nature seems to send a lot of signals that 'ethical, responsible' sex belongs in stable, marital relationships."

"I see what you mean, Micah," replied Bianca. "Dr. Platt pointed out how hard it can be to interpret Natural Law. This looks like a case in point. Sex without boundaries seems natural, but if one does not put various unnatural safeguards in place, sex comes with significant risks."

"Some of the respondents said they had premarital sex simply because they wanted to," Lauren stated, launching a new train of thought. "It seems like it's a freedom issue for them. Even if there are risks, they are adults and believe they should have the right to choose for themselves in such a personal matter."

"Is this an example of Ethical Egoism?" asked Micah. "Are they saying that premarital sex is morally right because it benefits the people involved?"

Lauren answered, "Filipovic certainly claims that there are many personal benefits when she writes, 'People with active sex lives live longer. Sex releases stress, boosts immunities, helps you sleep and is heart-healthy.' Unfortunately, she does not clarify whether these benefits come primarily to people with 'active sex lives' within marriage or those who have multiple partners. She speaks of the benefits of sex as though they apply whenever people have sex, regardless of the circumstances."

"I'm glad you pointed that out," responded Micah. "No one, at least in our current conversation, is questioning whether sex is good when it is moral. But it's another thing to say sex is moral whenever it's good."

"Micah! That was a nice turn of phrase," exclaimed Bianca.

"Your shock isn't all that flattering," deadpanned Micah. Lauren laughed, thankful for a break in the tension of discussing such a tough topic.

"Ethical Egoism also has to deal with the very real possibility of an unwanted pregnancy," said Bianca. "Sexual relations always involve two people, and a third person may be produced as a result. It seems like Ethical Egoists will have a hard time proving that everyone involved will benefit from what benefits the individual, when in fact unwanted pregnancies by definition create hardship, or at least inconvenience."

"That raises the question of more general benefits that come from premarital sex," Lauren injected. "A lot of the reasons we see in the survey and the arguments in the articles focus on the consequences involved. For instance, Filipovic makes this claim: 'People who marry early and/or hold traditional views on marriage and gender tend to have higher divorce rates and unhappier marriages.' She doesn't cite any studies, so I'm not sure what to make of her claims."[4]

Micah added, "Seidensticker, who also defends premarital sex, says that girls become sexually mature at age fifteen or sixteen and boys about a year older, five years after puberty in each case. In America the average marriage age is twenty-seven for women and twenty-nine for men. This gap of twelve or thirteen years is a long time, he says, for people to maintain virginity. If people marry young, they are more likely to divorce (Filipovic makes that point too, you'll notice), and the suffering people go through as a result of abstaining from sex for over a decade is unnecessary and immoral, he says."

"There's another dimension to their argument," added Bianca. "Marriages fail because of what Filipovic calls 'mismatched sex drives and bad sex lives.' The solution is what is commonly called the 'test drive.'"

Micah was sucking his vanilla shake at that moment and snorted a bit when he heard the phrase. After collecting himself he said, "So we're comparing getting married to buying a car now?"

"Follow the logic, Micah," Bianca went on. "No one would buy a car without taking it for a test drive. But people sometimes marry—a much bigger decision—without knowing by experience whether they are sexually compatible with their spouse. Filipovic—and many others, including many students on our campus—thinks that's a really bad idea and just asking for a failed marriage. Premarital sex allows two people to discover if they are compatible."

"I saw the logic immediately," retorted Micah, perhaps a bit defensively. "We've already seen the significant health risks people take in having multiple sexual partners. If the 'test drive' doesn't work out, then presumably a person goes on to options two, three, four, and so forth. To avoid the risk of marrying the wrong person, one embraces the risks of STDs, unwanted pregnancies, and possibly abortion. I guess I reacted as I did precisely *because* marriage is

---

4. While Filipovic does not cite a study, the following website refers to a study by "Family Studies" that claims that divorce rates drop from 32 percent for people who marry for the first time under twenty to 20 percent for those aged twenty to twenty-four, and finally to 15 percent for people who first marry between the ages of twenty-five and twenty-nine. See https://www.fyi.tv/relationships/the-arguments-for-and-against-saving-sex-for-marriage.

so much more significant than buying a car. Test driving several people and then picking the one that gives you the best sex seems to trivialize marriage."

"I see what you're saying, Micah," responded Lauren, "but you didn't exactly deal with the principal concern, that two people might find themselves married who are sexually incompatible."

Micah answered, "It's hard for me to respond to that without bringing in some of my Christian theology. The Bible teaches that sex is more about giving oneself to the other person than getting one's own needs satisfied.[5] If two people go into marriage with that mindset, then I would think they have a very good chance of having a fulfilling sex life."

"That's a beautiful thought, Micah, but I don't see how that proves that people should not test drive their sexual compatibility. Couldn't people do that to see how well they give themselves to each other?" asked Lauren.

"Well at that point I would appeal to Divine Command Theory, I suppose," admitted Micah.

"Which we should discuss," interjected Bianca, "but do you think we should continue to work through these other theories first? Were we done with Utilitarianism, the supposed benefits of premarital sex to society at large?"

"The discussion of benefits seems to focus primarily on personal benefits," observed Lauren. "Lower divorce rates for those who marry later, a better chance of a satisfying sex life for those who test drive, and the like. I suppose advocates would argue that a sufficient number of people enjoying such benefits would lead to overall advantages for society. Filipovic, if I'm reading her right, seems to have written her article not just because she wants to help frustrated individuals, but because she also thinks society would be improved if we were no longer pestered by the . . . what's the phrase?" At this point, Lauren looked through the articles again. "Yes, if Western society was no longer pestered by 'purity peddlers' who have constructed a 'false universe' that is basically making life miserable for everyone else."

"Against those supposed benefits," Micah countered, "in addition to the dangers of STDs and unwanted pregnancies, are other negative consequences. For instance, one of the studies here that presents pros and cons of premarital sex cites a study published in the *Journal of Family Psychology* that claims

---

5. See, for instance, 1 Cor. 7:3–5.

that couples who delay sex have better relationships.[6] Both sides seem to be claiming benefits based on who is surveyed and what they're asked. In short, I'm not sure the Utilitarian Ethic is going to resolve this issue very clearly."

"I agree," responded Bianca, "but it's an important part of the debate, as people on both sides regularly appeal to the consequences to justify their position."

"One of the points made by the advocates of premarital sex," said Lauren, "is that everyone is already doing it. So why make people feel bad about doing it? If it's the norm, why not just embrace it as ethical?"

"That sounds like one of our ethical systems," Bianca observed. "Micah, do you know which one?"

"Are you quizzing me, now?" asked Micah, furrowing his brow in mock concentration. "If it's right because the majority in a particular culture has decided it's right, then the ethical standard must be relative to the culture. Voilà! Cultural Relativism."

"Very good, Micah. I knew you could do it," intoned Bianca like a kindergarten teacher.

"Dr. Platt pointed out quite a few problems with Cultural Relativism," Lauren asserted.

"Wait, Lauren. I think I know these," Micah spoke up excitedly.

"I wasn't quizzing you, Micah."

Ignoring her, Micah went on, "Since the majority in the culture decides what is ethical, the opinions of minorities tend to be overridden. For instance, in our situation, those who believe premarital sex *is* wrong—the 25 percent who are 'purity peddlers'—would be unethical for holding this position because it conflicts with the majority. But if they moved to a more conservative country—say, Latvia. . . ."

"Latvia!" exclaimed Bianca and Lauren almost simultaneously.

"It's just an example. Stay with me here. If a purity peddler moved to Latvia, where most people are (hypothetically) opposed to premarital sex, the same behavior that was unethical in America would be ethical there. Dr. Platt pointed out how unlikely such a conclusion is. Ethics shouldn't depend on geography," finished Micah.

---

6. See https://www.fyi.tv/relationships/the-arguments-for-and-against-saving-sex-for-marriage.

"Interestingly, though," observed Bianca, "a lot of students on our campus gave as their number-one reason for engaging in premarital sex the fact that everyone they hang out with does it."

"Whatever people believe about premarital sex," Lauren replied, "they should probably have a better reason than that."

"Amen!" Micah answered.

"You sometimes use that word, Micah. What does that even mean?" Lauren asked.

"Oh, I'm sorry. It's a religious word that people use when they agree with something. I'm not actually sure what it means," admitted Micah.

After a brief pause, Bianca said, "Google says it's a word originally from Hebrew that means 'so be it.' So you're right, Micah. Agreement is the basic idea."

"Amen."

Lauren groaned. "Whatever. Which systems do we still need to consider?"

Bianca answered, "Virtue Ethics, Duty Ethics, Situation Ethics, and Divine Command Theory, if we try to do all the major ones."

"Whew! I think we need to take a break. I've got some other things to do this afternoon," said Micah. "Do you mind if we meet tomorrow to finish up?"

Lauren answered, "I've got nursing clinicals all day tomorrow. How about on Friday?"

"That works better for me too," responded Bianca. "I've got a test in one of my educational methods classes to study for. Will this same time on Friday work for you guys?"

Lauren and Micah replied, "Perfectly."

Lauren added, "That will give us time to review the articles and survey results further as well. See you guys then."

***

Two days later, the three friends gathered in the Student Center once again to resume their analysis of the topic of premarital sex.

"Hey guys," greeted Bianca, who was already positioned with a soft drink and snack when Lauren and Micah joined her. "I think we should start with Situation Ethics."

"Why's that?" asked Micah.

"I found out that premarital sex was one of the famous examples used by Joseph Fletcher when he wrote his book *Situation Ethics* back in 1966. He argued that in a given set of circumstances—perhaps, irrational opposition from the parents to young people getting married—it might be ethical for the young people to have sex in order to force their parents to come around. The situation would make the action the most loving thing possible and, therefore, ethical," Bianca summarized.

Lauren nodded and said, "So when campus students gave as their reason for premarital sex that it seemed like the most loving thing to do, they were probably influenced by Situation Ethics. Basically, if it's loving, then it is ethical."

"Do you remember how Dr. Platt guided the class discussion on this model?" asked Micah. "He raised the question about how one can determine in any particular set of circumstances what the most loving thing is."

Bianca chimed in, "If by 'most loving thing' is meant a thing that is motivated by love, it is hard to see how anything a person wanted to do could be ruled out. I mean, couldn't we rationalize just about any behavior as being loving? On the other hand, if by 'most loving thing' is meant the action that produces the most loving results, we're back in Utilitarianism with a sentimental twist."

"For most of the students," added Lauren, "I suspect that their appeal to love is not a careful, philosophical conclusion based on Fletcher's reasoning. They think they're in love. Therefore expressing their love sexually seems appropriate, even ethical."

"I agree," said Bianca. "Fletcher's conditions for premarital sex being ethical are pretty specific and limiting. I'm certain he would not view every one-night stand in the dorms as expressing love and, therefore, ethical."

Micah spoke up, "Kant's Duty Ethics was designed to remedy the subjectivism of approaching ethics as depending on circumstances or consequences. Maybe it can help us escape the problems with Situation Ethics."

"Do you see how the categorical imperative would apply, Micah?" asked Lauren.

"Not at the moment. Let me think about it," Micah responded. After a few moments, he said, "If I'm remembering the classroom discussion correctly, didn't Professor Platt say that Duty Ethics teaches that an action is moral if it is a reasonable thing for people to do?"

"Yes," Bianca responded, "but reasonable in a particular way. If I want to do an action, I should ask if it would make sense for everyone to do the action. If it is logically inconsistent, then it is immoral. If it is moral, it will be logically consistent."

"I'm not sure I see how this would apply to premarital sex," observed Lauren.

"How about this?" prompted Micah. "If everyone had sex before and apart from marriage, then marriage would no longer be necessary. It would disappear as a societal convention. But if marriage did not exist, then there would be no such thing as premarital sex. So premarital sex becomes self-defeating. Pretty good, huh?"

"Micah, unfortunately your argument assumes that marriage exists only for the purpose of sex. You don't really mean to say that, do you?" replied Lauren. "I mean marriage could still have significant cultural purposes even if everyone had sex before they married. I don't think your argument follows."

"Lauren's right, Micah. Nice try, though," Bianca tried to encourage him. He looked a bit disappointed.

"However," Bianca went on, "the second formulation of the categorical imperative is much more promising, I think. I say that because I just looked up Kant's view of premarital sex on my phone, and listen to what he says: 'If . . . a man wishes to satisfy his desire and a woman hers, they stimulate each other's desire; their inclinations meet, but their object is not human nature but sex, and each of them dishonors the human nature of the other. They make of humanity an instrument for the satisfaction of their lusts and inclinations, and dishonor it by placing it on a level with animal nature. . . . Human love is good-will, affection, promoting the happiness of others and finding joy in their happiness, but it is clear, that when a person loves another purely for sexual desires, none of these factors enter into the love. . . . The sole condition on which we are free to make use of our sexual desires depends upon the right to dispose over the person as a whole—over the welfare and happiness and generally over all the circumstances of that person . . . each of them undertaking to surrender the whole of their person to the other with a complete right to disposal over it.'"[7]

"Yes," Lauren affirmed. "That's good, Bianca. I've found the second formulation on my phone too. It's called the 'Formula of Humanity': 'Act in such a way that you treat humanity, whether in your own person or in the person of any other, never merely as a means to an end, but always at the same time as an end.'"

"So Kant believed that premarital sex implies that people are having sex just for what they can get out of it, and that means using another person as a means to an end rather than as an end," concluded Micah. "That makes good sense. It would be our duty, then, not to engage in premarital sex."

"I see that," agreed Lauren, "but I can still imagine a pushback. Couldn't a couple say they were having sex not just to satisfy some animal urge but because they loved each other and were preparing for marriage? So they were regarding their partner as an end, not merely as a means. Kant's argument does not strictly require marriage; it just requires people not to have sex only for the sake of the sex. Right?"

"I see what you mean," replied Bianca. Even Micah acknowledged Lauren's point with a slow nod of his head.

"So it is our duty to have sex for noble, unselfish reasons, otherwise we are using people, but that may or may not require marriage," summarized Bianca.

"Speaking of noble and unselfish motives," said Micah, "some of the best stuff I read over the last two days relates to Virtue Ethics."

"Good," Lauren responded. "Let's take that up next. What did you learn, Micah?"

Micah began, "As you know, Virtue Ethics directs our attention away from the things we do to the persons we are as we are doing them."

"You mean, like our motivations and that sort of thing, right?" clarified Bianca.

"Yes. An action is virtuous when it is done for virtuous reasons," Micah continued. "In class we talked about Aristotle and other Greek thinkers who thought the virtues could be defined in terms of what a good person

---

7. Bianca is quoting Kant's *Lectures on Ethics,* trans. Louis Infield (New York: Harper & Row, 1963), 163–65. His whole discussion (162–68) is worth consulting.

does. For example, habitually telling the truth doesn't make a person honest. Rather, an honest person habitually tells the truth. Looking at consequences, according to these thinkers, is getting the cart before the horse. And this discussion of premarital sex seems to focus largely on consequences, doesn't it?"

"Kant's Duty Ethics tried to get us away from that, but generally I agree with you," responded Lauren. Bianca nodded, indicated she was tracking with it as well.

"Paul Flaman, a Roman Catholic ethicist and professor at the University of Alberta in Edmonton, Canada, wrote a book entitled *Premarital Sex and Love* in 1999, and I found extensive extracts from it on the internet," continued Micah. "He focuses on what he calls the virtue of chastity.[8] Chastity, he says, is having 'holistic or properly ordered love.'"[9]

"Holistic, as in the whole person?" asked Bianca.

"Only you would know that," responded Micah. "I had to look that up. Yes, a whole person is involved in acts of love. With one's mind, emotions, will, and body, one gives of himself or herself to others—and Flaman of course says to God—not just with the body. This puts sex into proper relation to other human values. Flaman lists some of these values as 'the great dignity of human persons, self-giving and faithful love, justice, friendship, marriage, human life and health, procreation, truth, God, and the integrity of persons, including integral development of the person and bodily integrity.'"[10]

Lauren commented, "This really broadens the discussion. Having sex with another person according to this argument is about a lot more than merely the physical encounter."

Micah nodded, "Exactly. More specifically, sex should be viewed as a component of love, not a physical appetite like food or drink." To emphasize

---

8. See http://www.newadvent.org/cathen/03637d.htm for the definition of chastity from the standpoint of Roman Catholic Virtue Ethics.

9. For Flaman's argumentation, see Paul Flaman, "Some Contemporary Arguments against Premarital Sexual Intercourse," in *Premarital Sex and Love: In the Light of Human Experience and Following Jesus* (Ottawa: Justin, 2015), https://sites.ualberta.ca/~pflaman/PSAL/Ch6.pdf.

10. Flaman, "Some Contemporary Arguments," in *Premarital Sex and Love*, 3–4, https://sites.ualberta.ca/~pflaman/PSAL/Ch6.pdf.

his point, Micah waived a french fry in the air. "Love, properly understood, should place value on the other person ahead of oneself. It is more about giving than it is about receiving." He emphasized his point by handing the french fry to Lauren. Sensing a slight tension in the room, Micah quickly gave a french fry to Bianca as well.

"So if I say I love a person but really only want what that person is going to do for me, I'm just loving myself," observed Lauren. "We're back to Ethical Egoism with all its flaws."

"Pope John Paul II actually argued that premarital sex is dishonest," continued Micah.

"Dishonest? How?" asked Bianca.

"Let me quote him." Micah looked through his notes for a moment. "Sexuality, he says, 'is by no means something purely biological, but concerns the innermost being of the human person as such. It is realized in a truly human way only if it is an integral part of the love by which a man and a woman commit themselves totally to one another until death. The total physical self-giving would be a lie if it were not the sign and fruit of a total personal self-giving, in which the whole person, including the temporal dimension, is present: if the person were to withhold something or reserve the possibility of deciding otherwise in the future, by this very fact he or she would not be giving totally.'"[11]

Pope John Paul II at St. Mary's Cathedral in Sydney, Australia. Courtesy of Jason7825. Public domain.

---

11. Pope John Paul, as cited in Flamen, "Some Contemporary Arguments," in *Premarital Sex and Love*, 7, https://sites.ualberta.ca/~pflaman/PSAL/Ch6.pdf.

Bianca processed this for a moment and then said, "So the dishonesty, if I'm following the argument, is that two people who engage in premarital sex are claiming to be giving themselves entirely to the other person. But if they do not intend to be bound together by marriage, they are actually withholding something from the other person, and that is dishonest. Have I got his reasoning correct?"

Lauren spoke up, "I don't think Filipovic or the other defenders of pre-marital sex would accept the premise that the people engaged in it intend thereby to be giving themselves entirely to the other person."

"They probably wouldn't," agreed Micah. "But that simply shows that they are denying that sex is linked to love, and therefore they are tacitly assuming that sex is simply about what a person can get out of it for himself. Virtue Ethicists say it is unethical for a person to use another person for his own benefit in this way. I found another excellent quote that expresses this idea. Bear with me while I find it."

"It sounds again like Kant's second formulation to me," Bianca said while Micah was riffling through his notes.

"Yeah, kind of. Here's that quote. It's from a guy named William May, who, back in 1981, wrote *Sex, Marriage, and Chastity*. Listen carefully; this is a mouthful. Two people who engage in premarital sex, he says, 'have not established the uniqueness and exclusivity of each other. They are, in principle, replaceable, and substitutable. The "love" they offer is not an unconditional, irrevocable gift of self, but a love that is far from being total, far from being oblative'—I looked up this word; it means 'sacrificial,'" inserted Micah helpful-ly—"'and unconditional. It is a "love" focused on the benefit that each can gain from the other and contingent on this gain. It is a depersonalized kind of love.'"[12]

"That last statement is interesting," observed Bianca. "The logic seems to go like this: premarital sex separates sex from genuine love, because real love gives while premarital sex only takes. When one is only taking from another, he is treating her like an object rather than like a person."

"Exactly," said Micah. "Virtue Ethics says a person who takes rather than gives, while calling it *love*, is not virtuous, and the process of taking is not an ethical act."

---

12. Flamen, "Some Contemporary Arguments."

"You're not a Roman Catholic are you, Micah?" asked Lauren. "Do you Protestants agree with this argumentation? I'm a little surprised to hear you quoting a pope."

Micah shrugged. "We're willing to take good argumentation wherever we find it. Protestants tend to emphasize Divine Command Ethics, and Roman Catholics, as I understand it, tend to go to Natural Law, but Virtue Ethics has insights that both groups draw on quite a bit. Any seriously religious person is going to think that what we are on the inside is ultimately more than the sum of our actions."

Bianca chimed in. "As neither Protestant nor Roman Catholic, I agree with Micah. Virtue Ethics predates the New Testament, and a lot of what the Bible says about right and wrong fits with Virtue Ethics pretty well. The difference, as I see it, is that Aristotle thought he could figure out right and wrong on his own, while the New Testament writers believed they needed God to reveal it to them."

"Precisely," said Micah. "And that brings us to Divine Command Theory, our final system. Right?"

Lauren spoke up, "I'm not a Christian, but I'm well aware that religion has traditionally been against premarital sex. You guys call it 'fornication,' right? The perception of a lot of people outside the church is that your Puritanical rules are just designed to stifle enjoyment in life. How would you respond to that?"

"On the one hand," began Micah, "we aren't confident that people have the capacity to figure out what is best for them apart from God's commands. So I'm not sure I'll ever succeed in convincing someone who enjoys premarital sex that obeying God's commands to abstain from it will actually make her happier and more emotionally fulfilled. It might not unless she loves God and wants to please him."

Bianca chimed in, "For instance, if I'm not convinced that the long-term, holistic—I like that word—benefits of staying away from doughnuts are worth it, I may go ahead and eat the doughnuts and find them very pleasurable. The power to resist and interpret the resistance as beneficial comes from believing certain things about the doughnuts."

Lauren looked dissatisfied. "That seems mystical. You seem to be saying that I won't find God's commands good for me until I believe they're good for me. Why would I embrace them if I didn't already think they would be good for me?"

"That brings me to my second point," responded Micah. "The Bible teaches that obeying God's commands brings joy and fulfillment. We don't obey them in order to get fulfillment, but Christians are convinced that God's commands are ultimately beneficial to us."

"Yes. God does command people to abstain from sex until they marry,"[13] added Bianca, "but most Christians believe that obeying this command enables them to have more fulfilling relationships, relationships based on giving their whole selves to the other person rather than merely satisfying a physical desire."

"As for why you would embrace such an idea," Micah looked directly at Lauren, "like everything else in Christianity, it starts with faith in God's revelation, and then leads on to the obedience part."

"Okay," Lauren concluded. "So Divine Command Theory, at least in Christianity, would forbid premarital sex on the grounds that God doesn't think it is good for us."

Micah and Bianca nodded in agreement.

"Very good," Lauren concluded. "Are we ready to compile our analysis?"

Bianca and Micah gave thumbs-up. The hard part—the thinking—was done; now they just had to write it.

---

13. For instance, Heb. 13:4.

QUESTIONS TO PONDER

- Do you believe Natural Law, on the whole, favors or militates against premarital sex?

- What are consequentialist arguments for and against premarital sex?

- Relative to premarital sex, compare and contrast the approaches of Ethical Egoism and Situation Ethics.

- Micah unsuccessfully attempted to evaluate premarital sex via Kant's first formulation of the categorical imperative. Do you see a better way of doing it?

- The students' discussions of Kant's second formulation and Virtue Ethics overlapped quite a bit. Do you see differences between them relative to premarital sex?

- The discussion of Divine Command Theory focused on Christianity. What are the views of premarital sex in Islam and Buddhism?

TERMS TO KNOW

- Premarital sex
- Consensual
- Sexually transmitted disease
- Formula of Humanity
- Chastity
- Holistic

FOR FURTHER READING

Feinberg, John S. and Paul D. Feinberg. *Ethics for a Brave New World*. Wheaton, IL: Crossway, 2010, chapter 6: 267–306.

Geisler, Norman L. *Christian Ethics: Contemporary Issues & Options*. Grand Rapids: Baker Academic, 2010, chapter 15: 260–79.

Grenz, Stanley. *Sexual Ethics*. Dallas: Word, 1990.

Rae, Scott B. *Moral Choices: An Introduction to Ethics*. Grand Rapids: Zondervan, 2009, chapter 10: 270–301.

12

HOMOSEXUALITY

Synopsis: In this chapter Bianca and a friend Sophie discuss Sophie's discovery that her roommate is homosexual. Bianca and Sophie share the same religious background and a significant part of their discussion revolves around trying to understand what Christianity teaches about homosexuality and how a Christian should react in Sophie's situation. Eventually Bianca ends up discussing some aspects of the issue with Lauren, who brings a nonreligious perspective into the conversation.

* * *

The hiss of the espresso machine and the powerful, alluring aromas of coffee and spiced tea greeted Sophie as she opened the door and entered The Grey Earl. She was not a frequent visitor, but this is where Bianca suggested that they meet. Sophie had asked her if they could talk as they were leaving church on Sunday.

She looked around: The Grey Earl was an interesting shop. It had a very eclectic interior, decorated with things old and new. Bright, well-lit areas suitable for reading or school work were offset by dimly lit, more private areas, well-suited to personal conversations or solitary meditation. She spotted Bianca waiting for her in a corner of the room. Her friend had selected a location that was private while not seeming reclusive. *It's perfect*, Sophie thought. *We'll be able to have a private conversation without it looking like we're doing anything out of the ordinary.* She stopped to order a cappuccino and made her way over to the table. "Hi, Bianca. Thanks for agreeing to meet with me."

"Anytime," Bianca responded. "When school's in session we don't get much time together, but it's always nice to see one of my Eastern European sisters! Are you going to get something to drink?"

"They're making my cappuccino now," she replied. "What are you working on?"

"Actually," Bianca explained, "I'm reviewing the notes from my ethics class. We have a test coming up, and the material has been rather philosophical. This isn't one of those classes where you can bluff your way through the exams: you need to know the terms and understand the concepts or it will be very clear that you haven't done your homework."

"I didn't know that you're taking ethics. That's perfect timing!"

"It is? How so?" Bianca's curiosity was clear.

"Well, what I wanted to talk about is sort of an ethical issue," Sophie explained. "I'll get my cappuccino and be right back to explain." She left to retrieve her drink, leaving Bianca in momentary suspense. When she returned, Sophie seemed to be avoiding eye contact. She took a very careful sip of her drink and then stared at it for a few seconds. She reached for a napkin, unfolded it, spread it on her lap, and attempted again to take a sip. "This is too hot to drink," she said, finally looking at Bianca. "I'm going to get a straw." When she returned with her straw, she still seemed fidgety, so Bianca decided that she'd begin the conversation.

"How is your semester going?" she asked. "Are your classes OK?"

"It's a pretty normal semester, I guess. Or at least it's normal from an academic perspective."

This was the opening that Bianca needed. "Is there some perspective from which it's not normal? Is that what you wanted to talk about?"

"Yes, there's a new twist in my housing situation. It's not necessarily a problem. It's just something that I could use some help thinking through. I'm not quite sure how to respond to it—or how to feel about it. And you know, I just don't have many other friends who are Orthodox who I can talk to."

"I understand that!" Bianca responded heartily. Although the Orthodox church in town had been founded more than half a century earlier and had a nicely diverse congregation, very few college students attended it. "Are you having some kind of religious conflict with your roommates?"

"No," Sophie replied. "It's nothing like that. It's . . . well . . . one of my roommates is homosexual." She said this with a very controlled voice, carefully keeping her tone and volume level. "She hasn't made an announcement about it or anything, but she's not hiding it either. She's had her girlfriend over a few times, and you can see that they're more than just friends. A few days ago I saw them together in town, and I just happened to catch them in a kiss. I don't know if she plans to tell us or not. Since five women share our apartment, it seems like it might be appropriate for her to inform us. Then again, it's her private life, and perhaps it's none of our business. I'm torn on this issue in so many ways. . . ."

"I'm sure you are," Bianca empathized. "You guys have a good thing going. With the five of you sharing expenses, you live cheaply, and you all get along fine and pull your weight with the chores and everything. It's rare to find five people who can live together so successfully. I hope this doesn't cause problems."

"Yeah, we do have a very good situation. I'd hoped that we'd stay together right through graduation, though I know that's rare. Honestly, although Brandi's always been the least socially involved part of our team, she's also been the least trouble. I really don't expect that to change. I mean, I know that people can change in some pretty surprising ways, but she doesn't seem to have changed at all. She's still quiet, neat, and very polite. Maybe I'm overreacting—maybe there's nothing to worry about."

"It's Brandi? I've met her. She struck me as levelheaded and serious. Quiet, but nice."

"She is. What prompted me to ask you to meet was actually a remark that Father Gheorghe made on Sunday. Do you remember when he said that 'God loves all people, regardless of profession, political views, race, or sexual orientation'?" Bianca nodded her head. "I believe that, of course. But I also know that the church views homosexuality as sin.[1] I've read the Bible, and I

---

1. In Christian thought, considerable overlap exists between the meanings of the terms "sinful" and "immoral," but their connotations differ in a subtle way. An immoral act is any act that is contrary to the will of or to the moral nature of God.

know places that name homosexuals among those who will not inherit the kingdom of God.[2] I'm struggling to reconcile these things in my mind: God loves homosexuals, but the church views them as sinners. God loves them, but he won't let them into the kingdom. How can both sides be true?"

"Those are good questions, Sophie. No doubt about it. Have you tried talking to Father Gheorghe about them?"

"No, I haven't. I guess maybe I should, but I've never been very comfortable talking to clergy. They seem so—I don't know—aloof, I guess? They're just not like regular people."

"Actually," Bianca countered, "Father Gheorghe is very much a regular person. I've had some great personal talks with him. In fact, he's got one of the best senses of humor of anyone I know! I love talking to him. You should give it a try."

"That's interesting. I wasn't expecting to hear that. Perhaps I'll try to talk to him about it. But can we talk too? Do you mind?"

"Of course we can. I wasn't trying to get rid of you or anything. But when it comes to theology, I'm not all that strong. I grew up in a Christian home and try to live the Christian life, but you probably know as much about the Bible and what the church teaches as I do."

"That's OK," she said with a laugh. "You know more about ethics than I do, so between the two of us, we may be able to solve a problem or two."

"Sophie," Bianca began hesitantly, "what do you think of the old phrase 'Love the sinner, hate the sin'? Might that apply to God's attitude toward homosexuals?"

"I guess in theory it could," she granted. "But it always struck me as kind of cliché. If you really think that someone is heavily involved in some sort of sinful behavior, then you're going to have a hard time not thinking of them in light of what they're doing, aren't you? I mean, if someone is involved in

---

A sinful act is an immoral act, but there is the additional connotation that it is an act deserving of divine judgment. In this chapter, though, the terms will be used as synonyms since this is an ethics discussion rather than a theology discussion.

2. "Do you not know that the unrighteous will not inherit the kingdom of God? Do not be deceived. Neither fornicators, nor idolaters, nor adulterers, nor homosexuals, nor sodomites, nor thieves, nor covetous, nor drunkards, nor revilers, nor extortioners will inherit the kingdom of God" (1 Cor. 6:9–10 NKJV).

scamming senior citizens and taking their life savings, that's going to have a pretty major impact on how you view that person, right? And it will shape how God views them too, won't it?"

"Well, yes, of course it will," Bianca agreed. "But it doesn't necessarily mean that God will hate them for it. But maybe we're begging the question—or at least getting ahead of ourselves. Maybe we should begin by talking about whether or not homosexuality is actually immoral."

"OK, that's logical. I'll begin. One reason that I believe that homosexuality is immoral is that it's what the church teaches. The Orthodox Church, that is. I don't know all that much about what Roman Catholics and Protestants believe, but I imagine that it's similar to what Orthodoxy teaches on this subject. The Orthodox view is that when God originally created the world and everything in it, it was good. There was no sin, no evil, and no immorality. But then humans rebelled against God, and that rebellion introduced sin into the world. All of the moral problems that exist today are a result of humanity rebelling against God.[3] Homosexuality is just one example of this rebellion.

"Let me back up a little and explain that statement. Orthodoxy sees heterosexual marriage first and foremost from a soteriological perspective.[4] The Bible says that God first created Adam, and then because it was not good for Adam to be alone, God created Eve as a counterpart to Adam, a 'helpmate.' According to this picture, the original purpose of marriage isn't pleasure or procreation but rather an interpersonal relationship wherein a man and a woman complete each other. In this way, marriage pictures the Holy Trinity, three distinct persons forming one unified God, each divine person of the Trinity perfectly complementing the other two. Hence marriage has an inherently religious signification. It's a holy symbol, one that should not be tampered with.

"Orthodoxy sees homosexuality as an example of humanity's rebellion against God because practicing homosexuals have rejected God's original plan for marriage. And this rejection has many practical consequences, such

---

3. Thomas Hopko, *Christian Faith and Same-Sex Attraction: Eastern Orthodox Reflections* (Ben Lomand, CA: Conciliar, 2006), 24–25.

4. *Soteriology* is an area of theology. It is the study of the doctrines having to do with salvation from sin and sin's consequences and the resulting restoration of humans to a right relationship with God.

as undermining God's plan for procreation, which includes sexual pleasure as a means of creating children and encouraging loving, nurturing families that contribute to the flourishing of the human race. Homosexuality rejects God's plan, and as a result it deprives homosexuals of these natural benefits of God's wisdom."

"So then," Bianca interjected, "from the perspective of an Ethical Egoist, would you argue that homosexuality is immoral because it's not in the best interest of homosexuals?"

"Pardon me?" Sophie responded. "What's an 'Ethical Egoist'?"

"Sorry," Bianca apologized. "It's just one of the theories from my ethics class. Don't worry about it. I'm sure that's not where you were headed anyway. Are all Orthodox scholars in agreement that homosexuality is immoral?"

"Well, I didn't actually say that homosexuality is immoral, and I'm not sure that all Orthodox scholars would either. Some people make what may be an important distinction between homosexuality as a tendency toward same-sex attraction and homosexuality as an active lifestyle. I think nearly all Orthodox scholars probably hold that the latter, which implies actually committing homosexual acts, is sinful. I think there may be less unanimity on the former issue, though. Is it immoral to feel a sexual attraction for someone of the same sex if you don't do so willingly? I mean, I wish that some things that tempt me didn't. I can't help it that they do, and I don't give in to them. Jesus was tempted by Satan in the wilderness, but he never sinned, so I don't think being tempted by something is inherently sinful."

"I'm not sure that argument works, my friend. I love that you look to Jesus as your moral guide—so do I—but I think we're in danger of equivocating here. When Satan tempted Jesus by offering him bread when he was famished or power when he was humble, I doubt those things really tempted Jesus at all. Satan performed the act of tempting him, so to speak, but Jesus saw right through it and didn't seem to find any of the offers at all appealing.

"I agree with your earlier point, though. We shouldn't conflate same-sex attraction and living a homosexual lifestyle. For one thing, they can have very different consequences. But I don't think I want to lapse into a consequentialist way of thinking about this—that's something else from my ethics class. You know, you really should take this class sometime: it's opened my eyes to many different ways of thinking about morality.

"Anyway, I agree that homosexuality in the first sense and homosexuality in the second are two different things. But I'm not completely sure that even the first kind of homosexuality would be viewed as completely innocent by theologians. Do you remember Jesus saying that if a man lusts after a woman in his heart, it's as if he had already committed adultery with her?[5] And how he compares being angry at someone to killing that person, as if what's in a person's heart is as important as what a person actually does?[6] It seems like Jesus is just as concerned with our intentions as he is with our actions, which is, now that I think about it, consistent with his statement that 'out of the abundance of the heart the mouth speaks.'"[7]

"You're definitely not theologically illiterate, Bianca. You were being overly modest! You seem to know the Bible pretty well." Sophie was genuinely impressed with her friend's knowledge.

"Yeah, I've been taking a greater interest in it since I've been hanging around Micah. He takes the Bible very seriously."

"I've noticed that the two of you are spending some time together lately," Sophie observed. "Are you guys dating?"

"No . . ." Bianca responded, her voice trailing off.

"Oh, I see. So you're thinking about it, perhaps?"

"We'll see. For right now, we're just good friends. I think he may be interested in someone else, but I'm not sure."

"Oh, too bad. He seems like a real nice guy—and smarter than some too. He's not Orthodox, though, is he? I've never seen him at church."

"No," Bianca quickly responded. "He's very involved in an evangelical Protestant church. I visited it once with him, and it was nice. It's different from the Orthodox Church, but not in a bad way."

"Of course. I didn't mean to imply that everyone has to be Orthodox. It's having a heart for God that's most important."

"Amen to that!" Bianca replied. Sophie gave her a strange look.

"So back to our topic," Bianca continued. "I've heard of Christians who take a more progressive approach to the issue—Protestants, Catholics, and

---

5. Matt. 5:28.
6. Matt. 5:21, 22.
7. Luke 6:45.

even a few Orthodox.[8] The traditional view isn't the only view, you know. And being the traditional view doesn't always make it right."

"That's not a very Orthodox thing to say, is it, Bianca? Don't go all Protestant on me now that you've got a Protestant boy-interest!" Sophie was giggling as she said this. She and Bianca were close enough friends that their friendship could take a little ribbing once in a while.

"This isn't really a Protestant thing," Bianca replied, wanting both to defend and to explain herself. "There's a fallacy that we learned about in our ethics class called 'the appeal to tradition.' If everything is true that is a long-standing practice or belief, then traditional beliefs like the old-fashioned belief that bleeding people can cure diseases or the belief that the earth is the center of the solar system would be true.[9] But they're obviously not, so we need more than just tradition in order to determine whether homosexuality is immoral."

"I see your point—clearly. But how does that apply to theology? Don't we base our theology on the traditions handed down through the church, which has for two millennia preserved the teachings of Jesus, the apostles, and the church fathers? Is the church committing the fallacy of appealing to tradition?" Sophie's tone of voice indicated that she didn't think this was likely.

"Not necessarily," Bianca reassured her. "But we have to be careful how we reason or we might. If we have some good reason for thinking that the church is correct in its view, then we're not simply appealing to tradition, we're appealing to the church as an authority of the topic. Of course, that brings about another possible fallacy: the appeal to authority. But once again, if we're careful we can avoid it. The church believes what it believes because

---

8. An example of a progressive Christian position on homosexuality is that found in the statement of the United Church of Christ, "In Support of Equal Marriage Rights for All," which can be found on the UCC web page, http://uccfiles.com/pdf/in-support-of-equal-marriage-rights-for-all-with-background.pdf.

9. Until the seventeenth century, the standard view of the arrangement of the solar system was that the sun and the other planets revolve around the Earth. This is called the Ptolemaic theory, named after the Greek astronomer Ptolemy. It's also called the heliocentric view of the solar system. The standard view today is that the Earth and all the other planets revolve around the sun. This is called the Copernican theory, named after the Polish astronomer Copernicus. It's also called the geocentric view of the solar system.

God has revealed it. Since God knows everything that can ever be known, and since God doesn't lie, we can be certain that whatever God reveals is true. So as long as the church is rightly interpreting and faithfully teaching what God has revealed, we're on solid ground."

"Great!" Sophie responded, enthusiastically. "So our discussion returns to what God has revealed about homosexuality. And as I pointed out at the beginning, the Bible is clearly against it."

"Yes you did. However, in the interest of avoiding setting up any straw men—you're familiar with that term?" Sophie nodded her head affirmatively, so Bianca continued. "In order to avoid setting up a straw man, we need to at least consider the more progressive interpretation of what the Bible says on the issue."

"I don't have any idea how progressive Christians interpret the Bible on homosexuality," Sophie confessed.

"That's OK," Bianca assured her. "I read up on it for my class. First, let me address an argument that you alluded to a few minutes ago. You talked about heterosexual relationships being beneficial to a couple and to humanity because they result in procreation while homosexual relationships cannot. This is a common argument in the Natural Law school of thought. Natural Law ethicists think that what's moral can be discovered by carefully examining the way God made us and the way that we fit into the natural world in which God has placed us. This approach is especially common among Roman Catholic ethicists. They reason that God has a perfect plan—a design—for everything that he has created. All of the pieces of God's creation fit together like the pieces of a puzzle. If we look carefully at God's creation, including ourselves, it's often possible to figure out how the pieces fit together. In other words, we can figure out God's design plan.

"Now if we apply this theory to sex, it seems obvious that one of the primary purposes of sex is reproduction, like you were saying. God created sexual intercourse—with all of its pleasure—to encourage the flourishing of the human race. But if reproduction is the only reason that God created sex, then people should only have sex in order to reproduce, right? Otherwise they're corrupting God's purpose. But that doesn't seem right. That would mean that couples who don't want to have any more children—and even couples who can't have children—shouldn't make love. So it seems likely that there's more than one purpose behind sex. Another possible purpose is to encourage bonding between couples through the shared experience of physical and emotional intimacy. Furthermore, it's completely possible that God created human sexuality in part because of the intense pleasure that it brings: after all, God is the author of all good things, and pleasure, when not abused, is a good thing.

"Progressive Christians who want to make space for homosexual relationships in Christian teachings can point to these things to undermine the Natural Law argument that you used. A homosexual couple can fulfill several of God's purposes for sex, even if they can't fulfill the one pertaining to reproduction. And they can argue that it's not necessary to fulfill that one if they're fulfilling the others. If heterosexual couples aren't sanctioned for having sex without producing children because such love-making deepens their relationship and produces healthy pleasure, then homosexual couples shouldn't be sanctioned for love-making that deepens their relationship and produces healthy pleasure."

"Wow!" Sophie responded in surprise. "That actually makes a lot of sense! How come I never thought of that on my own? That's actually a pretty good argument! I think I've always taken it for granted that Christianity clearly opposes homosexual activity and views it as sinful. Apparently there's more to this issue than I knew!"

"I'm not saying that I think homosexual sex isn't immoral," Bianca quickly clarified. "I'm just trying to help you see it from the perspective of Christians who hold to that view. It's not my own view, though."

"Of course," Sophie agreed. "I figured that. But I want to know more about the progressive perspective. What other arguments do they use?"

"Well you also mentioned some Bible verses that condemn homosexual activity. Verses that cast homosexuality in a negative light span both testaments. Progressive Christians, however, accuse people who use these verses to oppose homosexuality of failing to interpret them according to their context. Take, for example, the apparent homosexuality of the men of Sodom. You remember the story, don't you?"

"Of course," Sophie affirmed, nodding her head. "Abraham's nephew Lot was living in this town called Sodom, but it was so wicked that God decided to destroy it. He sent two angels to warn Lot and his family of the coming destruction. Apparently they looked like ordinary men, and while they were speaking to Lot, the men of Sodom attempted to abduct them and rape them. The angels struck the men with blindness and made their escape. This is where we get the term 'sodomy.'"

"Right," Bianca confirmed, "that's it. People who oppose homosexuality often point to this passage as showing that homosexual activity is immoral. Why did God want to destroy Sodom? Because the Sodomites were evil. How were they evil? Well the one thing we know for sure is that they practiced homosexual intercourse. But that leaves out an important fact. This was homosexual *rape*. It was forced homosexual intercourse. Progressive Christians argue that what this story really shows us is that involuntary homosexual activity is immoral—just as involuntary heterosexual activity is immoral. But that doesn't mean that all homosexual activity is immoral any more than biblical condemnation of involuntary heterosexual activity means that all heterosexual activity is immoral."

"Wow, that's a new way of looking at the passage," Sophie said, with a hint of amazement in her voice. "I never even thought of that."

"I think it shows how easy it is to assume that a passage supports your position and how important it is to try to step back from your presuppositions and try to look at things from a neutral perspective. After all, we want the Bible to tell us what it means, not us tell the Bible what it should be saying, right?"

"Yes of course. I wonder how many Bible verses I've misunderstood because of faulty presuppositions. . . ." Sophie's voice trailed off as she reflected on this. Thoughtfully she asked, "Do you think there are any passages at all in the Bible that oppose homosexuality? Or are they all disputable like this one?"

"I personally think there are quite a few passages that oppose homosexuality, Sophie. I hope you didn't get the impression that I think the Bible isn't clear on this issue. I was merely trying to help you see that there are significant considerations on both sides of the debate. In the final analysis though, I think the person who wants to hold to the biblical view on the issue will have to be opposed to homosexual activity, even when it's completely voluntary.

"For example, near the beginning of the book of Romans, the apostle Paul writes about a whole list of sins, but he focuses on homosexuality more than any of the others. In this context there's no suggestion that the homosexual acts being condemned were involuntary. On the contrary, Paul writes that the participants 'burned in their lust toward each other,' suggesting that it was an act of mutual sexual gratification. Nonetheless he considers it sin."[10]

"OK," Sophie responded, "I'm somewhat familiar with that passage. Or at least I've read it, though it would probably be good to read it again. But if it's consensual, what makes it immoral?"

"Well for starters, if it's extramarital, that would be a problem. But even within marriage—if homosexual marriage was legal—Paul would view it as immoral. He gives two reasons for this: first, it goes against God's design; and second, it's not good for those who practice it. The first reason may relate to the Natural Law type of argument that we were discussing earlier: God's original plan, as seen in Adam and Eve, was one husband and one wife, which is a good recipe for a stable family that leads to and nurtures children and enables people and the human race to prosper. When a man and a woman make a long-term commitment to each other, they form a team that instantly makes them stronger than if they were alone. They support each other, they take care of each other, they share expenses and chores and help each other in a myriad of ways. When they have children, that increases their interdependence. A healthy family is a reward in itself. Eventually grandchildren come along, and the children and grandchildren give the original couple a reason to go on living after their careers have ended and eventually contribute to caring for them."

"This reminds me of a beautiful passage in Ecclesiastes," Sophie interjected. "It's so poetic that I have it memorized:

"Two are better than one,
Because they have a good reward for their labor.
For if they fall, one will lift up his companion.
But woe to him who is alone when he falls,
For there is not a second one to help him up!
If two lie down together,
Both stay warm.
But how can one stay warm alone?
If one is added strength,

_____
10. Rom. 1:24–32.

Two will stand before him.
And a threefold cord is not quickly broken.[11]

"But most of these advantages could be had by homosexual couples if they're in a stable, long-term relationship, couldn't they?"

"Sure," Bianca replied. "Historically, homosexual relationships have tended to be less stable and enduring than heterosexual relationships, but I imagine that cultural factors contribute to that. Yet when a couple has children, that introduces a special bond that is hard to replace. Homosexual couples will never have that. It could be one of the greatest benefits of following God's plan."

"Wait," cut in Sophie. "How about if they adopt? Or how about artificial insemination for lesbian couples and surrogate mothers helping gay men to have children of their own?" Sophie, catching on to the dialectical nature of ethical thinking, was starting to anticipate objections and counterarguments on her own.

"I guess those options would come pretty close," Bianca granted. "Adoption is a great one: it meets the needs of both the adoptive parents and the adopted child, and I understand that the bonds between adopted children and their parents can be as strong as the bonds between natural children and their parents. So this brings me to Paul's other argument: that homosexual activity itself has undesirable consequences. I imagine what he has in mind includes the health problems that are sometimes associated with homosexual activity. Since homosexuals have typically been less monogamous than heterosexuals, who tend to get married and tend to be more monogamous—not implying, of course, that no straight people are ever unfaithful to their partners—homosexuals have tended to be more susceptible to sexually transmitted diseases. A monogamous heterosexual marriage has health benefits for both the husband and the wife."

"OK, I can see that," Sophie allowed. "Still, if society encouraged monogamous homosexual marriages as much as it encourages monogamous heterosexual marriages, and if as a result homosexual practice was typified by monogamous relationships to the same degree that heterosexual relationships

---

11. Eccl. 4:9-12, *The Orthodox Study Bible* (Nashville: Thomas Nelson, 2008).

are, do you think the rate of STDs and the like would be the same among homosexuals as it is among heterosexuals?"

"I really don't know, I'm sorry to say," Bianca admitted. "I'm not a nursing student. I wish my friend Lauren were here. She might be able to answer that question."

"Well, I think I'd like to keep this conversation private for the time being anyway, OK?" Sophie asked.

"Of course," Bianca replied. "I'm sure we can find the answers to such questions in the library or on the internet, anyway. We don't need to bring anyone else into the conversation if you're not comfortable with that."

Just then the wreath of pinecones and bells that festooned the front door of The Grey Earl jingled. Looking up, Bianca glimpsed Lauren's blond hair and large, poufy down jacket entering the shop. She immediately looked away, but it was too late: Lauren had spotted them, but she headed straight to the counter. "Speaking of the devil . . ." Bianca said softly.

"What? Who?" Sophie queried.

"It's Lauren. See, over by the counter? The blond-haired girl? She's not the devil: she's actually quite angelic, though oddly enough she's also an atheist. But it's funny that she'd show up just after I mentioned her. We hang out here pretty often, though, so I guess it's not so strange. We could ask her about the medical side of the issue . . . do you want to?"

"Only if we can do it in a very general way, without bringing up my roommate. I don't want to be starting rumors about her."

"OK, we'll be discreet," Bianca assured her. "She saw us, so maybe she'll come over. If she does, I'll invite her to join us, and if she doesn't, we'll just let it pass."

Sure enough, once Lauren had purchased her drink, she made her way over to the small table where Bianca and Sophie were sitting. "Hi, guys," she greeted them, smiling and making a little twist with her body and a little nod with her head, conveying a friendly greeting while being careful not to spill her hot jasmine green tea. "May I join you?"

"Sure, please do!" Bianca replied. "This is my friend Sophie. Sophie, this is my good friend Lauren. Coincidently, Lauren and I are in the same ethics class."

"It's nice to meet you, Lauren," Sophie responded. "Bianca tells me that you're studying nursing."

"That's true. Are you in nursing too?"

"No, I'm a math major."

"Oh wow, you're one of those smart people! I'm not much good at math. It may be my worst subject. I respect people who have the mental focus to actually major in it." Lauren sounded sincere, and Sophie took it as a genuine compliment.

Feeling more positive about Lauren gave Sophie the courage to open up a little about what she and Bianca had been discussing. "Bianca and I were just talking about her—your—ethics class."

"Ahhh, that's why it's a coincidence that we're in the same ethics class. I was wondering what you meant by that, Bianca."

"Yes," Bianca explained, "that's the coincidence. You came in at just the right moment! We were talking about some things that Father Gheorghe, our priest, said about homosexuality on Sunday. That naturally led me to tell Sophie about our ethics class. In fact, I even mentioned you. We were wondering if there are any health problems that stem from homosexual activity even if that activity occurs only within the bounds of a monoga-mous relationship. And that's why I told her that you're a nursing major: I said that you'd probably know more about this than I do and that we should ask you."

"Well, I do know a bit about the medical issues related to homosexuality," she volunteered. "I've studied it some in my nursing classes and then a little more in ethics. But most of what I've read had to do with problems involving multiple partners rather than strictly monogamous relationships. I guess in monogamous male homosexual relationships there will still be issues relating to anal intercourse . . . but those same problems can happen in heterosexual relationships. Anal sex is risky business.[12] Other than that, I can't contribute much to this discussion, I'm sorry to say."

"That's OK," Sophie declared. "I appreciate your expertise. I've got to get going anyway: I have a lot of homework. One of the down sides of my major is that there's homework every—single—night! Math homework is fun, like solving a puzzle, but by this point in the semester, I'm ready for a break. So

---

12. For more on this, see WebMD, "Anal Sex Safety and Health Concerns," WebMD.com, https://www.webmd.com/sex/anal-sex-health-concerns#1.

thanks for talking, Bianca, and it was nice meeting you, Lauren. I hope I'll see you around."

***

Lauren and Bianca bade Sophie farewell. When she had gone, Lauren turned to Bianca a little quizzically and asked, "Was that just a theoretical discussion, or is there something that I should know?"

"It was purely theoretical," Bianca assured her. "Mostly. From the Orthodox perspective, homosexual activity is sinful. However, Orthodoxy also teaches that God loves all people, and that all people are created in God's image and thus deserve to be treated respectfully, as having inherent worth. Sophie wanted to talk about how we reconcile all of that, and what with my bringing in stuff from our ethics class, the conversation turned into quite a discussion. I ran out of tea a long time ago, so if you don't mind, I'm going to get a refill. Can I bring you anything?"

"No, I'm fine," Lauren responded, and Bianca went off in pursuit of another chai latte. Lauren blew gently on her steaming tea, deep in thought. When Bianca returned, Lauren asked, "Would you mind talking a bit more about Orthodoxy and homosexuality? I'd like to understand your position."

"Not at all," her friend responded. "Where should we begin?"

"Well, I assume that your position is rooted in the teachings of the Bible as historically interpreted in the Orthodox tradition. That seems rather old-fashioned to me, but we've already had that discussion, and I understand the logic of how you defend your approach. But when you say that homosexuality is a sin, aren't you faulting homosexuals for something that's completely out of their control? After all, people don't choose to be gay any more than you chose to be straight, or female, or Caucasian for that matter."[13]

---

13. While today it is often assumed that sexual orientation is genetically determined, there is some debate on the issue within the medical community. Environmental factors may also play a role. For example, one study investigated 409 pairs of homosexual brothers and found evidence of both genetic and environmental influences on a person's sexual orientation. See A. R. Sanders et al, "Genome-Wide Scan Demonstrates Significant Linkage for Male Sexual Orientation," *Psychological Medicine* 45, no. 7 (2015): 1379–88.

"That's actually one of the things that Sophie and I were discussing. It's a good question, but I think there's a pretty reasonable answer to it. Orthodoxy doesn't say that being a homosexual is sin, but it does say that homosexual intercourse is sin. There's an important difference. While it may be the case that some people have a genetic predisposition to homosexuality, having such a predisposition does not necessitate that someone act on the predisposition any more than having a predisposition to heterosexuality demands that someone act on that predisposition. Lots of single heterosexual people abstain from sex. Surely homosexuals can too."

"But you're forgetting something, aren't you? A straight person who abstains from sex has the hope that it's not permanent. A gay person who abstains because he thinks it is sinful must resolve to abstain for his or her entire life. That's asking a lot!"

"Well, yes, it would be," Bianca granted. "But some heterosexuals abstain for their whole lives. Plus, not all people who are homosexual remain that way for their entire lives, and some are actually bisexual and can have fulfilling relationships with the opposite sex. So the situation isn't as severe as you make it seem."

"OK, I agree with you," Lauren allowed. "But that still leaves some people who must resign themselves to a life of celibacy simply because the church says that it's sinful to live life the way they were naturally born to live it. For such people, the Orthodox position is a pretty hard pill to swallow, don't you think?"

"No harder than it is for heterosexuals who remain celibate—priests, nuns, and people who just never meet the right person. God calls us to a higher standard: permanent, monogamous, heterosexual relationships. He knows that's what is best for us in the long run."

"This is part of Divine Command Theory, right? That's the ethical theory that you prefer?" Dr. Platt had drilled the importance of getting to the theoretical root of ethical disagreements into his students rather effectively.

"Actually," Bianca replied, "It's Divine Nature Theory, but at this point in the discussion the difference is irrelevant. If you believe that, one way or another, morality is determined by an all-knowing, all-wise, all-loving God, then it makes sense to conclude that what is morally right is also what's in everyone's best interest."

"Hmmm . . . ," Lauren reflected. "There seems to be an undertone of Utilitarianism there too, isn't there?"

"Yes and no, I guess," Bianca admitted. "The feeling that I get from Utilitarian authors like John Stuart Mill is that an act that maximizes benefit and minimizes harm is moral simply because it maximizes benefit and minimizes harm. It seems like Utilitarianism assumes that the nature of reality is such that things that are beneficial are automatically moral. That leaves me with the feeling that something still needs explanation. Why is it that in a world without God, an act that maximizes benefit is superior to one that doesn't? I don't know if Utilitarianism has an answer for this question. I think theistic theories do a better job of explaining why maximized benefit is always the moral choice: it's because the world was set up by an omnibenevolent being who wants everything to work out for the well-being of all of his creation and all of his creatures."[14]

"Huh. That's interesting—I mean, you've got a pretty good critique of Utilitarianism there. You should talk to Dr. Platt about it. He'd be able to tell you if you're really on to something."

"Thanks!" Bianca was beaming. She hadn't expected Lauren to agree with her, let alone pay her such a high compliment. "So have I convinced you to abandon Utilitarianism, then?"

"No," she responded. "I wasn't a Utilitarian to begin with. And Dr. Platt's criticisms of relativism have pretty much convinced me that relativism isn't a viable option either. So since I don't believe in God, I'm strongly leaning toward Kantian Duty Ethics. It combines the strengths of Ethical Realism, a high regard for logical consistency, and a rational justification for the Golden Rule, which is perhaps what I like best in the world's great religions but without the mystical element.

"Since I'm a Kantian," she continued, "I need to adopt an attitude toward homosexuality that is consistent with Kantian ethics. Therefore I need to base it on a principle that can be universalized. That leads me to want to grant a lot of leeway to those who want to practice alternative lifestyles. Live and let

---

14. A good introduction to the debate over whether or not God is necessary in order to have a comprehensive explanation of morality is R. Keith Loftin, ed., *God and Morality: Four Views* (Downers Grove, IL: InterVarsity Press, 2012).

live seems to be a maxim that is easy to universalize. Do you remember that article by Robert Nozick that we read for class? The one where he argued for a libertarian reading of Kant?[15] I think that's the basic direction that I'd want to go."

"I do remember the article," Bianca confirmed. "It wasn't that long ago that it was assigned reading. But how is it relevant to the morality or immorality of homosexual relations? I don't follow your argument."

"Well, a big part of the discussion about homosexuality is about whether or not homosexual acts should be prohibited by law, and whether same-sex marriages should be legal. As you know, many states used to have laws against homosexual acts. But homosexual marriage has been legal in all fifty states since 2015. It seems to me that the categorical imperative requires that we adopt an attitude that allows people to decide for themselves whether homosexuality is moral and whether same-sex marriage is right.[16] The principle could be something like this: 'It is right for all people everywhere to decide for themselves whether to be involved in a heterosexual relationship, a homosexual relationship, or no relationship at all.'"

"I see," Bianca affirmed, slowly and thoughtfully. "It seems to me that you come pretty close to conflating morality and legality there. You'll have to be careful to avoid that. I see the question of the morality of homosexual acts as being distinct from the question of the legality of homosexual acts. I think it's a mistake to assume that everything that is immoral should automatically be illegal, though there are some Christians who seem to think this way. Perhaps I'm a little bit libertarian too. It seems to me that because the Bible teaches that each person is accountable to God for how he or she lives, we need to allow people the space to make up their own minds about what's right and what's wrong. This is what Christians call 'freedom of conscience.' And if we do that, then we must grant them the right to live by their decisions, as long as their decisions don't harm those around them. So in the end, it seems like

---

15. The class had read excerpts from Robert Nozick's *Anarchy, State, and Utopia* (New York: Basic Books, 1974).

16. The categorical imperative is Kant's key moral principle. The most common formulation in Kant's work is "Act only on that maxim which you can at the same time will to be a universal law." Immanuel Kant, *Foundations of the Metaphysics of Morals*, trans. Lewis Beck (Indianapolis: Bobbs-Merrill, 1959), 422.

you and I might disagree on the morality of homosexuality but even so we might agree on the question of its legal status. What do you think?"

"I'm pretty sure we'll disagree on the morality part of it!" Lauren agreed, laughing just a little. "I'm a bit surprised by your approach to the legal aspect though. If that really is the Christian teaching, then I'm pleasantly surprised and also a little impressed! I was expecting you to argue that homosexuality is sinful and consequently should not be allowed by law. Is your view peculiar to Orthodoxy, or is it common to all denominations of Christians?"

"It's not particular to Orthodoxy," Bianca explained, "but it's not accepted by all Christians either. All Christians that I'm aware of affirm the doctrine of freedom of conscience, but some of them qualify it to such an extent that it loses some of its impact. And many who do not qualify it out of existence would still argue that homosexual activity should be illegal because of its harmful impact on society. I guess I'm just a little bit progressive on this one aspect of the issue. But how about Kantians? Are Kantians agreed that the decision about the moral and legal status of homosexuality should be completely left up to the individual?"

"You know, I really can't say, Bianca. This is, after all, my first-ever ethics class. You know about as much about Kantian ethics as I do. But I can imagine that some Kantians would argue that we cannot universalize the principle of homosexual activity without undermining procreation and that therefore homosexuality is immoral. Really, where would we be if our ancestors universalized the principle, 'All people everywhere should be homosexuals?'"

Obviously they wouldn't be anywhere, but Bianca was so surprised to see Lauren undermining her own position in this way that she didn't know how to respond. For herself, Lauren was having trouble holding in a laugh at Bianca's look of bewilderment. Finally Lauren collapsed into uncontrolled laughter, which got Bianca laughing too, and their serious conversation was over. The rest of the evening they spent talking about lighter topics until eventually the need to get some schoolwork done forced them to part company, go home, and get back to work.

QUESTIONS TO PONDER

- If you think homosexual acts are immoral, why do you think that?

- If you think that homosexual acts are moral, do you think that there are any limits on what constitutes a moral homosexual act?

- Do you think that same-sex marriages are moral? Why or why not?

- Do you think that same-sex marriages should be legal? Why or why not?

- Do you think that people in same-sex marriages should be legally permitted to adopt children?

TERMS TO KNOW

- Homosexual
- Heterosexual
- Gay
- Lesbian
- Progressive Christians
- Monogamous
- Procreate
- STD (sexually transmitted disease)
- Appeal to tradition fallacy
- Appeal to authority fallacy

FOR FURTHER READING

American Psychological Association. "Answers to Your Questions: For a Better Understanding of Sexual Orientation and Homosexuality." Accessed 5/16/2020, www.apa.org/topics/lgbt/orientation.pdf.

The APA views homosexuality as a normal lifestyle devoid of moral difficulties.

Dallas, Joe and Nancy Hecke, eds. *The Complete Christian Guide to Understanding Homosexuality.* Eugene, OR: Harvest House, 2010.

The articles in this anthology generally view homosexual acts as immoral.

Hopko, Thomas. *Christian Faith and Same-Sex Attraction: Eastern Orthodox Reflections.* Ben Lomond, CA: Conciliar Press, 2006.

This volume also views homosexual practice as immoral.

Lehmiller, Justin J. *The Psychology of Human Sexuality*, 2nd ed. Hoboken, NJ: John Wiley & Sons, 2017.

This is a scientific discussion of various sexual issues including homosexuality.

Myers, David and Letha Dawson Scanzoni. *What God Has Joined Together: The Christian Case for Gay Marriage.* New York: HarperOne, 2006.

This volume argues that homosexual practice can be moral.

13

GENDER IDENTITY

Synopsis: In this chapter the reader follows Micah into his adult Sunday school class at his church. The class is studying the book of Matthew in the Bible. The day's lesson is on the first half of chapter 19. The passage may have implications for the controversial issue of gender identity, and the discussion of this topic gives Micah much to think about. The next day Micah is still thinking about it when he is joined at The Grey Earl by Bianca and Lauren. Naturally, Micah shares his thoughts with his two friends, and the discussion that follows brings out additional facets of the issue.

* * *

"Good morning, everyone," Don began. "It's time to get started. Please join me in prayer."

Don Moyer was the teacher of the adult Sunday school class at the church Micah attended. He wasn't an ordained minister. Instead he was a businessman and dedicated Christian who taught the class as a way of serving God. While he didn't have any formal theological education, he had a good mind and had studied the Bible and theology informally for many years. Furthermore, he practiced what he preached by living out his faith. Because of this, people in the church naturally looked up to him.

Sunday school always began with Don leading the group in prayer. "Heavenly Father, we thank you for this day—another Lord's Day. We thank you for the freedom that we enjoy to meet together openly, without fear of persecution. We thank you for your Word and the ability to study it together. We ask that you would please guide us in our study: help us to understand what you are trying to teach us. Please use this hour to make us more like you. For that is why we are here: we're not here just to fellowship with each other; we're here because we want to know and to do your will. And we ask these things in the name of Jesus Christ, God incarnate. Amen."

The class had been studying the book of Matthew, the first book in the New Testament. They'd progressed all the way up to the 19th chapter. Don asked for a volunteer to read the first twelve verses. Jessica stood up and read:

> Now it came to pass, when Jesus had finished these sayings, that He departed from Galilee and came to the region of Judea beyond the Jordan. And great multitudes followed Him, and He healed them there. The Pharisees also came to Him, testing Him, and saying to Him, "Is it lawful for a man to divorce his wife for just any reason?" And He answered and said to them, "Have you not read that He who made them at the beginning 'made them male and female,' and said, 'For this reason a man shall leave his father and mother and be joined to his wife, and the two shall become one flesh'? So then, they are no longer two but one flesh. Therefore what God has joined together, let not man separate." They said to Him, "Why then did Moses command to give a certificate of divorce, and to put her away?" He said to them, "Moses, because of the hardness of your hearts, permitted you to divorce your wives, but from the beginning it was not so. And I say to you, whoever divorces his wife, except for sexual immorality, and marries another, commits adultery; and whoever marries her who is divorced commits adultery." His disciples said to Him, "If such is the case of the man with his wife, it is better not to marry." But He said to them, "All cannot accept this saying, but only those to whom it has been given: For there are eunuchs who were born thus from their mother's womb, and there are eunuchs who were made eunuchs by men, and there are eunuchs who have made themselves eunuchs for the kingdom of heaven's sake. He who is able to accept it, let him accept it." (NKJV)

"Thank you, Jessica," Don replied. "That was well read. Obviously this passage touches on a number of important theological and moral issues. The most obvious of these is divorce, followed by remarriage, and then marriage itself as opposed to a life of celibacy. We've already talked about most of these issues as they arose in earlier chapters, so today I want to discuss an issue that has recently become a prominent point of discussion in America: transgenderism. Who can tell us what transgenderism is?"

A young lady—perhaps college age—sitting near the front raised her hand, and Don called on her. "Transgenderism is a movement that argues that gender and biological sex are not the same thing, and that someone's gender and sex can sometimes disagree."

"Very good, Leah!" Don responds. "That's a great start. I'd like to add one additional thing: the transgender movement views gender as a fluid continuum rather than fixed and binary. Let me explain what I mean by that, and then we'll talk about how our Scripture passage relates to this issue.

"First, I need to clarify some vocabulary. There's a difference between the meaning of the word 'sex' and the meaning of 'gender.' The way these words are used in twenty-first-century English, the word 'sex' refers to a person's physical makeup: you're either male or female, and that is determined by your biology. The word 'gender,' on the other hand, refers to a person's psychological makeup, which can range from strongly masculine to strongly feminine, with many gradations in between. Most often people who are biologically male also fall somewhere along the masculine side of the gender spectrum, but not always. Likewise those who are biologically female usually but not always fall along the feminine side of the gender spectrum.

The possibility that biological sex and gender are not the same and should not be conflated—should not be treated as if they are identical—raises some difficult questions for society and for Christianity. For example, how should a pastor—or any Christian, for that matter—counsel someone who feels like she's a woman trapped in a man's body, as was claimed by the famous Olympic athlete who used to be known as Bruce Jenner? Should we tell such people that their gender was determined by God when he assigned their biological sex? Or should we view sex and gender as completely distinct and therefore embrace the possibility that a person might have a gender that is different from his or her biological sex?"

Jessica raised her hand, and Don called on her. "Isn't that question answered in our passage?" she asked. "When Jesus told the Pharisees that God made only two sexes, 'male and female,' he didn't say anything about other sexes besides those two or about a person being both male and female at the same time."

"Great question," he replied. "When Jesus said, 'he which made them at the beginning made them male and female,' he didn't seem to leave much room for anything in between, did he? Biologically speaking, things seem to be pretty cut and dry: there are two sexes and that's it. But I need to reiterate that there may be a difference between sex and gender. Even if God created only two sexes, that doesn't necessarily mean that he created only two genders, right?"

"Let me back up a little and explain something that I mentioned earlier. I basically laid out two positions that people take on gender identity. Some see gender as *binary*—there are only two options—masculine and feminine. Others see gender as a *continuum*—with varying degrees of masculinity and femininity possible. Many of those in the latter camp think that not being at either extreme is perfectly fine: there's nothing wrong with being somewhere in the middle. So a boy who likes to wear pink shirts and play with dolls would be fine, as would a girl who likes to play with toy soldiers and the like. But while a person's biological sex is a fairly binary issue, that may not be the case concerning a person's gender. Does that make sense to you, Jessica?"

She nodded her understanding and added, "I guess I was getting confused by the vocabulary. I'm used to thinking of sex and gender as synonyms."

"I think we all are," Don granted. "The term 'gender' actually comes from linguistics, where some languages have masculine, feminine, and neuter noun and verb declensions. It's sometimes also used to refer to a person's biological sex, however, which is why it's so confusing. Today many people use the term 'sex' to refer to a person's biological characteristics and 'gender' to refer to a person's psychological ones."[1]

---

1. While the terms "sex" and "gender" are sometimes used interchangeably, in more nuanced usage they are not exact synonyms. The term "gender" originally referred to a linguistic distinction applied to nouns, pronouns, and syntactically associated words that are inflected, usually in forms designated as masculine, feminine, or neuter. More recently it has been adapted to refer to psycho-social character traits

A young man in the middle of the room raised his hand. "Yes, Jin?"

"This doesn't really seem very controversial to me," Jin said. "I'm sure some fathers pressure their sons to be as masculine as is conceivable, and I know that there are societal pressures on girls to be very 'ladylike,' as they used to call it, but most people today are at least aware that there's nothing wrong with striking a balance that includes the positive traits of both men and women, don't they? And as Christians, wouldn't we say that God himself epitomizes whatever is good in both men and women?"

"Wow, Jin, you've got a powerful argument there," Don answered. "But I'd like to continue my response to Jessica before considering your points because I want to explore how Matthew 19 does and does not apply to the subject. We'll return to your points before we're through, though, okay?"

Jin nodded his head, and Don continued. "So Jessica, when Jesus says that God created humans 'male and female' he does seem to affirm some sort of binary view. The question, though, is whether he's talking about their biological sex, their gender, or both."

"Yes, I guess you're right," she granted. "I think I'm just used to thinking along the lines of biological sex and assuming that sex and gender automatically correspond."

"I imagine that many of us are used to thinking like that," Don conceded. "But we don't want to beg the question, do we?"

"We don't want to do what?"

"Sorry: what I mean is that we don't want to assume that biological sex determines one's gender, since that's one of the things that's being debated. To 'beg the question' means to assume a certain answer is true rather than actually proving it. Simply assuming that biological sex determines gender certainly doesn't prove that biological sex determines gender. We need to get past our assumptions and come up with good reasons for what we believe."

"Now I want to be very clear that *if* Jesus thinks that biological sex determines gender, then we have a very good reason to embrace a binary view of gender. After all, if Jesus Christ is God incarnate, as we believe, then everything he believes has got to be true, for God does not make mistakes.

---

that are associated with but not identical to biological sex. *Oxford Living Dictionaries*, "Gender," https://en.oxforddictionaries.com/definition/gender.

So let's look at Jesus's words again in order to see if they actually support the binary view. Jesus said,

> Have you not read, that He who made them at the beginning made them male and female, and said, "For this cause a man shall leave his father and mother and be joined to his wife, and the two shall become one flesh?"[2]

What do you think? Is Jesus implying something here about sex or gender?"

Jessica hesitated to reply—she needed time to think.

Colton, a broad-shouldered man with a deep, slow voice, raised his hand, and Don called on him. "It seems to me that Jesus is at least implying something about biological sex, because we know that God first created a man, Adam, and then a woman, Eve, and that they procreated and fathered the human race. Procreation is pretty strong evidence that there were two biological sexes involved. But I'm not seeing any strong argument here about gender, if we accept that gender is distinct from sex."

"But should we accept that?" Jessica blurted out. She appeared to have significant reservations about the direction in which the discussion was going.

"Well, I haven't really thought about this much before, but it seems to me that we should," Colton answered, "because biological sex does seem to be binary while gender does not. Lots of people very clearly belong to one or the other biological sex but have psychological traits that fall somewhere toward the middle of the spectrum or even align with the opposite gender, like the Reverend Mother at the Catholic school I attended as a child—her personality was definitely that of an alpha male. Or the case worker who handled my adoption: he was as caring, gentle, and sensitive a person as I've ever known. Those are typically viewed as feminine character traits, aren't they?"

"Maybe this is a good place to invite Jin back into the discussion," Don suggested. "Jin, you pointed out that God's character traits include both feminine and masculine traits. That certainly makes sense, since anything that is good in men and women, respectively, ultimately comes from God.

---

2. Matt. 19:4–5 (KJV).

Would you like to tell us a bit more about this idea? Which of God's traits are usually thought of as masculine, and which are feminine?"

"Well," Jin responded, "in the Old Testament, God is depicted as a general, a judge, and a ruler, all of which are usually masculine roles. I suppose that there are some masculine character traits that accompany being a good general and a good ruler: a general needs to be confident, firm, and authoritative, able to lead and to inspire others to follow him. We definitely see that in Jehovah too: he is firm, commanding, and supremely self-confident. But the Bible also depicts God as loving, merciful, caring, and comforting, all of which seem to be more feminine than masculine."

"Thank you, Jin. I believe you're right: the biblical depiction of God shows him to have characteristics that are typical of both human genders. Perhaps God is bi-gendered? But don't tell Pastor that I said that," Don entreated, with a laugh. "Since God isn't a biological organism, he doesn't have a sex, even though we traditionally refer to him using masculine pronouns. God is a spirit being. As such, he does have a psyche—or perhaps it would be more accurate to say that he *is* a psyche. In fact, one of the Greek words for 'soul' is *psuche*, which is where the English word 'psyche' comes from. In ancient Greek this word referred to the energizing force of a living being. The Greek word *pneuma* is also used in reference to God and often translated 'spirit.' *Pneuma* is the word used to refer to the Holy Spirit. Since God has a psyche, he could have a gender in the sense in which we're using the term. But I'm inclined to agree with you, Jin, that God includes all that is good in both genders.[3]

"But I need to add a disclaimer here. Our discussion has made it sound a little like only men are firm, authoritative, confident, and so forth, and that only women are loving, caring, and so on. That's undoubtedly an unfortunate stereotype, for women can be firm and confident and they surely can be excellent leaders just as much as men can. Conversely men can be quite caring, loving, and sensitive, as Colton pointed out. Does anyone think something is wrong with women being confident or men being caring and sensitive?"

---

3. On the meaning of *psuche*, see Timothy Friberg, Barbara Friberg, and Neva F. Miller, *Analytical Lexicon of the Greek New Testament* (Victoria, BC: Trafford, 2005), 414; on the meaning of *pneuma* see 318.

Don paused, looking around, but no one seemed inclined to argue this, so he continued. "Let's return to discussing our passage. What we want to know is whether Jesus said anything that bears directly on the issue of gender identity. As you are well aware, a very important step to understanding a literary passage is examining the context in which the passage occurs. Our passage does not have extensive context that helps us to understand what's going on, though. In the previous chapter Jesus was in Galilee teaching his disciples on a range of topics, but the beginning of our chapter tells us that he left Galilee and went south into Judea, where he was ministering to a great crowd of people. During this ministry the Pharisees came to him and asked him about what the Law, the first five books of the Old Testament, taught about divorce. This is the immediate context of Jesus's statements. Since the verses preceding this discussion took place in a completely different setting and concerned very different topics, it does not help us to interpret what Jesus is saying here. Nor is the context that follows these words any help, for there Jesus moves on to other topics."

"Are you saying that the Bible doesn't address the issue of gender identity, Don?" Leah had been following the discussion intently. She was very curious to know what Don thought the biblical view was.

"Not exactly, Leah. I'm merely agreeing with Colton that while this particular passage may support a binary view of human sexuality, it doesn't address the issue of gender identity. I do think it supports a binary view of sexuality, though. When Jesus says that God 'made them male and female,' he is alluding to the creation of the human race as recorded in the first two chapters of Genesis. In fact, Jesus's words 'For this cause shall a man leave father and mother, and shall cleave to his wife: and they twain shall be one flesh' are a quotation from Genesis 2:24. The Bible records that God originally created only two sexes, and Jesus's appeal to the Genesis record as an authority for settling moral issues like divorce indicates that the basic order instituted by God at the beginning of the human race is still true today. Hence if sexuality was binary back then, it's still binary today.

"As we've already seen, though, sex and gender are not the same thing. One relates to the body, while the other relates to the soul. The question about gender identity is whether gender automatically corresponds to sex. If someone has a male body, does that person automatically have a male soul? This is a tricky question. What exactly is a male soul? Since a soul is immaterial, we can't be talking about having male sex organs or anything like that—those are material. What would constitute having a male soul?"

The class looked puzzled, and no one raised a hand. Don prompted them: "This is something that we've already talked about today, in this very class. What characteristics stereotypically distinguish men from women and vice versa?" Several hands went up at once. Micah's was one of them, and since he hadn't been involved in the discussion yet, Don called on him.

"Earlier you said that we stereotypically think of men as firm, authoritative, and confident and of women as loving and caring. So if those stereotypes are accurate, then would that mean that a male soul is one that has the character traits like firmness, authoritativeness, and confidence, while a female soul would be one that is loving and caring?" Micah's voice had a tone of genuine questioning in it, as if he was unsure of his answer.

"Yes, Micah, that's correct." Micah's hand was already shooting back up, so Don nodded for him to continue.

"But didn't you—and perhaps Colton—kind of imply that these characteristics aren't intrinsically masculine and feminine, since God has all of them and since some men have the feminine traits and some women have the masculine ones?"

"Very good, Micah," Don replied. "Colton, Jin, and I discussed that these character traits don't fall into two neat categories."

"What is it that determines how such character traits are viewed?" Micah asked. "Are these mere cultural judgments, or is there something else at work?"

"As far as I can tell," Don said reflectively, "the way we view such character traits seems to be a function of our culture. In white American culture, we traditionally expect the man to be the leader of the home and as a result to be the more outspoken and the more assertive person in a relationship, but in African American culture, it's pretty common for women to be outspoken and take leadership roles. In southern European cultures, people show their emotions openly, but in northern European cultures people are more private and less outwardly impassioned. Some Asian cultures are even more stoic: self-control is highly prized. I'm sure we could come up with a very long list of such contrasts.

"Of course, being stoic or being an extrovert is not usually a moral issue. There's nothing wrong with being quiet, private, or self-controlled. Nor is there anything wrong with being outspoken, as long as you're not rude. These are just personality traits, and variety is the spice of life. The point is that each culture has its own ideals about what men and women should be like. Failure to live up to those ideals can give rise to issues that may be spiritually and morally significant."

"Finally we're getting to the moral side of the issue," Jessica murmured, just loudly enough for Don to hear. "Yes we are," Don responded. "How does this become a moral issue, Jessica? Would you like to clarify that for us?"

Although a little embarrassed that Don had heard her comment, Jessica didn't hesitate to respond. "I imagine everyone's heard about transgender people, people who are physically male but maintain that their gender is female, or who are physically female but aver that their gender is male. Some of them want the right to use public restrooms that correspond to their gender rather than their sex, to play on sports teams that correspond to their gender, and other such things. But it seems immoral to be a man but claim that you are a woman . . . isn't that lying? And doesn't it give an unfair advantage to athletes who are really men but insist on competing against women?" Someone murmured support of her questions. Clearly she had hit a nerve.

Don was tempted to answer this question himself, but instead he volleyed it back to the class. "What do you think, class: would that be lying?"

Jin raised his hand and asked, "Wouldn't it be lying only if we assume that biological sex and psychological gender automatically correspond?"

"Explain what you mean, Jin, would you?" Don replied.

"Well," Jin began, "Two distinct issues are involved in this discussion. The first is whether gender and biological sex are the same thing. It seems that many of us are inclined to think that they're not. But if we accept that conclusion, other issues arise: If gender and sex are different, such that one could in theory be biologically female and at the same time have male gender, how do we know that a person's sex and gender always correspond? Will someone who is biologically male always have male gender? Or is it possible that someone who is biologically male could have female gender? And if that's possible, is it healthy? Is it moral?"

"You're on a roll today, Jin. These are very important points—and difficult questions. But what about Jessica's question about lying?" Don was not easily sidetracked.

"Sorry: I lost my train of thought for a moment. If it's possible for someone to have male biological sex and female gender, or female sex and male gender, then it's possible for someone with a male body to also be female, female in the sense of having female gender. So in this scenario, it would not be lying for such a person to claim to be female if she's referring to her gender rather than her biological sex."

"Excellent, Jin! That was a great explanation. Jessica, what do you think? Is Jin on to something here?"

"I can see what he's saying," she replied. "It does make sense, once we grant the distinction between sex and gender. But I feel somehow uneasy about a person with a male body claiming to be a female. Couldn't that open the door to a whole range of problems?"

"Problems such as those that you mentioned earlier, you mean?" Don asked.

"Yes. I think those need to be taken seriously," she answered emphatically.

"I agree with you, Jessica. But since this is a Sunday school class, and since we're running out of time, rather than focusing on these admittedly important practical aspects of the issue, I'd like to bring up one more relevant Scripture verse: Deuteronomy 22:5 (KJV) says, 'The woman shall not wear that which pertaineth unto a man, neither shall a man put on a woman's garment: for all that do so *are* abomination unto the Lord thy God.' In this passage God, through his servant Moses, seems to indicate that it is wrong for a person to dress according to a gender that does not correspond to his or her biological sex. By extension we could say that it is wrong for a man or woman to do anything that does not correspond to his or her biological sex: that although there are areas in which gender is a sliding scale, there can be areas where gender is fairly binary and in such areas sex and gender should correspond. Apparently in ancient Israel dress was one such area."

Micah raised his hand and asked what the context of the verse was. "We wouldn't want to take the verse out of context," he affirmed.

"No we wouldn't," Don replied. "This verse occurs in a section of Deuteronomy that provides a rather long list of principles that God gives to guide the ancient Israelites in their daily lives. Some are practical and some are moral in nature. The verses immediately preceding verse 5 are about helping your brother when he is in need, and the verses immediately following verse 5 are about how to treat wild animals. Hence in this case the context does not shed a whole lot of light onto the meaning of the verse."

Micah had a follow-up question. "Are these principles normative for all people, or do they apply only to the ancient Jews? I believe I remember you saying in a previous lesson that not everything contained in the Old Testament applies to people living today, like circumcision, temple sacrifices, and keeping the Sabbath on Saturday."

"You remember correctly, Micah," Don granted. "And I still affirm that. Some things in the Old Testament are timeless truths that apply equally to all people, and other things apply only to the person or people to whom they were addressed. We need to think carefully about the context and the sort of principle introduced in order to determine which kind of passage we're looking at. In this instance I think we are dealing with a principle that applies to all people because we see Paul applying the same principle to Gentile Christians in 1 Corinthians 11. In Deuteronomy 22:5 God seems to be telling the Israelites not to diminish the differences between the sexes by having men wear women's clothing or having women wear men's clothing. In 1 Corinthians 11 God, through Paul, seems to be telling Christians not to diminish the differences between the sexes by having men pray with their heads covered or having women pray without a head covering. Apparently during that time it was customary for women to wear head coverings but for men not to.

"I want to reiterate that we have to think carefully about what we're reading in order to avoid confusing the cultural elements with the normative elements, those that apply to all people. I don't believe there is any clear command in the Bible that says that all women everywhere must wear head coverings, though some people would disagree with me. But if a person lives in a culture where head coverings are a customary part of a woman's dress, then I believe that a woman should wear one. In North American culture, it's normal for women to wear dresses but it's not normal for men. Hence if you are a man living in North America, you shouldn't wear a dress. But if you're a man living in Scotland, it would be fine to wear a kilt!" At this statement several people chuckled.

"Clearly," Don went on, "cross-dressing goes against this principle of not diminishing the differences between the sexes. We can transgress this principle in many other ways. But just because some controversial things can be seen by some individuals to transgress this principle doesn't necessarily mean they do. For example, we've already discussed the fact that gentleness and sensitivity are usually viewed as feminine character traits in our culture but are actually good character traits for men as well as women. The same could be true of athleticism, intelligence, artistic ability, and many other qualities."

Don paused and looked at the class. "We've certainly not answered all of the questions that were raised in this class, and the questions that were raised barely scratch the surface of the issues related to transgenderism. Unfortunately we're out of time today. Hopefully our discussion will help all of us to think at least a little more clearly about some of these things. Next week we'll look at Jesus's interaction with the rich young ruler that is recorded in verses 16 through 30. Can I have a volunteer to lead the class in a closing prayer?"

The woman sitting next to Leah raised her hand. Don called on her, and she rose and bowed her head, the rest of the class bowing their heads too. "Almighty God, you are all-wise and all-knowing. We know that you love us and want what is best for us. Sometimes it's not easy for us to figure out what is right and what is wrong—especially as societal values shift and change. But we thank you for your Word, which offers us guidance through these complicated issues. We pray that your Holy Spirit would bless and guide all of us as we study your Word and strive to live lives that reflect your love and holiness. We pray this in the name of our savior Jesus Christ. Amen."

***

When Bianca and Lauren entered The Grey Earl, Micah was already seated at their usual spot. He had a Bible open on the table and he was obviously deep in thought. "Hi, Micah," Bianca said. "Are you busy? Should we sit somewhere else?"

"No, by all means, join me," he responded. "We had a really interesting discussion in Sunday school yesterday, and I wanted to give the issue some more thought. Have either of you given much thought to the transgender movement?"

"You were talking about that in church?" Bianca asked incredulously.

"Yes, we were," he answered. "We're studying the book of Matthew and the issue came up in our study of chapter 19."

"I think it's neat that you talk about such heady and contemporary issues in church, Micah," Lauren volunteered. "I didn't know that churches do that. Does yours, Bianca?"

"Not really," Bianca replied. "My church is very liturgical. We don't very often have classes like Micah's church does. I can see the value in educational ministries, though. It would be nice to learn more about the Christian approach to such issues and the reasons behind it. What position does your church take, Micah?"

"Well," he began somewhat hesitantly, "I don't think my church has an official position on it. Our approach is simply to try to understand what the Bible says about an issue and then adopt that as our position. . . ."[4]

"That sounds pretty old-fashioned, if you don't mind me saying. . . ." Lauren interrupted.

"Well, that's our approach. We believe that the Bible is inspired by God and that God knows all there is to be known about every possible issue, past, present, or future. If we're right about that, then although the Bible is old, it's never mistaken."

---

4. Christian denominations have taken a range of stances on gender identity. For example, in 2003 the theologically progressive United Church of Christ published a statement that views transgender people and transgenderism positively, "affirming the participation and ministry of transgender people within the united church of Christ and supporting their civil and human rights." See United Church of Christ, "Affirming the Participation and Ministry of Transgender People within the United Church of Christ and Supporting their Civil and Human Rights," whttp://religiousinstitute.org/denom_statements/affirming-the-participation-and-ministry-of-transgender-people-within-the-united-church-of/. In 2014 the theologically conservative Southern Baptist Convention passed a resolution that while attempting to be positive toward transgender people is negative toward transgenderism itself, stating that "gender identity is determined by biological sex and not by one's self-perception—a perception which is often influenced by fallen human nature in ways contrary to God's design (Ephesians 4:17–18); and . . . we extend love and compassion to those whose sexual self-understanding is shaped by a distressing conflict between their biological sex and their gender identity. . . ." See Southern Baptist Convention, "On Transgender Identity," www.SBC.net, https://www.sbc.net/resource-library/resolutions/on-transgender-identity.

"OK, I see the logic of that," she granted. "So what does the Bible say about transgenderism?"

"I guess I have to admit that it doesn't address the issue directly. But it does say various things that have implications for the issue. For example, the book of Genesis records that God created the human race 'male and female,' which affirms the two biological sexes, but the Bible also teaches that humans have a nonbiological, immaterial side, and it's not clear to me whether the traditional binary division of humanity into male and female applies to that. Perhaps the distinction that psychologists make between sex and gender corresponds in some way to the biblical distinction between the physical body and the incorporeal spirit, but I'm still thinking through this and trying to figure it out."

"When the Bible says that God created the human race 'male and female,' is it referring to Adam and Eve? Do you believe that they literally existed?" Lauren asked, a note of surprise in her voice.

"Not all Christians do, but yes, I'm inclined to," Micah replied.

"OK, I'll just assume you have good reasons for that and move on, since I know that you're an intelligent person. But without intending to disparage your religion in any way, may I point out some medical objections to the binary view of biological sex?"

"Definitely!" Micah responded. "I'd like to hear them. I didn't know that medical objections to it existed."

Recognizing the beginning of a long and intense discussion, Bianca interrupted. "Perhaps we should order our drinks?"

"Good idea," Lauren agreed. Micah continued searching through his Bible while the girls went to the counter and ordered their beverages. Micah had gotten Bianca hooked on chai latte, and she ordered one for herself and a refill for him. Lauren ordered ice water with a slice of lemon, quietly explaining to Bianca that she realized that she could cut calories and save money at the same time by drinking more water and less fancy tea and coffee.

When they got back to the table, Micah resumed the discussion immediately. "I've got a few more ideas about transgenderism and the Bible, Lauren, but I'd really like to hear the scientific side of the issue too. Tell us about it!"

"OK, to begin with, everyone knows that the male genotype is characterized by having one X and one Y chromosome, while the female genotype has two X chromosomes. But some people are born with two X chromosomes and a Y chromosome, and others are born with one X and a missing or irregular second X chromosome. As a result, such people sometimes appear to be neither male nor female, and sometimes they appear to be both. These people used to be called *hermaphrodites*, but now they're usually referred to as *intersexual*. Although it's an unusual condition, it's not as rare as you might think."[5]

"Wow, Lauren, that's fascinating! I didn't know about that!" Micah exclaimed excitedly. "So if a person's physiognomy is intersexual, that might have important ramifications on his . . . um . . . hey, should I say his, her, or what? How do you know what gender of pronoun to use?"

"Typically," Lauren responded, "you should use whatever pronoun the individual self-identifies with. Most of the time a person who is intersexual will have a greater tendency toward one sex or another and as a result will self-identify as that gender."

"OK, thanks. I think you've already partially answered the question that I was going to ask. If an intersexual person has more masculine than feminine physical attributes, is he likely then to also self-identify as having male gender? And someone who has more female physical attributes is more likely to self-identify as having female gender?"

"I'm not a psychology student, Micah, so I don't know as much about the psychological side of things as I do about the medical side. But I think gender identity is determined by both physiological and psychological factors. It's the old 'nature *and* nurture' one-two punch. The traditional view used to be that a person's gender identity is determined by his or her biological sex. This view emphasizes the role of nature and doesn't see much of a role for nurture in determining gender. There may be evidence that supports this view. I remember hearing about someone who had his genitals accidentally removed during circumcision when he was an infant. A psychologist convinced the

---

5. One study estimated that this sort of atypical chromosomal pattern occurs in greater than 1 percent of the population. See Melanie Blackless, et al, "How Sexually Dimorphic Are We? Review and Synthesis," *American Journal of Human Biology* 12, no. 2 (March 2000): 151–66. For a discussion of the range of such atypical patterns, see Kun Suk Kim and Jongwon Kim, "Disorders of Sex Development," *Korean Journal of Urology* 53, no. 1 (January 2012): 1–8.

parents to raise him as a girl, but in spite of their efforts he never felt like a girl. During his teen years his parents told him what had happened. He elected to have his genitals reconstructed and went on to live as a man. To me, this suggests that there is a strong connection between biological sex and gender identity.[6] But others have argued that when a baby is born, its psychological gender is undetermined. This view says that gender identity is a result of nurture rather than nature. Perhaps the truth is that it's a combination of both kinds of factors."[7]

"It doesn't make sense to me," Bianca said thoughtfully, "that an omniscient and loving God would create someone in such a way that he or she would have male sexual organs but female gender. That's sure to cause problems!"

"That's called 'gender dysphoria,' Bianca," Lauren stated. "I understand that it can be very distressing. Sometimes it even leads people to get surgery to change their sexual identity so that it matches their gender. That's called 'gender reassignment surgery.'"

"Mmmmmm . . . " Bianca murmured after a long, slow sip of her chai. "Maybe they should try chai instead."

"Very funny," Lauren replied, Micah suppressing a laugh in the background. "This really isn't something to joke about. I had a friend who looked for all the world like a guy, but she was definitely a girl. She didn't particularly have male personality traits either, but people were always mistaking her for a guy and it understandably bothered her, sometimes very deeply. I can only imagine what it's like for someone who has more severe dysphoria. I feel bad for such people!"

"Of course, Lauren. I do too. I didn't mean to be insensitive," Bianca said apologetically. "But that brings me back to my point about God: How is it that God creates people with such problems?"

"Well, if God 'creates' each person, then he 'creates' people with all kinds of deformities and diseases, some of them terminal, doesn't he? After

---

6. John Colapinto, *As Nature Made Him: The Boy Who Was Raised as a Girl* (New York: HarperCollins, 2006).

7. Carol Martin, Diane Ruble, and Joel Szkrybalo, "Cognitive Theories of Early Gender Development," *Psychological Bulletin* 128, no. 6 (2002): 903–13.

all, people are born all the time who are suffering from cerebral palsy, spina bifida, heart defects, and many, many other serious health problems. That's one of the reasons why I find it difficult to believe in God: if an omnipotent God exists, then he's got to be the cause of all of the evil in the world as well as all of the good. And I'd rather live in a world without God than in a world that has an omnipotent God in it who is going around causing all kinds of pain, suffering, and evil."

"Whoa, hold on a minute, Lauren," Micah interjected. "It's not necessary to believe that God creates each individual person directly and thus is responsible for all of the diseases and other problems that people are born with. The Bible teaches that God created the human race, but he created that race with the ability to perpetuate itself through natural, sexual reproduction. And because of sin, genetic defects and various environmental factors corrupt human nature and result in diseases and defects. We can't blame all of that on God. It's humanity that sinned, not God. Humans are responsible for the evil in the world."

"Micah," Bianca asked, "do you think that gender dysphoria is a result of the fall of humanity and the corruption of human nature that results from the presence of sin in the world?"

"It could be," he granted.

"That doesn't sound good, my friends: it sounds mighty bigoted. I think you need to be careful where you go with this." Lauren said this in a cautionary way, not wanting to attack her friends but concerned with the direction their ideas were headed.

"What do you mean?" they asked.

"Well, think about it: If gender dysphoria is a result of sin, then doesn't that mean that those who suffer from it are wicked sinners who perhaps should be punished, or at least shunned?"

"I don't think so, Lauren. According to Christian theology," Micah explained, "all humans are sinners. I'm a sinner, Bianca's a sinner, and so are you. We all suffer various results of the presence of sin. For example, I have mild scoliosis, and Bianca wears corrective lenses, but that doesn't make us any more wicked than anyone else. And we don't get punished for these things that are beyond our control except for the normal unpleasantness of having to live with a weak back and having to wear glasses to read."

"So tell me this: would someone with gender dysphoria be welcome in your church, or would such a person feel unwelcome or be asked to leave?" Lauren was looking straight into Micah's eyes as she asked this question, earnestly desiring to know if he was telling the truth.

Micah looked right back at her: "I think—and I hope—that they'd be welcomed. I really do."

She turned to Bianca: "How about in your church?"

"They would be welcomed."

QUESTIONS TO PONDER

- Is it possible to change your biological sex?

- Is it possible to change your gender?

- Does biological sex automatically determine psychological gender?

- Does your religion have specific teachings relating to gender?

- Is it moral to attempt to change your sex and/or your gender?

- How should we respond to people who are experiencing gender dysphoria?

TERMS TO KNOW

- Biological sex
- Gender
- Gender identity
- Gender dysphoria
- Transgender
- Intersexual
- Conflation
- Begging the question

FOR FURTHER READING

Hiestasnd, Gerald and Todd Wilson, eds. *Beauty, Order, and Mystery: The Christian Vision of Sexuality* (Downers Grove, IL: InterVarsity, 2017).

Janssen, Aron and Scott Leibowitz, eds. *Balanced Affirmative Mental Health Care for Transgender and Gender Diverse Youth: A Clinical Guide* (Portland, OR: Springer, 2018).

Koch, Michaela. *Discursive Intersexions: Daring Bodies between Myth, Medicine, and Memoir* (Bielefeld, Germany: Transcript-Verlag, 2017).

Yarhouse, Mark A. *Understanding Gender Dysphoria: Navigating Transgender Issues in a Changing Culture* (Downers Grove, IL: InterVarsity Press Academic, 2015).

INTERNATIONAL
ISSUES

ENVIRONMENTALISM

Synopsis: At the encouragement of her friend Shamar, Lauren joins the Lone Mountain College environmentalism club. Fortunately, their topic for her first visit is environmental ethics. After an interesting discussion with the club, Lauren shares her thoughts with Micah and Bianca.

* * *

It had been only a few weeks since Lauren and Shamar, a fellow nursing major, had begun hanging out and discovering that they had many mutual interests. She believed he was interested in her, but it was still early in their relationship. When he invited her to attend a meeting of the Lone Mountain Environmentalism Club, called Ecology Today (affectionately referred to as ET on campus), she gladly accepted. The group met Wednesday evenings at seven, and Lauren joined Shamar and about two dozen others in a medium-sized classroom in Branson Hall.

"So glad you could come, Lauren," greeted Katherine, the president of the club, who was about Lauren's age. "Shamar told us he was bringing a friend, and we are happy to have you join in our discussions."

"Thank you," replied Lauren. "I've always recycled and tried to treat nature respectfully but talking to Shamar about what you do here has caused me to think I have a lot to learn about environmentalism."

"You will find we are very zealous about introducing our ideas to new people," chimed in a young man standing near Katherine. "I'm Johnson— that's my first name—and I've been in ET since first arriving on campus three years ago. It's a great group, and we have an important mission."

"I think I can guess what your mission would be," Lauren stated, "but how would you put it into words?"

Johnson began to answer and quickly was joined by Katherine and several others who were nearby. They chimed in unison: "To inform, educate, and agitate until all people respect and protect Mother Earth as she deserves."

Lauren chuckled. "I gather that's ET's official mission statement." Johnson and several others nodded.

"I'm going to call our meeting to order, Lauren," announced Katherine, "and then you will learn a lot more about what we are trying to accomplish."

After a few moments, Katherine successfully got the group to take their seats—they sat in a circle of chairs facing one another—and announced their topic of discussion for the evening. Lauren was thrilled to learn that they had decided to discuss Environmental Ethics. The subject had not yet been raised in Dr. Platt's Ethics class, and she wasn't sure he was planning to cover it. At the beginning of class, Dr. Platt had explained that certain niche topics, like Business Ethics, would not be included, and perhaps he considered the ethics of environmentalism to be such a topic. In any event, Lauren was extremely interested and was happy she had chosen this evening to attend the group. She was beginning to think she would have enjoyed the evening even without Shamar sitting next to her. Win-win!

Katherine launched the conversation. "Most of us are aware that there are differences of opinion even in our group here tonight about the best way to approach environmental issues. What I propose for tonight is that we discuss different approaches to the subject and come up with something of a taxonomy for environmental ethics. This will clarify how the different ap- proaches relate to each other—what we have in common and where we differ."

A young man spoke up, "I'm sorry, Katherine, but what do you mean by *taxonomy*?" Lauren learned later that he was Charles, a freshman criminal justice major.

Katherine smiled and answered, "Don't apologize, Charles. You probably just helped several of the upperclassmen in here who wondered the same thing but were afraid to ask. It's not a word we use every day. A taxonomy is a classi-fication in which a subject is divided into its subtopics so that one can see the relationships between them.[1] From our previous discussions, we know there are several distinct opinions in this group about how to handle environmental questions. Let's talk about them and see how they relate to each other."

"Well, you all know where I stand on this issue," began an older-looking student—he had to be at least thirty!—sitting almost directly across from Lauren.

"Actually, Darrell, we have a visitor tonight, so feel free to spell out your position, although, yes, most of us know it," instructed Katherine.

Darrell continued, "Any stance that regards one living organism as having a superior status to any other living organism is immoral. Why should hu-mans have the right to exploit plants and animals for their own purposes? We all share this planet together. We all evolved over millions of years in unique ways. Sure, industrialization has improved *our* standard of living, but at what cost? Millions of trees and other plants who had the same right to life that we have, millions of animals—vertebrate and invertebrate, insects and—"

"You don't swat mosquitos, do you Darrell?" interrupted a young man (Shamar whispered to Lauren that he was Jonah, the club jokester).

"No, I don't!" roared Darrell. "What right do I have to—"

"Maybe the right to keep it from sucking your blood," rejoined Jonah. "Mosquitos don't seem to share your sensibilities."

"Thank you, Jonah," inserted Katherine. "But please don't interrupt as members present their views."

"Thank you, Katherine," Darrell huffed.

"Do you know what your view is officially called, Darrell?" Katherine went on.

Darrell responded, "I am a biocentric egalitarian. *Biocentric* because I support all life, and *egalitarian* because I support all life equally. And by the way, the fact that other life-forms don't share my sensibilities doesn't lessen

---

1. The New World Dictionary defines *taxonomy* in this way: "1. the science of clas-sification; laws and principles covering the classifying of objects. 2. *Biol.* A system of arranging animals and plants into natural, related groups based on some factor common to each, etc." Katherine is using the word in the second sense but applying it to a subject other than biology, which is commonly done.

their rights." Darrell glared at Jonah but then, to Lauren's surprise, smiled at him. Apparently, this kind of banter was common in ET.

Katherine concluded, "Thank you, Darrell. On one end of our environmental ethics spectrum is biocentric egalitarianism."

Looking at Lauren, Katherine continued, "Darrell is rather ferocious with his views because he doesn't have many—if any—allies in the club. We're not going to let this turn into a debate"—she glared at Darrell as she said this—"but does anyone have objections or, better, concerns about egalitarianism in environmental ethics?"

A soft-spoken young woman, sitting a few chairs down from Lauren and Shamar, spoke up. "It's an impractical ideal. Some plants encroach on other plants; some animals eat plants; some animals eat other animals. Humans cannot survive without shelter, which involves killing plants to build homes, for instance, and we also can't make it without food, all of which is either vegetable or meat. Egalitarians can talk all they want about all life-forms being equal, but that's not how the evolutionary process works. The fittest survive, and they cannot do so without some form of killing."

Lauren whispered to Shamar, "She's impressive. Who is she?"

Shamar whispered back, "Elise, a physics major. Yeah, she's really smart."

"Would you like to give a calm response to Elise, Darrell?" Katherine moderated.

Darrell thought for a moment and then responded, "You are correct that this is an ideal. I'm not trying to convince plants and other animals to recognize their equality with other life-forms, and some killing is unavoidable in the circle of life. My conversation is with humans. Killing plants may be necessary for our survival, but the way we have gone about raping and pillaging our planet is disgraceful. The ideal is not intended as an achievable goal. It is motivation for humans to reconsider how we take advantage of other life-forms for our own benefit."

A new speaker, later identified as Shaun, another physics major, spoke up, "So really, Darrell, you can talk about egalitarianism, but the only species that is in a position to make a *decision* about how to treat other life-forms is *homo sapiens*. *Sapiens*, if my high school Latin doesn't fail me, means 'wisdom.' Mankind has the wisdom to determine when killing plants and other animals is appropriate. Only we have evolved with that capacity.

"Therefore, Elise and I are biocentrists but not egalitarian. We believe that humans can discern a scale of value in evolutionary development that aids us in ethical decision-making relative to the environment."

Elise was nodding and chimed in at this point, "Exactly. Animals are superior to plants. Vertebrate animals are superior to invertebrates. It's morally acceptable to swat a mosquito that is preying on you or to domesticate cattle for their milk and, perhaps, their meat. It may be justifiable to cut down trees to build a town, but the overall welfare of our environment is the highest consideration."

Katherine asked, "Does your variety of biocentrism argue for the superiority of humans to other animals?"

"You mean except for egalitarian biocentrist humans?" quipped Jonah. Katherine hushed him.

Elise answered, "As Shaun mentioned, humans have an evolutionary advantage over other animals that means we will naturally make choices that enhance our probability of survival, even if that means disadvantaging some other animal species."

"But we are not anthropocentrist in the usual sense of that term," Shaun interjected.

"What do you mean?" Katherine prompted.

Charles spoke up again before Shaun could answer. "I'm sorry to interrupt again, but what does 'anthropocentrist' mean?"

Shaun answered. "It means human-centered, Charles. To answer your question, Katherine, we do not believe humans have the right to do whatever appears to advantage them. We have a responsibility to care for the environment for its own sake. Mother Earth was here before we were and no doubt will still be around after we are gone, if we don't destroy her. Elise simply meant that a responsible relationship with nature will involve humans making some choices that favor humans over other species," Shaun concluded. Elise smiled and nodded her agreement with his summary.

Based on the low chatter in the room, Lauren guessed that, while Darrell's extreme position had few sympathizers, many seemed to agree with the version of biocentrism advocated by the two physics majors. She wondered where Katherine herself stood on the issue. She soon found out.

Getting everyone's attention after a pause to let Shaun and Elise's points sink in, Katherine asked if there were any anthropocentrists in the group. To Lauren's surprise, a number of hands went up—in fact, a majority in the room. After Katherine asked them to define their position, one of them said, "Why don't you do it, Katherine? You express our position better than any of the rest of us."

Katherine smiled and responded, "Okay. I'll take off my moderator hat for a moment. Many environmentalists hold to some version of anthropocentrism, in which care for the environment is approached from the standpoint of human need as the highest priority. The position can be argued from either a Christian or naturalistic stance. Most Christians believe the world was created for humans, and humans were given the responsibility to care for the world. This leads to environmentalism with humanity as the principal focus. I believe we have a few members who would espouse that position." Lauren looked around the room and saw a head nodding. It was Shakira, whom she recognized from her ethics class. She hadn't realized Shakira self-identified as a Christian. She wondered if Bianca and Micah knew they had a fellow Christian in class. "Shakira, have I expressed the Christian position accurately?"

"Yes," Shakira responded. "We aren't thrilled with the word *anthropocentrism*, though. We believe our care for the earth is in obedience to God, so he is at the center of our ecology." Lauren noticed that the room had grown quiet. Shakira did not have many Christian allies in the club. Lauren was impressed by her courage to speak up.

Katherine went on, "Thank you, Shakira. Others, such as myself, argue for a similar position from a naturalistic standpoint. Because ethics relates to human behavior, it makes sense to us to make decisions relative to the environment primarily based on human factors. However—and this is the key point—we believe what is best for humans is to conserve and respect the environment in which we live. If we harm our habitats, we harm ourselves."

Several people literally clapped when Katherine said that line. Katherine, however, quickly returned to her moderator's role and asked, "Does anyone have concerns about the anthropocentrist positions I just briefly summarized?"

Lauren had determined not to participate during this first visit to the club, but her impulses got the best of her, and she suddenly spoke up, "We accused Darrell of having an impossible ideal a few minutes ago. Isn't it rather idealistic to say that human welfare and environmental benefits will usually coincide? It seems like most of what humans do to eat, shelter themselves, and produce energy is destructive of the environment. Doesn't anthropocentrism inevitably end up undermining ecology?"

"Precisely!" Darrell interjected. "If we're going to be idealists, we might as well go all in. Once man assumes his superiority to other life-forms, he can't be trusted to make decisions that are safe for the environment."

Katherine responded, "Since we've already established that humans *must* sacrifice some plants and animals to flourish on this planet, it is counterproductive to say responsible, conservative care of our habitats is impossible. Our track record may not be good, but modern people are much more sensitive to environmental concerns than even a generation or two ago. With information, education, and agitation, we can make a difference. To respond to Lauren's concern, good decisions can be made both to further human flourishing and protect our environment. Ecology need not be undermined by a responsible anthropocentrism."

"Future generations are counting on it," Johnson observed. "We must bequeath to our children a better planet than has been handed down to us." Everyone seemed to agree with that sentiment.

"Can I be a devil's advocate?" asked Lauren, feeling bolder because of the warm reception her previous question had received.

Katherine nodded affirmatively, and Lauren continued. "Why do future generations have rights? They don't exist anymore than past generations exist. Why should we care what the earth will be like for future people? What is the ethical basis for your feeling that you have a responsibility to them to preserve and even improve the environment?"

Katherine smiled and responded, "That is a very perceptive question. Some environmentalists think our responsibility to the earth outweighs our duty to our species. We discussed this group a couple of weeks ago in our meeting. Can anyone remember that discussion?"

"I can," Shamar spoke up. "We discussed the Voluntary Human Extinction Movement,[2] led by a British fellow whose name escapes me."

---

2. For more information on VHEM see https://www.unilad.co.uk/featured/man-campaigning-for-human-extinction-concerned-for-every-baby-he-sees.

"Les Knight," Katherine offered.

"Yes, thank you." Shamar continued, "They believe that the damage humans have already caused will take the earth millions of years to recover from. Therefore, they believe humans should voluntarily stop producing children so that the species will die out over the next generation. Their motto is 'Live long and die out.' Their founder had a vasectomy when he was twenty-five years old, I suppose in order to show how committed he was to the cause."

Katherine said, "That's a good summary, Shamar, and it shows I think that not all environmentalists take the rights of future generations into consideration."

"I know we discussed this a few weeks ago," Shaun offered, "but for Lauren's sake or anyone who was absent that night, I'd like to point out the logical flaw in the VHEM program. Because they insist that humanity's extinction is purely voluntary, the only people who will follow their program and voluntarily die out are those who agree with them. The net result of their approach will be fewer environmentalists on the planet. The only way they could succeed would be somehow to drop the voluntary part and wipe humanity out. Fortunately, they deny they wish to do so, and if they change their minds, they are insufficiently numerous to succeed."

Lauren was impressed with Shaun's logic and appreciated learning about VHEM, but she wasn't sure her original question had been answered. Apparently, this club of environmentalists took it for granted that each generation had a responsibility to later generations to care for the earth. She decided to let it drop.

Katherine asked, "Does anyone else have a question or observation about varied approaches to environmental concerns?" A brief pause ensued.

"I think I can summarize our findings," announced Jonah. Everyone looked at him rather skeptically. "At one end of the spectrum are the anthropocentrists who think human needs always outweigh environmental considerations. I don't think any of them have joined our club. Next to them are Katherine and her crowd, who want a responsible, ethical anthropocentrism. We should care for the environment so humanity can flourish. Next to them are the biocentrists, who believe care for the environment is the highest good, only rarely sacrificed for human needs. Finally, on the other end of the spectrum is Darrell, who wouldn't harm a fly."

"Wow, Jonah!" exclaimed Katherine. "You were listening!"

Jonah smiled. "Well, actually, Shakira allowed me to read her notes. I added the part about the fly, though." Everyone laughed.

When the room settled, Katherine continued, "It sounds like we are a pretty diverse group. What do we hold in common that allows us to function as a club?"

Several people started speaking at once, so Katherine pointed to a young man who had not yet spoken (Shamar told Lauren he was Lorenzo, a good friend of his).

"First, we are all passionate about conservation and preservation of the environment. We conserve natural resources because we recognize that the earth does not have an unlimited supply of fresh water, oil, coal, natural gas, or anything else. This motivation, of course, is primarily anthropocentric. But we all also agree that habitats[3] ought to be preserved free from human contamination. As ecocentrists argue, habitats are good in their own right and should not simply be viewed as collections of resources for humans. Conservation prevents humans from wasting precious resources, and preservation keeps us from destroying irreplaceable habitats, which destruction inevitably displaces and sometimes eliminates other life-forms with whom we are sharing the planet," Lorenzo concluded.

Shamar interjected, "Way to go, man! That was good." Lauren also smiled at Lorenzo and hoped Shamar's friends would become her friends in time. Those thoughts aside, Lauren found Lorenzo's definitions helpful. Avoiding the wasteful use of fossil fuels, like coal, was an example of conservation, and deciding to set aside a forest and refuse to allow loggers or developers into it was preservation.

"Thank you, Lorenzo," said Katherine. Addressing the group, she continued, "Lorenzo's statement expresses the central concern of ET. If we care about the environment, we will inform others about dangers to it; we will educate others about how to care for it; and we will agitate the government

---

3. A habitat is a natural environment for particular organisms. Examples of habitats on earth include desert, meadow, forest, seashore. Habitats can be large or small and include within them other habitats. For instance, a desert habitat might include within it an oasis habitat, with desert organisms adapting to the oasis environment.

to enforce policies that protect it. Our main aims are conservation and preservation of earth and her resources. What word best expresses this concern to maintain a balance between human need and ecological well-being?"

Shaun responded, "I believe you are speaking of *symbiosis*."[4] When Katherine smiled and nodded, Shaun continued. "Most scientists and environmentalists today believe life on earth—animals and plants—live in symbiotic relationships to one another. So while some of us emphasize biocentric thinking and others emphasize the human side more, the truth is all of the species on earth are interconnected and will live or die together."[5]

Katherine spoke again, "Understanding life as existing in a vast network of symbiotic relationships prevents us from being cavalier about the death of any living creature, but it also helps us recognize how the circle of life functions. Death and life flow together, resulting in mutual benefit to all species. Humans simply need to discover our place."

Lauren could feel the energy in the room as Katherine completed her statement.

After a pause, Katherine continued, "More specifically, though, what are current issues in environmentalism and ecology? How about each of you who wants to mention one and say a brief word about it, so Lauren will get an idea of what we're about?"

Darrell, who was never bashful, spoke first. "The biggest problem is air pollution. Our factories, automobiles, airplanes, aerosol bottles, and who knows what else are constantly pumping toxins into the air we breathe."

"Some progress has been made, right, Darrell?" broke in Katherine.

"Yes, some. In 1970 Congress passed the Clean Air Act, which set out to control hazardous air emissions from factories and automobiles, among other things. It was revisited in 1977 and then again, I believe, in 1990.[6] Cars don't burn lead fuel anymore, and factories must comply with limits on how

---

4. Symbiosis is "a close connection between different types of organisms in which they live together and benefit from each other" (https://dictionary.cambridge.org/us/dictionary/english/symbiosis).

5. For an interactive approach to examples of symbiosis in nature, see https://www.nationalgeographic.org/activity/ecological-relationships.

6. For information on the Clean Air Act, see https://www.epa.gov/laws-regulations/summary-clean-air-act.

much stuff they can pump into the sky. None of it seems adequate in my view, but I suppose things are better than they were before."

"Along the same lines," Johnson spoke up, "is the problem of water pollution. Especially in the developing world but even in the United States and Europe, clean fresh water is becoming scarce and expensive. The main culprits are industrial and agricultural processes. Again, the US government has tried to eliminate the most egregious offences by means of the Safe Drinking Water Acts."[7]

"Thank you, Johnson." Then Katherine prompted, "What else?"

Shaun spoke next, "Obviously, the most talked-about issue today is climate change.[8] Over the last seventy-five years or so, humans have released so many greenhouse gases into the air that the temperature on earth has increased measurably. Scientists fear that the effects will be catastrophic in time."

Lauren spoke before she could stop herself. "Do you guys actually think climate change is real?" She knew immediately that the credibility her earlier questions had garnered her evaporated with this query.

After a few awkward moments, Shaun responded, "Not to seem unkind, Lauren, but that's like questioning whether the earth is round or man descended from a lower life-form. ET accepts recognized science and bases our thinking on it. Climate change is a fact."

Katherine spoke in her usually soothing way, "But we all admit that there are plenty of people—we believe for political reasons—who don't want to accept the clear findings of modern science. No doubt their noisy propaganda led to Lauren's question. What are other issues?"

"Having grown up in Alaska," said Jonah, "I'm personally very passionate about deforestation. Our forests are important in producing oxygen, helping to manage temperatures, and contributing to precipitation. But across the globe, the human desires for space and for timber are leading people to decimate forests at an alarming rate. I'm really thankful that President Carter signed the Alaska National Interest Lands Conservation Act (ANILCA) in

---

7. See https://www.epa.gov/sdwa.
8. For a thorough discussion of climate change, see https://climate.nasa.gov. For an alternative viewpoint that discounts the danger of climate change, see https://www.forbes.com/sites/larrybell/2012/07/17/that-scientific-global-warming-consensus-not/#617b2e5e3bb3.

1980,[9] right at the end of his presidency. With a stroke of a pen, he designated over 100 million acres—about the size of the state of California—for preservation. Of course, the oil tycoons and the lumbermen went crazy and said it would ruin the state. Instead, we've got a booming tourist industry and the most beautiful place to visit in the world. If only people in the lower 48 and in other countries would catch that vision."

Katherine smiled and said, "Jonah, you just spoke for several minutes and didn't crack a single joke. That may be a record."

Jonah grimaced. "Oops. But did you hear about the two hikers in Alaska talking about what to do if they ran into a grizzly bear?"

"Yes, Jonah. 'I don't have to outrun the bear. I just have to outrun you.' That's the oldest joke in the book," groaned Shamar.

"Next topic?" cut in Katherine.

Elise answered, "I'm concerned about GMOs, Genetically Modified Organisms.[10] Scientists may have had good motives—trying to eliminate loss to climate and insects—but fooling around with the DNA of our food is a bad idea. I'm convinced it will have harmful long-term effects. I personally refuse to eat anything that's been genetically modified."

"I don't mean to sound combative," offered Lauren, although she was very nervous to speak up again, "but I thought this club trusted science. Aren't GMOs an attempt to use science to overcome weather, insects, and other threats to our food supply? Can't GMOs help us feed the millions of people in the developing world who are underfed?"

Lorenzo blurted out, "Shamar, dude, you better hold onto her. She's a lot smarter than you are!" Shamar actually looked pleased by his friend's outburst.

Lauren smiled and blushed, but she hoped Lorenzo's comment wouldn't prevent someone from actually answering her question. She wasn't disappointed.

Elise paused and then answered, "You've raised a legitimate point, Lauren. I would say two things in response. Scientists are not universally convinced that

---

9. For information on ANILCA, see https://www.nps.gov/locations/alaska/anilca.htm.
10. For information on GMOs (from the standpoint of opposition to them), see https://www.nongmoproject.org/gmo-facts. For a thorough discussion of the pros and cons of GMOs, see https://www.nature.com/scitable/topicpage/genetically-modified-organisms-gmos-transgenic-crops-and-732.

GMOs are a good idea or worth the risks they may entail. Certainly, there isn't nearly as much unanimity as there is relative to climate change. Second, climate change is descriptive; scientists are very good at telling us what *is*. GMOs are prescriptive, making changes in an attempt to improve the future and doing so, I might add, in very unnatural ways. That's where I trust science a lot less."

"Good exchange," chimed in Katherine. "We are about out of time. Would someone be so kind as to list a few more issues before we close?"

"I can," answered Shakira. "Soil pollution, overpopulation, acid rain,[1] nuclear waste, urban sprawl, and littering are also major problems.[2] There are so many ways humans are messing up the planet."

"Yes," Katherine responded, "but we can do something about it. Let's close the meeting by mentioning all the little ways individuals can make a difference. We'll go around the circle, and each of us just mention one. I'll start: it is important to recycle."

"Save water."

"Use less electricity. One way to do this is avoid leaving appliances plugged in while not in use."

"Don't use plastic straws."

"Drive less."

"Use a programmable thermostat."

"Stop using disposable items."

"Protect endangered species."

"Oh, yes," Katherine interjected, "we could say a lot more about that one. Very good."

"Grow your own food."

"Resell and donate."

"Buy fair-trade products."[3]

---

1. "Acid rain, or acid deposition, is a broad term that includes any form of precipitation with acidic components, such as sulfuric or nitric acid that fall to the ground from the atmosphere in wet or dry forms. This can include rain, snow, fog, hail or even dust that is acidic" (https://www.epa.gov/acidrain/what-acid-rain).
2. For a list of key environmental concerns, see https://www.conserve-energy-future.com/top-25-environmental-concerns.php.
3. "Fair trade" refers to products that are produced in developing countries and purchased for a fair price.

"Eat less meat."

"Use LED lightbulbs."

"Eliminate plastic from your life and go to glass as much as possible."

"Shop locally and eat natural foods."

When it came around to Lauren, she had no idea what to say. Fortunately, Shamar saved the day. "Make sure your closest relationships are with people who are ecologically conscious." Then he smiled at her. It was a nice way to end the meeting.

SELECTED ENVIRONMENTALISM ORGANIZATIONS	
Organization	**Website**
Environmental Defense Fund	https://www.edf.org
Forest Stewardship Council	https://us.fsc.org/en-us
Friends of Earth	https://foe.org
Greenpeace	https://www.greenpeace.org
National Audubon Society	https://www.audubon.org
National Geographic Society	https://www.nationalgeographic.org
National Resources Defense Council	https://www.nrdc.org
National Wildlife Federation	https://www.nwf.org
Sierra Club	https://www.sierraclub.org
The Intergovernmental Panel on Climate Change	https://www.ipcc.ch
The Nature Conservancy	https://www.nature.org/en-us
US Environmental Protection Agency	https://www.epa.gov
World Wildlife Fund	https://www.worldwildlife.org

Two days later, Lauren met Bianca and Micah at The Grey Earl. She hadn't told them about Shamar yet, and considering how she had occasionally flirted with Micah over the last several months, she was a bit nervous about it. When she entered the teahouse, all of that was forgotten as her friends graciously greeted her and invited her to join them at their usual table.

"Hi, Lauren!" said Bianca. "What's up?"

"Have you guys heard of the campus ecology club, ET?"

Micah shook his head, but Bianca replied, "Yes, I've seen their materials around campus. Why?"

"A friend of mine took me to their weekly meeting Wednesday night. It was really interesting."

"Tell us about it," said Micah.

For the next several minutes, Lauren summarized her experience at ET for Micah and Bianca.

Lauren concluded, "I was wondering if you guys would like to discuss the ethics of environmentalism from the standpoint of what we've learned in Dr. Platt's class?"

Micah looked doubtful and was probably about to ask what the academic benefit would be of such a conversation, but Bianca spoke first, "We'd love to, Lauren. Applying the principles to another area of thought will help us review what we've learned in class. Right, Micah? We'd love to?"

"Um, yeah. Absolutely!" said Micah, apparently trying to drum up conviction.

"If it will sweeten the deal," Lauren added, "I asked Dr. Platt yesterday if we could do this as an extra-credit project for class. He said we could." This comment had the desired effect, and Micah perked up noticeably.

"I suppose," began Bianca, "we should ask what the ethical basis is for caring for our environment. It seems like the right thing to do, but let's assess this feeling in terms of our ethical systems."

"Exactly," said Lauren. "That's what I was hoping we could do. The members of ET, in my opinion, assumed a number of things that they felt didn't need to be questioned. But Dr. Platt has taught us to ask such questions."

Surprisingly, Micah got the ball rolling. "Ethical Relativism would say we should care for our environment because that's what our community believes is the right thing to do."

"That doesn't work," rejoined Lauren. "One of the cornerstones of ET and most environmentalists, so far as I can tell, is that they constantly agitate for change. Clearly, they are appealing to a standard that they think all communities or cultures ought to conform to. I really enjoyed the meeting with them, but they are a very dogmatic group of people, at least when it comes to ecology."

"Natural Law would certainly appear more promising," affirmed Bianca. "Isn't it common sense to conclude that nature would teach us that we ought to preserve her? Nature is all about life, and the destruction of nature would contradict nature's basic orientation."

"That's interesting," replied Micah, "but I'm not certain the signals are that clear. Part of nature is human nature, and humans have been utilizing natural resources for their own benefit for all of human history. How could nature itself tell us that it is wrong to cut down a forest, if doing so would help advance a human community?"

"Once again," Lauren said, "nature is hard to interpret on its own. Would the same objection arise if we tried to apply Virtue Ethics to the problem?"

"Seems like it," replied Micah. "How can we necessarily know how a virtuous person would handle environmental concerns unless we have some prior knowledge about what's the right thing to do relative to the environment?"

"Not so fast," Bianca interjected. "Aristotle would argue for a golden mean relative to environmentalism. On the one hand, it would hardly seem virtuous to be wasteful, destructive, and selfish. On the other hand, care for people would seem to require the use of nature. Perhaps, the virtuous person is the one who can find the balance between human needs and responsible care for the planet."

"That's very helpful, Bianca," said Lauren. "What about Duty Ethics?"

Micah replied, "I think that could be promising. Let's try to formulate the categorical imperative relative to care for the environment. Can poor treatment of nature lead us to a logical contradiction?"

"I think so," Bianca chimed in. "Suppose every person destroyed his or her habitat. Theoretically, every habitat would be destroyed. There would cease to be habitats, and it would be contradictory to say that people destroy their habitats. I'm trying to frame this just like we analyzed telling the truth. If everyone told lies all the time, there would be no truth. And that means telling lies would become meaningless. Does the logic work for ecology?"

Lauren nodded. "Sure. I should treat the environment the way I want everyone to treat the environment. If I want you to preserve beautiful nature so I can enjoy it, or I want you to responsibly use resources so they will be available to me, then I should do the same for you."

"I think we can safely say it is our duty to act responsibly toward nature," concluded Micah, "although what that will look like precisely would have to be worked out."

"Perhaps Utilitarianism can help us with the details," offered Bianca. "What will be the consequences of squandering natural resources or releasing toxins into the air, water, and ground?"

"I'm glad you brought that up," said Lauren. "ET was convinced that it is our duty as a species to preserve the planet for our children. I raised the question of why generations who do not yet live should have rights. I don't think they really appreciated my question. They certainly didn't answer it. What do you guys think?"

"So far we've carried on the conversation from a secular standpoint," answered Micah, "but you had to know you were going to enter religious territory at some point. Christians are commanded by God to love our neighbor and put his or her interests ahead of our own. Since Jesus taught us that every person is our neighbor and deserves our love,[4] we regard future generations as our neighbors too. Therefore, we should preserve the environment for future generations because of our unselfish love for them."

Bianca added, "If one believes ethical commitments arise from evolution and reflect survival of the fittest, I suppose you could make a case that one should care about future generations out of a desire to see one's species survive. It's not entirely clear to me, however, why this conclusion would necessarily follow."

Lauren spoke up, "Okay. Back to Utilitarianism. If we were trying to make a decision about whether to cut down a certain forest, would the consequences settle it for us?"

"I think I see your point," answered Micah. "The apparent consequences for the human community might encourage us to cut down the trees and build the town; the consequences for the forest and forest animals would no doubt point in the opposite direction. Something other than the consequences would have to push us in one direction or the other."

---

4. This is the main point of Jesus's parable of the Good Samaritan in Luke 10:25–37.

"As usual," Bianca conceded, "Utilitarian considerations are useful but almost never sufficient."

Micah spoke again. "That leaves Divine Command Theory."

"Katherine, the leader of ET, mentioned at the meeting that some Christians are environmentalists. In fact, did you know that Shakira from Ethics class is a Christian?" Lauren asked.

"No," answered Bianca and Micah, almost in unison. "And she's in ET?"

"Yes," Lauren replied. "She said Christians believe God has commanded them to care for their environment."

Micah nodded and said, "That is a command God gave to Adam and Eve, the parents of the entire human race. God commanded them to populate the earth and to have dominion over the earth. Theologians often call this the Dominion Mandate."[5]

Bianca added, "Most Christians believe this mandate makes care for the earth a stewardship that God has entrusted to humans. On the one hand, there is a clear priority: the earth is for the benefit of humans, so environmentalism should never put lower life-forms in a position of rivalry to human need."

"On the other hand," Micah continued for her, "the earth actually belongs to God. So humans have a responsibility to use earth's resources wisely. Finding the balance between these two commitments is, of course, crucial and quite difficult."

"Wow, you guys have a lot more reason to be environmentally conscious than I thought," exclaimed Lauren. "Maybe you would like to come with me to our next ET meeting this coming Wednesday evening."

Micah replied, "I usually attend a prayer meeting at my church on Wednesday evenings, but I might be able to sneak away to attend ET some time. It sounds like it would be informative."

"And I have actually been going with Micah to his church the last few Wednesday nights," Bianca stated, much to Lauren's surprise. "The worship is very different from what I have been used to,[6] but I'm enjoying it. And I enjoy being with Micah." She smiled at him, and Lauren suddenly felt very comfortable telling them both all about Shamar.

---

5.   See Genesis 1:26–28 and David's brief commentary on the mandate in Psalm 8.
6.   Recall that Bianca affirms Eastern Orthodoxy, and Micah is an evangelical.

QUESTIONS TO PONDER

- If humans have the right to use or dispossess other life-forms on earth, what are the bases for this right?

- How might an evolutionist and a Christian who was not an evolutionist approach the questions of conservation and preservation of the environment differently?

- Does government have a role in protecting the environment? In general, do you think more regulation or less regulation is appropriate as the government interacts with businesses relative to this issue? Why?

- Is waste or abuse of the environment sinful? Why or why not?

- Can you think of specific ways you could change your life to better care for the environment?

TERMS TO KNOW

- Environmentalism
- Ecology
- Taxonomy
- Biocentric egalitarianism
- Biocentrism
- Anthropocentrism
- Conservation
- Preservation
- Habitat
- Symbiosis
- Pollution
- Climate change
- Greenhouse gas
- Deforestation
- Dominion Mandate

FOR FURTHER READING

Bouma-Prediger, Steven. *For the Beauty of the Earth: A Christian Vision for Creation Care.* 2nd edition. Grand Rapids: Baker Academic, 2010.

Enger, Eldon D. and Bradley F. Smith. *Environmental Science: A Study of Interrelationships.* New York: McGraw Hill, 2013.

Geisler, Norman L. *Christian Ethics: Contemporary Issues & Options.* Grand Rapids: Baker Academic, 2010, chapter 18: 314–34.

Hayward, Steven F. *Mere Environmentalism: A Biblical Perspective on Humans and the Natural World.* Washington DC: AEI Press, 2010.

Moo, Douglas J. and Jonathan A. Moo, *Creation Care: A Biblical Theology of the Natural World.* Grand Rapids: Zondervan, 2018.

Schaeffer, Francis A. *Pollution and the Death of Man: The Christian View of Ecology.* Wheaton, IL: Tyndale House, 1970.

Schmidtz, David and Elizabeth Willott. *Environmental Ethics: What Really Matters, What Really Works.* New York: Oxford University Press, 2002.

Toly, Noah J. *Keeping God's Earth: The Global Environment in Biblical Perspective.* Westmont, IL: InterVarsity Press 2010.

U.S. Environmental Protection Agency. https://www.epa.gov.

Wilson, Gordon. *A Different Shade of Green: A Biblical Approach to Environmentalism and the Dominion Mandate.* Moscow, ID: Canon Press, 2019.

WORLD HUNGER

Synopsis: In this chapter Bianca and her family "adopt" a child through Compassion International. When she tells Lauren and Micah about it, they are supportive but also ask questions about things that Bianca had not considered. This leads to soul-searching and interesting discussions.

* * *

"It came!" Bianca yelled. "Hey everybody, the mail's here, and it came!" It was Friday afternoon. Bianca had come home for the weekend and had picked up the mail before coming inside. She was holding a large envelope and was very excited. The rest of her family hurried into the living room.

"Well, open it up!" Her little brother, Jon, was also excited to see what had arrived.

"Mom, Dad, do you want to open it?" she asked, looking at her parents.

"You open it, honey. That's fine," her Mom replied.

She slid her finger under the flap at the top of the envelope and tore it open, unceremonious in her haste to see its contents. Inside was a large amount of printed material from Compassion International, a Christian NGO (non-governmental organization) that works with poor families in developing nations around the world. Compassion's signature ministry is pairing American families with poor children around the world. Through Compassion, an American family can "adopt" a child and provide a monthly stipend that provides food, other essentials, and after-school education to the child. It's a non-governmental approach to combating global poverty.[1]

Bianca carefully removed the contents of the envelope and spread it out on the coffee table. She seemed to be looking for something in particular—and then she found it: a glossy four-by-six picture of an preadolescent male. He looked to be no more than ten years old, with an olive complexion, black eyes, and short, dark hair. His name was Jhimmy, and he was their first-ever Compassion adoption.

"He's handsome," she said, studying his face. "Look how dark his eyes are! And his skin has a nice, warm olive color."

"Why is his name spelled with an 'h'?" Jon asked.

"That must be how they write it in Bolivia," Mom responded.

"But why?" Jon insisted.

"Why don't we let Bianca put her books in her room and then we can all sit down and read about Jhimmy together," Mom said. "I'll fix us a snack, and maybe in the meantime your father will come home."

While Bianca carried her things to her room, Mom carried the information from Compassion into the kitchen, depositing it on the table so that she could get out milk and the last of the homemade chocolate chip oatmeal cookies. Jon sat down and started looking through the material. Some of it was about Compassion and some was about the sponsorship experience, but Jon was interested in the stuff that talked about Jhimmy.

Before Bianca made it to the kitchen, they heard the sound of someone coming in the front door. It was Dad. "Honey, come to the kitchen, please," Mom called. "We have a surprise!"

Leaving his coat and hat in the hall closet, Dad arrived in the kitchen right behind Bianca. "What kind of a surprise? Oh, cookies! I like that kind of surprise!"

"No, not the cookies, silly: those are here all the time. We got the information on our new son!" Mom responded, showing him the mess of literature that Jon had managed to scatter all over the tabletop.

---

1. Compassion International is an actual NGO. For more information about what they do, see their webpage: https://www.compassion.com.

Dad was immediately drawn to the picture, as well. "He's a good-looking lad!" he said appreciatively. "He has a very straightforward look to him. What do we know about him?"

"His name is Jhimmy and he spells it with an *h*," Jon informed him. 'He's from Bolivia, which is in South America. He has a family and he plays soccer."

"You were supposed to wait for us to read about him together," Bianca remonstrated.

"You took too long!" Jon complained. "I've been waiting for weeks to learn about my new brother!"

Mom and Dad exchanged a look of approval. They were happy that their kids were excited about helping someone less privileged than themselves. "OK," Mom said, "Everyone sit down and have some cookies. Let's find out all about the newest member of our family."

***

On Monday afternoon Bianca was the first to arrive at The Grey Earl. She had invited Lauren and Micah to join her so that she could share her excitement about Jhimmy with them. She had previously mentioned to Micah that her family was considering such an initiative, but Lauren didn't know anything about it, so Bianca was eager to share the news with her best friends. She had even brought Compassion International pamphlets with her in case either of them seemed interested in considering an adoption of their own.

Soon Bianca heard the jingle of the bells on the front door and, looking up, saw Lauren entering and Micah sprinting up behind her to catch the door before it closed. They greeted each other happily and then chatted cheerfully as they made their way to what had become their habitual corner. "Hi, guys!" Bianca was full of smiles. "How are you?"

"Great!" Lauren responded.

"Famished, actually," Micah added. "I'm going to get something to eat."

"I will too," Lauren said. "We'll be right back."

As the two hurried over to the counter, Lauren reflected on what close friends the three of them had become. It wasn't that long ago that they first met, but in the course of a single semester they had gotten to know each other very well. It occurred to her that taking ethics together—and having such a nice place to hang out and talk—had the effect of accelerating the rate at which their friendship evolved. And now that the occasional, slight tension between her and Lauren over Micah's attentions was gone, she was feeling really good about things.

Micah came back with the largest chai latte on the menu and a truly giant blueberry scone. Lauren was back to drinking water, but she had bought a small scone too. "I couldn't resist," she said, winking at Bianca. "So what's the big news that you were so excited to share with us?"

"Well, I'm going to have another brother!" Bianca told them, almost gushing. Micah and Lauren responded at the same time, congratulating her and sharing in her happiness.

"When is the due date?" Lauren asked.

"Oh, he's already born," Bianca replied.

This answer stopped Lauren in her tracks: she had no idea what Bianca meant. Then Micah figured it out. "Are you adopting a child from overseas?"

"Yes—well, sort of," she answered. "My family has decided to sponsor a child in a developing country. It's not literal adoption, but we will donate money to his account every month, and it will be used to provide food and clothing for him, plus other necessities and supplemental education. We can write to him and he can write to us, so we can get to know each other and develop a personal relationship almost like he's part of our family. We'll support him until he graduates from high school. They say that this kind of sponsorship can make a huge difference in the lives of children in the developing world.

"His name is Jhimmy, and he lives in Bolivia, one of the poorest countries in the Western Hemisphere. He has a mom and dad and brothers and sisters, but they are rural agricultural workers who live at the poverty level in an area with few educational opportunities. The organization that we're partnering with is called Compassion International. It runs an after-school program that provides extra education, food, and clothing to low-income children like Jhimmy. Here. I brought brochures for you so that you can read about it," she said as she handed a brochure to each of them. Lauren and Micah took the brochures and looked at them curiously.

"This is neat, Bianca," Lauren said sincerely. "What got you interested in doing something like this?"

"Well, it flows at least in part from the experiences that my own family has had. We moved to America when I was very young, before my brother was born. We left Romania because of the oppressive, nearly inescapable poverty that followed on the heels of communism. Through hard work my parents were able to make a good life for us here in America. So we know firsthand what it's like to be trapped in a situation where no matter how hard you work, you just can't make a go of it. It's a terrible feeling! Now that we're financially stable, we want to help others to whatever degree we can. I know that adopting one child is a mere drop in a bucket, but I think it's a good first step, and maybe in the future we'll be able to do more."

"I really admire how hard your parents have worked, Bianca," Micah confided. "They're model immigrants: they're honest, they're hard-working, and they have embraced America as their new home. In light of that, I'm wondering why your family has chosen to help someone outside of America when there are so many needy people right here. That doesn't seem like a very good way to repay the good will that America has extended to you."

"That's simple, Micah," she replied, attempting to overlook Micah's not-so-subtle criticism of her family's charity. "My parents found that it was nearly impossible to escape poverty in an economic situation like the one prevalent in Romania, but also that it was very possible to escape poverty here in America. We want to help people who can't help themselves, and our experience leads us to think that living in American makes it much more possible for people to help themselves than is true of people in many other countries."

Wanting to make sure that she understood Bianca correctly, Lauren asked, "Are you saying that, in America, anyone who is hard-working like your parents are can improve their own lot, but that's not true in other parts of the world?"

"Yes, I guess so," Bianca agreed.

"I think that might be an oversimplification, if you don't mind me saying so," Lauren replied. "I'm not downplaying what your parents did, of course. In fact, what they did is all the more remarkable because many Americans have not succeeded in working their way out of poverty. America has a serious poverty problem. Sure, we're 'the land of opportunity,' but that's less true if you are disabled, come from a family with a poor educational background, are born into poverty, or have the bad luck of growing up in an area without good schools. And there are systemic problems like racism and classism too. In my public health class we learned that one in every hundred children in America suffers from malnutrition[2] and that 13 percent of Americans live below the poverty level.[3] In light of that, what your parents did when they moved here is rather amazing!"

Bianca smiled at this compliment of her parents. She was very aware that they were exceptional people. Nonetheless she was not convinced by Lauren's argument. "Thanks, Lauren. I do have great parents. But while malnutrition is a problem in America, actual starvation is a problem in some other parts of the world. Similarly, the poverty level in the US would be considered middle-class elsewhere. I don't think most Americans realize how good we have it.

"When we were looking into what country we wanted to adopt our Compassion child from, we came across some startling statistics. Did you know that worldwide, over 700 million people live below the poverty line, and that annually about three million people die of starvation?[4] Three million people each and every year! That breaks my heart! I recognize that there are Americans who face significant challenges like those that you described, and that there's a lot more that could be done here to combat poverty, hunger, and inequalities of income and opportunity. Maybe as a teacher I'll be able to contribute in some small way to overcoming such problems. But in other countries the same problems exist on a scale that the U.S. hasn't seen since the Great Depression. I'm not ungrateful to America, Micah—I'm very grateful—but it seems to me that the right thing to do is to focus on addressing the greatest needs first, and it seems to me that the most acute needs exist outside of the US. It's that simple."

---

2. "Malnutrition," Johns Hopkins Medicine, https://www.hopkinsmedicine.org/health/conditions-and-diseases/malnutrition. For a comparison of the effects of malnutrition in the US and other parts of the world, see "Child Nutrition," World Health Organization, https://www.who.int/gho/child-malnutrition/en.

3. The US Census Bureau reported that 13.1 percent of Americans lived below the poverty level in 2018, the most recent year for which the data is currently available. Craig Benson and Alemayehu Bishaw, "Poverty: 2017 and 2018," *American Community Service Briefs*, November 2019, https://www.census.gov/content/dam/Census/library/publications/2019/acs/acsbr18-02.pdf.

4. "2018 World Hunger and Poverty Facts and Statistics," WorldHunger.org, https://www.worldhunger.org/world-hunger-and-poverty-facts-and-statistics.

> "*Without food, man can live at most but a few weeks; without it, all other components of social justice are meaningless.*"
> —**Norman Borlaug**

"OK, Bianca, I can grant that point. You know I've never been outside of the U.S. I've seen a lot of poverty inside the U.S., especially in areas of urban blight. In fact, I've volunteered in a soup kitchen several times. But I know enough about the outside world to believe what you say about the poverty and hunger being even worse in other parts of the world than it is here. Nonetheless I see social ethics as including a hierarchy of moral obligations, like a set of concentric circles: a person needs to take care of himself first—not because he is motivated by egoism, but rather because by taking care of himself he is able to help others. Then he has an obligation to take care of his family, as the apostle Paul wrote in 1 Timothy.[5] Then he has a moral duty to help his neighbors, as Jesus said when he summarized the Old Testament law as 'love God with all your heart and love your neighbor as yourself.'[6] Then he has a duty to his nation, because God has instituted the government for the well-being of those who live under its rule.[7]

"This is a very practical approach to caring for others," Micah continued, "focusing on needs that are near at hand and that you can address personally rather than simply paying someone else to do your charity work for you. And I think that's important: when you do the work yourself, you are transformed by the experience. Not only do the people you are helping get helped, but you yourself are helped. You're helped to become a more caring, more other-oriented person. And that leads you to do more and more. If we'd all take this approach, who knows what sort of place our world would become?"

"Huh, that's really interesting!" Lauren stated, with a bit of surprise in her voice. "At first it sounded like you were combining your Christianity with some

---

5. "But if anyone does not provide for his own, and especially for those of his household, he has denied the faith and is worse than an unbeliever" (1 Tim. 5:8 NKJV).
6. Matt. 22:39, loosely paraphrased.
7. Support for this idea might be found in Matthew 22:20–21 and Paul's instruction in Romans 13:1–7, though Micah's position goes further than these passages.

kind of egoism in an improbable way, but I was misjudging where you were going. You know, I've heard that international relief efforts can be very inefficient. Direct food aid—importing large stocks of grain and the like—are a logistical nightmare. The expense of gathering, shipping, storing, and distributing such aid is tremendous. I've read that it's more than the cost of the foodstuffs themselves. The supplies often don't get to those who are in the greatest need, and flooding local markets with free or inexpensive foodstuffs overwhelms local food production, driving local farmers and merchants out of business. This can create exactly the opposite situation from the one desired: it can make populations dependent on international aid and unable to feed themselves.[8]

"Problems like these have led some NGOs to argue that indirect food aid—in other words, financial aid so that people or their governments can buy food—is more efficient. But such aid can lead to financial corruption and other evils.[9] And it is difficult to get the governments of wealthy nations to adopt such programs because direct food aid is a popular way of underwriting a wealthy nation's farmers, so politicians have a vested interest in supporting direct food aid."

"Wow, this isn't the sort of response I was expecting when I asked you to join me today," Bianca replied, somewhat taken aback. She had come to The Grey Earl full of exuberance about her family's adoption and had expected her friends to share in her happiness. And they were happy for her, but they were in such a habit of examining issues from an ethical perspective that the old, familiar pattern was exerting itself reflexively. "I never expected my friends to be critical of our attempt to help someone in need."

"I'm sorry, Bianca," Micah apologized. "We weren't intentionally raining on your parade. When the three of us get together, we seem to have a habit of turning every discussion into an ethics debate. But we're happy about your family's decision to adopt Jhimmy. Right, Lauren?"

---

8. A very interesting article on this is Eban Harrell, "CARE Turns Down U.S. Food Aid," *Time*, August 15, 2007, https://www.nytimes.com/2007/08/16/world/africa/16food. html. A scholarly discussion of the strengths and weaknesses of food aid is Randy Schnepf, "U.S. International Food Aid Programs: Background and Issues," Congressional Research Services, September 14, 2016, https://fas.org/sgp/crs/misc/R41072.pdf.

9. A good introduction to the problems of indirect food aid is Dambisa Moyo, *Dead Aid: Why Aid Is Not Working and How There Is a Better Way for Africa* (New York: Farrar, Straus and Giroux, 2009).

"Yes we are," Lauren confirmed. "In fact, it seems like Compassion International may succeed in avoiding the pitfalls that Micah and I mentioned. For example, Micah mentioned the importance of personal involvement with the work that you are financing. Compassion's approach seems to encourage the development of an actual relationship between your family and Jhimmy, and you'll get to know him better and better as the years go by. I imagine that personal relationship will encourage and motivate both him and you. Plus, this pamphlet seems to be claiming that Compassion avoids the pitfalls of both direct and indirect food aid by working through a carefully cultivated network of locally owned and locally staffed relief centers. If Americans are going to help needy people in other parts of the world, this seems like a pretty good approach."

"Thanks, guys," Bianca responded, grateful to have their support for her family's initiative. "I was hoping that you'd approve—well, actually, I was assuming that you'd approve. I hadn't thought about all of the pros and cons and all of the issues that might be related to helping the poor. If you approve of Compassion, do you think you might be interested in adopting a child? There are literally hundreds of children waiting for sponsors at any given time."

This invitation caught Micah and Lauren a little by surprise. As college students, they didn't have a lot of discretionary income. After a moment, Lauren responded, "Actually, I might want to talk to my parents about this the next time I go home. I don't have the money to sponsor a child on my own, but as a family we could afford to do it. We often make contributions to medical research organizations like the American Cancer Society and the Cystic Fibrosis Foundation, but I'm afraid that we don't really do anything to help the poor outside of America. We probably should consider diversifying and reaching out beyond America's borders."

Micah was wishing that Lauren hadn't been so ready to accept Bianca's invitation, for he was less inclined to. "Bianca, I think it's great that you want to help needy people. I do too. But as I explained, I think it's best to help those near at hand. I don't judge you for doing what you think is right—I want you to do what you think is right. But I'm still inclined to think that the Christian thing to do is to work within the schema of concentric circles that I described earlier. I hope you won't judge me if I decline your invitation."

"Micah, my dear friend," Bianca responded softly, "I know you to be a kind, sensitive, and generous person. I know that you have sympathy for people who are in need. I know that you go out of your way to help people. I certainly won't judge you if your conscience tells you that you shouldn't sponsor a child. I do wonder, though, whether your position really fits with what the Bible teaches.

"The passages that you cite may support your idea that we have moral obligations to care for ourselves, our families, our neighbors, and so on. I'd have to read them in context to know whether or not they do, but that certainly wouldn't be surprising. But most of us can afford to help people both near at hand and far away. It's not like you have to choose between helping your neighbor and helping an impoverished child in another country. Look at Lauren here: her family already donates to medical research, and now she's entertaining the possibility of sponsoring a child through Compassion.

"Do you remember the parable of the Good Samaritan?[10] Jesus told that story in response to the question 'Who is my neighbor?'[11] I think it can be shown that Jesus did not understand the biblical neighbor to be those who are in our geographic proximity. Rather he understood the neighbor to be those who are in our 'charitable proximity,' those whom my charitable acts can efficiently affect. Jesus's response to this question clearly uses the term in a symbolic way. The following verses contain Jesus's answer in the form of the parable of the Good Samaritan.

"In a day when travel was by foot, the Samaritans lived a significant distance from the inhabitants of Jerusalem. They were not literal neighbors. But it was not primarily geographical distance that separated the wounded Jew and the good Samaritan pictured in the parable: it was a mixture of religious, racial, and perhaps political prejudices. In his parable Jesus drives home the point that all human beings are our neighbors, regardless of such differences. The very point of this parable is that we have a moral obligation to feel compassion for all people, regardless of our differences."

"Whew, sister, that was a powerful argument!" Lauren exclaimed, very impressed by Bianca's persuasiveness. "I'm not a believer, but if I was, I'd be kneeling at the altar right now!"

---

10. Luke 10:30–37.
11. Luke 10:29.

"I definitely see your point, Bianca," Micah granted. "I'm sure that many Americans could afford to help needy Americans and also help needy non-Americans. For such people, viewing the situation as necessarily involving a choice between the two is a false dilemma."[12]

> "But whoever has this world's goods, and sees his brother in need, and shuts up his heart from him, how does the love of God abide in him? My little children, let us not love in word or in tongue, but in deed and in truth."
> —1 John 3:17–18 (NKJV)

"I'm glad that you two Christians are a step closer to reconciliation," Lauren joked. "But actually, Micah, I think you need to go a step further. It seems to me that there may be a good argument for prioritizing help to the most needy over help for those with lesser needs even if the neediest live farther away. Think about this: people tend to move in circles that reflect their own cultural, social, and economic status. Rich people don't usually hang out with homeless people; they tend to socialize with other rich people. Poor people tend to be found among other poor people. Likewise, rich people tend to come from rich families, and poor people tend to come from low-income families. For various reasons, poverty tends to be passed from generation to generation.

"If we adopt the theory that we are morally obligated to prioritize helping those in our family over those outside of our family whenever it's not possible to do both, and that we should help our neighbors rather than the more distant needy whenever it's not possible to do both, and that we ought to help those in

---

12. A "false dilemma" is a fallacy that occurs when an argument or scenario makes it appear like one must choose between two options when in fact one could choose both. (A false dilemma can also involve limiting the number of options to fewer than are really possible, but that's not the version of the fallacy involved here.)

our own country rather than people in other countries when it's not possible to do both, then because of the aforementioned fact that people tend to surround themselves with people like themselves, we are in effect saying that rich people should help rich people and poor people should help poor people. Since a rich person's family is likely to be rich, and a poor person's family is likely to be poor, the rich will be helping the rich and the poor will be helping the poor. Unfortunately, though, poor people are not able to provide much help to the poor, so the poor go unassisted. Conversely, rich people enjoy a very substantial, albeit unofficial, safety net. The same thing is true on an international scale: rich nations have considerable resources to help themselves and in national emergencies can appeal to other nations for loans, but poor nations have few resources to help themselves and, because of that very fact, in times of emergency they find it difficult to secure international loans.

"The unfortunate result of this is that the rich get richer and the poor get poorer.[13] Addressing this problem is, I think, one of the strengths of John Rawls's concept of the 'veil of ignorance.'[14] Dr. Platt didn't mention it in class, but I came across it while reading about Kantian ethics. Rawls was a prominent American ethicist during the second half of the twentieth century. He was a classical liberal—not in the sense of the Democratic Party or the Green Party, but in the sense of John Locke and Thomas Jefferson. His early work was very much influenced by Kant, which is why he caught my interest."

"Yes, I remember that you said that you're attracted to Duty Ethics more than Utilitarianism," Bianca broke in.

"Right," Lauren continued. "Rawls thinks that a central concern of ethics should be 'fairness.' He doesn't necessarily think that making sure that everyone has the same amount of wealth should be our goal; rather our goal should be to make sure that everyone is treated fairly. If that is done, then wealth imbalances should take care of themselves.

"The veil of ignorance is basically a thought experiment that Rawls created in order to test whether an action or solution that is under consideration

---

13. Economist Robert Reich argues that this is true for individuals in *Saving Capitalism: For the Many, Not the Few* (New York: Vintage, 2015).

14. John Rawls, *A Theory of Justice* (Cambridge, MA: Belknap, 1971); *Justice as Fairness: A Restatement* (Cambridge, MA: Belknap, 2001).

would be moral.[15] He recognized that it's very difficult to be completely detached when making decisions about things that will influence the distribution of wealth and opportunity. Self-interest has a way of sneaking in unnoticed (which is probably why lower-income people are usually more favorable toward economic arrangements that redistribute wealth than upper-income people are). So Rawls proposes that whenever considering such issues, we take into consideration the most likely outcomes of the various scenarios or solutions and how they will impact people, but we not take into consideration our own life situation: we block that information from having any influence on how we evaluate the scenarios. That's the 'veil of ignorance.' We make ourselves ignorant of our own situation so that we do not favor solutions that will benefit ourselves at the expense of others.

"Maybe it would be easier to understand if I illustrated it for you. We're talking about global hunger and whether it's best to prioritize the needs of those nearby or the needs of those whose plight is the most desperate. Imagine that you somehow find yourself in a position to determine how all aid in the world is distributed, and you are also somehow strangely ignorant of your own living situation: you don't know if you are rich, poor, or middle class, and you don't know what part of the world you live in. In such a scenario you won't know how the administration of food aid will affect you because you don't know whether you need food aid or not. But because, as Bianca pointed out, there are over 700 million people in the world who are living below the poverty level, and over three million people die of starvation every year, there's a significant chance that you are one of the impoverished, perhaps even someone who is in danger of starvation. In light of this, you will probably favor a system that is designed to assure, as much as possible, an even distribution of wealth and opportunity. That way, regardless of what your actual situation in life is, there's a good chance that you will have at least some chance of surviving."[16]

---

15. A thought experiment is an experiment that is conducted in your imagination rather than in a laboratory. It is a way to test theories that cannot be tested physically.
16. Another example involves the morality of slavery. In a society where half of the people are slaves and the other half slave owners, a person who is a slave owner will benefit from the system of slavery and will find it difficult to evaluate the morality of slavery objectively. This can be seen from the history of slavery around the world: slave own-

"That's really interesting!" Bianca responded, sincere appreciation in her voice. "I like it! It's Kantian? It's not Utilitarian? It seems like it would be a consequentialist approach, doesn't it?"

"It certainly does have consequentialist elements, I agree," Lauren granted. "But the central principle is Kantian. It's basically the Categorical Imperative: can a maxim be consistently universalized? In our case, we're asking whether a truly objective person would want to universalize the maxim of helping those near at hand or those in greatest need. Such a person would recognize that there could be situations where universalizing the former would end up helping those who don't need help and ignoring those who desperately need it, and hence the latter maxim would win out."

"Well, this veil of ignorance seems problematic to me, regardless of what school of thought it best aligns with," Micah objected. "It seems like a pipe dream. How are we supposed to actually step behind such a veil? Wouldn't that require that we be able to detect and set aside our preferences and prejudices before we step behind it? This seems like a nonstarter to me."

"Some of Rawls's critics have made exactly that objection, Micah," she replied. "It's insightful of you to come up with it so quickly. Rawls's defenders have argued that all that is needed is to set aside all prejudices and preferences that would privilege some people over others, but whether or not that is a sufficient rejoinder is debated."[17]

"It seems to me," Bianca observed slowly, "that this discussion of Rawls has shifted the focus of our discussion somewhat. We were originally talking about what would be right from the perspective of individuals. Am I mistaken, or has our discussion shifted toward what would be right for societies and governments?"

"That certainly seems like a relevant topic, regardless of whether we

---

ers developed elaborate ways to rationalize slavery as moral. However, if one was to evaluate the morality of slavery from behind a veil of ignorance (that is, without the knowledge of whether he or she would be slave or slave owner), then the person would be more objective and as a result would attempt to design a system that maximizes the freedom of all people. (Rawls discusses slavery in several parts of *A Theory of Justice*, especially, 247, but he does not explicitly give this illustration of the veil of ignorance.)

17. See the discussion of Rawls and the veil of ignorance in Michael Moehler, *Minimal Morality: A Multilevel Social Contract Theory* (Oxford: Oxford University Press, 2018).

were already moving in that direction, so let's talk about it, shall we?" Micah suggested.

"Sure," Lauren agreed. "If the veil of ignorance is a coherent approach to ethical issues, then I think its application to government involvement is natural. Governments ought to set aside prejudices and preferences and treat all people as equals. They should help those with the greatest needs regardless of race, religion, nationality, or any other criteria. I imagine that's what Rawls would argue, and *prima facie* I'm inclined to agree."

Micah was quick to respond to this line of reasoning. "Slow down, my friend. Even if the veil of ignorance turns out to be a coherent approach to such issues, I'm not sure that you're applying it correctly. The very reason for the existence of governments is to care for the citizens of the respective country. Hence governments have a greater responsibility for the welfare of their own citizens than they do for noncitizens. Perhaps we could agree that all governments have responsibilities for their own citizens, which would mean that every citizen is some government's responsibility, but you seem to be saying that all people everywhere are the responsibility of all governments everywhere. That seems obviously mistaken to me."

"OK, I see your argument, Micah," she replied. "But I'm not convinced that there is a set of universal rules that somehow applies to all governments. As a theist, you might think that God has a set of ideals that he expects all governments to live up to. As an atheist, I'm much more inclined toward contractualism, the view that societies decide for themselves what the responsibilities of their governments are. I think that a government is responsible for whatever its citizens decide that it's responsible for. Therefore I'm inclined to think that a government is responsible for whatever poor people its citizens decide it's responsible for. And I'm inclined to think that if the citizens of a country are morally sensitive, then they will tell their government to help those who are not able to help themselves, regardless of sex, race, nationality, and any other criteria. Need should be the only relevant criterion." Lauren said this with a quiet but firm note of conviction in her voice.

"I see the logic in that, Lauren," Micah said, almost acquiescently. "If you don't have a God to determine what the proper role of government is, then I guess it's going to have to be decided by the people. But the people could decide for a view like mine, where each government cares for its own rather than neglecting its own in order to care for someone else's."

"Whoa, Micah, that's a bit of a straw man!" Bianca objected. "I didn't hear Lauren advocating that anyone be neglected. If you can't defend your view without resorting to straw men, perhaps you should reconsider it. Personally, even though you and I agree that the role of government is established by God, I find myself leaning more toward Lauren's position in some areas. It seems conceivable that God left many things up to humans to decide—not right and wrong, but cultural things and practical things, like what form of government to have, and perhaps to some extent what laws to enact. Furthermore, it seems to me that American Christianity sometimes has a tendency to conflate theology and the American political culture without being aware that it's happening. Christianity outside of America is, at least in my experience, much more globally oriented, often less nationalistic, and generally more sensitive to cultural differences and socioeconomic disparities."

"Is that so, Bianca?" Lauren sounded surprised. "I'd like to hear more about that. Since I have two pals who are ardent Christians, I'd like to understand Christianity a little better."

"I'd like to hear more about it too," Micah admitted. "As I've stated before, I've never been outside of America. I love my country, as both of you know very well, but it doesn't hurt to see things from another perspective. Could we talk about that some other time, though? I've got to get started on my homework."

"Sure!" Bianca replied, happy with this conciliatory resolution of a discussion that seemed like it might be heading toward an argument. "Thanks for sharing my excitement with me today. You guys mean a lot to me. Lauren, if you want more information on Compassion, just let me know."

"Will do!" Lauren replied as they grabbed their things and headed toward the door.

QUESTIONS TO PONDER

- Is there a moral obligation to help the needy if it is within your power?

- If there is such a moral obligation, where does it come from?

- How should we decide how much help to give and to whom we should give it?

- Does civil authority come from God, from the citizens, from both, or from neither?

- If civil authority comes from the citizens of a country, does that entail some sort of cultural relativism?

TERMS TO KNOW

- Compassion International
- Direct food aid
- Indirect food aid
- False dilemma
- NGO
- Veil of ignorance
- Thought experiment
- Contractualism

FOR FURTHER READING

Alston, Philip. *Report of the Special Rapporteur on Extreme Poverty and Human Rights on His Mission to the United States of America*, United Nations, General Assembly, Human Rights Council, 4 May 2018. http://undocs.org/A/HRC/38/33/ADD.1.

Lappé, Frances Moore and Joseph Collins. *World Hunger: 10 Myths* (New York: Grove Press, 2015).

Sider, Ronald J. *Rich Christians in an Age of Hunger: Moving from Affluence to Generosity* (Nashville: Thomas Nelson, 2015).

Wilkinson, Richard and Kate Pickett. *The Spirit Level: Why Greater Equality Makes Societies Stronger* (New York: Bloomsbury Press, 2009).

16

WAR

Synopsis: Micah is preparing for a debate on the topic of "War and Pacifism" in his university debate class. Because it is an ethics issue, he seeks out help from his friends Bianca and Lauren, and Lauren's friend Shamar.

* * *

"I really appreciate you guys taking time out to help with this project. I've read so much stuff on this topic that my head is about to explode," Micah said as Bianca, Lauren, and Shamar settled into their seats in the back of the Student Center.

Micah and Bianca had recently announced their relationship on social media, and, since Lauren and Shamar were also dating, the four friends had begun hanging out quite a bit as the semester was coming to an end. This was not a normal dating occasion, however.

"Let me get this straight, dude," began Shamar, who had become a good friend to Micah since he had begun hanging out with Lauren, "this isn't for Ethics class?"

Micah responded, "We had a short discussion of war in Dr. Platt's class" (at this, the two girls nodded), "but right now I'm preparing for the final project in my debate class. I chose the topic of war since I found it interesting in Ethics class and thought it would be fun to dig a little deeper into the topic. I was also motivated by some family dynamics. Two of my uncles are in the military and are very gung-ho about defending our country. They can sound quite militaristic at times. Another of my uncles is a Quaker; he and his wife are extremely committed to pacifism. Family reunions can be interesting, and I've always kind of wondered who was right."

"Dr. Herschel didn't mind your double-dipping, as it were?" asked Bianca.

Micah thought Bianca had a strangely sensitive conscience about weird things sometimes. In this case, though, he had checked that out. "No, I checked with her. Once she saw the limited scope of our ethics notes on the subject, she was fine with my going more deeply into it in her class. I also told her a little about my family situation, and she said she liked 'the existential quality' of my addressing the topic, whatever that means."

Bianca said, "It means it's not just an abstract debate topic for you. You're personally involved."

Lauren spoke. "We're, of course, happy to be here, Micah, but what exactly are you hoping we can do for you?"

Micah breathed deeply. "I know this is a big request, but I would like to go through all the arguments I've compiled on both sides of this issue—Dr. Herschel doesn't tell you until you show up for the debate which position you will be taking—and see if you think I am making sense. It may take a while, but you guys are sharp thinkers, and I don't want to make a fool of myself next Tuesday."

Shamar spoke first, "I'm really glad you invited me and not just your Ethics class friends. A few of my ET[1] friends are also pacifists, so I've had several discussions along these lines over the last year or two. I'll enjoy hearing both sides."

"And of course, we're here for you, Micah," Bianca said as Lauren smiled and nodded. "We know how you can think sometimes. You definitely need our help."

Micah grimaced, but he didn't defend himself. That's exactly what he himself was thinking.

"Which case do you want to make first?" Bianca asked.

Micah gathered his note cards, consulted them for a moment, and answered, "I think I should deal with a third position first, in case it comes up while addressing the other two. Some have argued historically for a militaristic or jihadist position that affirms that war is appropriate to achieve national or religious objectives. I think it is important to mention this because, as we'll see, the just war position is at pains to deny that it is pro-war."

---

1. ET is Ecology Today, the campus environmentalism club featured in chapter 14.

"Who would argue that war is good?" asked Lauren.

"I didn't actually find theorists arguing that war is good. What they argue is that war need not merely be defensive. Machiavelli, for instance, argued that war is an extension of politics, a useful way for a strong state to impose its will on a weaker state," responded Micah.[2]

Bianca asked, "Did he claim this was ethical?"

Micah answered, "He wasn't much concerned about whether something was ethical. A state is either strong and able to impose its will on weaker states, or it is weak and will inevitably be imposed on. Offensive war, then, is ultimately the way to safeguard the state."

"The best defense is a good offense," offered Shamar.

"Precisely. Remember, Machiavelli was writing at a time when Italy was divided into a bunch of small states vying with each other for land and wealth. Even so, in his book *The Art of War*—"

"Wait," interrupted Shamar, "I thought some Chinese guy wrote *The Art of War*."[3]

"Yeah, that's true, Shamar," responded Micah. "That's the famous one, but Machiavelli wrote a book with the same title.[4] His book gives advice for waging war that clearly seeks to limit casualties and make sure one doesn't go to war without a reasonable chance of success, ideas present in just war theory. One gets the impression, though, that Machiavelli would have no problem with offensive war if it secured the safety and security of the state."

"You mentioned jihad," said Lauren. "You're speaking of militant Islam, right?"

Micah nodded and replied, "One reading of the Koran is that offensive warfare against infidels—non-Muslims—is not only moral but commanded by God. Of course, most Muslims worldwide read the Koran differently, but as you know, there are radical Muslims today who embrace the concept of Jihad."

---

2. See *The Prince*, chaps. 10, 12–14, and 21, for examples of Machiavelli's rhetoric. He does not urge expansion, but he speaks of successful conquerors as good examples and says of princes, "A prince should therefore have no other aim or thought, nor take up any other thing for his study, but war and its order and discipline" (chap. 14).

3. Shamar is speaking of Sun Tzu, *The Art of War*, a classic on military theory.

4. See https://onemorelibrary.com/index.php/en/books/social-sciences/book/military-science-201/the-art-of-war-239.

"Divine Command Theory," commented Bianca.

"Yes. Those who hold to Divine Command Theory as their ethical system do not believe they have the right to question what God commands. Whatever He commands is moral," explained Micah. He then directly addressed Shamar, "As you know, Bianca and I are Christians. We believe divine commands are nonnegotiable. But we don't believe God commands Christians to engage in offensive warfare."

"Even though your God commanded the Israelites to exterminate people in the Old Testament?" asked Lauren.

Micah winced a bit at the question, but he answered, "That's actually a big subject, but I can summarize the answer and discuss it more thoroughly with you later, if you want. The teacher in my college-and-career class at church went over this issue a couple of weeks ago. First, God has authority over life and death and is never wrong to take life if he deems it wise to do so. Therefore, he has the right to order a holy war if he so desires. Second, he had promised the land of Canaan to the Israelites hundreds of years before and wanted them to live there. Third, He gave the inhabitants of that land—most of them were called Canaanites—opportunities to repent and turn to him, but they sank into great wickedness.

Their extermination should be viewed as widespread capital punishment decreed by a just Judge. Fourth, the Canaanites who did repent—such as Rahab of Jericho—were not killed but instead were incorporated into Israel. Presumably, others would have been spared had they too repented. Fifth and finally, Israel was God's chosen nation and operated as a nation, fighting wars, making treaties, and so forth, none of which applies to Christians today. We are not a nation, we are not promised any specific property on this earth, and we are never told in the New Testament that we are to achieve our goals through violence.

Niccolò Machiavelli by Santi di Tito.
Public domain.

"I know that was a mouthful, but I don't think Christians today can justify offensive warfare because God commanded the extermination of the Canaanites in Joshua's time," Micah concluded.[5]

Bianca looked admiringly at Micah (he thought she looked surprised) and said, "If I may add two points. Violence is not intrinsically wrong. Some day we believe Jesus is going to return and destroy his enemies, and that will be justice.[6] Second, even the Old Testament prophesies of a time when violence will no longer exist. Swords will be beaten into farming implements.[7] That time of peace is what we look forward to, but Christians are not told to bring that time to pass through warfare."

Shamar and Lauren looked doubtfully at each other.

"Okay," Shamar began, "but what about the Crusades? If Christians could do that, how can you condemn Muslims for doing the same thing back at you?"

"Fair question," responded Micah. "I don't know many Christians today who would endorse the Crusades as ethical or moral. Just because people who called themselves Christians did them, doesn't mean they were a Christian thing to do. When I get to just war theory, I'll point out that the basic principles of it were stated by St. Augustine over five hundred years before the First Crusade, yet the crusaders rarely paid any attention to the standards for just war that Augustine affirmed."[8]

"Anyone else affirming the positive value of war?" asked Bianca, trying to get the conversation moving again.

Micah responded, "No doubt there have been many militaristic states that have launched offensive warfare without qualms about whether the war was moral. I didn't try to run all of them down and figure out their justifications. My point in bringing militarism up was to say that advocates of the just war position strongly reject that perspective."

---

5. For a brief discussion of the ethics of the extermination of the Canaanites that makes some of the same arguments, see https://www.desiringgod.org/interviews/what-made-it-okay-for-god-to-kill-women-and-children-in-the-old-testament.

6. See Rev. 19:11–21.

7. See Isa. 2:4. Many Old Testament prophecies envision a future time of peace.

8. For a balanced and interesting discussion of the morality of the Crusades, see https://www.thegospelcoalition.org/blogs/kevin-deyoung/what-about-the-crusades.

"Fair enough," Lauren spoke for the three listeners. "Then let's try again. Which are you going to cover first: just war or pacifism?"

Micah answered, "Pacifism is a little more complicated, so let's talk about it next."

"What's complicated about it?" asked Shamar.

"Well first, there are a surprising number of ways to be pacifist. Then there are both Christian and secular versions of pacifism, and people use both consequentialist and non-consequentialist arguments for it," Micah answered.

Shamar asked, "What do you mean by 'consequentialist' and 'non-consequentialist'? Remember, I'm not in your Ethics class."

"Trust me," Micah answered, "we'll get to that."

Lauren asked, "Is pacifism mostly a modern phenomenon?"

"Frankly, it's hard to find in ancient times outside Christian circles. States warring against one another was a fact of life. Plato argued that peace is better than war, but he did not argue that war is morally wrong.[9] As I'll point out later, Cicero argued that rules of justice ought to apply to warfare,[10] but he wouldn't have gotten far telling his fellow Romans that war itself was wrong. Secular pacifism does appear to be a largely modern construct."

"But not Christian pacifism?" asked Bianca.

"That's a different story," answered Micah, "although scholars are divided on the question." He glanced down at his note cards. "Several early church writers of the second and early third centuries—Athenagoras, Tertullian, Origen, and Lactantius—appear to be opposed to war and violence in general. They didn't think Christians should serve in the army, and they emphasized the way of love as distinguishing Christians from others in Roman imperial society."[11]

Shamar observed, "That seems pretty airtight. What's to disagree about?"

"It turns out," said Micah, "that serving in the Roman military required offering sacrifices to Roman gods. Similarly, the gladiatorial contests and other aspects of the violence of the Roman culture were blended with paganism and idolatry."

---

9.   Plato, *Laws*, 1. Cited in Arthur F. Holmes, ed., *War and Christian Ethics* (Grand Rapids: Baker Academic, 2005), 20–23.

10. Plato, *De Republica* 3. Cited in Holmes, *War and Christian Ethics*, 24–25.

11. See Holmes, ed., *War and Christian Ethics*, 37–54, for the relevant documents.

"Whoa," interjected Lauren. "I hang around you guys a lot, but you may need to explain to Shamar what idolatry is."

Shamar turned to Lauren, "I watch *American Idol*. I know what idolatry is, thank you very much."

Micah laughed and said, "The idols I'm talking about were not generally other people—although they did worship the emperors, come to think of it—but rather gods and goddesses like Zeus, Apollo, Venus—"

"What Micah is trying to say," Bianca inserted, "is that idolatry is the worship of artifacts as though they have divine powers or have divine powers behind them."

"Thank you, Bianca." Micah cleared his throat. "To return to my point, Christians had a lot of good reasons for repudiating all of that without necessarily being pacifists. That is, if the Romans had fielded a secular army with no religious strings attached, it is not certain that Christians would have objected to serving. Even the pacifists will admit that Christians began showing up in the Roman army in the third century despite all the religious challenges involved. That's hard to explain if the churches were generally agreed about a policy of nonviolence."[12]

"What you're saying is that we don't really know whether the early Christians were fully pacifist or not," concluded Lauren. "When did full-blown Christian pacifism show up?"

Micah answered, "There are examples of opposition to war in the Middle Ages, including some famous names like St. Francis and John Wyclif. But full-blown Christian pacifism probably appears during the Reformation of the sixteenth century. When the Reformers began breaking away from the Roman Catholic Church that had dominated Western Europe for centuries, new state churches were founded across Northern Europe. Churches working with governments to manage societies are never pacifist because states believe they must have arms to defend themselves. The Lutherans in Germany; the Reformed states that arose in Switzerland, the Netherlands, and Scotland; and the Anglicans in England all viewed war as necessary to protect themselves from the Catholics and each other."

---

12. Arthur Holmes makes this case in *War: Four Christian Views*, ed. Robert G. Clouse (Winona Lake, IN: BMH, 1986), 126–7.

Lauren spoke up again. "Nothing much had changed, then. The Middle Ages had a lot of fighting—if I'm correctly remembering my Western Civ— and the breakup of Europe into a bunch of separate states was not likely to ease the tensions."

"True, but some Christians objected to state churches. They believed the union of church and state leads to persecution of others because of their beliefs. They extended this opposition to include violence in general and, therefore, warfare," Micah observed. "History books call them *Anabaptists*; today, they are the Mennonites and Amish."[13]

Shamar asked, "If they're Anabaptists, are they related to the Baptists? I know lots of Baptists, although I don't think any of them are pacifists."

Micah answered, "The Baptists share many teachings with the Anabaptists, but my understanding is that they came along later. The Anabaptists' motive in rejecting all violence, including warfare, was the desire to make the church totally separate from how things are done in the secular world."[14]

"That's a noble desire," Bianca observed, "but it doesn't seem very realistic. If a government took that position, the state would be defenseless against its enemies."

Micah nodded, "That's true, but a Mennonite pacifist would typically respond in a couple of ways. First, this is a theology for the church, which will always be a minority in every state. Most pacifists of this kind wish their governments would avoid war, but they do not expect their governments to be Christian. Christians, they say, are not called to rule in this age; they are called to suffer. Second, being defenseless against one's enemies means being exactly like Jesus Christ, who was a lamb led to the slaughter. He could have used force—"

---

13. The Amish actually split from the Mennonites in 1693 and, therefore, did not exist during the Reformation. Micah is probably unaware that other descendants of the Anabaptists include the Hutterian Brethren, the Bruderhof, the Church of the Brethren, and the Dunkard Brethren Church. All of these churches have official pacifist positions. See http://www.hutterites.org/; https://www.bruderhof.com; http://www.brethren.org; and https://www.dunkardbrethrenchurch.com/index.html. The Amish seek to be preindustrial and therefore do not maintain a website, but helpful information can be found here: https://www.britannica.com/topic/Amish.

14. See https://themennonite.org/feature/mennonite-peace-witness-across-spectrum for an interesting discussion of the modern Mennonite "peace witness."

"Doesn't one of the gospels say he could have called down legions of angels to help him?" inserted Bianca.

"That's right." Micah glanced through his cards. "Jesus says that in Matthew 26:53, just as the soldiers are arresting him. In the verse right before that, he ordered Peter to put away his sword because 'all who draw the sword will die by the sword.' Anabaptists use this passage quite often to argue that following in Jesus's steps means being willing to suffer and die rather than defend oneself. From a national standpoint, this obviously would rule out war."[15]

"It would seem to rule out not being conquered by neighboring states that disagree," intoned Shamar.

"There's that," agreed Micah.

"But what if every country did embrace this viewpoint?" Bianca wondered. "Wouldn't that be beautiful?"

"I'm sorry," Shamar replied. "I can't help but think of a Jack Handey Deep Thought: 'I can picture in my mind a world without war, a world without hate. And I can picture us attacking that world because they'd never expect it.'"[16]

Micah and Shamar started laughing, but Lauren elbowed Shamar rather aggressively and said, "Bianca was being serious, Shamar. Peace is a beautiful goal, and we shouldn't make fun of people who are willing to suffer to achieve it."

Micah straightened up, glanced at Shamar, and said, "We weren't trying to make light of their aspirations. Shamar's point is that states can't function that way. No country, Bianca, is going to embrace this viewpoint. Even the Mennonites don't expect them to. That's why they're prepared to suffer for their pacifism. They don't expect their theology to spread around the globe until Jesus comes back. In the meantime, they hold to it precisely because it is countercultural and helps them stand out as peaceful folks in a violent world."

Bianca seemed to accept Micah's semi-apology and asked, "Are there other significant pacifist groups besides the descendants of the Anabaptists?"

Micah nodded. "That brings me to my aunt and uncle, who I mentioned earlier. The Friends, better known as Quakers, have always affirmed pacifism.

---

15. For an able defense of the pacifist position by a modern Mennonite scholar, see Myron S. Augsburger, "Christian Pacifism," in Clouse, ed., *War*, 81–97.

16. https://www.deepthoughtsbyjackhandey.com.

They emerged in the seventeenth century in England, and from the beginning they were committed to nonviolence. They still have a strong reputation for opposing war and, for most Quakers, opposing violence in general. My aunt and uncle prefer to call their position 'peacemaking.' While *pacifism* sounds entirely passive, *peacemaking* communicates an active idea of opposing warfare with peaceful alternatives."[17]

"What kinds of peaceful alternatives are they talking about?" Lauren asked.

"What you would expect. My uncle believes governments should be willing to compromise, negotiate, appease, or whatever it takes to save lives. In general, pacifists think life should be valued more than political objectives."

Shamar stirred when he heard that. "What if the political objective is preventing one's country from being overrun by a militaristic neighbor? Isn't it a bit naive to set political objectives against valuing life as though the two are always in conflict?"

"You sound like my other two uncles," said Micah with a smile.

Bianca, however, countered, "You've got to admit that wars are often fought over political objectives that hardly seem more valuable than human life."

Micah said, "We're going to get to just war theory soon, I promise. One of the main reasons people developed just war ideas was to prevent wars over insignificant matters or for immoral reasons. But yes, I agree that history has lots of examples of unjust wars."

"In addition to the Anabaptists and the Quakers, are there any other significant Christian pacifists?" asked Bianca.

Micah replied, "The three biggest names in religious pacifism of the twentieth century are the Russian novelist Leo Tolstoy, the Hindu reformer Mahatma Gandhi, and Martin Luther King Jr. It seems that Tolstoy influenced Gandhi and King, and Gandhi further influenced King."

"So their arguments must not have been strictly Christian if Gandhi is in the list," observed Shamar.

"Actually, Tolstoy grounded his opposition to war directly in his interpretation of the gospels. His opposition to the Russian government got him

---

17. For a video explaining nonviolence from the Quaker perspective, see https://www.fgcquaker.org/resources/end-violence. The classic expression of this viewpoint from the Mennonite perspective is *The Politics of Jesus* by John Howard Yoder.

kicked out of the Russian Orthodox Church, and he developed his own very personal and unique approach to Christianity. He was convinced that Jesus Christ taught complete nonviolence and that individuals can be agents for social change only if they refuse to allow human systems of government to force them into non-Christian attitudes and actions. So he rejected all violence not on consequential but on moral grounds.[18] What's the ethical word I'm looking for here, Bianca?" asked Micah.

"I think you mean 'deontological,' where the ethical decisions are made based on what is right and wrong without regard to consequences," answered Bianca.

Micah nodded his head. "Exactly. Thank you, Bianca. What is surprising is how much Tolstoy's staunch opposition to official violence influenced people around the world who did not agree with his basic theology, Gandhi among them. When Gandhi went to South Africa to oppose apartheid early in his career, he started an educational commune that he named Tolstoy Farm. It functioned from 1910 to 1913, and Gandhi began developing his own version of pacifism."

Leo Tolstoy. Public domain.

"Gandhi named his community after Tolstoy!" interjected Lauren. "That's remarkable. I have heard that Gandhi respected Jesus. Is this what that is about?"

"At least partly, I think," replied Micah. "After reading the Sermon on the Mount, Gandhi decided that Jesus was a great teacher. He even said of him, 'Jesus was the most active resister known perhaps to history. His was nonviolence par excellence.' Obviously, Gandhi was uninterested in becoming a Christian and told people that his Hinduism was open to all the great teachings of the other

---

18. See Colm McKeogh, *Tolstoy's Pacifism* (Amherst, NY: Cambria, 2009).

religions. But like Tolstoy, he interpreted Jesus as a pacifist and used Christ's teachings as support for his own practice of nonviolence."[19]

"Can you tell us more about Gandhi's Pacifism?" asked Shamar.

Micah consulted one of his note cards and responded, "Gandhi didn't like the word 'pacifism' and came up with his own word to describe his position: *Satyagraha* (I'm pretty sure I mispronounced that). He believed nonviolence begins with one's own soul coming to such a peaceful state that it would never seek to solve a problem by means of violence. He did, however, believe that nonviolent means of protest were essential for bringing attention to the needs for reform. This is very similar to what Tolstoy believed. Violence should be protested using nonviolence."

Bianca asked, "Is this a consequentialist ethics in which nonviolence was the best way to achieve good results?"

"I don't think so," answered Micah. "Gandhi realized that the authorities might crush him and his associates as they protested, but his basic principle was noninjury to any living being in thought, word, or action. I think it's pretty—I've forgotten the word again."[20]

"Deontological," Bianca, Lauren, and Shamar said in unison.

"Oh, yeah. You guys can't come to my debate, can you?" Micah pleaded. All three smiled but shook their heads.

"And Gandhi influenced MLK?" asked Shamar.

"Big time." Micah explained, "King toured India in 1959, specifically to learn more about Gandhi and his philosophy. Of course, King was a Baptist minister and had Christian reasons for nonviolence, but in his report of his visit to India, he wrote, 'I left India more convinced than ever before that non-violent resistance is the most potent weapon available to oppressed people in their struggle for freedom.'[21] Of course, he grew in fame as a prophet of peace over the next nine years until his assassination in 1968."

19. For the above quote and other information about Gandhi's attitude toward Jesus Christ, see https://www.mkgandhi.org/articles/gandhi_christ.html.
20. For a detailed study of the varieties of nonviolence by a Gandhi scholar, see https://www.mkgandhi.org/g_relevance/chap02.htm.
21. For complete text of King's description of his India tour, see https://kinginstitute.stanford.edu/king-papers/documents/my-trip-land-gandhi.

"Fascinating!" said Lauren. "But a while ago you suggested that there are also non-Christian pacifists, by which I'm thinking you meant people who are pacifists without explicitly Christian reasons. Can you explain that line of thinking?"

Micah responded, "Many in the last century or so have argued against war without necessarily appealing to religious reasons. An influential example of this kind of secular pacifist is the philosopher and mathematician Bertrand Russell. Russell is a good example of someone who was a pacifist on consequentialist grounds. He believed that war is bad because it fails to effectively solve problems, it has terrible costs in lives and other resources, and it cannot really be carried out in a just fashion."

Bianca added, "We studied Russell in Introduction to Philosophy. He certainly would not have had Christian reasons for pacificism. He was

strongly opposed to religion. He was an interesting thinker, though, and a really good writer."

"Yes, he's famous as a philosopher and writer," rejoined Micah, "but he also gained notoriety for his war protests. He was fired from Cambridge and served some time in jail for publicly protesting the First World War, and then over forty years later he was arrested again for protesting nuclear weapons."[22]

Shamar asked, "What were his main reasons for opposing war? Was he opposed to all violence?"

"He wasn't even opposed to all war, actually. Early in his career, he wrote an article on the different

Bertrand Russell. Public domain.

---

22. For an interesting take on Russell's pacifism, see https://newhumanist.org.uk/articles/4709/bertrand-russells-lofty-pacifism. For a more thorough and positive assessment of Russell's pacifism, see Alan Ryan, *Bertrand Russell: A Political Life* (New York: Farrar, Straus and Giraux, 1981).

kinds of war and argued that wars of self-defense are usually justifiable since the consequences of a nation not defending itself against attacks by an enemy would be bad for everyone concerned. But he went on to argue that most wars are alleged to be self-defense when in fact they are not. His consequentialism is really evident in this article. Wars of conquest are obviously immoral, except, he said, for when there is a substantial gap in cultural advancement between the conquering country and the people being conquered. For instance, he believed the conquest of the North American Indians by Westerners was justified by the huge advantages everyone received by the more advanced culture triumphing."

"That's certainly not politically correct!" reacted Bianca. "And it certainly doesn't sound like pacifism."

Micah continued, "He became more liberal in his politics over time and probably moved away from that early position. The point is, though, that he believed World War I was unjustifiable by any standard, he joined and became a leader of an anti-war group called the No-conscription Fellowship, and he traveled around the country urging people not to support the war effort. As I said, this got him fired from Cambridge, arrested, and labeled by one British politician as 'one of the most mischievous cranks in this country.'"[23]

Lauren asked, "What did he do when World War II came?"

"He supported Chamberlain's appeasement efforts as long as he could.[24] When it became evident that the Nazis were a threat to all of Europe, Russell reluctantly agreed that force would be necessary and supported the war effort. His convictions were entirely shaped by what he thought the consequences would be. That also explains his later antinuclear career, in which he became famous for demonstrating with much younger people against the government's nuclear program. He even got himself arrested again."

Bianca offered, "Let me guess. He believed the consequences of a nuclear program would be the annihilation of mankind, so he opposed it on that ground."

---

23. Quoted in https://journals.openedition.org/rfcb/308, another assessment of Russell's pacifism.
24. Neville Chamberlain, the Prime Minister of Great Britain 1937–1940, sought to avoid war with Nazi Germany through a series of compromises. Obviously, he was ultimately unsuccessful.

Micah nodded. "Very perceptive. He often spoke of the irrationality of any program that threatens the survival of the species. By the 1960s his opposition to war had become more pronounced and perhaps consistent, and he vigorously spoke out against the Vietnam War."

Shamar said, "Wait a minute. He protested the First World War and the Vietnam War? How old was he in the 1960s?"

"He was in his nineties when the Vietnam War started. He lived to be ninety-seven," Micah concluded.

Lauren then said, "Micah, you seem pretty well versed in the history of this topic. But what if you are asked to summarize pacifism in two minutes. Can you do it?"

Micah took a deep breath and said, "I'll try. The four main kinds of pacifism are (1) Absolute Pacifism, in which all violence is wrong, personal or national; (2) Christian Pacifism, in which Christians are forbidden to participate in any form of violence, but it is understood that secular society will do so; (3) Private Pacifism, in which nations or other God-ordained authorities can rightly wage war but individuals should never employ violence (Augustine taught this one, but not many have followed him on it); and (4) Antiwar Pacifism, in which individuals may have the right to defend themselves, but nations should never use war to solve problems.[25] As we've seen, Quakers, Tolstoy, Gandhi, and others hold to number 1; Mennonites typically hold to number 2; and most secular pacifists espouse number 4. The arguments for numbers 1 and 2 are almost always religious and deontological"—Micah smiled at his friends as he finally got the word out—"and arguments for number 4 are usually consequential, having to do with the horrors and costs of war. How was that?"

Bianca clapped, and Lauren and Shamar each gave him thumbs-up and a big smile.

Then Shamar asked, "There is a Kingdom Hall a few blocks from campus, and I've met a few Jehovah's Witnesses from there. Aren't they pacifists too?"

"I didn't study them," answered Micah. "Sorry."

---

25. For these categories see the discussion of pacifism in John S. Feinberg and Paul D. Feinberg, *Ethics for a Brave New World* (Wheaton, IL: Crossway, 2010), 637–38.

"I've got this," Bianca spoke up. "They are conscientious objectors who refuse to serve in secular militaries. They say they should fight only God's battles. But they are not pacifists. They do not oppose their governments going to war, and they do not personally reject violence."[26]

"Thanks, Bianca," Micah said. "How in the world did you know that?"

Bianca replied, "I read an article about it a couple of months ago. No big deal."

"I wish you were doing my debate next Tuesday." Micah's statement made his friends laugh, but he didn't think it was funny.

"Shamar and I are going to get some coffee," Lauren said as she and Shamar rose and headed for the Student Center coffee bar. "When we get back, you can explain just war theory to us. This first part was interesting, Micah, but do you think you could keep this last part shorter?"

"Will do," Micah responded.

Ten minutes later, Lauren and Shamar returned with cups of coffee for everyone. Once they were settled into their chairs, they directed their attention to Micah.

"During the first century before Christ, a Roman orator and ethicist named Cicero argued—"

"Whoa, dude!" exclaimed Shamar. "More history? Do we really need another history lesson?"

Micah smiled and said, "This one will be short. I promise." He placed his hand over his heart, unfortunately the hand that was holding his coffee cup, which spilled all over his notes and shirt.

After order was restored (for some reason, his friends were amused), Micah began again, "Cicero built on some things Plato had said in a couple of his political writings and argued that war should be carried out in a just manner. He said self-defense is reasonable, but wars should have rational limits, treachery or revenge should be forbidden, and prisoners should be treated humanely. Ethicists consider Cicero's writings to be the foundation of just war theory."[27]

---

26. For an official statement of the conscientious objector position of Jehovah's Witnesses, see https://wol.jw.org/en/wol/d/r1/lp-e/1951080.

27. The relevant documents are cited in Holmes, ed., *War and Christian Ethics*, 13–31.

Bianca commented, "That seems like a brave thing to do during the Roman Empire. Talk about a militaristic state!"

Micah agreed and said, "Perhaps not surprisingly, it was the Christians who picked up on these ideas and further developed them. The key thinker was St. Augustine, who lived four hundred years after Cicero. He modified and expanded the criteria for deciding whether a war is just, and during the Middle Ages St. Thomas Aquinas endorsed and further explained the theory. By the time of the Reformation, just war theory was well established."

"But for modern times," Lauren inserted, "you don't need to give us a play-by-play of all the historical developments, do you? You can just tell us what just war theory is. Right?"

Micah smiled, "As a matter of fact, correct. Although there have been some modern developments that we will have to consider. But without further ado, just war theory says that ethical criteria are needed both for determining when wars are just and for figuring out how to justly fight a war. These are distinguished as *jus ad bellum,* the justice of war itself, and *jus in bello,* carrying out war justly."

Bianca patted Micah's arm—the dry one—and said, "You don't pronounce the Latin *j* as in *jelly*; it sounds like a *y* as in *you*: 'yoose ad bellum' and 'yoose in bello.'"

Micah looked annoyed and said, "Does that really matter?"

Bianca responded, "We *are* trying to limit how much people laugh at you, right?"

"Tough job, dude," added Shamar with a grin.

Micah groaned and continued, "There is no universal agreement on the criteria for either one, but I've compared a number of lists. They agree in their fundamental ideas. For a war to be just, it must satisfy the following criteria:

1. Legitimate authority must exist to determine whether the rest of the criteria are met. Individuals can't just decide to declare war on someone.
2. War must be the last resort. Other good-faith efforts to solve the problems must be attempted before declaring war.
3. A formal declaration of war must be made.

4. There must be reasonable hope of success. It is not a just war to throw a bunch of soldiers into a conflict in which many on both sides will die when the outcome is already obvious.

5. There must be proportionality between the goal to be achieved and the destruction necessary to achieve it. This idea of proportionality receives a lot of attention. Wars to achieve trivial goals or protect minor assets have decimated populations and ruined economies.

6. There must be just cause. Just war ethicists believe self-defense is a sufficient cause. Protecting an ally under attack is similar, since nations often have treaties with one another for mutual defense. Very few just war ethicists in modern times argue for offensive wars ever being just. By the way, this principle suggests that many conflicts are just wars for the nation defending itself and unjust wars for the aggressor. Of course, some wars are unjust on both sides. It is hard to envision a truly just war on both sides, although nations tend to interpret situations in accordance with their own interests.

7. There must be right intention: to secure peace. This principle rules out wars of conquest, wars to overthrow oppressive political systems, wars to advance political or economic agendas, etc."[28]

Lauren commented, "There's a lot to talk about there. Just off the top of my head, it seems like one could question what makes an authority legitimate. How many good-faith efforts are necessary before declaring war? Is it ever right to make a preemptive strike before declaring war?"

Bianca continued the thought. "Some of these seem very subjective. When is hope for success reasonable? Who decides how much destruction is the right amount for achieving some goal? Are intentions—especially of a nation—ever that clear-cut? Couldn't someone say he's just seeking to secure peace but also be trying to protect oil fields that his country needs or be seeking to overthrow a dictatorship?"

Shamar concluded, "I think, Micah, that the ladies are pointing out that these criteria are too slippery and subjective actually to prevent wars. One

---

28. This list is adapted from Feinberg and Feinberg, *Ethics for a Brave New World*, 654–55.

could almost always find a way to justify the war he wants to fight." Lauren and Bianca nodded to affirm Shamar's assessment.

Micah replied, "Just war advocates are well aware of these problems, and many of them admit to no easy solution. It is important to frame the discussion properly, though. As Arthur Holmes says in arguing for this position, 'The just war theory *does not try to justify war*. Rather it tries to bring war under the control of justice so that, if consistently practiced by all parties to a dispute, it would eliminate war altogether.'[29] It is unlikely that there will be general agreement among all nations on these principles, but to the extent that nations embrace this ethic, war will diminish or even vanish. After all, not all people follow the Golden Rule, but it remains a legitimate measure by which to determine whether behavior is ethical."

"What about the other criteria?" Lauren asked. "The ones for evaluating the justice of how war is carried out?"

"*Jus in bello*," Bianca clarified.

Micah answered, "Here they are:

1. There must be a limited objective: restoration of peace. This is similar to the criterion for an entire war. Each military operation should have a similarly restrictive goal. If wiping out an installation or garrison or whatever would not help win the war, then it would be unjust to do it.
2. The object is the restraint of enemy soldiers, not their death. This principle argues that it is never right to kill people that can be captured or to kill people that have been captured. Even in the grim business of war, life should matter.
3. Direct attack on noncombatants is illegitimate. People have recognized this idea for a long time, but warfare has a poor track record of recognizing and honoring the boundary between soldiers and civilians. This principle is also difficult to apply in guerilla warfare, where virtually everyone is mobilized for the war effort. Nevertheless, killing people who are not trying to kill you is immoral.

---

29. Clouse, ed., *War*, 119–20. Italics original.

4. One should not inflict unnecessary suffering. Various warfare conventions have passed laws against torture and other 'cruel and unusual punishments.'

5. The principle of proportionality may justify indirect effects on civilians. That is, the good achieved by winning the war must be measured against attacks on infrastructure, etc. Destroying a munitions factory, for instance, may kill civilian workers and will certainly put many of them out of work, but if doing so shortens the war, it may be justified."[30]

"Have you had a chance to share these criteria with your two militaristic uncles?" asked Shamar.

Micah smiled and answered, "As a matter of fact, I ran this by one of them last night. He agreed with some of the principles involved, but overall he said these rules demonstrate the difference between an ethicist in an office and a soldier carrying a weapon on a battlefield."

Bianca said, "How did you respond to that, Micah? If these rules are impossible to obey, what good are they?"

"Obviously I wasn't going to lecture my uncle on what's appropriate on a battlefield. But I did tell him that I wouldn't want thousands of soldiers marching through a countryside with modern weapons without *any* rules. As I said before, rules for conduct may be ideal, but at least they set a standard that soldiers can seek to meet."

"When you say 'soldiers,'" Shamar observed, "you talk like each private is making these decisions. Soldiers are taught to do what they're told by their officers. Again, these criteria don't seem realistic."

Micah replied, "I thought about that. The military can't suspend ethics to the extent that a soldier is morally justified in doing evil because his commander tells him to, can it? Doesn't he have to reserve the right to say, 'I won't shoot that civilian, sir,' even if it costs him his life?"

"Maybe," Shamar said and became quiet, thoughtful.

"The fact is," Micah went on, "most of the decisions to evaluate situations and try to honor the criteria for just fighting will be made by generals and

---

30. Feinberg and Feinberg, *Ethics for a Brave New World*, 655.

other officers or even politicians rather than by foot soldiers. I was using the word 'soldier' in the general sense to include everyone actively engaged in the fighting. Most privates will not be thinking about ethical considerations when they're being shot at. The US military—not to mention various international tribunals—have adopted similar standards. They call them 'rules of engagement.' They're pretty complex—as most government or military things tend to be—but they use a lot of the same concepts as I just listed."[31]

Shamar nodded and said, "Fair enough."

"There's one more aspect to just war theory," Micah added. "Just war ethicists give reasons pacifism doesn't work. If pacifism is refuted, the alternative is that war is sometimes justifiable."

"Can we try to guess some of the arguments against pacifism?" asked Bianca.

Micah nodded. "Go for it."

Bianca began, "Relative to Christian Pacifism, it seems that arguing for nonviolence from the Scriptures is open to many objections. God commanded violence in the Old Testament, as we saw before, and Paul says the government has the right to use the sword against criminals.[32] I'm pretty sure even Jesus can be interpreted as not being a pacifist. Don't many interpreters say he preached against revenge but not against self-defense in the Sermon on the Mount?"

"On Tuesday," Micah answered, "I'm going to try not to get bogged down with a lot of delving into biblical interpretation, but the majority of interpreters of Scripture throughout history have rejected the idea that Jesus or anyone else in Scripture taught pacifism. Most Christians since the Reformation have believed that a person can be a citizen of heaven while also being a faithful citizen of the earthly state he or she belongs to."[33]

Shamar then said, "I alluded to this earlier, but it seems to me that war is inevitable when evil nations attack their neighbors for unjust reasons. A nation has to have the right to defend itself."

---

31. For the official Rules of Engagement of the U.S. Military see https://www.loc.gov/rr/frd/Military_Law/pdf/OLH_2015_Ch5.pdf.

32. Rom. 13:1.

33. See Feinberg and Feinberg, *Ethics for a Brave New World*, 644–49, for careful handling of the scriptural material.

"And I'm glad," Lauren said, "that you guys" (she directed this comment to Micah and Bianca) "don't agree with the Jehovah's Witnesses and Anabaptists who say war is wrong for them but okay for the countries they live in. That seems like freeloading to me. I can't imagine allowing others to die so that I could have my own personal freedom."

"We agree with you, Lauren," Bianca responded. "But in fairness to those folks, they do believe their allegiance to God outweighs their responsibility to defend their country."

"And I did read Mennonites," added Micah, "who explicitly said they would be willing to die for their country but not to kill for their country. But you bring up a legitimate concern, Lauren. Let me add one more point. A primary argument of pacifists is that respecting the value of life demands it. Just war advocates reply that if one really respects life, then one will defend it. Or to put it another way, the right to life presupposes the right to defend one's life and the lives of those one loves."

"I know we've been here for a while," Bianca said, "but I imagine the pacifist side on Tuesday will bring up nuclear war. What are you going to say about that, Micah?"

Micah looked at Bianca and said, "You really know how to bring up the tough issues, don't you? Many just war ethicists believe nuclear war cannot be justified because it is inevitably disproportional, doing more damage that can ever be justified, and it always kills noncombatants in large numbers."

"Does anyone try to justify nuclear bombs, like what we dropped on Hiroshima and Nagasaki to end World War II?" asked Lauren. "I've read that the bombs saved millions of lives, both Allied and Japanese."

"You've nailed it, Lauren. Nuclear warfare can be morally justified only on consequentialist grounds, that it saves more lives than it costs. I don't see how one could ever justify it on the basis of the just war criteria most people recognize."

Shamar said, "In that case, the just war program is seriously undermined. We are in the nuclear age, and the major international players have nuclear arsenals. What's the point of arguing about just war if just wars are now impossible?"

Micah replied, "Fortunately, the many wars that have been fought since the close of World War II have seen the use of only conventional weapons.

Both sides having stockpiles of nuclear weapons has been a deterrent to anyone actually using them. Therefore, the rules of war have still applied."

"And have still been broken," added Bianca.

"True. Everyone—for the most part—agrees that war is terrible. If everyone respected the criteria for just war, war would cease, since no nation would have to defend itself if there were no aggressors. Pacifism says everyone should agree not to fight; just war says everyone should agree only to defend oneself. The difference between the two positions is this: What do you do when a nation breaks all the rules and attacks you? Pacifists say protect life by refusing to kill. Just war advocates say protect life by refusing to die and refusing to let others you love die with you," Micah concluded.

"Another line of thought," said Lauren, "might relate to application of your just war principles in other areas. Off the top of my head, it seems like you could discuss how this idea relates to personal self-defense and what proportionality looks like if someone threatens you or your family. I read an article once about people who were bombing abortion clinics because they said they were protecting life. I bet they'd say they were fighting a just war.[34] Gun rights and the lawful limits on police violence are other areas to consider. And what about—"

"Whoa!" interjected Micah. "Yes, the discussion can bring up all those things, plus capital punishment, and more. There are no easy answers, but one needs to decide what one's fundamental principles are. Is violence and therefore war always wrong, or are they sometimes justified? Once a person settles that question, he or she is ready to work out all the implications. And that central question is really what my debate Tuesday is about."

"We think you're ready, Micah," Lauren concluded. Shamar nodded his agreement, and Bianca gave Micah's hand a gentle squeeze.

---

34. In rejecting this claim, one could appeal to the idea that it is never right to break good laws in order to protest bad laws, or even to a more sweeping generalization: ends do not justify means.

QUESTIONS TO PONDER

- In Micah's summary of pacifism, he lists four versions of the idea. Which of these seems the most consistent and logical to you? Why?

- Review the criteria for *jus ad bellum* and *jus in bello*. Which are most essential? Are any too subjective?

- Choose a war in American history and, to the best of your knowledge, assess it relative to just war criteria.

- Some ethicists believe just war theory should be extended to allow for preemptive strikes. The argument is that it would be foolish to allow an enemy a first strike that crippled one's ability to respond. When certain that the enemy was preparing just such a strike, a preemptive strike would be ethical.[35] What do you think of this idea?

- Does just war theory have any bearing on the morality of torture? Why or why not?

- Is just war possible in an age of nuclear weapons? Could the use of nuclear weapons ever be justified ethically?

---

35. A much debated example of such a preemptive strike is Israel's attack on Egypt in the Six-Day War of 1967, which Israel claimed was necessary to prevent Egyptian invasion. For details see Michael B. Oren, *Six Days of War: June 1967 and the Making of the Modern Middle East* (Novato, CA: Presidio, 2003).

TERMS TO KNOW

- Militarism
- Jihad
- Divine Command Theory
- Consequentialism
- State church
- Pacifism
- Deontological
- Appeasement
- Absolute Pacifism
- Christian Pacifism
- Private Pacifism
- Antiwar Pacifism
- Just War Theory
- *Jus ad bellum*
- *Jus in bello*
- Proportionality
- Rules of engagement
- Nuclear war
- Conventional weapons
- Deterrent

FOR FURTHER READING

General:

Coates, J. *The Ethics of War.* Manchester: Manchester University Press, 1997.

Reichberg, Gregory M. Henrik Syse, and Endre Begby, eds., *The Ethics of War: Classic and Contemporary Readings.* Hoboken, NJ: Wiley-Blackwell, 2006.

Shaw, William H. *Utilitarianism and the Ethics of War.* Abingdon, Oxfordshire: Routledge, 2016.

Christian:

Clouse, Robert G., ed., *War: Four Christian Views.* Winona Lake, IN: BMH Books, 1986.

Feinberg, John S. and Paul D. Feinberg, *Ethics for a Brave New World.* Wheaton, IL: Crossway, 2010.

Geisler, Norman L. *Christian Ethics: Contemporary Issues & Options.* Grand Rapids: Baker Academic, 2010.

Holmes, Arthur F., ed. *War and Christian Ethics: Classic and Contemporary Readings on the Morality of War.* Grand Rapids: Baker Academic, 2005.

Rae, Scott B. *Moral Choices: An Introduction to Ethics.* Grand Rapids: Zondervan, 2009.

CONCLUSION

For many years the head of the math department at the university where I teach kept a notice posted outside his office: "Theory is when you know everything, but nothing works. Practice is when everything works but you don't know why. In our classes, theory and practice come together: Nothing works, and you don't know why."[1] While a bit cynical, this motto expresses a truth: people struggle to integrate theory and practice. Teachers of upperclassmen often remark that students who supposedly passed English composition in order to qualify for their classes often seem unable to write thesis statements or construct clear sentences. Upperclassmen often remark that university teachers who are supposed to be professional educators often cannot construct a compelling PowerPoint or deliver a lucid lecture. In every field of knowledge and learning, both theory and practice are necessary and mutually informing.

The existence of this book—practical ethics—speaks to the need of turning ethical theory into practice. Learning ethical systems but never actually confronting practical questions, such as those discussed in chapters 2 through 16 of this book, has dubious value. The authors trust that you have seen the extraordinary practical value of engaging these important issues with careful thought and sustained conversation.

Nevertheless, the main theme of this book has been the opposite concern. It is easy to jump into practical ethical issues, employ what one feels is common sense, and begin drawing conclusions and asserting "truths." Chapter 1 laid a foundation for the conversations in the rest of the book by insisting that ethical decisions ought to flow out of sound ethical principles.

---

1. See https://www.reddit.com/r/ScienceJokes/comments/8gmdwp/theory_is_when_you_know_everything_but_nothing/ for a version of this joke.

CONCLUSION

The time and effort it takes to understand the Categorical Imperative, the principles of Utilitarianism, the reasoning behind Situation Ethics, Virtue ethics, Ethical Egoism, and the rest are well worth it. Even those, like the authors, who are committed to Divine Nature Theory should recognize that life presents ethical dilemmas not always clearly resolved by simple appeal to scriptural mandate. While determined never to act contrary to the divine nature as God has revealed himself in Scripture, we believe other ethical systems often give substantial aid in unraveling complex ethical problems.

First, then, this book has sought to convince the reader that ethical theory and practice must come together. The better we understand the different principles and possibilities involved in making an ethical application, the more soundly we will reason and the more confidently we will be able to move forward. Bianca, Lauren, and Micah spent their semester in Dr. Platt's ethics class learning this lesson, and they would want you to learn it too.

Second, as suggested above, this book has tried to steer the reader away from simplistic solutions. The authors do not believe that utility—consequences—is ever sufficient of itself to render an action moral. If an action is immoral on other, firmer grounds, then the fact that it yields apparently favorable results does not justify it morally. Nevertheless, as several conversations pointed out, determining how the various deontological systems—such as Virtue, Duty, and Divine Command Theory—handle difficult cases often involves some appeal to the perceived consequences. For instance, the Christian God commands people not to deceive, and he commands them to value and protect life. It was no doubt a consideration of the consequences entailed by obeying one or the other command that guided the consciences of many who protected Jews from Nazi troops or fleeing slaves in the Underground Railroad, even if such action entailed deception.[2] Most of the chapters of this book have intentionally maintained a certain openness to various interpretations, partly to encourage thought in the readers and partly to illustrate that most controversial ethical issues admit of no easy answers.

---

2. For examples of the former, see Corrie Ten Boom, *The Hiding Place* (Grand Rapids: Baker, 2006). Relative to the Underground Railroad, see Eric Foner, *Gateway to Freedom: The Hidden History of the Underground Railroad* (New York: W. W. Norton, 2016).

Third, this book has sought to illustrate that serious ethical thinking is not the exclusive province of older people. Most people will face decisions relative to virtually every issue canvassed in this book before they turn twenty-five. On the one hand, young people do well to be teachable, to listen to older generations who have traversed various paths, perhaps several times, and humbly to accept help. On the other hand, this book has resolutely set itself against ethical relativism; the older people in your life telling you something is moral doesn't make it moral. The closest thing to a book of philosophy in the Christian Scriptures is Ecclesiastes, in which a teacher of wisdom urges young people to learn how to live now, before it is too late.[3] Establishing sound principles of ethical behavior—learning wisdom—is the safest way to navigate a world of myriad moral and ethical challenges. Regardless of one's age, a person can begin learning wisdom today.

Finally, the authors of this book are committed to wisdom beginning with the fear of the Lord.[4] We are happy for Lauren and Shamar, and we enjoyed learning from their perspectives, but in the final analysis, we believe that those who try to understand ethics without trying to understand God are working at a disadvantage. We believe that Divine Nature Theory—in which the nature of God is learned primarily through Scripture, although we also learn of him through nature and other forms of general revelation—is the bedrock upon which other ethical systems can build most successfully. It is a right view of God's nature that will show us what our duty truly is, what virtue really consists of, what love looks like in any situation, and how properly to assess apparent consequences.

It is on this firm foundation that Micah and Bianca eventually married and, we're reliably informed, lived happily ever after. At the same time, we firmly believe that civil and constructive conversation about ethical principles is possible between atheists, agnostics, and religious people, and that such conversation is in great need today. And on *that* foundation, Micah and Bianca have continued their friendship with Lauren and Shamar, and they even continue to talk about ethics once in a while.

---

3. See the powerful conclusion of the book in Ecclesiastes 11:9–12:14, which is directly addressed to the young.
4. Prov. 1:7; 9:10.

SELECT BIBLIOGRAPHY

Alcorn, Randy. *Pro-Life Answers to Pro-Choice Questions*. Colorado Springs: Multnomah, 2000.

Alston, Philip. *Report of the Special Rapporteur on Extreme Poverty and Human Rights on His Mission to the United States of America*, United Nations, General Assembly, Human Rights Council, May 4, 2018.

Baggett, David, and Jerry Walls. *Good God: The Theistic Foundations of Morality*. Oxford: Oxford University Press, 2011.

Baird, Robert M., and Stuart E. Rosenbaum, eds. *Punishment and the Death Penalty: The Current Debate*. Amherst, NY: Prometheus, 1995.

Bauman, Stephan, Matthew Soerens, and Issam Smeir. *Seeking Refuge: On the Shores of the Global Refugee Crisis*. Chicago: Moody, 2016.

Becker, Lawrence C., and Charlotte B. Becker, eds. *Encyclopedia of Ethics*. 2nd ed. New York: Routledge, 2003.

Beckwith, Francis J. *Defending Life: A Moral and Legal Case against Abortion Choice*. Cambridge: Cambridge University Press, 2007.

Blomberg, Craig L. *The Historical Reliability of the New Testament: Countering the Challenges to Evangelical Christian Beliefs*. Nashville: B&H Academic, 2016.

Bouma-Prediger, Steven. *For the Beauty of the Earth: A Christian Vision for Creation Care*. 2nd edition. Grand Rapids: Baker Academic, 2010.

Bourke, Vernon. *History of Ethics*. 2 vols. Edinburg, VA: Axios, 2007.

Breeden, Tom, and Mark L. Ward, Jr. *Can I Smoke Pot? Marijuana in Light of Scripture*. Hudson, OH: Cruciform, 2016.

Caplan, Arthur L., James J. McCartney, and Daniel P. Reid. *Replacement Parts: The Ethics of Procuring and Replacing Organs in Humans*. Washington, DC: Georgetown University Press, 2015.

Carens, Joseph. *The Ethics of Immigration*. Oxford: Oxford University Press, 2015.

Caulkins, Jonathan P., Beau Kilmer, and Mark A. R. Kleimann. *Marijuana Legalization: What Everyone Needs to Know*. New York: Oxford University Press, 2016.

Clouse, Robert G., ed. *War: Four Christian Views*. Winona Lake, IN: BMH, 1986.

Coates, J. *The Ethics of War*. Manchester: Manchester University Press, 1997.

Colapinto, John. *As Nature Made Him: The Boy Who Was Raised as a Girl*. New York: HarperCollins, 2006.

Colson, Charles W., and Nigel M. de S. Cameron, eds. *Human Dignity in the Biotech Century*. Downers Grove, IL: InterVarsity Press, 2004.

Dallas, Joe, and Nancy Hecke, eds. *The Complete Christian Guide to Understanding Homosexuality*. Eugene, OR: Harvest House, 2010.

Derrickson, Jason, ed. *Marijuana Legalization: State Initiatives, Implications, and Initiatives*. New York: Nova Science, 2014.

Dworkin, Gerald, R. G. Frey, and Sissela Bok. *Euthanasia and Physician-Assisted Suicide*. Cambridge: Cambridge University Press, 1998.

Enger, Eldon D., and Bradley F. Smith. *Environmental Science: A Study of Interrelationships*. New York: McGraw Hill, 2013.

Esposito, John, and Dalia Mogahed. *Who Speaks for Islam? What a Billion Muslims Really Think*. New York: Gallup, 2007.

Feinberg, John S., and Paul D. Feinberg. *Ethics for a Brave New World*. 2nd ed. Wheaton, IL: Crossway, 2010.

Foner, Eric. *Gateway to Freedom: The Hidden History of the Underground Railroad*. New York: W. W. Norton, 2016.

Foreman, Mark W. *Christianity and Bioethics: Confronting Clinical Issues*. Eugene, OR: Wipf and Stock, 2011.

Friberg, Timothy, Barbara Friberg, and Neva F. Miller. *Analytical Lexicon of the Greek New Testament*. Victoria, BC: Trafford, 2005.

Geisler, Norman L. *Christian Ethics: Contemporary Issues and Options*. Grand Rapids: Baker Academic, 2010.

Glover, Jonathan. *Choosing Children: Genes, Disability and Design*. New York: Oxford University Press, 2008.

Gorsuch, Neil. *The Future of Assisted Suicide*. Princeton, NJ: Princeton University Press, 2006.

Greasley, Kate, and Christopher Kaczor. *Abortion Rights: For and Against.* Cambridge: Cambridge University Press, 2017.

Greasley, Kate. *Arguments about Abortion: Personhood, Morality, and Law.* New York: Oxford University Press, 2017.

Greenberg, Karen J. *The Torture Debate in America.* Cambridge: Cambridge University Press, 2005.

Grenz, Stanley J. *Sexual Ethics.* Dallas: Word, 1990.

Grudem, Wayne. *Christian Ethics.* Wheaton, IL: Crossway, 2018.

Hayward, Steven F. *Mere Environmentalism: A Biblical Perspective on Humans and the Natural World.* Washington, DC: AEI, 2010.

Hiestand, Gerald, and Todd Wilson, eds. *Beauty, Order, and Mystery: The Christian Vision of Sexuality.* Downers Grove, IL: InterVarsity Press, 2017.

Hill, Kevin P. *Marijuana: The Unbiased Truth about the World's Most Popular Weed.* Center City, MN: Hazelden, 2015.

Hoekema, Anthony. *Created in God's Image.* Grand Rapids: Eerdmans, 1986.

Hoffmeier, James K. *The Immigration Crisis: Immigrants, Aliens, and the Bible.* Wheaton, IL: Crossway, 2009.

Holmes, Arthur F., ed. *War and Christian Ethics.* Grand Rapids: Baker Academic, 2005.

Hopko, Thomas. *Christian Faith and Same-Sex Attraction: Eastern Orthodox Reflections.* Ben Lomand, CA: Conciliar, 2006.

Hoyt, Joanna Michal. *A Wary Welcome: The History of US Attitudes toward Immigration.* Skinny Bottle, 2017.

Hume, David. *An Inquiry Concerning Human Understanding.* Indianapolis: Bobbs-Merrill, 1955.

Janssen, Aron, and Scott Leibowitz, eds. *Balanced Affirmative Mental Health Care for Transgender and Gender Diverse Youth: A Clinical Guide.* Portland, OR: Springer, 2018.

Jensen, Steven J. *The Ethics of Organ Transplantation.* Washington, DC: Catholic University of America Press, 2011.

Jones, Michael S. *Moral Reasoning: An Intentional Approach to Distinguishing Right from Wrong.* Dubuque, IA: Kendall Hunt, 2017.

Kant, Immanuel. *Grounding for the Metaphysics of Morals, with On a Supposed Right to Lie because of Philanthropic Concerns.* Trans. James W. Ellington. Indianapolis: Hackett, 1981.

_____. *Foundations of the Metaphysics of Morals*. Translated by Lewis Beck. Indianapolis: Bobbs-Merrill, 1959.

_____. *Lectures on Ethics*. Translated by Louis Infield. New York: Harper & Row, 1963.

Kilner, John F. *Dignity and Destiny: Humanity in the Image of God*. Grand Rapids: Eerdmans, 2015.

Klusendorf, Scott. *The Case for Life: Equipping Christians to Engage the Culture*. Wheaton, IL: Crossway, 2009.

Koch, Michaela. *Discursive Intersexions: Daring Bodies between Myth, Medicine, and Memoir*. Bielefeld: Transcript-Verlag, 2017.

Kuhse, Helga, and Peter Singer. *Should the Baby Live?* Oxford: Oxford University Press, 1986.

Lappé, Frances Moore, and Joseph Collins. *World Hunger: 10 Myths*. New York: Grove Press, 2015.

Lehmiller, Justin J. *The Psychology of Human Sexuality*. 2nd ed. Hoboken, NJ: John Wiley & Sons, 2017.

Levinson, Sanford. *Torture: A Collection*. Oxford: Oxford University Press, 2006.

Lewis, C. S. *Mere Christianity*. New York: HarperOne, 2002.

_____. *The Abolition of Man*. New York: HarperOne, 2002.

Loftin, R. Keith, ed. *God and Morality: Four Views*. Downers Grove, IL: InterVarsity Press, 2012.

Manninen, Bertha A., and Jack Mulder, Jr. *Civil Dialogue on Abortion*. New York: Routledge, 2018.

Marsh, Margaret, and Wanda Ronner. *The Pursuit of Parenthood: Reproductive Technology from Test Tube Babies to Uterus Transplants*. Baltimore, MD: Johns Hopkins University Press, 2019.

McKeogh, Colm. *Tolstoy's Pacifism*. Amherst, NY: Cambria, 2009.

Meitlis, Yitzhak. *Excavating the Bible: New Archaeological Evidence for the Historical Reliability of Scripture*. Savage, MD: Eshel, 2012.

Moehler, Michael. *Minimal Morality: A Multilevel Social Contract Theory*. Oxford: Oxford University Press, 2018.

Moo, Douglas J., and Jonathan A. Moo. *Creation Care: A Biblical Theology of the Natural World*. Grand Rapids: Zondervan, 2018.

Moyo, Dambisa. *Dead Aid: Why Aid Is Not Working and How There Is a Better Way for Africa*. New York: Farrar, Straus and Giroux, 2009.

Myers, David, and Letha Dawson Scanzoni. *What God Has Joined Together: The Christian Case for Gay Marriage*. New York: HarperOne, 2006.

Nozick, Robert. *Anarchy, State, and Utopia*. New York: Basic Books, 1974.

Pojman, Louis P., and Jeffrey Reiman. *The Death Penalty: For and Against*. Lanham, MD: Rowman & Littlefield, 1997.

Rae, Scott. *Moral Choices: An Introduction to Ethics*. 4th ed. Grand Rapids: Zondervan, 2018.

Rawls, John. *A Theory of Justice*. Cambridge, MA: Belknap, 1971.

_____. *Justice as Fairness: A Restatement*. Cambridge, MA: Belknap, 2001.

Reardon, David C., Julie Makimaa, and Amy Sobie, eds. *Victims and Victors: Speaking Out about Their Pregnancies, Abortions, and Children Resulting from Sexual Assault*. Irvine, CA: Acorn, 2000.

Reich, Robert. *Saving Capitalism: For the Many, Not the Few*. New York: Vintage, 2015.

Reichberg, Gregory M., Henrik Syse, and Endre Begby, eds. *The Ethics of War: Classic and Contemporary Readings*. Hoboken, NJ: Wiley-Blackwell, 2006.

Richardson, Herbert, ed. *On the Problem of Surrogate Parenthood: Analyzing the Baby M Case*. Lewiston, NY: Edwin Mellen, 1987.

Rollin, Bernard E. *A New Basis for Animal Ethics: Telos and Common Sense*. Columbia: University of Missouri Press, 2016.

_____. *Animal Rights and Human Morality*. Amherst, NY: Prometheus, 1981.

Ryan, Alan. *Bertrand Russell: A Political Life*. New York: Farrar, Straus and Giroux, 1981.

Sager, Alex, ed. *The Ethics and Politics of Immigration: Core Issues and Emerging Trends*. New York: Rowman & Littlefield, 2016.

Sandel, Michael. *The Case against Perfection: Ethics in an Age of Genetic Engineering*. Cambridge, MA: Belknap, 2007.

Scanlon, T. M. *What We Owe to Each Other*. Cambridge, MA: Harvard University Press, 1998.

Schaeffer, Francis A. *Pollution and the Death of Man: The Christian View of Ecology*. Wheaton: Tyndale House, 1970.

Schmidtz, David, and Elizabeth Willott. *Environmental Ethics: What Really Matters, What Really Works*. New York: Oxford University Press, 2002.

Sharp, Lesley. *The Transplant Imaginary*. Berkeley: University of California Press, 2014.

Shaw, William H. *Utilitarianism and the Ethics of War.* London: Routledge, 2016.

Sider, Ronald J. *Rich Christians in an Age of Hunger: Moving from Affluence to Generosity.* Nashville: Thomas Nelson, 2015.

Singer, Peter. *Animal Liberation: The Definitive Classic of the Animal Movement.* New York: Harper Perennial, 2009.

_____. *Practical Ethics.* 2nd edition. Cambridge: Cambridge University Press, 1993.

Skinner, Daniel. *Medical Necessity: Health Care Access and the Politics of Decision Making.* Minneapolis: University of Minnesota Press, 2019.

Smith, Owen M., and Anne Collins Smith, eds. *Taking Sides: Clashing Views on Moral Issues.* 14th ed. New York: McGraw Hill, 2016.

Soerens, Matthew, Jenny Yang, and Leith Anderson. *Welcoming the Stranger: Justice, Compassion and Truth in the Immigration Debate.* Downers Grove, IL: InterVarsity Press, 2018.

Sterba, James P. *What Is Ethics?* Medford, MA: Polity, 2020.

Sumner, L. W. *Physician-Assisted Death: What Everyone Needs to Know.* Oxford: Oxford University Press, 2017.

Ten Boom, Corrie. *The Hiding Place.* 35th anniv. ed. Grand Rapids: Baker, 2006.

Thobaben, James. *Health Care Ethics.* Downers Grove, IL: InterVarsity Press, 2009.

Toly, Noah J. *Keeping God's Earth: The Global Environment in Biblical Perspective.* Westmont, IL: InterVarsity Press, 2010.

Vasquez, Margie, ed. *Marijuana: Medical Uses, Regulations, and Legal Issues.* New York: Nova Science, 2014.

Weikart, Richard. *The Death of Humanity and the Case for Life.* Washington, DC: Regnery, 2016.

Wilkens, Steve. *Beyond Bumper Sticker Ethics: An Introduction to Theories of Right and Wrong.* 2nd ed. Downers Grove, IL: InterVarsity Press, 2011.

Wilkinson, Richard, and Kate Pickett. *The Spirit Level: Why Greater Equality Makes Societies Stronger.* New York: Bloomsbury, 2009.

Wilson, Gordon. *A Different Shade of Green: A Biblical Approach to Environmentalism and the Dominion Mandate.* Moscow, ID: Canon, 2019.

Yarhouse, Mark A. *Understanding Gender Dysphoria: Navigating Transgender Issues in a Changing Culture.* Downers Grove, IL: InterVarsity Press, 2015.

Yoder, John Howard. *The Politics of Jesus.* 2nd ed. Grand Rapids: Eerdmans, 1994.

INDEX